# Soundtrack Success: A Digital Storyteller's Guide to Audio Post-Production

Jeffrey P. Fisher

**Course Technology PTR**
*A part of Cengage Learning*

**COURSE TECHNOLOGY**
CENGAGE Learning

Australia • Brazil • Japan • Korea • Mexico • Singapore • Spain • United Kingdom • United States

## COURSE TECHNOLOGY
### CENGAGE Learning

**Soundtrack Success: A Digital Storyteller's
Guide to Audio Post-Production**
**Jeffrey P. Fisher**

Publisher and General Manager, Course
Technology PTR: Stacy L. Hiquet

Associate Director of Marketing:
Sarah Panella

Manager of Editorial Services: Heather Talbot

Marketing Manager: Mark Hughes

Executive Editor: Mark Garvey

Development Editor: Cathleen D. Small

Project Editor/Copy Editor: Cathleen D. Small

Technical Reviewer: Brian Jackson

Interior Layout Tech: MPS Limited, a
Macmillan Company

Cover Designer: Christopher Bodel

DVD-Video Producer: Brandon Penticuff

Indexer: Larry Sweazy

Proofreader: Carolyn Keating

For product information and technology assistance, contact us at
**Cengage Learning Customer & Sales Support, 1-800-354-9706**

For permission to use material from this text or product, submit all
requests online at **www.cengage.com/permissions**
Further permissions questions can be emailed to
**permissionrequest@cengage.com**

All trademarks are the property of their respective owners.

All images © Cengage Learning unless otherwise noted.

Library of Congress Control Number: 2006904401

ISBN-13: 978-1-59863-254-5

ISBN-10: 1-59863-254-X

**Course Technology, a part of Cengage Learning**
20 Channel Center Street
Boston, MA 02210
USA

Cengage Learning is a leading provider of customized learning solutions with office locations
around the globe, including Singapore, the United Kingdom, Australia, Mexico, Brazil, and
Japan. Locate your local office at: **international.cengage.com/region**

Cengage Learning products are represented in Canada by Nelson Education, Ltd.

For your lifelong learning solutions, visit **courseptr.com**

Visit our corporate website at **cengage.com**

Printed in the United States of America
1 2 3 4 5 6 7 13 12 11

*For Lisa. Always.*

# Acknowledgments

Huge thank you to Mark Garvey, whose patience and support made this project happen. Even when I was terribly late with the manuscript, he never lost faith in the project. I owe him my sincerest gratitude.

If only there were words to express how much I appreciate my editor, Cathleen Small. She also held onto this project over the long, long time it took to come to fruition. I owe her immensely for her editing work. This book is far better because of her hard work and dedication. Thank you, CS!

Thanks to Christopher Bodel for his friendship and the illustrations he contributed to this book, including the cover.

Special thanks to Tony Santona for his cartoons used in the text and for his invaluable assistance on the book's DVD.

Thanks to all my students, who continue to challenge me. I'm most proud when they take the audio journey that results in successful projects.

And thanks to all my clients and peers, who make leading my sound life so rewarding.

# About the Author

**Jeffrey P. Fisher** has built a 25-year career in the music, sound, and video industry. He has extensive experience and credentials as an award-winning, active musician, composer, trainer, and media specialist. He's been writing for the music, sound, and video industry for more than 18 years and is a highly respected and sought-after writer and lecturer. Fisher works from his project studio providing music, sound, writing, video, training, and media production and post-production services for corporate, cable, and commercial clients, including indie filmmakers. He writes about music, sound, and video for print and the Web, including 11 books. He has published his free email newsletter, Moneymaking Music Tip of the Week, since 1997. His library music CD, *Dark New Age* (Fresh Music 2004), along with his *Atmospherics* CD and two-volume, buy-out music library, *Melomania*, showcase his musical vision. He also teaches audio and video production and post-production at the College of DuPage Motion Picture/Television department in Glen Ellyn, Illinois, and at DePaul University Digital Cinema Program in Chicago, Illinois. He co-hosts the ACID, Sound Forge, and Vegas forums on Digital Media Net (www.dmnforums.com). For more information, visit his website at www.jeffreypfisher.com or contact him at jpf@jeffreypfisher.com.

Other books by Jeffrey P. Fisher:

- *Voice Actor's Guide to Recording at Home and on the Road* (with Harlan Hogan; Course Technology PTR, 2008)

- *Ruthless Self-Promotion in the Music Industry,* Second Edition (Course Technology PTR, 2005)

- *Cash Tracks: Compose, Produce, and Sell Your Original Soundtrack Music and Jingles* (Course Technology PTR, 2005)

- *The Voice Actor's Guide to Home Recording* (with Harlan Hogan; Course Technology PTR, 2005)

- *Instant Surround Sound* (CMPBooks, 2005)

- *Instant Vegas 5* (with Douglas Spotted Eagle; CMPBooks, 2004)

- *Instant Sound Forge* (CMPBooks, 2004)

- *Moneymaking Music* (Artistpro, 2003)

- *Profiting from Your Music and Sound Project Studio* (Allworth Press, 2001)

- *Ruthless Self-Promotion in the Music Industry* (Artistpro, 1999)

- *How to Make Money Scoring Soundtracks and Jingles* (Artistpro, 1997)

# Contents

Introduction. . . . . . . . . . . . . . . . . . . . . . . . . . . . . . . xv

## Chapter 1
## Crafting the Quintessential Soundtrack    1

Dialogue................................................................. 1
Background Sounds.................................................. 1
Sound Effects .......................................................... 2
Sound Design .......................................................... 2
Music ..................................................................... 2
Putting It All Together .............................................. 2
Workflow................................................................. 3
DVD Education......................................................... 4

## Chapter 2
## Audio Aesthetics    7

Dialogue Rules ........................................................ 7
Plan Ahead.............................................................. 7
The Final Mix Matters ............................................... 8
Narrative Elements................................................... 9
   Diegetic and Non-Diegetic Sounds ........................ 9
   Listening versus Hearing ...................................... 10
   Figure/Ground..................................................... 10
   Cause and Effect ................................................. 11
   Entrainment ....................................................... 11
Soundtrack Core Elements ....................................... 11
   Fixing and Sweetening......................................... 11
   Controlling Noise ................................................ 12
   Ensuring Consistency .......................................... 12
   Enriching the Listening Experience....................... 13
Checklist for Soundtrack Success ............................. 14
Sound Transitions ................................................... 14
Ear Candy .............................................................. 15
   Quiet Scenes...................................................... 15
   Sports-izing ....................................................... 16
Analyze This ........................................................... 16

## Chapter 3
## What Is Sound?    **19**

Components of Sound ................................................................................. 19
Analog Basics ........................................................................................... 21
Sound Perception ...................................................................................... 21
Digital Diatribe ......................................................................................... 22
Sound Starts ............................................................................................. 23
Sound Channels ........................................................................................ 24
Wrap Up ................................................................................................... 25

## Chapter 4
## Workflow    **27**

Picture Editorial versus Sound Editorial ..................................................... 27
Divvy Up the Work .................................................................................... 28
Workflow Approach ................................................................................... 29
    Spotting Session .................................................................................. 30
    Working with Production Dialogue ...................................................... 33
    Working with Sound Effects and Backgrounds ..................................... 33
    Working with Music ............................................................................ 34
    Putting It All Together ......................................................................... 35
Technical Issues ......................................................................................... 36

## Chapter 5
## Location Matters    **39**

Overcoming Production Woes ...................................................................... 39
    Location, Location, Location ................................................................ 40
    Capturing Room Tone ......................................................................... 40
Top Mistakes Made in the Field .................................................................. 41
Fix It in Post...Not! .................................................................................... 44
    Noise ................................................................................................. 44
    Distortion ........................................................................................... 44
    Acoustic Anomalies ............................................................................ 44
    Distant Miking ................................................................................... 45
    Live One-of-a-Kind Content ............................................................... 45
    Printed Effects ................................................................................... 45
More Noise Issues ...................................................................................... 45
    Practicing Noise Avoidance ................................................................. 46
    Wild Tracks and Shooting for Sound .................................................... 46
    Deadening the Sound .......................................................................... 47
    Adding Noise in Post .......................................................................... 47
    Dealing with Wind Noise .................................................................... 47
    Choosing a Mic .................................................................................. 48
    More Noise Sources ............................................................................ 48
Checklist for Production Sound Success ...................................................... 48

## Chapter 6
## Microphones                                                        51

Dynamic Mics ....................................................................... 51
Condenser Mics .................................................................... 52
Ribbon Mics ......................................................................... 53
Pickup Patterns .................................................................... 53
Mic Rules ............................................................................. 57
   Choose the Right Mic ................................................... 57
   The Fewer Mics, the Better .......................................... 57
   Only Record in Stereo When Appropriate ................... 57
   Move the Mic Closer .................................................... 57
   Avoid Built-In Mics ..................................................... 59
   Use Care with Your Mics ............................................. 59
   Be Careful When Placing Multiple Mics ..................... 60
Microphone Types ................................................................ 61
Boosting the Signal .............................................................. 62
Fisher's Hierarchy of Microphone Choices ......................... 64
Placement Options and Tips ................................................ 66

## Chapter 7
## Building the Location Sound Kit                                    71

Mixers, Meters, and Levels ................................................. 71
Separate Audio Recorders .................................................... 74
Cables and Connectors ......................................................... 76
Location Sound Field Kit ..................................................... 77
Recording Sound Effects and Backgrounds ......................... 78
Stereo in the Field ............................................................... 79

## Chapter 8
## CYA Tips                                                          85

Double-System Recording .................................................... 86
Slate Procedures .................................................................. 88
Audio Recorders .................................................................. 91
Shoot for Sound ................................................................... 92
Quality Control .................................................................... 93
What Is Wrong with This Scenario? ..................................... 93

## Chapter 9
## Hearing Sound                                                     95

Monitors ............................................................................... 95
Real-World Reference ........................................................... 97
Speaker Location .................................................................. 99
Speaker Calibration ............................................................. 101

Ruminations ................................................................................................ 104
Audio Interface/Soundcard ........................................................................ 107

## Chapter 10
## Making and Recording Sound    **113**

Computer Hardware Choices ....................................................................... 113
Software Choices ......................................................................................... 114
NLE to DAW .............................................................................................. 119
Gearing Up .................................................................................................. 120
    Strategy ................................................................................................... 121
    Research ................................................................................................. 121
    Set Goals ................................................................................................ 122
    Budget .................................................................................................... 122
    Buy/Pass ................................................................................................ 123

## Chapter 11
## Make Sound *Sound* Better    **125**

Using Effects ............................................................................................... 125
    Tone ....................................................................................................... 125
    Time ....................................................................................................... 126
    Modulation ............................................................................................ 127
    Dynamics ............................................................................................... 128
    Pitch ....................................................................................................... 130
    Time Compression/Expansion ............................................................. 130
    Other Effects ......................................................................................... 130
    Channel Strips ....................................................................................... 131
    Restoration Tools .................................................................................. 132
    Audio Analysis Tools ............................................................................ 132
    Multi-Effects ......................................................................................... 134
Must-Have Plug-Ins .................................................................................... 135
Links ........................................................................................................... 136
FX Workflow ............................................................................................... 136
The General State of Generic Advice .......................................................... 137

## Chapter 12
## Audio-Post Workflow Tips    **139**

Keeping Organized ...................................................................................... 139
Preparing the Project ................................................................................... 140

## Chapter 13
## Voiceover                                                    143

Scripting Voiceover ........................................................................ 144
Casting Voiceover ........................................................................... 145
Getting the Best Performance ...................................................... 146
Recording VOs ................................................................................ 148
  The Recording Environment ...................................................... 149
  The Porta-Booth .......................................................................... 149
  Engineering Equipment ............................................................. 151
  Mic Placement ............................................................................. 152
  Record Flat ................................................................................... 152
  Talent Placement ........................................................................ 153
VO Resources .................................................................................. 153

## Chapter 14
## Recording ADR and Walla                                     155

The Challenges of ADR ................................................................. 155
Getting Quality ADR ..................................................................... 156
Walla ................................................................................................. 159
  Defining Walla ............................................................................. 159
  Recording Walla .......................................................................... 159
  Handling Walla Challenges ....................................................... 160
  More Techniques for Effective Walla Recordings .................. 160

## Chapter 15
## Editing Dialogue                                             163

The Importance of Editing Dialogue .......................................... 163
Smoothing Dialogue ...................................................................... 164
JLX .................................................................................................... 166
Other Smoothing Techniques ...................................................... 170
Close Your Eyes and Hear ............................................................ 171
Dialogue and Phase ....................................................................... 172
Fixing Common Dialogue Ills ...................................................... 175
  DC Offset ...................................................................................... 177
  Sibilance ....................................................................................... 177
  Popped P's (and B's and T's) ..................................................... 178
  Mouth Noises (Breaths, Lip Smacks, and Other Vocal Garbage) ..... 180
  Expansion ..................................................................................... 183
  Too Much Reverb ........................................................................ 184
  Rumble and Hiss .......................................................................... 185
  Tonal Fixes ................................................................................... 186
  Better Speech Intelligibility ...................................................... 187
  EQ One File with Another .......................................................... 188

Clicks, Glitches, and Pop Removal ........................................................ 188
Repairing Clipped Peaks (Distortion) .................................................. 190
Hum ...................................................................................................... 192
Time Compression/Expansion ........................................................... 195
Pitch Shift ........................................................................................... 196
Volume ................................................................................................. 197
Compression ....................................................................................... 198
Dedicated Noise Reduction ................................................................... 199
Special Voice Effects ............................................................................. 205
Simulating a Telephone Line .............................................................. 205
Simulating Rooms and Spaces ............................................................ 206
Delay...Delay...Delay .......................................................................... 206
Reversing Dialogue ............................................................................. 206
Flanging, Chorusing, and Phasing ...................................................... 207

## Chapter 16
## Sound Effects                                                                                209

Oodles of Sounds .................................................................................... 210
Spotting Sound Effects ........................................................................... 211
Hunting and Gathering ........................................................................... 213
Your Sound Effects Library ..................................................................... 219
Production Tracks ................................................................................ 219
Sound Effects Collections ................................................................... 220
Sound Effects Websites ....................................................................... 221
Roll Your Own ..................................................................................... 222

## Chapter 17
## Foley and Backgrounds                                                                        225

Foley ........................................................................................................ 225
Recording Foley ................................................................................... 226
Footsteps .............................................................................................. 227
Clothing ............................................................................................... 228
Props ..................................................................................................... 228
Foley Sound Effects ............................................................................. 229
Software-Based Foley .......................................................................... 230
Backgrounds ............................................................................................ 230
Gathering BGs ..................................................................................... 231
Super-Size Your Stereo Backgrounds .................................................. 233
Surround BGs ....................................................................................... 235

# Chapter 18
# Sound Effects in Use                                            237

Write Once, Use Many Times .................................................... 237
Play to the Emotions ............................................................... 237
The Long Road ....................................................................... 238
Sound Saves Money ............................................................... 238
Movie Physics ........................................................................ 239
Think Cause and Effect .......................................................... 239
Remember the "See a Dog, Hear a Dog" Adage ....................... 239
Finding the Sync .................................................................... 239
Sync the Foreground .............................................................. 240
Don't Mistake Clip Edges for Sound Starts .............................. 241
Be Authentic .......................................................................... 241
Make 'Em Your Own ............................................................. 242
Get Real during Pauses .......................................................... 242
Use Layers ............................................................................. 243
Watch Out for "Noise" Sounds .............................................. 243
Beware of "Temp" Video ........................................................ 244
It's What the Sound Sounds Like, Not What It's Called ............ 244
And Then There's Sound Design ............................................. 244
Use the Non-Surround LFE .................................................... 246
Worldizing ............................................................................. 247
Include Some Ear Candy ........................................................ 248
Use Perspective Shifts ............................................................ 248
Pre- and Post-Lap .................................................................. 249
Beware the Exit-Sign Effect .................................................... 249
Throw in the Kitchen Sink ...................................................... 249
Never Close the Door to Creativity ......................................... 250
Futzing Around ...................................................................... 251
Premixing, Freezing, and Printing Audio Effects ..................... 251
Getting Notes ........................................................................ 252
A Few Short Case Studies in Sound-Effects Work .................... 253
    Cars in Motion .................................................................. 253
    Dream Phone .................................................................... 253
    Screams ............................................................................ 253
    Killer Drug ....................................................................... 254

# Chapter 19
# Music                                                           255

Music Fundamentals ............................................................... 256
    Why Are You Using Music? ................................................ 256
    What Emotional Response Do You Desire? .......................... 257
    What Is the Message? ........................................................ 257
    Who Is Your Audience? ..................................................... 257

What Style Is Appropriate to the Audience? ........................... 257
What Style Is Appropriate to the Message? .......................... 257
Where Will You Put the Music (or Not)? ............................ 257
Getting the Music .............................................................. 259
    Library (a.k.a. Production or Stock) Music .................... 261
    Indie Artists ............................................................... 263
    Creative Commons ..................................................... 264
    DIY Music ................................................................. 264
    Hire a Composer ........................................................ 266
    Music Budget ............................................................. 267
Editing Music .................................................................... 268
Further Music Studies ........................................................ 270
    Opening Titles/Show Theme ....................................... 270
    Motif and Leitmotif ................................................... 271
    POV ........................................................................... 271
    Building Tension and Foreshadowing ........................... 271
    Diegetic to Non-Diegetic and Back ............................. 271
    Music as Sound Effect ................................................ 271
    Offbeat, Atonal Music ................................................ 272
    Electronic Music ........................................................ 272
    Firewood ................................................................... 272
Case Study: Scoring *The Craving Heart* ............................. 272

## Chapter 20
## Mixing

                                            **275**

Housekeeping ..................................................................... 275
    Listen to What's There ............................................... 276
    Don't Mix Alone ........................................................ 276
    Premix/Predub ........................................................... 277
    Track Optimization .................................................... 278
    Audio Effects Optimization ......................................... 280
    Monitor Optimization ................................................ 282
    Have a Reference Mix ................................................. 284
Mix Secrets ....................................................................... 284
    Think WHOLE Mix, Not Individual Pieces .................. 285
    Dialogue Still Rules .................................................... 285
    Look beyond the Obvious ........................................... 286
    Find a Place for Everything ......................................... 286
    Fill the Entire Audible Frequency Range ...................... 287
    Watch Time ............................................................... 287
    Use Volume ............................................................... 287
    Use Frequency ........................................................... 288
    Use S-p-a-c-e ............................................................. 289
    Embrace Dynamics and Contrast ................................ 290

Apply Appropriate Effects ................................................................ 290
Use Automation ................................................................................ 291
Don't Watch the Screen .................................................................... 292
Trust Your Ears ................................................................................ 292
Tired Ears = Bad Mix ....................................................................... 292
Quality Control ...................................................................................... 292
Surround-Sound Issues .......................................................................... 294
Export and Encode Options ................................................................... 295
Render the Final Mix ........................................................................ 296
Dolby Digital AC-3 Metadata ........................................................... 297
Dialogue Normalization .................................................................... 299
Dynamic-Range Compression ........................................................... 299
Final Thoughts ...................................................................................... 300

Index . . . . . . . . . . . . . . . . . . . . . . . . . . . . . 301

# Introduction

Imagine today's movies, television programs, web clips, and video games without sound. They aren't quite the same, are they? From a mathematical standpoint, sound is half of the movie-going, television-viewing, and game-playing experience. From a cerebral standpoint, sound comprises something closer to 70 percent of the experience.

Don't believe me? Try this: Grab a copy of your favorite DVD and drop it in. Pop some popcorn, turn the lights down low, and snuggle up next to your significant other. Press play on the DVD and then mute the sound. And unless your favorite movie is *The Gold Rush* or some other film from the silent era, you'll find that without the sound, the movie isn't nearly as complete.

Sound makes a significant contribution to your enjoyment of a visual story. It will bring the same advantages to your work. If you don't use sound effectively and pay as much attention to it as you do to the images, your productions will suffer. Whether you make narratives, documentaries, news, training videos, podcasts, games, or some other means of communication, sound has a great impact on what we see, believe, and remember.

Of course, movies were never really silent. Even Charlie Chaplin's images were accompanied by music, usually a single piano or organ whose initial function was to cover up the annoyingly loud noise of the projector. Filmmakers soon learned to exploit the power of music, and later the entire soundtrack, to tell their stories better.

Thankfully, putting together a better soundtrack is the easiest, cheapest, fastest, and most effective way to make your movie look better. When you dedicate attention to every element that comprises the whole soundtrack—dialogue, sound effects, and music—your story will hold more meaning for the audience, and you'll deliver your message in a more memorable way. Audiences will often put up with "bad" visuals, such as a shaky camera, strange colors, grainy imagery (we call all that *style*), but they will never, ever put up with bad sound. A mic thump, a crackly cable, a noticeable presence jump, an indecipherable dialogue line, and any number of sound gremlins all conspire to ruin your audience's experience. Crummy sound interferes with the viewer's ability to suspend their disbelief. Unless you purposely want to break down that barrier, improving the sound of your productions should be a top priority. Audiences have high expectations for soundtracks, and as a digital storyteller, it is up to you to deliver a high-quality, intelligible, emotionally supportive, and high-impact soundtrack that audiences remember.

The irony of it all is that good sound goes completely unnoticed. Great sound might get a mention (and occasionally a gold statue), but simple, effective soundtracks are felt by audiences but rarely acknowledged. People notice sound moments when they are not there, such as when a character places a cup on a table but no clunk is heard. Add the clunk, and nobody pays attention, because the sound is expected. Leave the clunk out, and some may notice, while others may just come away feeling a sense of unreality about the scene—it won't "work" for them. Sound completes the experience, obviously adding other layers and complexity. But don't expect accolades from the average viewer. They'll comment on the characters, the story, and how your movie made them feel. They won't leave the theater humming your sound effects. Outside of your peers, soundtrack creation is a mostly unsung art. But that never diminishes its importance. Sometimes sound is nothing more than neutral background filler that contributes to the realism of a scene. Other times, sound is up front and in your face, almost exaggerating what's happening. This book's goal is to help you discover how to best use the entire soundtrack to deliver your message effectively.

Always remember this: Bad sound equals a less enjoyable movie (or TV, game, and so on) experience for your audience. Period.

One of my favorite comments came from someone who posted to a forum I co-moderate. I'll paraphrase the naïve individual who asked whether, after all the hard work spent pulling together a complicated and lengthy video project, there was a button to press to clean up the sound. In essence, what was the magic formula for getting the audio together? This person expressed his impatience with going through the audio piece by piece, as he did with the video.

You can imagine my reply. If you're not willing to bring the same care to your sound that you willingly bring to making your visuals look good, you need to re-examine your priorities. There are no shortcuts or magic formulas. Soundtracks take as much work—if not significantly more—than production and picture editing combined. Don't run away from the work. Instead, embrace the challenge, knowing that ultimately your story will be better.

Today's digital storytellers have access to incredible tools, from digital video and animation software to software-based editing and digital delivery, including high definition. The problem many face is forgetting that sound is more than half of the experience. You need to understand how to use audio to make your productions better and more effective. This book will provide you with that knowledge. It's a soup-to-nuts guide to the entire realm of audio post-production, with particular attention paid to fixing problems, sweetening sound, and pulling together a complete soundtrack. You will discover how to record, edit, fix, sweeten, mix, master, and deliver high-quality and high-impact soundtracks. Also, the DVD that comes with this book includes audio and video examples that further explain and demonstrate the many concepts and techniques described in the book.

Choosing this book means you take sound very seriously. Or at the very least, you think it's time to sharpen your audio skills. Whether your video is stunningly beautiful or gritty and arty, the right sound will make it better. A vibrant soundtrack combined with high-quality visuals makes a statement greater than the sum of its parts. This guide shows you exactly how to do this with the most useful and practical techniques available today.

Of course, your buying this book indicates that you're willing to learn and apply what you know. Kudos to you for recognizing your own shortcomings and taking the steps to expand your knowledge. Otherwise, as you discover all that effective soundtrack creation entails, you'll soon realize that you need to hire someone to take care of these chores for you.

So whether you DIY or farm out the work to another, this resource provides the primer you need to make high-quality and high-impact soundtracks that soar. You will discover how to make informative and entertaining audio-visual presentations by using dialogue, voiceover, walla, backgrounds, sound design, sound effects, Foley, and music to deliver your message effectively.

# Who This Book Is For

More and more video editing studios and corporate production environments are keeping the tasks of recording, mixing, and sweetening of audio in house. Audio chores that were often farmed out to recording studios now fall to video editors.

Today's nonlinear video editors are being asked to do more and more. Although they used to just cut the movie, now they color-correct, compress, handle graphics, and so much more. Many are being asked to do audio post, too. Also, music selection falls to many editors, and some even have to write music on their own, using products such as GarageBand and Sony ACID. Yowza! Some gleefully take on these tasks, such as Walter Murch, who did a lot of sound work on *Jarhead* as he cut the film. Others—and perhaps you are one of them—have to be taken kicking and screaming to the edit bay to work on audio. "I don't know anything about audio," is the mantra I usually hear shouted across darkened rooms. It doesn't have to be that way at all. You can tell your story visually and still have time, expertise, and creativity left over to massage the soundtrack in ways that viewers will appreciate.

This book is for storytellers who produce content for theaters, TV, video, games, and the web. It will also appeal to those who aren't audio pros but who still need quality sound work on their productions, such as independent filmmakers and other low- to medium-budget content producers. The book will also appeal to music composers and producers, game sound/music designers, animators, audio instructors and their students, and film/TV/video enthusiasts. Unfortunately, try as it might, this book can't contain everything about audio and soundtracks. As I gaze across my bookshelves, I see thousands of pages from books and websites, along with dozens of DVDs and the remnants of countless hours in classrooms and many days and nights in darkened rooms spent honing my craft. All of these resources have served as my education. What I endeavor to do here is to relate the key concepts, workflow, and practical techniques that you can apply to *your* soundtracks. This won't be the definitive guide to soundtrack creation and success—no single book ever could be—but this resource aspires to serve as a detailed primer and a welcome reference to use for your storytelling career. After all, it was William Yeats who said, "Education is not filling a bucket, but lighting a fire." As you work through this book, I hope it becomes just the spark you need.

Furthermore, you can stay connected with me beyond this book by visiting and participating at my blog (www.jeffreypfisher.com) and by following me on Twitter: @JeffreyPFisher. I look forward to hearing from you.

Jeffrey P. Fisher

May 2011

## DVD Downloads

If you purchased an ebook version of this book, and the book had a companion DVD, you may download the contents from www.courseptr.com/downloads. Please note that you will be redirected to the Cengage Learning site.

If your book has a DVD, please check our website for any updates or errata files. You may download files from www.courseptr.com/downloads. Please note that you will be redirected to the Cengage Learning site.

# 1 Crafting the Quintessential Soundtrack

The next time you're in the theater or watching your favorite TV show, pay careful attention to what you hear. There's far more there than meets the ear. So, what goes into a soundtrack? There are several different layers that, when combined, result in the complete whole.

## Dialogue

Dialogue is the primary sound element that most people recall first. This dialogue might be between actors in a scene, between people in an interview, or even voiced by an unseen narrator. Dialogue, with the possible exception of voiceovers, is usually recorded on location but is often tweaked in post-production because tracks can be noisy. By applying some special tools, you can transform the dialogue into something almost squeaky-clean.

Unfortunately, sometimes dialogue is so bad that it needs to be replaced in post-production. This process—called *automatic dialogue replacement* (ADR for short) or its better known name, looping—has the actors re-record their lines, one at a time, while watching and listening to their original performance. The re-recorded lines then replace the bad production audio. For some Hollywood films, as much as 80 percent of the dialogue recorded on location is replaced in post. That may shock you, but it is nevertheless quite true. It is also one of the main reasons why Hollywood films sound so good, and so many low-budget and indie films do not.

When you see a crowd in film, they are only pantomiming. Their sounds, called *walla*, are always added later. Why walla? Urban legend has it that to create the murmur of a crowd, groups of people uttered the word "walla" to render the din as unrecognizable speech.

Oh yes, and for musicals and music videos, the singers lip-sync to a pre-recorded track. But you knew that already, right?

## Background Sounds

Every place has its own unique sound. For example, an office might hum from overhead fluorescent lights, whir from computer fans, and have a jumble of other noises—human and mechanical. These sounds are usually ignored in production, where getting good dialogue is critical. However, without these background sounds, there's a sense of unreality to a scene. You must add them back in during post-production. Backgrounds (BGs) provide a solid anchor for all the other sounds. They give a sense of space, place, and even time period that serves to surround and reinforce the other sound elements.

## Sound Effects

The next layer consists of sound effects. Believe it or not, most, if not all, of the specific sounds you hear on a film or TV show are added in later. Other than dialogue, sounds kept from location recordings are rare. Putting this off to post gives the storyteller more control, focus, and freedom to build a more effective soundtrack. Sound effects are often captured during separate recording sessions or drawn from existing libraries available on disc or as web downloads.

Some sound effects are so specific that they get created and recorded while the technician is watching the film in post-production. Named *Foley* (after the man who invented the technique), sounds such as footsteps, props, and clothing noises get added to the mix.

## Sound Design

Another aspect of soundtrack creation is that of sound design—actually creating the sounds the audience will hear. Credited as the first true sound designer (for the original *Star Wars*), Ben Burtt came up with the entire world of sounds for the *Star Wars* universe, a legacy that continued through all six films. In the late '70s, though, Burtt had little more than some high-quality mics, analog recorders, and a few methods to manipulate sounds, such as varispeed, reverse, equalization and other filters, flanging, delay, and stacking/mixing. He relied mostly on his creativity and ingenuity to craft the sonic world of this sci-fi classic. Today, a single software tool, such as Sony Creative Software Sound Forge, lets you work more easily, faster, and at higher fidelity, and includes more sound manipulation tools than Burtt had at his fingertips (and probably dreamed about). Of course, Burtt has all the new tools now, too!

## Music

And finally there is music, with its infinite power to manipulate the emotions of a scene. Music sets the mood, supports the imagery, and drives the drama. What does the music say about the nature of a film? Think of examples from your favorite movies. Does the music evoke romantic comedy, perhaps? Action-adventure? How about the score in a horror film? Music has great power, and that is why it is so critical to every soundtrack's success.

## Putting It All Together

All of these elements get pulled together for the final mix. Very complex soundtracks usually require combining elements into groups before the final mix. This is called *premixing*, and the results are known as *premixes* or *stems*. Sometimes these are called *dubs*. There may be dialogue, effects, Foley, and background premixes. These all come to the final re-recording mix session, where the balance of elements is finally determined.

It is typical for a final mix to keep the three main elements—dialogue, music, and effects—separate, too. This DM&E mix is used for foreign-language dubbing. The D (dialogue) can be replaced, keeping the original mix of M (music) and E (effects). However, the foreign-language final mix can control the relative balance of these three elements, primarily for maximum speech intelligibility. You wouldn't want to remix the whole thing, though. Also, for some documentary work—particularly when there is an interview in another language that is then voiced by another native person—the interview goes to the effects stem while the voiceover stays in the dialogue stem. If the project is a surround-sound release, there will be 18 tracks to the DM&E. (5.1 surround equals six separate channels for each of the three primary elements.) A stereo downmix will also be created.

To recap: First comes dialogue; then walla; then backgrounds; followed by sound effects, including Foley; and finally the extra sweetener—music. These are the component parts that are combined into the final soundtrack. If you had to break down a soundtrack into its three most important considerations, dialogue would carry the message, sound effects would function as the reality (though they can be exaggerated, too), and music would provide the emotion. These roles may change, but generally they are true. The success of your soundtrack depends on how effectively you employ each of these elements. This book will help you master the basics and more, and it will lead you down the path toward better audio tracks for every production you do.

Take a look at Figure 1.1 for a graphical soundtrack overview.

## Workflow

The workflow critical to making your soundtrack function is deceptively simple. First, you must decide on all the sounds you need—dialogue, voiceover, walla, sound effects, Foley, background, and music. Next, you record, create, or otherwise acquire these elements. Then, turn your attention toward aligning or syncing these sounds appropriately with the visuals. Usually, you add other layers to build a convincing sonic environment. Next, balance and mix these sounds for the most impact. And finally, output and deliver the finished soundtrack.

Don't be fooled by this simplicity, though. There are many steps and procedures involved in every step of this outline. This book will fill in the gaps and offer the techniques you need to complete these major tasks.

If you take one thing away from this resource, it's this: Spend *at least* half as much time on your soundtrack as you do on making your video look fantastic. But if you really

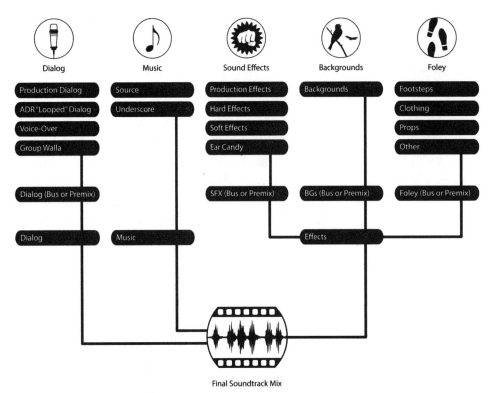

**Figure 1.1**  Soundtrack overview. Graphic courtesy of Christopher Bodel.

want to make a statement, spend the same amount of time on what people hear as you do on what they see. This will make your projects better than you ever could have hoped for or imagined.

## DVD Education

So where do you learn to craft effective soundtracks? Many movies have bonus features that can serve as an education in the art and science of sound for picture.

Start with the film *The Shop Around the Corner*, starring James Stewart. There's a wonderful bonus feature on the DVD that details the sound recording of the day. It's quite primitive by today's standards, but it's a fun exploration and history lesson nonetheless.

Many deleted scenes included with DVDs do not have the gloss of the completed picture and serve as great indicators of how atrocious many production sound recordings really are. You will have a new appreciation for the dialogue editor when you listen to the final scenes for comparison. My favorite example for this study, thanks to a tip from sound guru Tomlinson Holman, is the quirky *To Wong Foo, Thanks for Everything! Julie Newmar.*

*Forrest Gump* has a behind-the-scenes documentary that includes an interview with sound supervisor Randy Thom, along with examples from the film. *Star Wars:* Episode II *Attack of the Clones* gives a definitive look at sound post-production as sound designer Ben Burtt explains that films aren't released, they escape. This documentary shows a little bit of everything discussed in this book and is highly recommended.

Films that are worth studying for their outstanding sound include *Monsters, Inc.*, which has an alternate audio track that features the surround-sound mix of sound effects only (no dialogue or music). You should also check out anything by David Lynch, a director who is highly involved with the sound of his films, especially my particular favorite: *Twin Peaks: Fire Walk with Me*, with its quintessential horror-movie soundtrack. *Das Boot* is another amazingly well-done sound experience. The silence in the U-boat as they hide from Allied ships is particularly effective (especially in 5.1). *The Conversation*, though somewhat dated with its technology, is another film sound study priority. There are plenty of other examples—just look at the films that win Oscars for sound, and you'll know where to start, augment, and complete your education.

For an exercise in film music 101, grab *North by Northwest*, in which one of the extra audio tracks features only Bernard Herrmann's amazing score. Listen to how Bernie uses variations on the main theme repeatedly throughout the film.

On the web, check out FilmSound.org for further insight, especially their extensive collection of film sound clichés (http://filmsound.org/cliche). If you've never heard of the Wilhelm scream—though I know you've heard the actual scream—find out about it here.

# 2 Audio Aesthetics

So, what makes for good audio on your soundtracks? I have three edicts that I'd like to share with you.

1. Dialogue rules.

2. Plan for sound.

3. It's the final mix that matters.

Let me clarify these three points.

## Dialogue Rules

Most of your projects will be driven by dialogue—what characters say, what eyewitnesses report, what voiceovers explain, and so on. So, dialogue should be the primary focus of the sound experience. Dare I say that the whole soundtrack should be built around dialogue and be subservient to it? Yes! Dialogue rules, and everything else is secondary. Therefore, you must make sure the audience can fully understand what is being said. This can be problematic at times because you've heard the dialogue a hundred times already—you might even have written it—and there may be a tendency to bury it under other soundtrack elements. Resist this urge. You understand what's being said because you've heard it before. However, your audience will always be hearing it for the first time. Be kind to them and make dialogue clarity a top priority. (Also, it helps to get a fresh perspective on this issue from test audiences, even if that audience is composed of only a friend or significant other.)

## Plan Ahead

Too often sound is an afterthought. I urge you to think about sound up front, as you draft the story and pull together the project. Although many wonderful sound moments come together in post-production, many more come through scripts that are carefully crafted in the first place. If you build sound into your project, your final version will have a soundtrack with better impact. So few screenwriters use sound well as a dramatic tool. That continues to surprise me, because sound can (and should!) be an effective storytelling device. Resolve now to make sound part of the story, and you won't regret the decision.

Sound should enhance the story and add meaning to it. It should put you in an environment—indeed, a specific locale. It should reveal the time period. Sound can even reflect the thoughts and inner emotions of the characters. Sound, for the most part, is objective for the audience to hear. But sequences can be effective when we hear *as* the character hears it—in other words, from their particular subjective point of view. This can be an effective—even unnerving—way to get inside a character's mind.

The other side of planning involves visiting locations and listening to them *before* you bring the whole cast and crew for the typical shoot. Many issues of locations—noise, excessive reverberation, and other ills—can be mitigated in advance. You'll also get a better sense of what problems may arise, and you can then choose tactics and equipment to solve those problems. For example, planning the final scene to take place in Chicago's Buckingham Fountain? You won't get good dialogue recordings on the set with all the water rushing around. Therefore, you need to make other plans, such as ADR, to get the best sound for that important dramatic moment.

## The Final Mix Matters

I do not necessarily care what a single, unadorned soundtrack element sounds like on its own when it is only part of the overall mix. How everything fits into the mix as a whole is what really matters. For example, a piece of dialogue subjected to extreme noise reduction might sound less noisy, but otherwise be lo-fi on its own. However, when that same dialogue gets surrounded by sound effects, backgrounds, and music, it might work quite nicely. Don't focus only on individual elements when you need to keep your ear on the final mix. Each element is only part of the total orchestration. The exception, of course, is when a soundtrack piece must play on its own, without support from any other source. In this case, the sound must be at its best. Of course, you should always strive to make every sound you use as pristine as possible, but know that even good sound often needs sweetening to make it work with other sound elements.

Think of the whole soundtrack for the most depth and meaning. If your dialogue is a little sparse, fill in the missing elements with music, sound effects, and backgrounds to make a fuller soundtrack. In the early days of sound recording, tracks were limited in both dynamic range and frequency response. Dialogue was especially midrange-y (telephone-like). The use of music—arguably, the overuse of it—during that era helped fill out the soundtrack and make for a fuller sound. However, it was only marginally successful because the optical soundtracks of the day prevented the kind of truly high-fidelity recording and playback available today.

When you are thinking about the whole soundtrack, take a hint from audio pro George Massenburg. To paraphrase him: There needs to be an internal balance within the soundtrack itself—how the different elements fit together into a cohesive, related whole. However, there must also be an external balance—that is to say, a balance in how the sounds relate to the outside world. In other words, does it sound right upon playback? So, the internal balance is more creative and centered on storytelling, whereas the external balance is more technical and focused on levels, phase, and so forth.

In his book *Practical Techniques for the Recording Engineer* (Mix Books, 1989), Sherman Keene offered a list of mixing ideas. Even though this resource is somewhat dated and focused on music-only projects, his main ideas remain especially poignant. Keene comments that a good mix includes:

- Powerful and solid lows

- Proper use of midrange

- Clear and clean highs

- Proper, but not overburdening, effects

- Real acoustic information, not just electronic reverbs and delays

- Dimension with a sense of depth

- Motion and movement of the instruments (individual parts)

- One true stereo track, preferably up front

To this list, I would add "ear candy"—audio moments that stick in the minds of the audience members.

## Narrative Elements

Sound functions as more than just the other half of the audio-visual experience. It has a real place in the narrative that can make storytelling more powerful and meaningful for your audience. Keep these key aesthetic concepts in mind as you work on your soundtracks.

### Diegetic and Non-Diegetic Sounds

Authors David Bordwell and Kristin Thompson coined the language of sound and how it's used in visual storytelling today in their book, *Film Art: An Introduction* (McGraw-Hill, 2006). The sounds that are part of the scene, such as onscreen dialogue, footsteps, and traffic noises during a street scene, are called *diegetic* sounds. *Non-diegetic* sounds include elements that do not emanate from the scene itself, such elements as musical score and voiceover narration. For example, we don't expect the camera to pan over to reveal an offscreen orchestra playing, though Mel Brooks did this in his Alfred Hitchcock tribute, *High Anxiety*. As an example of diegetic sound, on the other hand, in *Groundhog Day*, Bill Murray's character awakens to the same Sonny and Cher song playing from an onscreen clock radio. This is the essence of diegetic music.

Don't confuse offscreen sounds with being non-diegetic, though. A unseen dog heard barking outside a window in a scene is still part of the diegesis of the scene. So, while all non-diegetic sound is inherently "offscreen," not all sources of diegetic sound are shown to the audience.

Consider also the movie *Amadeus*. The constant shifting from diegetic, onscreen music to non-diegetic underscore is a major theme and is one of my favorite examples. Mozart's music is used to support the drama as traditional non-diegetic underscore, and is also often heard performed onscreen in snippets from performances—pure diegetic. Especially noteworthy is the sequence near the end of the film. Mozart is too sick to physically write out his last music score. He enlists the help of peer composer Salieri and begins to dictate the score. Mozart hears the music in his head, which the audience also hears as a form of diegetic music. When he reviews the score written by Salieri, the music plays again as part of the scene. Then, the scene cuts away to Mozart's wife as she rushes to return to her husband's side. The very same diegetic music becomes the non-diegetic dramatic underscore to her fruitless journey instead. It's a brilliant sequence from which you can learn.

## Listening versus Hearing

Another distinction to make is whether you are forcing your audience to actually listen to your soundtrack. Listening is an active engagement, whereas hearing is passive. We hear all the time, but to be truly present and focused on the material, we need to listen. Your job is to highlight the important soundtrack elements your audience needs to listen to and specifically direct their attention and focus to them in an ever-evolving, carefully coordinated and choreographed dance of sound.

## Figure/Ground

Soundtracks are composed of many layers containing obvious and not-so-obvious sounds. The problem is that too much sound quickly degenerates into noise. Oscar-winning sound designer Walter Murch says that your audience can only focus on two simultaneous sounds. Adding a third element makes the whole indistinct. His analogy is that a person can focus on two trees, but three (or more) trees make a forest. This observation is akin to the Gestalt theory of figure/ground. In a dynamic mix, sound elements come and go, which usually works fine as long as no more than two primary figures (sounds) are present together. The other sounds simply become a part of the overall background element—the forest, if you will.

This does not imply that your soundtrack needs only two elements to work at any given time. On the contrary, you must augment these figures with other less-important audio flourishes that ground your audience. Without these added pieces, the soundtrack doesn't always work as a whole. It sounds unrealistic, thin, and as if it's missing something. Most people won't be able to explain what's wrong. The soundtrack simply won't "work" for them.

### Cause and Effect

Another factor to keep in mind as you assemble the audio elements is that of cause and effect. Often you will have one sound that relates to another. For example, a character throws a huge switch in a giant warehouse, and the lights come on with a big sound. Or this example: A gun fires, and the audience hears both the shell ejecting and hitting the ground and the bullet ricocheting off of a distant wall. I prefer to call some of these sounds "soft effects," as they are related to an obvious hard effect and serve to add a level of detail that contributes to the whole sound and makes it richer.

### Entrainment

Author David Sonnenschein talks about another critical element of soundtrack creation in his book, *Sound Design: The Expressive Power of Music, Voice, and Sound Effects in Cinema* (Michael Wiese Productions, 2002). Entrainment means that as humans we may perceive synchronization between elements where it doesn't exist. For instance, when music accompanies an action, the two appear to be in sync. In reality, there is no synchronization—just our mind trying to make sense of or create some order out of sheer chaos. This tendency by your audience to entrain is a valuable notion for the sound designer as you build sequences. Slight sync errors go unnoticed and can make some effects, such as Foley, work. Composers exploit this all the time. For instance, if just one music element—say, a cymbal crash—aligns with an onscreen action—say, the bad guy appears—the audience synchronizes those two events and feels that the whole music score is in sync with the picture. It won't matter if nothing else musically mirrors the action; the audience will entrain the rest.

Consider reading Sonnenschein's book to further explore these aesthetic principles in greater detail. It's not a technical book; it's an erudite analysis of narrative sound. I highly recommend it.

## Soundtrack Core Elements

Your job is to craft the audio in such a way that it adds meaning to the project and results in a better overall audience experience. Sometimes your work goes completely unnoticed as you add a layer of realism that simply supports and reinforces the concept. Other times, you may go for a more stylized approach that draws attention to specific actions and emotions. In both cases, you draw upon unique techniques and add a dose of your own creativity to make the best possible outcome.

### Fixing and Sweetening

To a certain extent there are only two aspects to soundtrack work: fixing and sweetening. You will spend a lot of time fixing mistakes, usually poorly recorded or executed location audio. After all that fixing, you will turn your attention to sweetening the soundtrack to make it better. You will add sounds, fill in missing elements, and otherwise create a believable and appropriate soundtrack. Always finish the fixing before the sweetening, but always keep the sweetening in mind as you fix things. Remember the third edict: It's the final mix that matters.

## Controlling Noise

Another crucial element to soundtrack success is the absence of noise. While a completely noise-free soundtrack may not be possible or even desirable, keeping distracting noise out of the audience's ears is key. Noise is all around us and finds its way into our work, intentionally or not. Although you probably won't eliminate noise completely, you *do* need to learn to reduce its debilitating effect. Sometimes you can get rid of it entirely, sometimes you can keep it from ruining the experience, and other times you can use it to make a point or to your best advantage.

## Ensuring Consistency

There needs to be a consistent level and "sound" to your soundtrack. Volume levels can't be all over the map, though using the full dynamic range (soft sounds to loud sounds) is a good tactic. If everything is really loud or really soft all the time, you need to revisit your soundtrack. Again, turn to Hollywood and study what is effective. Soundtracks aren't loud or whisper-quiet all the time; just when needed. It's this contrast that often makes the whole experience more memorable.

> **Note:** Remember to assemble a soundtrack that puts your personal stamp on the project, too. Sound doesn't have to be anonymous; it can also be artistic.

On long-form projects, you might find yourself revisiting the work you did earlier in the project. That's why I rarely work linearly; I work on the tough scenes first so that I have time to revisit them after more of the project is under my belt. I often discover particular fixes as I move along and can then return to other sequences and make them stronger and more effective.

Going back to apply what you've learned to work you did days or even weeks ago is a necessary evil. Embrace it, or the work you do late in the project might not match what you did early on. I know it can be boring to go over the same ground, but you'll like the finished product more. There will be a consistency to the production that will work better for your audience.

The first 10 to 15 minutes of a project sets the tone for the audience. They will apply its quality to the rest of the piece as their experience moves along. The last 10 to 15 minutes is what they will remember most about the sound. So, if your sound is bad at the start and finish, that's what your audience will notice. But come in strong and finish well, and your audience will feel that the whole soundtrack was good. If you are going to have to compromise sonically, do so in the middle, where it's least noticed or remembered (provided you started and ended with very good audio).

Another aspect of consistency is that the sounds you choose and the way you present them in the final mix must be appropriate to the message being delivered. Make mindful choices that support what you are trying to say. Sometimes you have to make really tough choices, too. Follow the three rules of work that Albert Einstein suggested: "Out of clutter find simplicity; from discord find harmony; in the middle of difficulty lies opportunity." Often soundtrack elements get left out of the final mix because there's a better way to reveal the story. It can be hard to let go of these—after all, you put a lot of work into them—but always go with what serves the story best and leave out any and all of the extraneous material.

## Enriching the Listening Experience

I'm a firm believer that the soundtrack alone should paint a picture in the audience's mind's eye. If the soundtrack needs the visuals to work, you aren't trying hard enough. Any soundtrack that can make an impact on its own makes the visuals that much stronger. Sound should add something that the image itself doesn't contain. As I said before, the presentation is greater than the sum of its parts.

Make sure you fill the entire frequency spectrum with sound—solid lows and clear and pristine highs. Humans hear from 20 to 20,000 Hertz (Hz), but most of what we hear falls into a narrow frequency range. The low note on a normally tuned bass guitar is 41 Hz, while the frequencies that help make speech intelligible range between 2 and 4 kHz. This is the real problem, because you have to make room for all the soundtrack elements, but you only have so many frequencies to deal with. Therefore, understanding and using the whole range can make your life easier. Dialogue fills a lot of middle, so surrounding it with low tones and high tones (from music, for example) can enrich the listening experience.

Hot on the heels of that last observation is to always make room for sound. You can't have the scream, the gunshot, and the music crescendo all happening at the exact same moment; it will sound like a jumbled mess. Remember the figure/ground discussion from earlier in this chapter. You have to avoid having sounds step on one another by separating them in time, frequency, and volume. A loud sound will always cover up a soft one, so be aware of how sounds cover up other sounds (called *masking*) and plan accordingly. Decide on the primary sound that should be present at any given moment and then downplay those sounds that serve a more secondary, supporting role.

You must employ a dynamic, ever-changing mix of elements. Use your creativity and make the right choices that show your audience what's most important sonically. Your work effectively says: "Listen to this first. Now listen to this. And now this." And so on. It's a tricky tightrope to walk, especially with a dense mix, such as in an action film. Too much sound going on makes for a soundtrack of noise. It's no less tricky on a quiet sequence, where a single sound can be magnified unintentionally and therefore change the nature of a scene and its emotion.

## Checklist for Soundtrack Success

To summarize what we've discussed so far, here is my soundtrack success checklist:

- Can your audience understand all the words?

- Did you paint a clear picture in the audience's mind's eye?

- Did you use sounds that are appropriate to the message?

- Have you filled the entire frequency spectrum (bass, mids, and highs)?

- Is there room for sound? Or is everything a jumbled mess?

- Is the soundtrack free from noise and distortion?

- Is there a consistent level and intentional sound?

If you can already answer yes to each of these questions, I applaud you. This kind of audio result is no easy task. However, achieving immediate soundtrack success is nearly impossible. So if you can't answer yes to all of these questions yet, you're in good company. And you should read on for the details you need to check these off your list.

## Sound Transitions

Other aesthetic choices include where a sound occurs in relation to other sounds around it. Some of these indications may be in the script, but they are more often arrived at in the edit suite, as scenes build and flow into one another. Sound often changes over time. Or, because of a location or other change, you often need to transition from one sound (or set of sounds) to another. There are four choices for transitions:

- Straight cut

- Sound before picture (usually for a location change)

- Sound dissolve

- Sound after picture

The general rule is to match the screen action. If there is an abrupt cut in the screen action, you can cut the sound accordingly. If there is a dissolve or some other visual transition, the sound from the previous environment can fade out while the subsequent sound environment fades in (called a *crossfade*).

Sometimes this dissolve goes through black, where the outgoing scene fades to black, holds in black for a brief moment, and then the incoming scene fades in. Here, you may choose to go to complete silence during the black interlude, or you may either carry some sound over or begin to introduce the new scene.

The previous sound can continue into the next shot, too. Although this is often done with music, sound effects can work, too. Alternatively, the new sound can come *before* the new scene. For example, a loud sound that typifies the new location can start before the audience sees the next shot. This is often used to jar an audience by cutting from a quiet scene to a loud, dense scene, such as a party. The party ruckus is heard before we see the action creating that sound. TV shows often do this musically by starting with a busy musical interlude, called a *bumper*, when returning to the drama following a commercial break. The TV cop drama *NYPD Blue* used this effect extensively.

A sound dissolve can also work, where one sound morphs to become another. Near the conclusion of the original *Manchurian Candidate*, a gunshot ends a scene and rings out in the large room, with its reverb tail continuing into the next scene. At the same time, a thunderclap extends the apparent gunshot into the next scene. In reality, the two sounds overlap or crossfade, one replacing the other. The gunshot sound is effectively lengthened by the long thunder sound effect. It's a powerful effect that supports the drama quite convincingly.

# Ear Candy

Sound design can be more evocative than you might readily perceive. For example, a single sound effect can be composed of several sounds, some acting subliminally. For *Monsters, Inc.*, Gary Rydstrom added a little bit of scream when cars zoomed by onscreen (known as a *car-by*). Because the power in the monsters' world came from children screaming, mixing in these sounds worked almost subliminally. There's an example of this on the movie's DVD bonus features.

I call moments such as these (along with other such intentional sound moments) *ear candy*. These sounds are not integral to the plot or used to support visible action. Instead, they act as diegetic sweeteners to help bring a scene to life. Much of the ear candy I add is for my own amusement—something to occupy my mind and ears, as a thinly disguised form of rebellion against my spending too many long hours alone in dark rooms. For one project, every time people opened or closed a door to a particular location (a coffee shop), I added a little tinkly bell sound. This wasn't on the original production takes, but I thought it added something more real to the scenes.

Most audiences don't notice this hard work, but it *does* work on a subconscious level and is therefore worth the extra effort. Time spent adding footsteps, prop noises, little sound effects, convincing backgrounds, and so on results in a better experience for the audience. Just don't expect the audience to acknowledge your hard work. Composers often add ear candy to their music, and sound editors should follow that precept and work to make their soundtracks more alive and vibrant.

## Quiet Scenes

One of the most difficult soundtrack tasks is to work on a quiet scene. Audio people are so tuned to piling up effects to build a scene that when faced with the opposite challenge, we go crazy. The complete absence of sound is rare—there is usually background (if only from the presence tracks and used primarily to smooth dialogue). Perhaps you might include an exaggerated focus on certain sounds, such as an overtly loud ticking clock.

For one film, it took the better part of a day to work on a one-minute quiet discussion in a bedroom. It's not that the production tracks were bad; it's just that any little noise was magnified and seemed too big and out of place. It required meticulous care to clean things up, reduce any noise elements, and keep the drama intact. To be honest, it's easier to do a big action scene than these quiet little moments. But be forewarned: These dramatic scenes stick in the audience's mind long after the credits roll. It is worth the extra effort to pull them off well. Fantastic examples of quiet scenes are many sequences in *Castaway* and the first 20 minutes or so of Pixar's *Wall-E*.

Music may function here, but music without natural sound (a.k.a. *nat sound*) quickly descends into music video. Keeping the nat going along with the music is more realistic. The sound, though greatly understated, keeps the audience believing, while the music enhances the emotion. Of course, almost everyone just notices how good the talent is (such is the storyteller's life), despite the fact that the soundtrack deserves at least *some* of the credit.

### Sports-izing

Many visual statements look better with sound treatment. TV sports programming is notorious for adding sounds to their television coverage. Every graphic entrance, every instant replay wipe, and more has some kind of ear-candy sound treatment. I affection-ately call it *sports-izing* your soundtrack. If you work in non-narrative TV or you do a lot of corporate/industrial work, enhancing visual sequences with sound is a mainstay. Logos swoosh in and slam when they stop center-screen. Lightning booms, crackles, and sizzles out. Noise sweeps and effects, as they are sometimes known, are part and parcel of radio spots, TV promos, sports, and other "reality" programming. Although it's acceptable to add these sounds after the visual is made, you can build them before, too. For example, Digital Juice (www.digitaljuice.com) offers Evolvers, which work like music. You lay them into your soundtrack and build your visual around them instead of post-syncing effects to an already built visual sequence. They are part of the Digital Juice Sound FX library.

## Analyze This

One of the best tactics for learning about soundtrack aesthetics is to watch, listen, and analyze as many films, documentaries, TV shows, and so on as you can. This is best done with something you've already seen. You are familiar with the story and other elements, so you can concentrate on just the soundtrack. It's best to ignore the music at this point and focus on the dialogue and effects. You can do a separate analysis of the music later. Listen critically and ask and answer these questions:

- What specific sound elements made an impression on you? Why?

- How does the sound enhance meaning, story, and plot and provide character insight?

- Does the sound detract from or otherwise change the meaning?

- Does the sound relay emotions? If so, how?

- Are there uses of diegetic and non-diegetic sound?

- Are there examples of subjective sound?

- Was the soundtrack as a whole effective or ineffective? How?

- Was the soundtrack realistic or stylized? In what ways?

In the next chapter, our discussion turns to the basics of sound and digital audio.

# 3 What Is Sound?

Stretch a piece of string or a rubber band tightly and then pluck it to see it vibrate until it runs out of energy. Sound is similar to this vibration. Sound doesn't move back and forth, but rather it spreads out in all directions from the source that created it, much like when you drop a stone into a calm pond. Sound waves also crest (called *compression*) and trough (called *rarefaction*), just like water waves. This wave analogy continues when you see sound represented on a computer monitor when you are using sound editing software. It looks like a waveform, and indeed it is. To share a few key terms with you, the high-quality audio file format used by computers is, in fact, called *WAV*. Sound traveling through air is called *acoustic energy*, and musical instruments that create their sound through vibration are known as *acoustic instruments* and include flute and acoustic guitar.

## Components of Sound

Sound has two primary components that we perceive: pitch and loudness, which are represented by measurements of frequency and amplitude (or volume), respectively. Other ways to describe sound are in terms of rhythm, timbre, fidelity, a sound's point in space (closer or farther away), and its time base. These are more subjective descriptions than the more quantifiable ones, though. Picture a calm pond, and then imagine throwing in a stone. The wave begins to move outward. One cycle of the wave goes from that calm water surface to the top of the wave (maximum compression), back through the surface to the maximum wave trough (rarefaction), and once again back to the calm, at-rest surface. When there are more cycles per second to the sound wave, the pitch is higher; when there are fewer wave cycles per second, the pitch is lower. Pitch is expressed as a frequency, with higher pitches having a higher frequency. This frequency is based on the number of cycles per second, expressed as Hertz (Hz). The normal human hearing range is from 20 Hz to 20,000 Hz (20 kHz).

The height of a wave crest and the depth of its trough reflect the power or amplitude of the sound. This amplitude is perceived as loudness, with higher amplitudes being louder and lower amplitudes being softer. We express loudness using the decibel (dB) scale. Decibels do not start at the complete absence of sound, but rather at the threshold of human hearing. They continue up through the threshold of pain—loud sounds that physically hurt. The typical home environment comes in at a mere 40 to 50 dB, but a loud rock concert can extend well over 110 dB. It is crucial to note that the decibel scale is logarithmic, which means that a 3-dB increase doubles the energy, so 93 dB is twice as loud as 90 dB. However, most people do not notice a sound being twice as loud unless they hear a 9- to 10-dB change. This discrepancy between measurable loudness and perceptual loudness is important to understand. Mathematically, making a sound effect twice as loud would indicate increasing its volume a mere 3 dB. But the audience might barely notice this level of increase. Therefore, you often need to make some sounds far louder than the math would indicate to have the impact you desire. Unfortunately, in a busy mix, there may not be enough room to make this sound so loud. Instead, you may need to decrease the level of other sounds to make this one sound as loud as you need.

The Fletcher-Munson equal loudness contours show a comparison between loudness and frequency as reflected by the human ear (see Figure 3.1). At lower volumes, the ear is less sensitive to low-frequency sounds. As a result, for a 100-Hz sound to be perceived *equally as loud* as a 1,000-Hz sound at 40 dB, the 100-Hz sound needs to be almost 20 dB *louder*! If your sound system has a loudness control, you've experienced this phenomenon. The loudness control should be engaged when you are listening at lower volumes because it compensates for the ear's reduced sensitivity to low-frequency sounds at lower listening levels. The loudness control, therefore, boosts the bass.

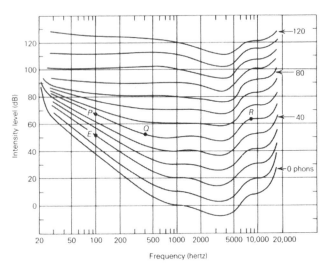

**Figure 3.1** Fletcher-Munson equal loudness contours.

It is no coincidence that the film standard for mixing volume is 86 dB. You should note that between 85 and 90 dB, the Fletcher-Munson plot shows a flatter frequency response by the ear. At this volume level, the ear generally perceives many frequencies as equally loud. Consequently, make all your critical sound decisions at this volume level because you can trust that your ears aren't lying to you. If you use other volume levels, you may compensate in the mix for your ear's less-than-ideal frequency response, and when you play your mix in other situations it might not sound right. For example, you might add bass that you feel is missing, when really it is just your ear's inability to hear it properly in relation to other frequencies. Remember this point; it will become important during the discussion of speaker calibration later in this book.

## Analog Basics

What are the primary sources of sound? There are only three: voice, music, and noise. When describing these sounds, people often resort to analogies, such as saying that a tire screech sounds like a baby crying. The term *analog* can be found as the root of *analogy*. An analog is something that is like another something—but not necessarily an exact copy. You need to understand this key concept of analog before you can grasp the fundamentals of digital audio. The analog world creates new representations of the sound, as when a microphone converts the acoustic energy first into mechanical energy and then into electricity. The mechanical/electrical energy are analogs—they are like the acoustic energy but not an exact copy. Similarly, digital audio is a mathematical representation of the sound but not an exact version of it.

Although we live in a highly digital world, there are still many analog components to sound recording, manipulation, and delivery. For examples, microphones and speakers are the obvious analog components of today's soundtrack.

## Sound Perception

No discussion of sound can be complete without a discussion of sound perception. How does the ear work? The outside of the ear—where many people hang their jewelry—is known as the *pinna*. Satellite-dish designs are based on the pinna—both serve to collect energy and funnel it to a single point. The ear gathers sound and sends it down the ear canal.

---

**Note:** It is interesting to note that the shape and size of the pinna serves to accentuate the consonants of human speech, making words more intelligible.

---

The end of the ear canal has a piece of tightly stretched skin called the *tympanic membrane*—otherwise known as the *eardrum*. When sound reaches the eardrum, it vibrates analogously to the sound energy. (There's that *analog* word again.) The *ossicles*—three tiny bones: the hammer, anvil, and stirrup—connect to the eardrum and transfer its vibration to the inner ear, or *cochlea*. Working like a piston, these bones serve to amplify the energy, too. The fluid-filled cochlea contains thousands of tiny hairs. The sound energy, now a mechanical energy, creates a wave pattern in the fluid that stimulates the tiny hairs. The result is an electrochemical response that travels to the brain and is interpreted as sound.

This conversion from one form of energy—acoustic sound energy—to mechanical energy and then to electricity is known as *transduction*. Microphones work the same way. Sound strikes a diaphragm, which vibrates, and the sound is then converted to electricity. As electricity, it can be amplified and recorded. In a tape-based recorder, electricity moves a magnet, which vibrates and in turn arranges tiny particles of metal on the tape into a pattern that creates an analog match of the original sound.

Keep in mind that there can be breakdowns in the system at any stage. This distortion, defined simply as the output differing in any way from the input, is a significant component to analog systems. What goes in and what comes out will differ. Sometimes this difference is pleasing and complementary; other times it sounds terrible.

## Digital Diatribe

In the world of computers, there are only two numbers: 0 and 1. However, the computer can combine zeroes and ones in ways that make today's complex computing power possible. The act of replacing an analog recorder with its digital equivalent requires that you somehow convert the electricity into zeroes and ones. Remember, you have to capture both the frequency (pitch) and amplitude (loudness) of sound to effectively reproduce it.

To capture frequency, the computer soundcard's analog-to-digital converter (ADC) analyzes the electrical waveform by taking tiny digital snapshots, known as *samples*, of it over time. The process is called *sampling*. The computer takes 44,100 samples each second for CD quality and 48,000 samples per second for digital video (DV). These sample rates are usually abbreviated as 44.1 kHz and 48 kHz, respectively. To prevent aliasing (a form of distortion), this sample rate must be twice the highest frequency sampled. Because human hearing ranges from 20 Hz to 20 kHz, a filter blocks any frequencies above 20 kHz from the computer. However, in the analog world, we can't make a filter that lets in 20 kHz and stops at 20.1 kHz on up; such a brick-wall filter is impractical. Therefore, the anti-aliasing circuit employs a gentler filter that limits the frequency response to 22.05 kHz, and then the sample rate is 44.1 kHz for CDs.

The ADC must also assign a value to each sample as an indicator of its amplitude. This is known as the *bit depth*. CD quality uses 16 bits for 65,536 possible amplitude steps ($2^{16}$). The sampling process means that values must round or quantize to the nearest value. This is another form of distortion known as *quantization error*. Obviously, the more values there are, the more accurate the results. For example, using 24 bits ($2^{24}$) gives a much finer and more faithful representation—16,777,216 possible values.

Note that converting from analog to digital takes a smooth waveform and creates a stair-step pattern in the final digital file. On output, the soundcard's digital-to-analog converter (DAC) reads the data and converts it back into electricity. The DAC also uses a special filter to help smooth the stair-step digital pattern back into the original wave shape.

CD-quality stereo sound—44.1-kHz sample rate and 16 bits—uses about 10 MB of space; a monaural file uses about half that. Several audio compression schemes, such as Dolby's AC-3 and the ubiquitous MP3, use psychoacoustic masking to reduce the file size while maintaining acceptable fidelity. When encoding, the software meticulously evaluates the file and then discards information the ear probably won't hear. For example, a loud cymbal crash often covers up or masks the other sounds for a brief moment during a song. By describing only the cymbal and ignoring everything else, you can reduce the file's size. Because this is a dynamic process applied over time, the ear/brain combination fills in what's missing. By throwing out information, significant file size reductions are possible. However, there is a substantial quality hit when you use these compression schemes—they throw out almost as much as they keep in the final output. However, MP3 and especially AC-3 use clever psychoacoustic principles to fool the ear/brain.

## Sound Starts

There were many attempts to synchronize moving pictures with sound. Success came in 1926, with *Don Juan*, though it was the Vitaphone process playing Al Jolson's music in *The Jazz Singer* that often gets the credit. Vitaphone used a Gramophone record player connected to the film projector, but was soon supplanted by using sound from microphones to modulate a light source that then exposed film. Optical sound became the standard and is still present on every film released. The single channel of monaural recording dominated for years, until *Fantasia* brought stereo front speakers and a rear effects track as a precursor to today's surround sound.

The 1940s brought magnetic tape recording to the movies, and that technology dominated for several decades until digital recording took over. Movie studios saw competition from TV and began to release widescreen Cinerama and CinemaScope movies that worked best with big soundtracks. Multichannel sound saw the addition of a third dedicated center channel, primarily to anchor the dialogue to the screen; two stereo speakers for effects and music; and a single special-effects speaker to the rear to immerse or surround the audience in the sound.

With the widescreen format of 70mm, there was space on the film itself to accommodate up to six discrete analog soundtracks: left, left-center, center, right-center, right, and a rear effects speaker. It was Dolby that really embraced this format, and it slowly evolved into the 5.1 format we know today. Dolby also brought Dolby Stereo, Dolby Surround, and then Dolby Pro Logic to 35mm film. Dolby Surround and Pro Logic used a clever matrix to encode left-center-right and a single mono surround (LCRS). VHS brought these theater soundtracks to homes.

Interested in more motion-picture sound history? Here's a terrific website to consult: www.widescreenmuseum.com/sound/sound03.htm.

## Sound Channels

Recordings come in several flavors: monaural (mono), stereo, and multichannel (surround). Mono requires only one speaker; stereo needs two; and surround (known as 5.1) typically requires at least six, although other formats also exist.

Monaural (1.0) requires one speaker, and as a result, there is not a sense of spaciousness because all the sound comes from a single point in space.

Stereo (2.0, left/right, or L/R) requires two speakers spaced apart, which creates a sound field between the two speakers and a space behind them. Most of us are familiar with the sense of depth and space in stereo recordings—many sounds seem to originate from the phantom center, though no speaker is really there. If the exact same sound comes from both speakers, that sound is heard in the center. This phantom center doesn't exist; hence the name—it is just an effect of stereo. A mono sound played on two speakers will have everything appear in this center, too. The stereo effect is pronounced on headphones because there is no interaction between the speakers (your head is in the way) as there is with speakers in an acoustic environment (a room).

The problem is that stereo only sounds its best and works if you are positioned in the sweet spot between the speakers. Ideally, that's your head and the two speakers forming an equilateral triangle. Outside of this area, the stereo doesn't quite work. The farther away you are from the sweet spot, the more monaural the sound is, too. Though the spaciousness from stereo sounds more pleasing than mono, it still comes from a single direction, typically from the front.

Hollywood added a center channel (3.0 or LCR) to help solve the problem of being outside of the stereo sweet spot. Using a discrete, dedicated speaker, soundtrack creators were able to keep the dialogue in the center of the movie screen, even if the audience sat to the sides in a large theater. By reinforcing stereo's phantom center, there were better directional cues and a sense of space for people sitting outside the stereo sweet spot.

To create a more immersive experience, one additional channel (4.0) positioned to the rear had sound come from behind the audience and helped to surround them with sound. This format is often known as Dolby Pro Logic (LCRS) and is still in existence today.

Adding rear-channel discrete left and right stereo surrounds (LCR and LsRs, or 5.0) expands the depth and spaciousness into a full 360-degree circle enveloping the audience. With stereo there is a sense of width and depth at the front of the room. With surround, there is a sense of envelopment, or being *in* the sound as it happens all around.

The final part of the surround equation is the dedicated low-frequency enhancement (LFE) channel (.1) positioned in the front, near the center channel. It only carries a tenth of the frequencies compared to the other full-range speakers (hence the .1).

The LFE's purpose is to provide additional bass content, and it is therefore sometimes called the *boom channel* or the *baby boom*. Good LFE effects, such as explosions, are felt more than heard. The LFE helps to compensate for the ear's lack of sensitivity to extreme low frequencies (as mentioned earlier).

It's important to note that surround can be a matrix (Pro Logic) or discrete (Dolby Digital, 5.1 LCRLsRs). The matrix approach uses special encoding tricks to add multi-channel information to the standard stereo mix, and decoders used during playback re-create the experience. Conversely, discrete multichannel sound keeps the six channels separate for encoding and delivery. The individual outputs are sent to the appropriate speakers, thus re-creating the original mix exactly. DTS Coherent Acoustics Audio, Dolby Digital (AC-3), DVD-Audio, and SACD are discrete surround formats.

Today's theatrical films include up to four separate soundtracks:

- There is a DTS timecode track to synchronize the visuals with the separate DTS-encoded CD-ROM.

- For maximum compatibility, there is always a stereo analog optical track.

- There is the typical Dolby Digital 5.1 and Dolby Digital EX (placed between the sprocket holes). The Dolby Digital 5.1 format, using Dolby's AC-3 format, has emerged as the standard for DVDs and digital television (DTV).

- There is Sony Dynamic Digital Sound (SDDS) in a 7.1 configuration, split to occupy both sides of the film outside the sprocket holes.

Both DTS-ES and Dolby Surround EX add a center surround channel, though it is matrixed with the regular stereo surrounds and not discrete.

## Wrap Up

Understanding and applying these mechanics of analog and digital sound will help make your work better. For example, many DAWs ask you to select a project sample rate before you can begin. You need to know the differences between, say, 44.1 kHz and 48 kHz to make sure your sync works. Keeping the Fletcher-Munson curve in mind will help you make better-quality judgments. Refer to this chapter when you need clarification on these and other discussed matters. Next, we'll focus on workflow and the personnel who work together to realize the final soundtrack.

# 4 Workflow

Now that you have a solid understanding of what makes up a soundtrack, let's focus on the people who actually do the work and lay down a workflow framework that's efficient and minimizes problems.

## Picture Editorial versus Sound Editorial

Although *you* may be your entire production department, it still makes sense to identify the typical people and positions involved with sound in audio-visual productions. On films and TV, picture editorial edits the material to tell the best story. Sound editorial works to enhance the sound. While the picture team cuts, the sound team can do some preparatory work, such as recording and/or gathering needed sounds. This may include sound effects, voiceover, and so forth.

However, the sound department rarely starts putting these sounds in until the picture cut is done and locked (a.k.a. *picture lock*). If you start too soon, changes to the picture affect the sound, sometimes necessitating a lot more work. A director who cuts out three frames from a shot to tighten a scene usually only works with a track of video and a track or two of audio. But the sound editors may have dozens of audio tracks, and removing three frames affects the sync and must be conformed across the project and rippled down the timeline. This can be scary and difficult to do manually. Thankfully, there are some methods for handling these conforms, which we'll talk about later.

I feel it's best to wait for picture lock before you dive into the nitty-gritty of putting together the soundtrack with the picture. That said, you should always be *thinking* about the sound and doing whatever you can to get ready for the real work. More on this later in this chapter.

In an ideal world, you would not start sound editing and building scenes before picture lock, but it doesn't happen that way. Directors and producers are forever massaging their art—and who can blame them, thanks in no small part to today's nonlinear editing systems (NLEs). But at some point, directors and producers have to let go so you can get on with the sound without worrying about any additional picture edits or changes that affect sync.

If you edit your own material, you can follow a similar workflow. Focus on the story-telling and performance first. Ignore the sound for the most part—unless it helps you tell a better story, such as for timing, to edit a montage, and so forth. Once you've completed the picture cut, then start to work on the sound proper.

## Divvy Up the Work

The leader of the sound team is known as the supervising sound editor. This person is in charge of the entire sound department for a project and oversees all its functions. There may also be a sound designer in charge of recording effects and locations and otherwise creating the sounds. Often these two people are one and the same, but not always.

Next, there are the sound editors, who usually divide their work between being dialogue editors and sound effects editors. Dialogue editors may take on ADR chores, while sound effects editors also cover Foley. However, there may be people assigned specifically to these roles—ADR editor, Foley editor, and so on.

The music supervisor may report to the supervising sound editor, but not always. Music supervisors are responsible not only for underscore, but also for securing rights to use popular music in projects. There are also music editors who conform tracks to match constantly evolving picture edits. Although underscore is typically recorded to picture (while watching the complete film), this doesn't mean that subsequent picture changes after the music recording session won't require additional editing of the already recorded musical score.

Additional people who specialize in mixing are often brought in for premixing (or pre-dubs) and the final mix. The head mixer is known as the *re-recording mixer* (or *dubbing mixer*), because the final mix itself is often called the *re-recording mix*. (The term *final dub* is often used to designate this, too.) There may be several mixers, with each one in charge of dialogue, effects, Foley, and music, respectively.

---

**Note:** Interestingly, the person who records the sound on location is called the *production sound mixer*.

---

**Supervising Sound Editor**

- Sound Designer
- Sound Editors
  - Dialogue Editor
  - ADR Editor
  - Foley Editor
  - Sound Effects Editors

**Music Supervisor**

- Music Editor

**Re-Recording Mixer**

- Dialogue Mixer

- Effects Mixer

- Music Mixer

# Workflow Approach

As supervising sound editor, it's time to begin the project. As mentioned earlier, it is best to think about sound before the script is written or finished. When you make sound a more integral aspect of the storytelling, the soundtrack—arguably the whole project—is typically better. If that isn't possible, consider reading the script before starting work on the project. There may be cues in the script that can stimulate your sonic creativity, including hints about the project's overall mood. Pay particular attention to the script's scene header information, which delineates places and times of day (even historical periods, depending on the project).

```
EXT. HOTEL - ENTRANCE - MORNING
```

There may be other specific sound references in the text, too.

```
An unseen phone RINGS and RINGS. Doors SLAM.
```

These script indications can provide clues to the kinds of sounds you need to acquire. In the above example, you will need sounds that evoke the busy hotel lobby, phone sounds, and the doors.

After reading the script, make it a point to meet with the director and/or producer(s) to discuss sound issues before the production, if possible. Often you can uncover potential problems and solve them before things go awry. Usually, the director is more relaxed at this point, because the stress of production and picture editing haven't started yet. This person may be more open to discussing the project and not be mired in the minutiae that rains down later.

It can be helpful to ask about the bigger-picture elements—the soundtrack as a whole—at this time. Be sure to inquire about mood and how it might change as the drama unfolds. Ask what the director and producer see as the sound's role. Perhaps they can suggest an existing film or other examples that you can use as a reference. All this discussion can help send you down the right path as you prepare for the actual work later.

---

**Note:** Subsequent chapters will contain more planning information and "gotchas," particularly in the world of location dialogue recording.

---

These meetings should help you build solid relationships with the director and/or producer—whoever the decision-makers are. You are an integral part of their vision, so it pays to have rapport. Also, make sure you communicate with everybody involved. For example, if you are handing over your tracks to a re-recording mixer, ask what she wants in terms of premixes and stems. You might want to send an early rough to these other people to test your workflow and technology compatibility, while there's still time to fix matters.

Also, make technology decisions and devise a suitable workflow for handling all the audio material at this meeting. Solve the technical issues right away. There are format and software compatibility issues during production, post, and delivery. Work these out before deadlines encroach. Anything you can get in advance, such as production audio, rough cuts, and so forth, can help you see what kind of work is involved. If the production audio is less than stellar, perhaps you can make suggestions before more shooting happens. If it's already too late, at least you'll know the kind of work involved, because you will spend a lot of time making the production audio cleaner.

Also, develop a schedule of what needs to be done and by when. I prefer to work backwards from a deadline, indicating specific milestones along the way. And when you develop a schedule, establish the division of labor in terms of who will be responsible for each task.

Again, cut the picture first and then work on getting the sound to work with that picture edit. There are exceptions—such as editing to a pre-recorded music track or voiceover—but for the most part, work with locked picture. If you don't wait for picture lock, you will redo the soundtrack multiple times as the director, editor, and producer continue to tweak the project. However, the reality is that most projects are never locked (until somebody takes the project away), so figure out a way to deal with this problem and work with locked picture as best you can.

---

**Note:** If you edit your own visuals, keep this crucial hint in mind: Edit the visuals and story pacing with sound in mind. You often need to leave some room and time for sound; otherwise, you make it really hard to do certain sound tricks later.

---

## Spotting Session

After the picture edit, it's time to hold a spotting session. It's acceptable to screen a rough cut here, though a nearly final locked cut is best, obviously. A spotting session is where you screen the project with the principals in attendance (the director, producer[s], composer, and other members of the sound team). I often prefer to screen the project on my own a few times and make notes before I schedule this spotting session.

---

**Note:** Make sure you give yourself one chance to enjoy the project. You should screen it first without interruption and without an eye or an ear on technical issues. You need to experience it as an audience would by immersing yourself in the world and going along for the emotional journey. Don't deprive yourself of this crucial screening. You will have only this one chance to record your first impressions. After that, you will be too close to the material to ever have the *first-time* audience's perspective again.

---

In his book *Sound Design: The Expressive Power of Music, Voice, and Sound Effects in Cinema* (Michael Wiese Productions, 2002), David Sonnenschein goes into great detail about developing what he calls the *sound map*. He suggests a multi-step process that can help you break down the sound for a project. The book is worthwhile reading, but the real value is in finding your own way to prepare a road map for the soundtrack's journey.

Remember that this is just a map. And as with any map, you may take a detour or an entirely new route when the actual sound work begins. Think of the map as preparation only and as a way to prepare the needed soundtrack elements. When you begin the work, the actual soundtrack replaces the map and is what is really most important.

For me, the first impression is vital. I just watch as if I'm in the audience seeing it for the first time. When I'm finished, I record my emotional response. Next, I watch again and start to lump sounds into broad categories, as suggested by Sonnenschein. These categories include environment, objects, actions, and emotions. As he further suggests, asking and answering the following questions is invaluable at this stage:

- What completes the scene?

- What would personalize the environment?

- Where is the emotion? Is it subjective (the character's) or objective (the audience's)?

After these initial screenings, it's time for the more formal spotting session. It helps to have timecode burned in to the video (see Figure 4.1). As you take spotting notes, you can write down precise timings. The previous screenings and other preparatory work, such as reading the script, will help you with more general sound matters. Now you need to get down to specifics.

As you watch the project with the others, ask yourself these two questions: What do you have? What you need? You must decide where, when, and why you will place the soundtrack elements. In essence, your spotting notes serve as a very detailed road map for building the dialogue, music, and effects. Typically, a music spotting session is different from a sound spotting session, so I'll talk more about music spotting in a later chapter.

**Figure 4.1** Timecode example.

These spotting notes may be simple lists of the sounds, or they may be tied specifically to the timecode values. It's up to you to decide what level of detail you want. Generally, the more people involved, the more detail is useful. If it's just you alone, a list and perhaps a few specific references may be all you need. Here's an example of some general spotting notes.

- Detective office
  - Computer running
  - Fan running
  - Ringing phone
  - Picking up paper
  - Scribbling on paper
  - Phone slamming
  - Getting up from chair
  - Door opening
  - Walking with paper (carpet)

- Squad room
  - Fluorescent lights humming
  - Computers humming
  - Typing noise
  - Phones
  - People talking
  - Papers rattling

- Drawers opening and closing
- Walking with paper (tile surface)
- Handing paper to other detective

After the spotting session, turn your attention to further study of what's already there and begin to gather the missing sound elements.

## Working with Production Dialogue

Go through the dialogue takes first and choose the best ones. Turn your attention toward fixing, cleaning up, and otherwise smoothing existing production dialogue. There will be gaps, so devote time to recording, creating, and/or finding needed parts, such as looking for alternative takes or wild tracks (recordings made on location separate from the usual dialogue tracks), or scheduling ADR and voiceover sessions. Group walla may also be required.

If you only get a rendered file or the NLE cut, you are missing audio that may be important, such as alternative dialogue lines, wild reads, room tone/presence, and other useful sounds, including production sound effects. Often location sound record-ists keep logs of such material, and the editor may have them as part of the video capture logs, so if you can get such material your job may be made easier.

It's also important to get the dialogue tracks with *handles*, those little bits of audio recorded before and after each and every picture edit. These handles give you flexibility for making dialogue editing and crossfading smoother. We'll discuss more about this later in the book.

It's best to focus on dialogue first and spend the majority of your time getting it clean, smooth, and great-sounding. After you've finished the dialogue, then move on to the other elements. I prefer to do backgrounds, sound effects, Foley, and then ear candy and other sweeteners, in that order. You need to discover the working method that's best for you.

Often it's hard to get a feel for how a scene is coming together until it fully comes together. That catch-22 is one of the more difficult challenges to contend with when working on audio. I may temp in a sound effect or background when working on the dialogue only if it gives me some perspective on the whole. For example, if a dialogue scene takes place outside in the city, I may temp in some city sounds to get a sense of the overall feel. Usually, these temp tracks get deleted, replaced, or augmented later, though.

## Working with Sound Effects and Backgrounds

Next, start hunting and gathering sound effects and material suitable for building backgrounds. You can purchase sound effects from various sources, though rolling your own is often the better tactic because you can build your own library of sounds. Many sound editors modify existing effects to put their personal stamp on sounds, too. Rarely is a single sound effect used—rather, most sounds and backgrounds are built by combining and layering many sounds to create a richer, more complex end result.

Matching the action requires sonic treatment, too—especially when it comes to little things, such as picking up and setting down objects, opening and closing doors, and using other obvious sounds. Footsteps, clothing rustles, and prop sounds—the Foley—are as important as (or often more so than) building convincing backgrounds, so you must also consider them.

Don't confuse room tone/presence (recordings of the sound of every space while on location) with building location backgrounds. They are separate. Room tone/presence is useful for gaps in dialogue and to help smooth dialogue edits. Backgrounds are the sounds of the environment you add intentionally to make a scene more realistic. For example, you might add traffic sounds to a city sequence. Remember, a foreign-language dub will *not* have your room tone, just the backgrounds. So, if you rely on room tone alone for all of your backgrounds, you are in for a shock! Use room tone to smooth dialogue and support the "sound" of a room—don't use it as the whole thing, unless the room is very quiet.

Similarly, don't rely on background sounds alone to cover bad dialogue editing. You should work hard on making the dialogue its best before you include the added layer of backgrounds. A director may decide to lose the background sounds in a scene during the final mix, and if you were using those noise elements to cover up other problems... well, that's not a good position to be in.

## Working with Music

Music should be your next consideration. More often than not, music and effects will fight each other due to a lack of communication between the people involved. You should seek active participation and collaboration between composers and sound supervisors. I often do both roles (and you may assume both roles, too), so I find thinking about sound effects as music and vice versa to be a very good approach. This way, the soundtrack is more unified and makes a better impact.

---

**Note:** I find if you put in the music too early, you rely on it to mask other missing soundtrack elements. Music should drive emotion, not fill in gaps in other sound areas.

---

If you use library music, keep a log of the tracks used. Although some library music is royalty-free, it may still require you to file cue sheets when it is played on TV, so the library/composer will still earn performance royalties. To be sure, record the appropriate information about the music you use. Later chapters will include more detail on music issues.

## Putting It All Together

At every stage, dialogue, sound effects, and music need to be tweaked and made to synchronize with the action and reflect the drama and emotion of the project. As the soundtrack comes together, premixing (or predubbing) helps reduce the number of tracks to more manageable numbers for the final re-recording mix. There, everything gets balanced into the final whole.

Make sure you share roughs and sequences early. Don't wait until you are completely finished to play your work for those involved. Keep them informed and in the loop so that they are part of the process. This is even more critical if you don't meet with them in person. If you use email, phone calls, and overnight packages, you need a lot of contact, because you won't be able to guide people as you would in an in-person work-in-process review. An FTP site for uploading large files can be helpful here.

Don't be married to anything. Try out ideas. Take a "kitchen sink" approach and put everything you can think of into the soundtrack. But put these experiments on their own tracks or busses so you can easily mute them or jettison them from the project. However, I never throw anything away. I've had whole scenes ADR'd—only to have the director decide he liked the original, albeit noisy, takes more. It was simple to mute the ADR lines and unmute the original dialogue work. Try ideas when you can—but, of course, this really depends on your relationship with the director and/or producer. If there is mutual respect and trust, you can be more creative and offer suggestions. I find it's easier to ask for forgiveness than to ask for permission. Put in everything and discuss your work together and then you can take out material and get to the core of what the soundtrack is trying to be and say.

Your job often is to offer possibilities that the others on the creative team may not have considered. Usually, the director and the editor have lived with the project for a long time, and your initial sound work brings them a fresh perspective that often rekindles their creativity. At this point, the project becomes highly collaborative.

Also, I find that end-of-day decisions, when you are tired and your ears have lost their perspective, rarely turn out well. Give yourself some time away (and rest) before you go with those last-minute changes. Your fresh ears will often expose mistakes and errors in judgment that you can correct before moving on—or, worse, before you play them for your collaborators. Be picky about what you keep and aggressive with what you lose. I once wrote a music track that accompanied a really interesting ear-candy sound sequence. I loved the music, but the scene worked better with just the effects. It was hard to delete the music—okay, I only muted it to appease myself psychologically—but it was ultimately the right choice.

If you are doing the final mix, take some time off between the sound editing and the mixing. You need to give your ears, brain, and creativity a rest. Come back to the mix when you are fresh. I find making DVDs and playing them in alternate locations (and for alternate audiences) can help expose errors and inspire ideas. Put it away and return. That is what works.

## Technical Issues

Before moving on, let's take a moment to discuss a few technical matters related to the overall workflow. I prefer using external FireWire/USB drives for projects. Some software, such as Pro Tools, requires this. It also keeps everything together in one portable place. When the gig is done, you can put the drive on the shelf and recall it if needed for changes. Buy a new drive that matches each project. Smaller drives are perfect for shorter, less comprehensive projects (and they're relatively cheap). You should reformat the drive as needed. For instance, Windows users must always reformat the drive to NTFS. Drives come preformatted for the antiquated and problematic FAT32 format with its 4-GB file-size limit. Don't use it. Reformat to NTFS and save yourself many headaches!

The more sophisticated the project, the more you need to be organized. Start by building folders on the hard drive for the project, and then use the subfolders wisely to hold dialogue, ADR, effects, backgrounds, music, notes, effects settings, and works in progress. Don't use a shoebox approach and lump everything into one place. Find an organization method that works for your brain, and use it wisely.

Learn your software inside and out, and don't be tempted to upgrade or bring in new software or equipment during the project. Stick with the tried and true. It's better to know a few toys really well than have a lot of stuff but very little knowledge of how to use it.

Before beginning your audio work, lock the video in your NLE/DAW. If it is an NLE project with many edits, lock them all down. This way, if you slide out of sync, it is only because of the audio, not the video. I once accidentally added some dissolves to a scene because I forgot to lock the video, and all the crossfades I added to the audio were reflected in the video. The director was not happy! So I learned to lock the video and unlock the audio from the video so it could be used without the risk of affecting any video.

I also duplicate any audio included and work on the copies. I place the original soundtrack elements at the bottom of my timeline and mute them. This way, I always have a reference to the originals should I need it. I'm not duplicating the media, mind you—just the reference to them in the project.

Use tracks wisely, too. They don't cost anything, and they often make your life easier, even if they start to use up a lot of screen real estate. The biggest mistake beginners tend to make is using too few tracks. It's often better to place specific dialogue on its own track, such as Actor 1 on Track 1 and Actress 2 on Track 2. This lets you alternate or checkerboard an onscreen conversation. Sound effects are often so dense that you have

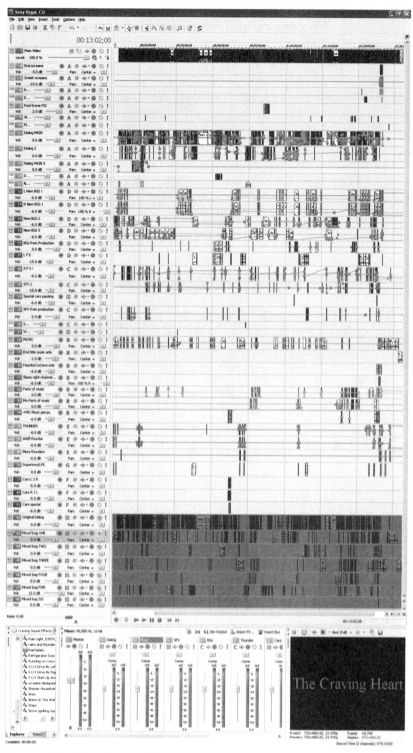

**Figure 4.2**  Timeline project.

to spread them out over several tracks to make them work. This checkerboarding approach makes it easier to do fades, too.

Moving elements to another track because you need to treat them separately or differently is a better choice. Even though you can automate many audio effects and volume/pan, I often just create a new track with the needed effect/volume/pan and move the sounds involved to it. Soundtrack timelines can get rather crowded and messy (as shown in Figure 4.2).

Save often. I save several works in progress—at least one a day—to several locations (drives, separate computers, flash drives, and so on). This way I don't risk losing anything important. It pays to document everything, too—especially the settings used for effects and special processes that you did. And don't forget to have backups of everything—preferably two backups kept in separate locations!

That wraps up the essential workflow of what it takes to pull together a soundtrack. It's missing a lot of the details you need to make every step work. You'll find that information as the book progresses. This served as your big-picture overview that you can follow as you learn the specific techniques that will make your soundtrack better.

# 5 Location Matters

Although this book is primarily a post-production resource, that doesn't mean you shouldn't take time to acquire the best sound possible at every stage. Proper field recording—whether you're capturing dialogue, an interview, natural sounds, or sound effects to be used later—requires some additional effort on your part. This chapter will provide guidelines for doing it right.

The on-location sound crew is generally small, consisting of the sound mixer, who sets levels, mixes the various microphones used, and often records the actual sound; a boom operator, who operates the fishpole boom and handles the actual placement and aiming of the mic during production; and perhaps additional sound utility people, who provide general help or run additional fishpole booms as needed.

## Overcoming Production Woes

As I've said before, audiences put up with iffy video, but they never put up with poor sound. There are quite a few post-production fixes available, but your best defense is, as the saying often goes, a strong offense. Get high-quality sound to begin with, and half the battle is over.

First and foremost, remember my number-one edict: Dialogue rules! You must focus on capturing top-quality voice in the field, even at the expense of missing other sounds. Make good mic choices and position the mics to capture the loudest, clearest, most noise-free human voice you can. But what about the other sounds? Most of them can—and should—be added during post-production. There are exceptions, such as one-of-a-kind vehicles, equipment, animals, and other natural (or *nat*) sounds. You might indeed need to record these sounds while on location. However, you can make most of these recordings before and after the crucial dialogue segments.

Sometimes you or a sound crew will return to the location to pick up these other necessary sounds, too. For example, I once put together a corporate video that featured a particular piece of factory machinery. I had to use the sound of that machine and not generic factory sounds from a sound effects library. Of course, most of the video was driven by interviews, so I still concentrated on their quality during production. I later went back to the location to gather the necessary machine sounds.

There is also the fallacy of perfection to consider. Many people point to Hollywood and say that their dialogue sounds so good—and indeed it does. However, most Hollywood dialogue is replaced in post via ADR. Getting great audio inside the confines of a recording studio is far easier than getting clean audio in the field. When you consider that some of the world's best boom operators and production sound mixers work on Hollywood films and television programs, and a large percentage of *their* audio gets thrown out and replaced, you quickly realize that getting good voice recordings in the field is no easy task. That doesn't mean you should roll over and give up. Nor should you live by the mantra, "We'll fix it in post." What you *should* do is get good basic sound. You wouldn't shoot a close-up out of focus, would you? Don't record the sound equivalent, either.

## Location, Location, Location

The first step is to really listen to the location. Our ear/brain combination is brilliant at filtering out unwanted sounds, letting us focus on what we feel is most important. Have you ever been in a loud restaurant with a friend, and yet you can still focus on your conversation, ignoring all the cacophony around you? If you choose, you can sort of "point" your ears, focus on any sound you want, and disregard the rest. Microphones are not as smart; they hear everything. Put yourself in the mic's position and really listen. Are there obvious problems, such as noisy air conditioners, traffic, room echo, loud people, and more? You must always listen for and to any noise and then take steps to combat it.

The best way to really hear the environment is to remove yourself from it. When you get back to the editing suite, have you ever just cringed when you've heard the audio? It didn't sound like that on location. Unfortunately, it did, but you just didn't notice or take the time to check. Invest in high-quality, good isolation headphones. You don't want to use the earbuds that shipped with your MP3 player or another pair of cheap, open-ear designs. You want headphones that filter out the surrounding sound, letting you really hear what the microphone hears. I suggest a closed-ear design, such as the Sony MDR-7506, or an in-ear model, such as the Etymotic ER-6. I also like the Direct Sound HP-25 Extreme Isolation Headphones for really high-noise locations.

Noise-canceling headphones are fine for airplane travel, but not on the set. You want to hear the noise so you can take steps to combat it. Besides, the noise-cancelling ones do not provide an accurate picture of the sound and tend to exaggerate certain frequency bands to make music sound better in high-noise environments. For field recording, you want accuracy and reasonable noise rejection—enough so you can hear the mic.

Make sure you listen loudly enough, too. Boost the headphone volume level enough so that you can hear the background noise that the mic hears. If you listen at too low of a level, you might miss these critical details.

## Capturing Room Tone

One key to fixing audio in post is the use of room tone or presence (called *atmos* in the UK) to smooth and hide edits, making the finished tracks sound better. Every location has a specific sound or background ambience that works its way onto your recordings. Outside there might be birds, distant traffic, and other noise. Inside might feature the hum of machinery, air conditioning, and so forth. Therefore, you should *always* capture room tone/presence at every location. What you want is a recording of the environment without any principals talking, using the same equipment and settings you used to get the voice recording. Essentially, tell everybody to shut up and not to move, and then record this atmosphere.

Don't skimp here. Get a solid thirty seconds to one minute. You won't be on your deathbed complaining that you wasted your life grabbing too much room tone. And if you stay at the same location for a long day, capture room tone/presence at various times—morning, afternoon, twilight, and night—and from various perspectives. Outdoor locations can change drastically as a day progresses—that one lone cricket at 6:00 p.m. becomes a chorus of crickets by 9:00 p.m. Sound can change over time, and you might miss these subtle (and sometimes not so subtle) variances in the heat of production. The change will be gradual to your ears, so you probably won't notice...until you hear the tracks back at your editing suite and these inconsistencies become glaringly obvious.

Keep this thought in mind: It is far, far easier to mess up good sound than it is to clean up bad sound! For example, suppose you have an actor talking 50 feet away from the camera. With a mic placed near the camera, this thespian will sound distant and thin. This might match what the camera sees, but getting quality audio that an audience can comprehend at this distance will be difficult. If you mic the actor closer, such as with a lavaliere, his lines will be clearer, but they won't match what the audience sees. However, adding a little reverberation to the lav track can mimic the distance, making the scene more real without sacrificing quality. So, I'd rather have good, clean audio that I can manipulate in post than have crummy audio that can never really sound good at all.

## Top Mistakes Made in the Field

Bad location recordings usually suffer because of several issues.

■ **Using the wrong mic and/or the wrong mic operator.** Use external microphones. Period. The built-in camera microphone is good for only one thing—picking up the noise of the camera (and camera operator). For most other tasks, it is unsuitable. Directional mics are the mainstay in the field, but when improperly used, they cause bad results. As for the operator, a joke I usually share with my college students goes something like this: "Who runs the mic boom on most student shoots? The person least qualified"—and that is a shame. Don't leave your sound to the whims of the underqualified and undermotivated. Microphone choice and placement, whether fixed in place or moving with the action on a fishpole boom, are critical to the success of your location sound. These are such important subjects that detailed explanations will come later in the book.

- **Not monitoring properly or quality-control checking while still on location.** I've mentioned this already, but it needs further addressing here. You have to know what you are getting before it's too late. Plug those headphones into the camera (or into another mixer or recorder you may be using) and listen—really listen. Because digital cameras and other recorders don't offer the ability to hear your recording as you record, you need to regularly rewind and listen. You can only monitor what is going to the camera/recorder; you can't monitor what's coming off the "tape" or card until playback. Something could go wrong, and you wouldn't know without spot-checking the actual recordings made. If you don't do this, you have no right to complain about how it sounds when you get back to edit.

- **Too many changing mic positions.** This is the most egregious error made in production. Just because a shot changes, that doesn't always mean the sound should. Often, mics get moved around to match camera angles or because of other issues (casting a shadow on a set, for instance). You don't want to be pointing the mic in different places or changing distances all the time. If you do, the quality will change from shot to shot. Resist the urge to always move the mic. Even going from a long shot to a close-up doesn't call for a drastic change in the mic perspective or its sound. A little goes a long way here. Stick the mic on a character for the whole scene and leave it there, even when you're shooting multiple angles and other coverage. That way, any spoken line you cut in post will sound similar. You'll love the result in the editing suite.

Although moving the mic sometimes makes sense, often it does not. For example, suppose your script calls for two people sitting at a table having a conversation. Typical coverage would be to shoot the entire scene as a two-shot and then shoot close-ups of the two actors. When edited, the scene would cut back and forth between the various angles, and thus matching the sound might be difficult. Why? You probably moved the mic with the camera. The mic points in a different direction for each shot, and therefore it might pick up different sounds in the room. You wouldn't notice this until the edit. If you had aimed the mic from one position and still moved the camera around, you'd have consistent sound on every take, making the dialogue editing a snap.

Another common mistake is to mix mics, such as putting a lavaliere on one actor and a boom on the other. These are very difficult to intercut and have them sound convincing.

- **Not getting close enough.** The farther away you are from your subject, the more room sound you record. This manifests itself in more distracting noise and the hollow, distant, and often echo-y sound of a voice bouncing around the room (known as *reverb*). The best way to record good dialogue is to get as close as possible to the subject. That helps take the room sound out of the recording and gives you a tighter, fuller sound.

Also, there is a fallacy that highly directional mics, such as shotgun mics, have more reach, meaning you can pick up sounds from farther away. This is simply not true. Despite what you may see private detectives and spies doing in some movies, mics have a limited range of use. In reality, directional mics work well in the field because they reject sound arriving from certain directions (the sides) and therefore let you focus the sound more on what you need. So, even with directional mics, you still need to get as close as possible. Learn to work with the camera operator and hug the frame line—get the mic as close to the talent as possible without dipping it into the frame and ruining the shot.

- **Not understanding signal-to-noise ratio.** We live in a noisy world, and that interferes with getting good location sound. Noise is a constant in a given environment, meaning that no matter where you are in the space, its volume level stays relatively the same. You can change the dialogue volume by simply getting closer to the talent. The closer you are, the louder they will be. There is a rule, known as the *inverse square law*, that says intensity is inversely proportional to the square of the distance. That means halving the distance between a sound source doubles its intensity. What makes this relevant is that as you move the mic closer to the talent, the talent gets louder. But here's the crucial bit: The noise in the room *stays the same*. It doesn't get any louder. Therefore, as you get closer, you improve the signal-to-noise (S/N) ratio, with signal being the good stuff you want (dialogue) and noise being everything you don't want. Getting the biggest S and the littlest N you can should be your goal. Similarly, control volume changes acoustically by moving closer to softer speakers and farther from louder talkers. Resist the urge to adjust levels at the mixer/recorder, because this changes the level of the background noise. Using mic distance to control volume levels keeps the noise the same from shot to shot and from take to take.

- **Not scouting locations in advance.** You need to do a site survey of the areas where you will record before the actual production takes place. This applies to both indoor and outdoor locations. Use the scouting opportunity to listen for noise and other potential problems and then develop ways to diminish their effects on your recordings. Record these location surveys and listen to them back at the studio. This can reveal noise issues that you might not notice when on location and that you subsequently need to address. For example, one room may have too much reverb in it, while a nearby space sounds better. It's easier to make these alterations ahead of time. Also, try to go on the same days and times as the shoot to lessen surprises. One student shoot did his site survey at a park on a Saturday, and all was well. When he returned to the location on Sunday, a nearby church—with traffic, music/singing, and more—made clear sound recording impossible.

# Fix It in Post...Not!

There are some location recording problems that simply can't be fixed satisfactorily during post-production. Excessive noise is one such issue, but there are a few other gotchas to watch out for, too.

## Noise

Noise falls into many categories. I define it simply as everything I *don't* want on my recordings. For example, when recording dialogue, everything that isn't the actor's speech is noise. But when recording sound effects, any human speech that leaks into the recording is noise. The hardest noises to deal with are water, wind, hum, and simultaneous sounds. Removing a waterfall from a voice track is nearly impossible. Wind gusts and hum are equally difficult to remove convincingly. When one sound steps on another sound, such as a clunk that is simultaneous with a word, separating them is nearly impossible. Problems such as plosives, sibilance, and most ticks, pops, and glitches are relatively easy to remove, but not without some other issues at times. The easiest noises to remove are high-frequency hiss and low-frequency rumble.

The best way to reduce and even eliminate noise is to do a little work at every stage. In pre-production, you can scout locations and choose those with the least interference and those that have good sound qualities already. Generally, if a location sounds good, then the recordings made in it will sound good, too. During production, you can make good mic choices and work hard to get those mics as close as possible at all times. And in post-production, you can use some audio tools to further clean up the noise that's left. With good S/N, minor noise-reduction fixes in post are amazingly successful. But it's always GIGO—garbage in, garbage out. If you start with bad sound, no post-production magic will make it miraculously perfect!

## Distortion

Distortion of any kind is almost always problematic. If a mic, mic preamp, or digital recorder distorts, the sound is clipped off. There is a loss of information that can't be recovered because it doesn't exist. Although some tools can restore or at least suppress the harshness of distortion, the tracks are never very good. Watch those levels when recording and do retakes when there is clipping.

## Acoustic Anomalies

Some acoustic anomalies, such as phase and comb filtering caused by multiple mics being too close together or having a mic too close to hard surfaces, can ruin recordings. There's an odd hollow sound to these recordings that is difficult, if not hopeless, to restore. Follow the 3:1 rule and keep multiple mics at least three times as far away from each other as they are from the source. For example, if a mic is one foot away from a person, the nearest other mic to that mic should be at least three feet away. Keep mics from getting too close to hard surfaces, such as walls. Sound arrives at the mic directly but also bounces off the wall, arriving slightly later. These two sounds are separated in time slightly, resulting in a recording that may sound bad.

When you are near hard surfaces, keep in mind the law that says that the angle of incidence equals the angle of reflectance. Sound, being a wave, follows this rule. If sound strikes a hard surface at a 45-degree angle, it will reflect away at the same angle. By positioning yourself carefully, you can keep reflected sound from a nearby surface from hitting the mic later (as described earlier). You might be surprised by how simply aiming the mic slightly differently will improve the sound in these situations. Often, the difference between good sound and great sound is a slight repositioning of the mic. Move the mic around and listen for the sweet spot where the sound is best; then leave the mic there.

## Distant Miking

The distant, hollow, swimming-in-reverb sound from too-distant miking and/or off-mic situations is another problem from which it is hard to recover. If you record too much room and not enough voice, eliminating the room and tightening up the voice is often not correctable. The reason home movies sound the way they do is because as little Adam opens his holiday gifts, the camera and its mic are at the other end of the living room. We hear the room, not the good stuff. If you simply close-miked little Adam, the sound would be so much better.

## Live One-of-a-Kind Content

If you miss getting live, one-of-a-kind content, there is usually no way to get a second take. Making good choices, preparing ahead of time, and using redundancy can save your butt from these unfortunate incidents. Also, plan for the mix. Get the primary elements you need to complete the soundtrack based on what you feel the final master will be. Nobody ever complains that they recorded too much sound on location!

## Printed Effects

Finally, if you print effects (reverb, compression, overcooked limiters, and so on) to your recording, they are tricky to eliminate in the future. Recording with effects makes the effect a permanent part of the sound, and what might sound good in the field may sound terrible later. I'd rather use effects to sweeten matters in the controlled environment of the post audio suite. If something doesn't sound right on location, change mics, locations, positioning, and so forth to make it sound clear and natural, rather than using effects.

# More Noise Issues

Because noise is the primary nemesis of location sound recording, you need some additional techniques to overcome it. Noise comes from many sources—the location itself, people (including the crew), electronic and mechanical noise, and a host of other gremlins that conspire to ruin your best dialogue takes. Overcoming noise at the source with a preemptive approach is a far better tactic than relying on post tools to massage audio. The following sections discuss some common ailments and ways to deal with them.

## Practicing Noise Avoidance

Noise avoidance is the first tactic to take. If the location is noisy, move somewhere else. A simple fix is to just relocate where the microphone points, because that can make all the difference. Just aiming from a different angle—say, below instead of above—makes for a better sound. I've discovered that in many situations, three feet makes a huge difference. Whether that's moving the whole shot three feet away or moving where the mic is by three feet (sometimes just turning 90 degrees), it results in a significant quality improvement. For example, we were shooting a news stand-up with a fountain in the background. Aiming the mic at the reporter from the camera's perspective picked up too much of the water. Moving perpendicular to the reporter (so that the less sensitive sides of the mic faced the fountain) made the water noise almost disappear. The change? A three-foot difference.

Another example is a project for which the CEO wanted to deliver his lines outside near the corporate sign, so he could show off the building and such. The problem was that there was an airport nearby, so nearly every take was ruined. Later, I re-recorded the lines in a quiet office and then used B-roll to show more footage. Simply relocating made all the difference. In another instance, a very noisy factory floor was the setting. It would've been impossible to pull a good vocal out of it. Looking up, I noticed a glass observation window. We moved up there and got great sound, and the factory and its coveted machinery were still visible through the glass, over the executive's shoulder.

Busy scenes need *not* be busy on the set. For example, suppose your scene takes place in a crowded restaurant. It would be a pain to grab good dialogue in the usual cacophony of a busy eatery. Instead, eliminate all these noises. Focus on getting the dialogue of the principals, and have all the background action be as quiet as possible. Background extras can mime talking, instead of actually producing the sounds, for instance. Have the actors whose dialogue you need act accordingly, of course. If they need to shout to be heard above the (imaginary) din, they should deliver their performance accordingly. After you've recorded clean takes, have the extras speak and act as if they are in an actual restaurant and record that for possible use later. Otherwise, in post-production add all the missing sound elements to the scene—extras talking (called *walla*), sound effects, general restaurant background sounds, and even diegetic music. Using this approach, production sound is relatively easy to capture, and then you can control the audience experience by rebuilding the soundtrack in post-production.

## Wild Tracks and Shooting for Sound

Another tactic for getting better location sound and reducing noise is to record extra takes on the set or nearby, away from the noise. You may do these with the actors repeating their lines without the camera involved. These are known as *wild takes*.

They let you focus on getting better sound in situations where the mechanics of the full production preclude that. These extra takes often work better than ADR because the actors are still on the set and in the moment. Wild tracks are a must for impossible-to-get dialogue, such as when the talent is too far way. Shoot the scene normally and then have the actors move closer to the mics and record the lines again. On a night shoot with generators running, shut them down temporarily and record wild takes free from the noisy racket.

Similarly, shoot the scene as usual, trying to get the best sound possible. Then shoot the scene again with the mics right in the shot. Even move the whole sound crew right into the scene and shoot the piece again for the sole purpose of getting better sound. If you record this sound-only take right after the first, the actors will repeat their performances relatively closely. During editing, you can use the visual from one scene and the audio from the other.

## Deadening the Sound

Some locations are just "live" and boomy with reverberation that hangs in the air. The only way to make these spaces usable is to get closer with the mic and deaden the sound somewhat. While you won't turn the sound of a stadium into the sound of a bedroom closet, you can significantly deaden the area around the person you are going to record. This can make the dialogue sound better. Look for the heavy quilted blankets favored by movers or those available from Markertek (www.markertek.com). Hang several on C-stands loosely, like stage curtains, for the best result. Position them around the subject or in the path of the direction they are speaking. For example, if they are speaking toward the camera, deaden the sound around the camera.

These blankets placed on the ground can also reduce footstep and crew noise. I once had to cut out all the footsteps made by the camera operator walking around during a dramatic scene. This took a lot of work during post-production that could have been prevented by placing some blankets on the ground for the camera operator to walk upon.

## Adding Noise in Post

You might need to use noise in post to make things sound better. If crickets are on one side of a two-person conversation but not the other, the only way to fix it is to add crickets to the dialogue track missing them and blend the noises together. Sometimes you have to mess up the audio to make it work, such as adding room tone/presence to tracks. As mentioned earlier, make sure you record suitable room tone/presence at every location.

## Dealing with Wind Noise

Wind noise is a definite field audio affliction. Foam windscreens—which I call *clown noses*—are only marginally effective. I prefer furry zeppelins, such as the Rycote Softie (www.rycote.com) or the high-tech DPA WINDPAC. Omnidirectional mics are less susceptible to wind noise than cardioids. And because you can point omnis away from the wind source (without sacrificing the quality of the source you want to record), they can be another choice for certain situations. See Figure 5.1 for an example of a wind-protection device.

**Figure 5.1** Wind protection.

## Choosing a Mic

Unlike our ears, which can discriminate sounds remarkably well, microphones hear everything in the room. Choosing directional mics offers a more focused sound. Directional mics tend to reject off-axis sounds arriving from outside the mic's primary pickup pattern. This means directional mics can suppress the noise you don't want. Mics are very important, so there's more detail on them in Chapter 6, "Microphones."

## More Noise Sources

There is also electronic noise, introduced by all the gear used to capture and record sound. Microphones, preamps, cameras, cables, and similar equipment can all contribute noise. Any breakdowns in the chain usually result in inferior recordings.

The people involved with your production are another potential noise source. Fidgety staff; noisy clothing; jangling jewelry; severe and not-so-severe health issues, such as sneezing and coughing; and the biggie, cell phones—all of these plot to create more work for you during post. Tell people to be quiet and turn off those cell phones. Putting phones on silent won't help either; they must be off, or they will dit-dit-dit-dit on your tracks. And that's a sound you can't disguise!

# Checklist for Production Sound Success

Getting good, clean, accurate production sound on location contributes greatly to the success of your overall soundtrack. If you follow these reminders, you will be 80 to 90 percent of the way there.

- **Dialogue rules.** Focus on getting the best dialogue recordings you can and worry about all the other sounds later. Have all your preparation, including the sound equipment you use, built around this one principle.

- **Get closer.** Move your mic as close to the talent as possible and get the strongest signal and the least amount of noise.

- **Choose directional mics.** Shotgun and hyper-cardioid mics reject sound arriving from the sides. This helps you focus on the material you want and, by aiming carefully, you can reduce the stuff you don't want.

- **Always get room tone.** It's important to record 30 to 60 seconds at every location and throughout the day if you're at the same location for a longer time. Use the same gear, have everybody shut up for a moment, and then record the material.

- **Wear headphones.** You need a good set of cans to separate your ears from the environment so you can really hear what the mic hears, and you can then make appropriate adjustments. On the set, the sound mixer functions as the critical ears upon which the whole crew relies for judgment to ensure high-quality sound acquisition.

# 6 Microphones

Location and studio sound starts in the analog domain, and therefore you need a way to pick up acoustic energy and convert it into something you can record. Of course, at any analog step there can be distortion. I define distortion rather simply: If what went in and what comes out are different in any way, there is distortion. Sometimes that distortion might be a lot, resulting in a gravelly, nasty sound; other times the distortion is minimal, with little impact on the resulting sound. Some distortion—usually the warm sound of a tube—actually sounds good to our ears. This distortion is what makes mics sound different. We choose some mics for the sound they impart to our recordings, whereas we prefer other mics because they capture the sound with little coloration. And we choose still other mics because they allow us to get the best sound, free from distracting noise, that we can in a given situation.

Recording good production sound on location starts with making good microphone choices. There are essentially two types of microphones: dynamic and condenser (a.k.a. *capacitor*). Much like the eardrum, all mics have a flexible diaphragm that vibrates in an analogous manner to the sound waves that reach it. This process of transforming a form of energy—from acoustic sound waves into mechanical energy—is called *transduction*. Microphones are occasionally referred to as *transducers*, too.

## Dynamic Mics

Dynamic mics have the moving diaphragm connected to a coil of wire that in turn moves inside or around a magnet from the motion caused by the sound striking the diaphragm. If you remember your basic physics, moving a magnet in a coil of wire generates alternating current—electricity! Therefore, dynamic mics are tiny electrical generators that convert acoustic energy first into mechanical energy and then into electricity.

Dynamic mics are quite rugged and can take abuse more than other types of mics can. Most can handle large sound-pressure levels (SPLs), too. If you need to record very loud sounds, a dynamic might be the best choice. However, by their very nature, they are less sensitive to the subtleties of sound. The inertia of the mechanical elements—they work like a piston—makes dynamic mics less able to respond to quieter sounds, and they miss some of the subtle, finer parts of a sound. Although a dynamic, such as the Shure SM57, is well suited to snare drums and blazing rock electric-guitar solos, I'd never use it for solo violin. If you have to record the sound of an explosion, though, a dynamic mic may be the way to go. They are also potentially noisier because they may require more level boosts to reach proper recording levels. This extra gain often boosts background noise, making it difficult to record quiet sources.

Because dynamic mics are hardier (which is especially useful in bad weather) and don't require a power source to work, it makes perfect sense to *always* have one with you in the field as a backup. For example, I carry a Shure SM57 or an Electro-Voice EV635a in my location kit.

## Condenser Mics

Condenser microphones work differently. There is, of course, a moveable diaphragm (often made of gold) that sits very close to a stationary back plate. Electricity is applied to both the diaphragm and the back plate. As the diaphragm moves in response to the sound waves striking it, electrons jump across the gap between the plates, creating an analogous electrical current. Two conductors separated by an insulator are known as a *capacitor* in the electrical world; hence the name "capacitor mic." Condensers come in large- and small-diaphragm designs. The large-diaphragm versions are well suited to studio voice recording, whereas the small-diaphragm condensers generally get used on musical instruments. In a shotgun design, small-diaphragm condensers really shine for location recording.

As should be apparent, condenser mics require a power source to function. This power source might come from a battery or from a separate power supply. Some other audio components might provide the requisite power, too. For example, mixers, stand-alone preamps, and even some video camcorders often have power for mics. This is known as *phantom power*, because it travels down the same cable as the sound without interfering with the signal you want to record. Standard phantom power is 48V direct current (DC). Some mics will work with less, but not all models will. Consult with your mic manufacturers if you're considering using lower-voltage phantom power.

A variation on the condenser microphone just described is the electret-condenser. It differs because it has a permanently charged element and can therefore operate on a smaller voltage—often a tiny watch battery. Electret-condensers can be manufactured quite small and rather cheaply, and consequently most low-end, inexpensive models are equally low quality.

Because they have less mass, condenser mics can respond to minute changes in sound, which makes them ideal for capturing the subtle nuances of our audio world. Many models capture sound with amazing detail, depth, and clarity. Condensers are the mainstay on sung vocal performances, many voiceovers, and quite a few musical performances. Some models are coveted for their sound. Why do certain mics consistently get called upon for certain tasks? It's because they sound right for the job they've been given. You'll see many a Neumann U 47/87/89 on vocal sessions and Sennheiser 416s on VO spots.

Condenser mics have another quirk. The mechanism puts out such a small amount of electricity that it requires a tiny amplifier inside just to get to mic level. This can make them a little larger than the typical dynamic mic. This on-board preamp can be either a solid state or tube device. The much-sought-after Neumann U47 is one such mic that uses tubes inside. The mic's temperature can get quite high, which is why you might see them hanging upside down on the ends of booms/mics stands—to help dissipate the heat. This placement doesn't make them sound better or different, though.

Condenser mics are often "hotter" than dynamic mics, meaning they can amplify soft sounds more, giving you a greater signal-to-noise ratio when recording. Because they are powerful, you don't need to use subsequent electronics as much, which usually results in a far cleaner, more noise-free sound.

The downside of condenser microphones used to be their cost. However, while most models remain more expensive than dynamic mics, there has been an influx of good-quality, low-cost models in recent years. Thanks to these prices, many people are willing to use condensers in circumstances that were once the exclusive realm of dynamic mics.

## Ribbon Mics

A ribbon microphone uses a corrugated ribbon of metal as its diaphragm, strung between the two poles of a magnet. It essentially functions just like a dynamic mic, but it is singled out here because of its fragility. A drop to the ground or a burst of air—even wind—can damage a ribbon mic. Unlike its dynamic cousin, ribbon mics are not rugged and are relegated to studio use only. I prefer them on some voiceover sessions because of their vintage sound.

## Pickup Patterns

Mics all have specific pickup patterns (a.k.a. *polar patterns*), which makes some less sensitive in certain directions. This directionality is important for field recording work because it allows you to reject undesirable sound—noise!—in favor of what you really want—mostly voice. Just because a mic is less sensitive to the back, that doesn't mean it still doesn't pick up some sound arriving from the rear. It does, but off-axis sounds are reduced in level, giving you choices in post. If only a brick-wall mic could be made that only worked in one direction and ignored everything else...alas, no.

Omnidirectional mics pick up sound equally in all directions. Picture a mic at the center of a globe to understand this concept. Sound arriving from any direction sounds the same (volume issues aside). There is no off-axis coloration. As a consequence, omnis pick up the most room sound. They sound more open and "roomy," and therefore they often record more noise than other pickup patterns. These are, therefore, the most useless mic for most field use. They have their purposes, but usually not for field voice recording. They can be useful for some ambience and sound effects recording, though.

However, omnis are less sensitive to wind noise, so they might be a good choice when all other methods fail. Another exception would be TV news, where the omni is often used by reporters for stand-ups, interviews, and press conferences when they want to be sure not to miss any speech, regardless of whether the mic is pointed at the source. The ubiquitous and incredibly rugged Electro-Voice EV635a is a TV news mainstay.

There are several flavors of unidirectional or cardioid microphones. These are more sensitive in one direction, picking up sound in a heart-shaped pattern; hence the cardioid moniker. Sound outside this zone, such as that arriving from the rear, is reduced in level, or attenuated, significantly. This ability to reject unwanted sounds is the primary reason why directional cardioid mics get picked. Note that as you move closer to cardioid microphones, there is a proximity effect that boosts the bass in your voice. This can make you sound boomy in certain rooms. This artifact can also make a thin voice sound more authoritative, though. Voiceover actors take advantage of this effect to sound fuller and more powerful.

Be aware that cardioid microphone designs vary greatly, and figuring out which is the business end can be tricky. Some pick up sound on top, while others are side-address. However, many side-address mics have the grill cloth on top and on the sides, making it even harder to figure out which end is which. For example, we have side-address mics in the studio at the school where I teach. One day, I walked in and saw these mics all pointed down. Obviously, the person thought the mics picked up on the top; instead, they were aimed at the lap, which isn't the right way.

On David Letterman's desk sits a dynamic Heil PR-40, which looks like, and is positioned on the set to be, a side-address mic. It's not. The Heil is a top-address and is actually pointed away from Letterman. However, the condenser Audio-Technica 2020 looks similar to the Heil design, but is a true side-address mic. Look for the little cardioid icon or the manufacturer's name to find out where you should be pointing it. If you're in doubt, consult the owner's manual that comes with the mic. See Figure 6.1 for a comparison of a side- versus a top-address mic.

It is possible to elongate the pickup pattern somewhat, thereby rejecting even more off-axis sound arriving from the sides and rear. This design is called a *hypercardioid*, and it not only reduces the level of sound arriving from less-sensitive directions, but it also severely colors the sound not arriving from the front. Only sound in the pickup pattern sounds right. Hypercardioids are well suited to dialogue recording indoors. If you further narrow the pickup pattern to the front, the mic is called a *super-cardioid*. Again, beware of off-axis sounds from the side and rear, because they sound thin and off.

Shotgun mics (a.k.a. *line* and *gradient* or *lobar* mics) are another breed altogether. They share some of the same characteristics of hyper- and super-cardioid designs, offering

**Figure 6.1**  Side- versus top-address mic.

narrow pickup patterns and rejecting sound from the sides and rear. Short shotguns, such as the Sennheiser 416, are the most used mics for quality outdoor location sound work. They have a tight pattern in front and a small lobe to the rear, but their real advantage is their insensitive sides. By having such a narrow pickup angle, they can help you really focus on the sound you want and attenuate all that you don't want.

Shotguns can get fooled in a really reverberant space and can actually lose their directionality, sounding more like an omnidirectional mic, very distant and roomy. It's best to avoid using shotgun mics indoors and instead choose a quality hypercardioid, such as the Oktava MK-012.

The long shotgun microphone is the audio equivalent of a laser beam, able to focus tightly on a sound source. Again, beware of off-axis sounds from the side and rear, because they sound thin and off. Due to a quirk in the long shotgun design, they actually pick up slightly to the sides and back (though they reject these sounds well in relation to front-arriving sounds). Therefore, the worst placement for a long shotgun is on or very near a camera, because it will pick up the sound of the camera and often its operator, too.

Also, because shotguns do pick up to the rear—it's the sides that reject sound—you can use them to your advantage. For example, if you're recording actors walking along a busy street, you would not want the rear aimed at the street (or the front, for that matter—obviously). You'd want the sides "facing" the street noise. Often just moving the angle of the mic slightly can make the noise go down in volume and increase the level of what you want. It's called finding the *sweet spot*—where the mic sounds best! It's the reason why the mic operator must wear headphones, because the slightest adjustment of the mic placement can make a huge difference in the sound quality.

Just to reiterate: Hyper- and super-cardioid mics and short/long shotguns do not have a longer reach. They still sound best when placed as close to the subject as possible. The advantage of these polar patterns is that they are less sensitive to sound arriving from the sides and to the rear. Through careful placement and aim, you can put the mic where it picks up the most voice and reduces the noise around it.

Another pickup pattern is the bidirectional microphone with its figure-eight pattern, often used for mid-side stereo recordings. Figure-eights reject sounds to the sides quite effectively, even better than a cardioid rejects to the rear. Bidirectional mics are usually side-address and appear like a side-address cardioid; look for the sideways 8 icon to be sure.

---

**Special Note:** Some mics—particularly some high-quality studio condenser microphones—have variable patterns. A selector switch on the mic itself or its external power supply (in the case of tube designs) allows you to choose from omni, through cardioid, to figure-eight patterns. Other mics—especially some small-diaphragm condensers—have interchangeable capsules in omni, cardioid, and hypercardioid patterns, letting you choose which "top" to put on the mic body. These special mics are very versatile for field and studio work.

Pressure-zone microphones (PZM) and other boundary microphones have a hemispherical pickup pattern because they were designed to be placed on a flat surface. Boundary mics appear similar to PZMs, but they can be a hemicardioid or half-hemispherical pattern, rejecting sound from the other direction (like a regular cardioid). You'll often see PZMs and/or boundary mics on the floor along the front of the stage during plays and musicals. Their unobtrusive design works well for many dramatic and documentary shoots, too. I once used a single PZM for a long office scene, placing it on the desk between my actors and hiding it from view by covering it with a single sheet of paper.

Because a boundary mic is essentially a cardioid mic running parallel to the ground, you could emulate it with any cardioid mic resting on the ground or other surface with cloth or a foam piece under it so it remains parallel. This gives the same hemicardioid pattern of a dedicated boundary mic.

There are also stereo mics and matched pairs or combinations of mic patterns designed for stereo recording.

---

See Figure 6.2 for an illustration of various microphone pickup patterns.

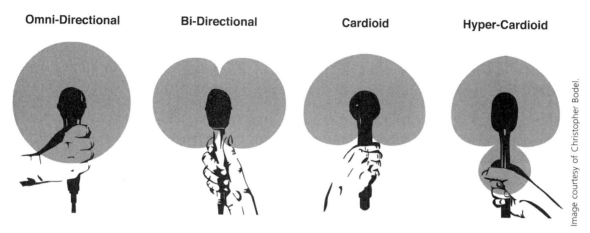

**Figure 6.2**  Microphone pickup patterns.

# Mic Rules

Entire books have been written about microphone techniques. They all boil down to a few simple rules.

## Choose the Right Mic

First, find the right microphone for the task. Different types and models are better suited for different situations. I suggest you try out a few different kinds, makes, and models until you discover the choice that works best for the work you do. For example, if you are a documentary filmmaker, a high-quality lavaliere will work well for interviews, and a decent hypercardioid or a short shotgun will suffice for capturing natural sound. Recording voice-overs? Try a studio condenser, though a short shotgun can sometimes work here, too.

## The Fewer Mics, the Better

Use a single mic for most recordings. Every human I've ever met has one mouth. Therefore, use one mic per mouth and one recording channel per mic. If you have multiple people in a scene, then more mics might make sense. Generally, the fewer mics the better, especially if you are combining them to a single channel. If you are recording voices to separate, discrete channels (multitracking), then this rule does not apply.

## Only Record in Stereo When Appropriate

Avoid recording single voices in stereo, too. Instead, use the stereo capabilities of recorders and cameras in other ways. (See the CYA techniques covered later in the book.) Stereo is best reserved for backgrounds and sound effects. Mono suffices for voice.

## Move the Mic Closer

The farther away you are from the voice to be recorded, the more room sound gets picked up. Translation: more noise. When the mic is closer, the voice dominates or masks the other room sounds. You want to maximize the level of what you want to capture and minimize all the other sounds around. That gives you more choices in post-production.

If you recall from before, proper mic placement enables you to record a better signal-to-noise ratio. To define that simply, the *signal* is the good stuff to keep, and the *noise* is everything else you don't want (which may or may not be actual noise). Maximize the signal to the surrounding noise by getting closer to the source of the sound. This means you will be getting a higher recording level with the effect of pushing the noise level far, far below that of the voice. With the voice much stronger or hotter than the noise, you can balance the dialogue much easier in post. You can reduce or eliminate it completely without adversely affecting the voice quality. If the noise level is high and therefore closer to the same level as the voice, it will be difficult, if not impossible, to reduce or eliminate the noise during post work without severely affecting the voice quality.

Figure 6.3 shows a bad signal-to-noise level. The noise itself is almost indistinguishable from the dialogue. It would be difficult to impossible to make this sound good. Conversely, in Figure 6.4 you can see a large separation between the noise and the good dialogue. There is still noise present, but it is so low in volume compared to the dialogue that it can be minimized easily.

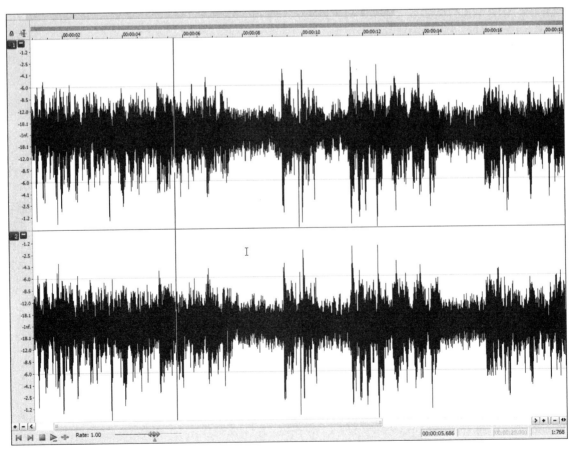

**Figure 6.3** Bad signal-to-noise ratio.

So, get closer...closer than you think. Don't forget the Inverse Square rule, which says that as you get closer to a sound source, the volume will increase (duh!), and as you move away, the sound level drops (double-duh!). It's hard to believe there is a law for this; however, it is a predictable occurrence. Double the distance, and the sound-pressure level drops 6 dB; halve the distance, and the sound is 6 dB louder. Keep that in mind as you fight levels on loud or soft sounds and general noise interference.

> **Note:** Fisher's secret microphone technique? Point the mic at the sound source and get closer.

In the studio, the proper distance from a mouth to the mic is the width of your hand—four to six inches. A close mic technique such as this results in a warm, clean, and natural vocal quality that is pleasing to listeners. When using a lavaliere, make the letter L with your thumb and pinkie. Place the top of your thumb along the lower lip. Where the pinkie rests is the right place for the lavaliere.

When using a shotgun on a boom (fixed or moving), try to get as close as possible to the subject—the closer the better. Booming from above (sometimes called *hanging*) often provides a more open, crisp sound. Booming from below, called *scooping*, can sound too heavy. Because aiming at the mouth can be difficult when using a moving boom, pick a target high on the chest. Remember ITSS (It's The Sternum, Stupid) and keep the mic aimed there. It's easier to keep the sound consistent aimed this way when the boom, the subject, or both is moving. The voice will still be in the pickup range of the mic, too.

## Avoid Built-In Mics

The crummy little mic that came built into your camcorder is best avoided for anything serious. The exception to this rule would be those pro and semi-pro cameras that come with an attached on-camera mic. These provide a marginally better sound than a built-in mic and can work well in a pinch, provided you are rather close to the subject. Learn from this example and instead invest in quality external microphones that you place near the sound source, not near the camera. However, many a documentary or event producer has been saved by the sound captured with a built-in or on-camera mic. Some sound is better than nothing in one-of-a-kind situations, such as breaking news or other unexpected opportunities. But for all other times, you need to get the mic away from the camera and close to whatever is making the sound you want.

## Use Care with Your Mics

Microphones are an investment. The technology doesn't change nearly as much as related production equipment. Therefore, you won't be changing them often. If you take care of your mics, they can last for many, many years. So, treat your mics well.

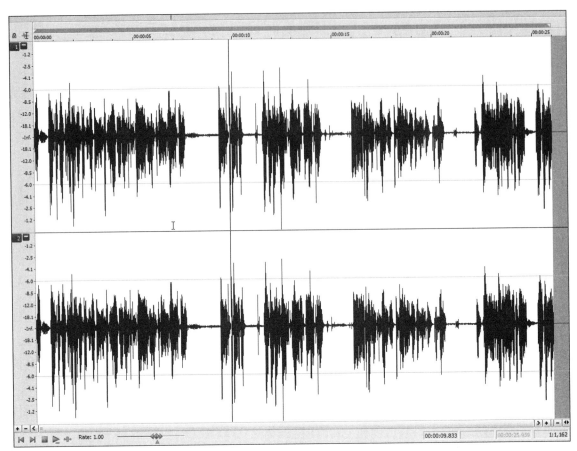

**Figure 6.4** Good signal-to-noise ratio.

Use quality storage cases. Many professional mics include a suitable case with the mic purchase. Mics are sensitive to moisture, so store your mics with a couple of those "Do Not Eat" silica packs to absorb excess wetness.

## Be Careful When Placing Multiple Mics

Though it might not seem apparent at first, using more than one mic can be far more trouble than it's worth. Multiple mics on the same subject can be more problematic than good. When mics are close to one another, they may interfere with each other and cause phasing issues—a swishy, hollow sound. Remember the 3:1 rule and place a second mic at least three times as far away from the first mic as that mic is from its subject. For example, if a mic is 10 inches from a subject, place a second mic at least 30 inches away from the first mic.

> **Note:** Always have a dynamic mic as a backup. When you use condensers, always have a backup power supply and/or extra fresh batteries, if applicable.

# Microphone Types

There are a further five primary microphone types. Handheld mics are, as the name implies, designed to be carried by its user. Typically, these are dynamics built to withstand rough handling. Two good cardioid dynamics are the Shure SM57 and SM58 (www.shure.com). Another popular choice is the Electro-Voice N/D767a (www.electrovoice.com) and the aforementioned EV-635a.

Studio condensers and many ribbons are larger and make more sense anchored to a stand or desktop microphone stand. Some small-diaphragm condensers are rather small, looking more like a handheld when they really aren't designed to work that way. There are many large-diaphragm studio condensers from which to choose, and an equally large complement of small-diaphragm condensers. On the high end are those made by Neumann, DPA, and Lawson; in the middle are plenty of options from Shure, Røde, Avant, and Audio-Technica. On the inexpensive side are plenty of good choices from companies such as Marshall with its MXL 909, M3, and others (www.mxlmics.com). Even some of the expensive mic manufacturers have inexpensive alternatives to explore, such as AT's 2020 and 2021 combo, comprising both a large- and small-diaphragm model.

Lavalieres are the tiny clip-on microphones worn by news anchors and used by most reality TV shows. These are commonly small, unobtrusive electret-condensers. Because they stay clipped in place on the body, they give a wearer greater range of movement. Lavs are an ideal choice for video interviews and "talking heads." Because cardioids suffer from proximity effect, most lavalieres are omnidirectional—they would sound too boomy placed on the resonant cavity of the chest. That makes them a little susceptible to noise, though being close to the mouth of the speaker usually overcomes this. That said, my favorite lavaliere is the Audio-Technica AT831b, which is a cardioid that includes a bass roll-off switch to overcome proximity effects. Lavalieres such as Sony's ECM series, the TRAM TR-50, and the tiny, easy-to-hide Countryman designs are all good choices. The Sanken COS-11 is another favorite, great-sounding lavaliere that is very easy to conceal, making it ideal for narrative use.

Headworn mics are gaining in popularity because they are unobtrusive—especially the DPA designs (www.dpamicrophones.com), which come in various flesh colors and are quite thin. Many are cardioids and placed very close to the mouth, making them suitable for noisy environments. I often see them worn by NASCAR commentators. Because they are close to the mouth, they can be susceptible to plosives, such as the letters *p*, *b*, and *t*. For news-gathering and some documentary work, this may be a decent alternative. The Crown CM-311A (www.crownaudio.com) and the Shure SM10A along with the aforementioned DPAs, are good choices here.

Shotguns are typically used at the end of a fixed or handheld fishpole boom in situations where mobility is needed and mics must be hidden, such as recording location dialogue for movies and TV. The ubiquitous Sennheiser 416 (www.sennheiser.com) is the *de facto* short shotgun standard, as are the other models they make. Shotguns from Sanken, Neumann, and Schoeps are equally sought after. Shotguns are tightly focused; aim carefully because anything off-axis doesn't sound as good. Point the end at the mouth, chin, or sternum, and you'll get good dialogue. Some other less expensive shotguns include the Audio-Technica 897 and those from Røde, including the NTG-1 and NTG-2. I prefer to use short shotguns outdoors for dialogue recording, and I'm fond of both the Oktava MK-012 and the Sennheiser MKH 50 supercardioid for indoor dialogue work. Handheld, lavaliere, and headset microphones come in both wired and wireless incarnations. The wired variety tethers the user to a cable, which can be annoying when movement is involved. Wireless offers more freedom, but is susceptible to interference. Don't forget to add suitable wind protection if you will work outdoors.

See Figure 6.5 for a shot of the various mic types.

**Figure 6.5** Microphone types.

## Boosting the Signal

Microphones put out a tiny amount of electricity, called *mic level*. The signal must be boosted before it can be used by other audio components, which use a higher voltage called *line level*. A microphone preamplifier—or *preamp*, for short—is included with most audio mixers and many recorders and camcorders, and there are some stand-alone preamps, too. Be aware that some wireless systems have the necessary preamp included so the receiver output is at standard line level.

You do not want to plug a mic into an input looking for the higher line level. You will not be able to boost the mic level enough to hear it properly. Similarly, plugging a line-level device into a mic input will overload the preamp, creating a distorted sound. Mic- and line-level inputs also usually have different impedance, which, when mismatched, can further deteriorate the sound. Most recording equipment has either separate plugs or a switch for choosing the correct input, either line or mic. When using a mic, recorders typically include a knob or slider to allow users to adjust the amount of preamplification, sometimes called *gain* or *level*.

Many consumer and a few prosumer camcorders use something known as *Automatic Gain Control (AGC)* to set incoming audio signal levels. This circuitry looks for sound, boosting levels until it finds some. Once it hears the sound, it adjusts the volume automatically. Unfortunately, this constant level adjustment can be heard as a sort of pumping and breathing sound on the final recording. Also, if it is very quiet, the AGC turns up the volume a lot, and if there is a sudden loud sound, it pulls the volume back rather sharply, resulting in a sucking sound—which is why I always say that AGC sucks!

If your camcorder allows it, defeating AGC is almost always the better choice. You are smart enough to set your own levels—smarter than any AGC, that is. With AGC, your recordings will be noisier and will suffer from the artifacts mentioned earlier. Without it, you risk recording too loudly and thus introducing distortion, but with some practice, you can control levels and leave the location with far better sound.

Alternatively (and sometimes additionally), a camera or recorder may have a limiter function. This device keeps the level from exceeding the 0 dBFS (decibels full scale—in other words, the digital scale) level that is the absolute top of the digital sound recording world. If it is set incorrectly, such as sending too much level to the camera and using the limiter to contain clipping peaks, it is just as bad as the AGC. However, a little limiting on just the loudest parts—and even then only occasionally—is acceptable. Instead of relying on these crutches, learn to set good levels and learn to ride the levels for material that warrants it. Turning the level up and down in response to changing audio is always better than using these electronic tools. Moving the mic closer to or farther away from the sound source as a way to control volume fluctuations is absolutely the *best* method, though.

While on the subject of camcorders, is your camera set up for recording audio correctly? Many DV models, especially consumer and even some prosumer models, ship from the factory with the wrong audio settings as the default. Your camera might be one of those set to record using only 12 bits. You want to choose the 16-bit setting. With 12 bits you have far, far lower resolution, which translates into a severe loss of dynamic range and the introduction of more noise into your recordings. Who needs that? Take a minute right now to pull up the menu on your camcorder, navigate to the audio settings, and make sure your audio will be recorded at 16-bit resolution.

If you are shooting HDV, understand that it uses a different audio scheme—MPEG-1, Layer II, 384 Kbps (kilobits per second), which is lossy compression. While the quality is acceptable for most voice and production work, you may prefer to use external recorders for more critical work, such as music (more on external recorders later in the book).

See Figure 6.6 for an example of camera mic inputs.

**Figure 6.6** Camera mic inputs.

## Fisher's Hierarchy of Microphone Choices

So now that you've learned a thing or two about microphones from this chapter and the previous one, what choices should you make? Here are my suggestions, from best to worst, for location sound recording.

1. Although I wouldn't use it for sound effects gathering, when recording human voice, you can't beat a lavaliere clipped to or hidden under the talent's clothing or placed nearby. This gives you a close, clean, in-your-face, dry sound. There will be very little room sound, giving you a lot of freedom in post. Lavs do suffer from off-mic sound, such as when a subject turns his head. This usually is not an issue for interview work, but for narrative projects this may pose a problem if an actor moves a lot. I love lavalieres for interviews and most actors, too. If you want a more open or roomy sound, move the mic a little farther away from the sound source. With lavs, there can be the perception that the sound you record won't match the shot people see (as mentioned earlier), and you may pick up clothing rustle, but overall it's hard to mess up good lav sound. As for models, try the Audio-Technica AT831 and AT899, Sony ECMs, the TRAM TR50, Sanken COS-11, and on the high end, Lectrosonics.

**Note:** The world of field recording is divided into two groups—those who love lavs and those who love booms. I'm a lav guy, which means I've insulted half my readers already. Sorry. Actually, I like booms, too, for many situations. I just do a lot of work alone, and lavs work well in these situations when I don't have a boom operator.

2.   Although hiding a mic in an actual plant is optional, the second best mic choice is a planted microphone, such as a hypercardioid, handheld, PZM/boundary, or even a lavaliere hidden on the set. As always, you want to be close to the talent. Planted microphones work well if there is minimal talent movement (though you could use multiple mics placed around the set, too). Obscuring the mic takes some creativity. I recall reading about how one savvy sound recordist hid a mic on another actor who didn't speak in a scene while the speaking actor walked around the human-planted mic. Omnis are sometimes useful here, such as the Shure VP64AL or Electro-Voice EV-675, though typical cardioids/ hypercardioids prevail, such as SM57/58 dynamics and both large- and small- diaphragm condensers, Crown PZMs or Audio-Technica boundary mics, or AT831/899 lavs. If two people are opposite one another, a figure-eight mic pointed correctly can be a very sound choice.

3.   If you don't want to see a mic, such as a lav clipped to your talent, and hiding it under clothing or on the set just won't work, consider putting a cardioid or hypercardioid (or even a short shotgun) on the end of a fixed microphone boom. If your talent is seated or if movement will be minimal, fixing the mic in place results in a great open sound. Many people don't have the spare human needed for moving a fishpole boom, so using a fixed mic instead makes sense. There are many mic stands from which to choose; the heavier, sturdier ones are best, but are not very portable. If you use a long boom and a heavy mic, be aware that the mic stand might tip, so you need a counterweight to keep it from slamming to the ground—or worse, slamming into your talent. Use a small bag filled with rice or sand and tie it on to the opposite end. For interview or training situations, consider a large-diaphragm studio condenser on the end of the fixed boom. If the room is rather live, avoid this, but in a typical office or other small space, the result can be a clean, almost recording studio–like quality with a little more openness than a dry lavaliere would provide.

4.   If your subject is moving or if you'll be moving around a lot, such as for news gathering, documentary, and event production, a hypercardioid or short shotgun on the end of a fishpole boom pole operated by another person is the next choice. Frankly, it can be just as good as the preceding suggestion, but because it requires a dedicated staff addition, it's listed as number four. In reality, though, the boom is where most people begin, because that's what they see Hollywood doing. Good boom work can be fantastic, but for the novice, it can be a nightmare. Don't cut your teeth using a boom on a critical shoot. It takes practice to move the boom quietly, keep it from hitting people and things, get good sound, and more. Changing mic perspectives, usually through boom work, makes cutting dialogue in post difficult. Plus, a shotgun mic has such a narrow pickup pattern that aiming incorrectly can result in far, far worse sound than if another choice were made. With a windsock over the mic, it can be hard

to tell where the shotgun is indeed pointed. Therefore, I feel that mediocre lav sound is often far superior than bad boom work, given the choice. That said, for sound effects gathering, I prefer to use a pistol grip with a short shotgun. If you decide to use a boom, make sure the operator has headphones to hear clearly what he or she is doing. Small adjustments make all the difference, especially with longer, more focused shotguns. For models, try the Audio-Technica AT835ST or a Sennheiser ME 66 or 416. Or, if you're inside, try the Oktava MK-012 or the Sennheiser MKH 50. Also, get shock mounts made by Audio-Technica or K-Tek and boom poles made by K-Tek, too.

5.  Last on my list is the use of wireless mics. Though wireless promises convenience, that comfort is usually for the talent, not for the audio engineer. I'd rather have a mic on a cable any day! Virtually any mic can become wireless with the addition of a transmitter and a receiver. Most wireless systems use handhelds and lavalieres, though. Wireless mics are prone to interference, and in our increasingly wireless world, the possibility of having a take ruined by something outside your control is quite prevalent. Some of the bandwidth reserved for the wireless mics was sold off by the FCC as part of the DTV transition. Any wireless mics operating at 700 MHz and above are technically illegal. Look for proprietary digital systems to emerge in the near future. If you decide to go wireless, avoid the cheap systems. Look for UHF, dual-diversity systems such as those made by Audio-Technica, Sony, or Lectrosonics.

---

**Note:** The Microphone University at DPA Microphones (www.dpamicrophones. com) is packed with a wealth of free, helpful information. There are details on mics, applications, stereo and surround techniques, and a detailed pro audio dictionary, too.

---

## Placement Options and Tips

If you decide to go with body mics (a.k.a. lavalieres), the best placement is to make the letter L with your thumb and pinkie, placing the top of the thumb along the lower lip, and the lav even with your pinkie. That's higher than most people place them, so start there and move down, always with an eye for "the closer, the better."

You don't always have to hide a lavaliere under clothing when simply moving it out of the frame is better. For example, a lavaliere clipped out of shot near a belly button will almost always sound better than a badly operated shotgun on a boom pole. Not going under clothing also prevents rustles and other noise from ruining the sound. With small lavalieres, you can get rather creative, such as hiding it in the talent's hair, taping it to their glasses, clipping it to the brim of a hat, attaching it to a dashboard or rearview mirror in a car, hiding it in a book, hiding it on furniture, and so forth.

When you are working with flimsy clothing material that won't support the mic, use a business or credit card behind the lavaliere to strengthen the hold. There are also some magnetic clips available for sensitive fabrics, such as silk, where the clip's teeth might cause damage. For strain relief, loop the mic's connecting cable around the mic, about 1 inch in diameter, and run that end back through the clip. This is known as the *broadcast loop*; you'll see a lot of news anchors using this scheme. Also, use care so the clip's teeth won't cut the cable.

The TRAM lavaliere is a little easier to obscure under a shirt or blouse. Its kit comes with several different clips that add extra versatility. For example, use the vampire clip to attach the mic under the clothing, facing the mic capsule outward. The way the mic sits in the vampire clip minimizes clothing rustle. Another tactic is to use moleskin (available in the foot-care section in your local pharmacy) to wrap around the mic and then apply the moleskin to the underside of the fabric. You can use this trick with other mic styles, too—not just the TRAM.

If the talent stands or moves while wearing a wired lavaliere, consider taping the belt-pack power supply to the leg, just above the ankle. This way the cable comes out the pant leg with fewer tangles, trips, or restrictions.

If only under clothing will do, you need to invest in some surgical tape or adhesive bandages for attaching the mic (somewhat) painlessly to skin. Simply loop the tape or bandage around the mic and secure it to the skin. A little extra tape here is a good idea—about an inch or two away from where the cable connects to the mic, create a loop in the cable and tape it down, too. This provides a little buffer strain relief for when the cable inevitably gets tugged. Rycote (www.rycote.com) makes great products called Undercovers, Overcovers, and Stickies that are ideal for this kind of work.

When hiding a lav on female talent, *CSI* sound recordist Mick Fowler offered this advice in a *Mix* magazine interview (www.mixonline.com): "I take advantage of Marg Helgenberger's and Jorja Fox's physiology and place the mics between the breasts using surgical tape. [Actor] Gary Dourdan...has a good set of pecs. So, I use the same technique on him, too." Clipping or taping the mic to the inside of the bra band between the cups is an alternative placement option. There is typically a little gap there for the mic to sit. Leaving a blouse button open can reduce clothing rustle and result in a strong, clear sound. Obviously, this placement should be performed by the talent herself, following your instructions.

Don't rush up to the talent and clip on a mic without first asking permission. Placing body mics requires building rapport with the talent. Many people don't like their personal space invaded. You have to be the diplomat. Remind people that you are there to make sure they sound their best. Don't be confrontational. I'm not antagonistic; we're a team. Although I prefer to place mics myself, sometimes you have to let the talent do it themselves. In this instance, give complete instruction and details. Stick around to supervise, if possible.

If this applies to your situation, such as if you make narrative or documentary reenactments, check with the wardrobe department to determine mic placement options. Some fabrics are noisier than others, and a simple textile swap could make all the difference in the world. Be wary of accessories, too, such as jewelry and some props, because they can jingle, jangle, and otherwise ruin good dialogue takes.

The proper way to hold a fishpole boom is to stand straight with your feet slightly wider than shoulder-width apart. Bend your knees slightly, as if you were sitting on a horse. Tai Chi aficionados will know this as the horse stance. Grip the pole firmly, spreading your arms apart about the same distance as your feet, one hand on the base of the fishpole and the other along its length. Don't grip it with the supporting hand; just cradle the pole in your palm. You should look like a letter X. Raise the pole up high so that the mic is aimed down at the talent. Try to minimize moving your feet and instead pivot at your waist. Most people can pivot 270° easily. If you have to turn, start in the stretched, uncomfortable position and move into the comfortable one. Bend at the elbows and shoulders to tilt the mic down or up.

Make friends with the camera operator so that you know what the shot is going to look like. This can give you ideas for the best placement of the mic without interfering with the visual. Obviously, you want to choose the placement that gives you the best overall sound, but if there is a camera involved, you might need an alternative location. Make sure you stay out of the shot and prevent your mic and fishpole boom from casting shadows on the set or the actors.

Aim the mic at the mouth for the best sound. That can be difficult, especially if the subject is moving. In that case, aim at the sternum, which is an easier target to hit and sounds natural even if the talent's mouth moves away slightly. Aiming at the sternum still keeps the mouth in the pickup pattern of the mic.

To cue the boom is to rotate it in place to capture needed lines, usually with multiple people on the set simultaneously. To swing the boom is to physically move it through space. You always want to minimize swing and instead position yourself so all you need to do is cue the mic. If you must swing inside, place a foam windscreen over the mic, as moving it will create wind that can ruin your recording. Outside work necessitates wind protection at all times, regardless of whether you are standing still or swinging the mic.

Get closer to the softer speaker in any given scene and use distance to adjust levels between multiple speakers—closer to soft talkers and farther away from the loud people. Find the right placement that gives you the best sound for most of the scene without having to make major adjustments.

Consider *scooping*, which is positioning the boom pole below the talent instead of the more conventional method of hanging it from above the talent's head. Scooping gives a heavier, darker tone but may be the only alternative in some situations, such as when the mic casts a shadow on the set when positioned above. Scooping can also reduce footstep noise when actors are walking and the camera moves along with them.

Always catch the line start for the next speaker, even if that means leaving the current speaker a bit early. Voices that trail off slightly sound more natural than speech that fades in slowly. If you move too late, the next voice will get louder gradually as the mic gets closer. That's a difficult fix in post. The audience can almost hear the mic moving as it tries to catch the lines. You might be better off using more than one mic in such a scene if it requires too much swinging to get all the words.

Making the right microphone choice is a major factor that can deliver the quality sound you need when on location and in the studio. Understanding how mics work —especially their pickup patterns—can help you make good decisions for the kinds of audio situations you face. But there are other aspects to keep in mind, too, and they are the subject of the next chapter.

# 7 Building the Location Sound Kit

Though they are very important to the quality of sound you record, microphones are only part of the equipment you need for successful production sound recording. In this chapter we'll look at the other pieces of gear and begin to pull together a solid toolbox that can help you secure good field recordings.

## Mixers, Meters, and Levels

You might see many location sound recordists using a mixer, which is a piece of electronic equipment that allows you to combine multiple sound sources. Mixers come in both A/C- (see Figure 7.1) and battery-operated models. Some, like the one in Figure 7.1, are used in more controlled environments, such as a recording studio or an editing suite, while the portable field mixers are better built for the demands of on-location production sound.

If you will be recording only one or two mics or other sources, there is no need for a mixer. You can use the mic inputs on the camera or recorder itself. Why add another piece of gear when it's not warranted? This is something that adds another layer of complexity and can break down. That said, some people prefer the sound of using mixer preamps on their mics to what a camera provides. Some cameras simply do not sound very good, even when high-quality mics are used. A separate mixer can give you additional controls and potentially a better overall sound. Plus, you won't be bothering the camera operator.

Worse still is that the mixer levels may be mismatched with the recorder or camera electronics, introducing the potential for more noise in the workflow. If this is the case, be sure to match the mixer output to the camera input. This is usually the line out feed from the mixer into the line in at the camera. It's crucial to monitor sound at both locations—though monitoring the sound at the camera makes the most sense, because it's the last stage doing the actual recording. Some mixers support a return monitor feed from the camera, which lets the operator check both what the mixer sounds like and what the camera is "hearing."

Also, the output of most portable mixers can be switched between mic and line level. If you plug the mic out of the mixer into the mic in of the camera, you will run through two mic preamps. If you plug a mic out into the line input, there won't be enough gain,

**Figure 7.1** Mixer example.

and you'll record low levels and noise. If you match the line level out of the mixer into the mic in of the camera, you risk overloading the circuit and recording distorted, clipped sound. You must match the gain staging correctly for the best results. Note that the actual physical outputs/inputs may *not* be different on either device, but a switch may adjust the functionality of the input/output. Refer to the manuals that shipped with your gear for specifics.

Next, you have to calibrate the output of the two devices. When you set levels with the mixer, you need to know that the camera isn't adding to or subtracting from the level. You should use a test tone—most portable mixers generate the necessary tone—that reads the mixer meters to adjust the levels and match the meters on the camera. If your mixer does not generate a test tone, create or acquire one and play it back using another device, such as an MP3 player connected to the mixer. My favorite tool for this is the Gold Line GL14 sine wave generator, which plugs into an XLR input and generates a series of tones ideal for calibrating levels. Be careful—one of the devices might have a different meter scale. For example, the mixer might have analog-style VU meters, which read, essentially, an average level over time and ignore most signal peaks. The camera may be a digital peak scale or peak program meter (PPM), using the decibel full-scale standard (dBFS). The problem with these two different meters is that there are two zeroes, which are different. A 0-dB level on the VU scale is not equal to 0 dBFS on a digital scale. Instead, 0 VU is equal to one of two digital settings: –18 for EBU and –20 for SMPTE, as shown in Figure 7.2. Neither standard is better, but you need to be consistent and accurate and record which one you use in your field notes. Run a 1-kHz test tone sine wave through the mixer and set it to read 0 dB VU. Set the peak meter on the camera to read –18 or –20. If both meters are the same, and you are sure of this, they should read the same.

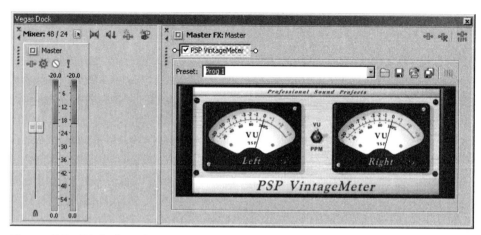

**Figure 7.2**  Digital and VU meters with test tone.

With the two devices calibrated properly, you can trust that what you see on the mixer meters will be what the camera records, with no level mismatches. Of course, it still behooves you to monitor from the camera to make sure all is well. It also makes sense to rewind the tape or otherwise play back what you've recorded during lulls to confirm that the audio is going down fine. Remember, you are monitoring the signal *before* it is recorded. Rare is the recorder or camera that gives you confidence recording—that is, hearing what you recorded right after you record it. Instead, you need to listen back to the recordings to ultimately check their quality.

Finally, how loud should your recordings be? Keep the two meters in mind. An analog VU has a zero on its scale, but it is acceptable to exceed that zero because there is headroom above the zero to handle louder peaks without distorting. A VU shows a more average level. Digital meters also have a zero, but it is the absolute top of the scale; there is no headroom above that zero. It is never good to exceed 0 dBFS, or you will distort and clip the waveform, something you can never recover from—it sounds nasty (see Figure 7.3)! Therefore, *never* exceed 0 dB on a digital recording. You have to set levels to keep the loudest parts always below that zero. Try keeping the majority of the sound between –6 and –10 dB below digital 0 when using meters set to the digital scale. With VUs it is tricky to set levels because you don't see the peaks, and they really matter when recording! Keep the average hovering just around or below the 0 VU. See Figure 7.4 for an example of an audio waveform that has too low of a level.

Unfortunately, setting levels is not something that is easily learned; it takes practice and experience. I suggest you do a series of test recordings that let you see and hear the difference that setting levels makes. You want to squeeze the maximum level you can, but you don't want to distort. The louder the good stuff is means that the noise is that much lower. But too loud is a distorted mess. I'd rather have slightly lower levels get recorded than have harsh and impossible-to-fix distorted audio.

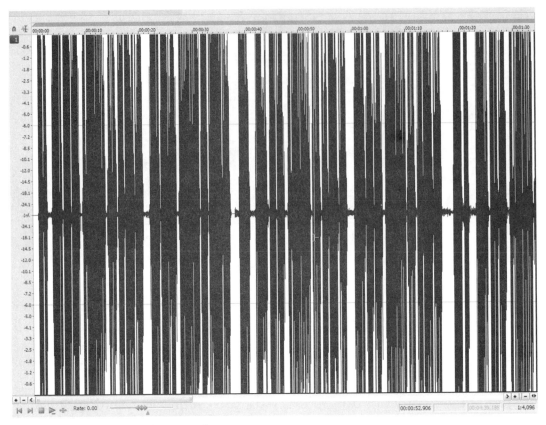

**Figure 7.3** Clipped audio waveform.

A limiter in the camera or a mixer can help catch occasional peaks, but don't rely on a limiter to do your work for you. There's a reason why level knobs and faders move—so you can change them while recording by boosting and cutting as needed in response to the changing volume of sounds you want to capture.

## Separate Audio Recorders

In addition to (or in lieu of) a mixer, many production sound people use a separate recorder instead of the camera. Those who shoot using the HDSLR cameras must record to a separate device, as the onboard audio tools are low quality for serious work. The advantage to this workflow is having a dedicated piece of hardware that's designed solely for sound (unlike the camera, where manufacturers typically cut audio corners). There's also the possibility of redundancy by being able to record to the audio device and send the same sound to the camera. If one fails, the other fills in. Recorders can give you multiple recording tracks, which add flexibility to the location recordings. For example, different actors in a scene can get their own isolated tracks (called *split tracks*). The Edirol R-44, shown in Figure 7.5, is a four-track, solid-state recorder and mixer. It has great-sounding preamps and a bevy of useful tools, including phantom power, a limiter, and more. The next chapter covers more on using recorders and recording separate (called *double-system*) sound.

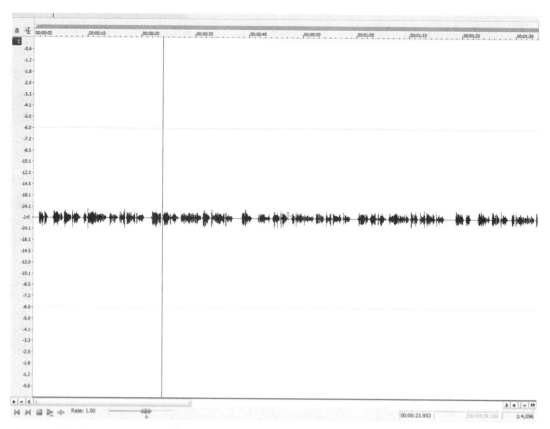

**Figure 7.4**   An audio waveform with too low a level.

**Figure 7.5**   Edirol R-44 field recorder/mixer.

## Cables and Connectors

By far the most overlooked link in the analog chain is the cabling used to connect mics to cameras, mixers, preamps, and other recorders. Don't cheap out on me here! Spend a little money buying high-quality cables, such as those made by Mogami and Monster Cable. I prefer to use the shortest cable I can when connecting gear, so having a few different lengths makes the most sense. Learn how to properly coil and store cables for maximum reliability and longevity, too.

Microphones, not to mention camcorders and other audio recorders, connect in a variety of ways. Mics usually do not include a cable, and virtually every professional mic terminates in a male XLR connector. Some consumer microphones may have an attached cable that typically ends in a male 1/8-inch or 1/4-inch connector. Here's a clue: If the mic you're using ends in an 1/8-inch plug, it's not going to be very good quality (sorry).

Most cameras are two-channel stereo, though DV supports four channels (two of inferior quality). Consumer cameras, if they even accept external mics, have a female 1/8-inch input. Some prosumer camcorders are similarly outfitted. Pro cameras usually have XLR inputs. Cameras that lack XLR inputs can still use professional mics with either an adapter cable or a breakout box, such as those made by BeachTek (www.beachtek.com) or Juiced Link (www.juicedlink.com).

The 3-pin XLR connector is important because it is a balanced system that rejects RF and A/C line noise. Still, if your audio cable has to cross a power cable, try to do it at 90 degrees and avoid parallel runs. Balanced cables work well when connected to mics. They are low impedance (meaning they don't resist the flow of electricity much) and are therefore suitable for very long cable runs. When you need to run long cables, pro mics and XLR cables are the way to go. Line-level signals should always be short runs regardless of the cable type.

When it comes to 1/8-inch and 1/4-inch connectors, there are two varieties: mono and stereo. When the male connector has only one black ring on it, the signal is mono. When two black rings exist, the signal can be either stereo or balanced. In the stereo configuration, you might use such a connector to plug into an MP3 player. However, the stereo configuration can also mimic the three connectors of the XLR. When used this way, the 1/4-inch connector is also balanced—called *TRS* for *tip, ring, and sleeve*.

The problem comes when you're using an XLR on one end and a mono 1/8-inch or 1/4-inch on the other to interface to a camera or recorder. This configuration is not balanced and is therefore susceptible to interference. But an even greater problem can exist with this scenario. XLRs work their magic by having one of the two main connectors (the third is the ground) 180 degrees out of phase. If wired incorrectly, the regular and out-of-phase signals get recorded on the two separate channels at the camera or recorder. When played back, there is a wide stereo image that completely disappears when summed to mono—the two channels, being exact opposites, add up to nothing! Listen for this phenomenon when you are editing dialogue in post if you use such a cable. You will need to delete one of the channels and keep the remaining one. This is a big problem when you are trying to interface pro mics with consumer gear. Use a breakout box instead, as mentioned earlier.

See Figure 7.6 for an example of five types of connectors.

**Figure 7.6**  Five types of connectors: 1. stereo 1/8-inch (3.5mm), 2. RCA, 3. mono 1/4-inch, 4. stereo 1/4-inch or balanced Tip-Ring-Sleeve (TRS), and 5. XLR.

When it comes to cables, always have some redundancy. When there's a problem, often cables are to blame. As a rule, check everything before critical recordings and inspect regularly for loose connections, cuts, and so forth. Hook up those mics and cables, perform some tests, and listen back. Make sure everything is right before you leave for a shoot.

## Location Sound Field Kit

So what gear do you need to acquire to build your location sound recording kit? Here's a handy list:

- Quality closed-ear headphones for both mixer and boom operator.

- Several different mics (dynamic, hypercardioid, short shotgun, lavaliere, PZM/boundary).

- All the hookup cables you may need...and a few extras, just in case.

- Fishpole boom and a pistol grip with mic shock mount.

- Foam windscreens and wind "socks"—perhaps a full-blown mic "blimp" system.

- Batteries and spares.

- Weather protectors. Cotton batting, sold in fabric stores, is ideal for combating the noise from rain that pelts the mic. It will get wet and heavy quickly, though.

- Radios (for the boom operator and the sound recorder to communicate). Avoid cell phones because their annoying dit-dit-dit when the network tries to find them will ruin your recordings. Of course, you can also communicate via the mics and a mixer, depending on the gear you select.

- A ditty bag full of a collection of plugs, cables, adapters, and tools for unusual situations. Here's a list of what I carry with me:

    - Y-adapters.

    - Headphone splitter, headphone distribution amp, and extra headphones.

    - Various adapter combinations, such as 3.5mm to 1/4-inch, RCA to 1/4-inch balanced, RCA to mono 1/4-inch, RCA extenders, RCA to 1/4-inch and 1/8-inch 3.5mm adapters. Have opposites and right-angle versions, too.

    - Various cable combinations, such as patch cables, adapter cables in various lengths, Low-Z and High-Z converters, pads and attenuators, and a ground lifter.

    - Tools such as a burnishing tool for cleaning jacks, screwdrivers, needle-nose pliers, gaffer's tape, cable ties, and a flashlight. (There are carry-on restrictions if you travel by air with many of these items. Make sure you are not talking about your pistol grip and shotgun when you are in line at airport security, either.)

    - Mic clips, booms, stands, and such.

## Recording Sound Effects and Backgrounds

Many of the same techniques already discussed apply when you hit the road, hunting and gathering custom sound effects. Condenser mics and short shotguns work quite well on boom poles and with pistol grips. You can record to a camera or another digital recorder and bring that material into your editing suite.

Keep in mind that getting a single recording of something that makes sound is not as valuable as having multiple perspectives of it. Think as you would for camera angles, such as close, medium, long shot, and extreme long shot. Some sounds have a different texture depending on where the mic is (and what mic you use!). Just like shooting video, you want to get maximum sound coverage.

Also, think about the progression of a sound and record all those variations. You'll never regret recording too much of some sounds, because it affords you more choices and better accuracy when you include the sounds in the final mix. For example, suppose you need to record a certain vehicle. A partial list of sounds would be:

- Record various car-bys of the vehicle moving toward and away from the mic at different speeds and angles. Tire/brake squeals are optional. Don't forget turns, pulling up, backing up, and such.

- Include different surfaces (gravel, asphalt, concrete, dirt) if the script requires.

- Get various perspectives of the car starting, idling, running, and pulling up and away.

- Capture doors and trunks opening and closing and at different speeds and power.

- Get inside perspectives of starting, idling, running, and driving in various areas, on pavement, at various speeds, and more.

- Record everything you can think of and then some, and then record these again from different perspectives (close, long shot, very far away, and so on). Try different microphones for additional textures and perspectives.

Stereo can be quite useful here, especially when you are recording ambient backgrounds and certain effects that work well in stereo (such as a car-by). True surround sound recordings, such as using a multichannel recorder in conjunction with a dedicated surround sound microphone, like the Holophone (see Figure 7.7), are also useful. The little Zoom H2 records four channels at once using its built-in mics, and I've found it to be a fantastic sound effects gathering tool, too, particularly ambiences and backgrounds.

**Figure 7.7** Holophone surround microphone.

## Stereo in the Field

Voice is best left mono so that it appears in the center of a stereo image, anchored to the screen. Stereo, though, is great for music and some sound effects and is certainly well-suited for backgrounds.

With the acceptance of multichannel surround sound, it makes even more sense to do more stereo recording in the field. Obviously, it makes sense to record some real surround, too. However, few of us have access to surround microphones or the ability to record five to six channels of discrete sound simultaneously. That said, the aforementioned Zoom H2 brings four-channel recording to your toolset with a minimal investment. And also, real stereo is a good compromise and far easier (and often cheaper) to attain.

Ambient backgrounds recorded in stereo work well for two-channel mixes and in either L/R or Ls/Rs in multichannel sound delivery. For instance, a decent stereo recording of city sounds placed in the surrounds will envelop the audience, leaving the stereo front and center channels available for additional effects and/or music and dialogue, respectively. A fully surround recording for backgrounds would rarely be applied (never say never, though); however, many music tracks are delivered this way, especially in orchestral music. It's rare that rock/pop/hip-hop does true surround recordings, unless the project is a live concert recording. Sporting events recorded for TV often benefit from full surround recordings of the audience.

So, stereo is a good tactic. True surround is useful, too, because it can be converted quickly to stereo.

There are several ways to record stereo. The basic requirements include a recorder capable of recording in stereo, which is virtually every professional and semi-professional recorder today, including every camcorder from mini-DV through XDCAM and beyond. You will also need either two microphones or a dedicated stereo microphone. There are different stereo techniques to employ, as shown in Figure 7.8 and discussed below. Each technique has advantages and disadvantages.

- Spaced omnis use two identical, or matched, omnidirectional mics spaced using the 3:1 rule—at least three times as far apart as the distance to the sound source. You might want to match the size of your stereo image to your project. For example, space them 40 inches apart for a TV production and 10 to 15 feet apart for a film. This creates a stereo image that matches what the audience sees.

- X/Y uses two matched cardioids positioned nearly on top of one another but pointed opposite, 90 degrees away from center.

- ORTF separates two matched cardioids by about 17 cm and 110 degrees in a V pattern.

- Mid-side recording uses a cardioid and figure-eight mic in a special configuration (detailed a bit later in this chapter).

- There are several dedicated stereo mics, including the Audio Technica AT822/825 and the Røde NT4. All three use the X/Y technique. The mics in the Zoom H2 use two different X/Y patterns. The Zoom H4n uses an X/Y pattern, too.

- In an attempt to mimic how the ears function, binaural recording uses mics in the "ears" of a dummy head. Alternately, you can clip two lavalieres to eyeglasses or a hat for surprisingly good binaural recordings. I use the Core Sound (www.core-sound.com) binaural mic set with an M-Audio MicroTrack 24/96 for field stereo recording to great success. Binaural recordings sound best played back on headphones where the sense of truly being there is faithfully reproduced. The effect gets diminished somewhat playing on speakers, but it is still a good, strong stereo sound.

■ Dedicated surround microphones, such as those made by Holophone (www. holophone.com), support multichannel recording by positioning five mics in a football-shaped mount that is really just a binaural variation.

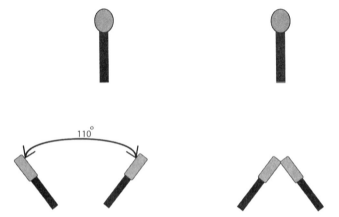

**Figure 7.8**   Stereo microphone techniques. Clockwise from top: spaced omnis, X/Y, and ORTF.

With any stereo technique, you trade having a wide stereo image with more localization of the sound source. In short, some techniques give a spacious sound but lose definition, and others portray the sounds accurately but don't sound as full or wide. For instance, the X/Y approach indicates where things are well, but has a small spatial impression, while ORTF loses the directionality of sounds, but there is a better sense of space.

The best stereo technique is mid-side (M/S) because it provides adjustable stereo and is fully mono-compatible. Not all stereo collapses or sums to mono well. And mono compatibility is very important because you never really know where or how your project will play. Mono-stereo-surround and the whole arena of downmixing is equally important, and we'll visit these ideas in detail as we discuss mixing later in the book. The nature of M/S allows you to choose the stereo image, and when summed to mono, the mono sound remains robust.

M/S works by using a cardioid mic and a figure-eight mic arranged and recorded in such a way that it creates an adjustable stereo image. One such pair comes from Beyer as their M160/M130 combination. Its only major drawback is that to monitor it on location requires a special matrix. If you don't mind *not* monitoring correctly, you can still employ the technique in the field and extract the stereo in post. This is the workflow I recommend.

Two mics, cables, a stereo recorder, and headphones are all that you need. And although in the field you will hear a funky stereo-ish sound in your ears, it's good enough for making level and quality decisions. You won't hear the real M/S stereo in the field, but you will in post, once you know how to process the recording. I like the M/S technique for grabbing sound effects and backgrounds on location. This gives me post choices ranging from mono to wide stereo, which no other stereo technique really allows. I also like it as a stereo miking technique on many musical instruments. I wouldn't use it for dialogue or singing, though group walla and background vocals (including choirs) benefit from it. I rarely use it for Foley because so much of the work is close-up, and mono works well in this case. Of course, there's nothing wrong with miking everything M/S because you can always throw out the stereo and keep the mono!

With M/S you point the cardioid at the sound source and position the figure-eight just above or below the cardioid with its nulls pointed toward the sound source. Its sides pick up the sound. Sound arriving at the front and rear of the side mic is out of phase, which is what creates the sense of stereo. The cardioid reinforces the phantom center with a solid center monaural image. Record the mic output to two separate channels, routing the cardioid (mid) mic to the left and the figure-eight (side) mic to the right.

In post, you bring up the left (mid) and right (side) on two separate NLE or DAW tracks. Copy the side channel to a third track. Flip the phase on this track 180 degrees out of phase with the original side track. Hard pan these tracks left and right, respectively. Keep the mid channel panned center. Figure 7.9 shows how this might look in your NLE/DAW. Playback reveals the widest stereo image. Pulling the pan controls back toward center on the side channels gives you a kind of wideness control. Turning off those channels gives you the single mono mid channel. Go back to full stereo, and

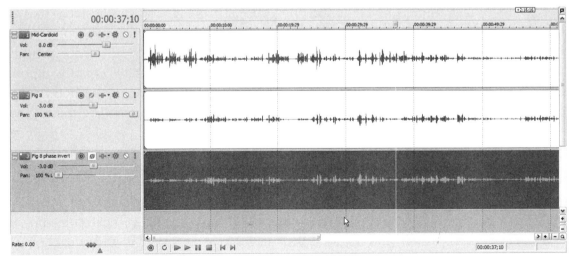

**Figure 7.9** Processing mid-side.

then listen to the recording in mono. The side channels cancel each other out, leaving, once again, the mono center.

In surround you could route the sides to the surrounds and the mid to either the center channel or phantom center for a super-wide enveloping sound with clear imaging to the front. Collapse this surround mix to mono, and the Rs/Ls disappears, leaving your center-panned mono sound.

That wraps up the gear and some of the techniques you need for successful on-location work. There are several other situations you may need to deal with—those are the subject of the next chapter.

# 8 CYA Tips

Often production sound is a one-shot affair, so there isn't a chance or enough time to go back and get it right the second time. Therefore, I've developed a few tips to cover all the bases.

- Most professional cameras targeted for corporate, event, documentary, and indie film use include solid audio recording tools: balanced XLR connections, phantom power, level meters, and other needs. This does mean that the camera operator and sound recordist must fight for camera time. If the camera records the audio, the sound recordist needs access to it, along with having headphones plugged in. This is not a problem when the camera operator and sound recordist is the same person, but when multiple personnel are involved, crowding around a camera can pose problems. Work it out beforehand to prevent professional clashes and potentially problematic audio. A simple headphone splitter so more than one person can be on headphones might be all that's required. Working with a mixer that you calibrate to the camera can be helpful here, as you can control levels and such without touching the camera repeatedly.

- Use the camera mic channels effectively. Camcorders offer two mic inputs, which can be used for stereo but more often are better used as dual-mono/two-track. Stereo can be true stereo or it can be two separate channels suitable for separating talent onto a discrete track for redundancy, two different mics, and/or two levels. Therefore, splitting mic assignments, such as routing a lavaliere to Mic 1/Left and a shotgun to Mic 2/Right or a wireless lav to 1/L and a planted, wired mic to 2/R provides redundancy and individual control. This is known as *split track recording*. Similarly, if you have two performers in a scene, mic each one individually, route their audio to individual channels, and set levels accordingly: Actor 1/L and Actress 2/R. In post, your NLE/DAW can let you choose between the channels. Having separate tracks offers greater flexibility as you pull the soundtrack together.

- Another tactic is to split the same mic to both camera input channels and set one input 12 to 15 dB lower than the other. This lets you handle a sudden volume change that might distort on one channel, giving you wiggle room on the other. The problem with heavy distortion from having the levels set too hot is that there is nothing in the recording to recover. With this two-level setting, the alternate channel should replace the badly distorted one.

---

**Tape Redux:** Recently, some students working on an advanced project asked me for help with an audio problem. Their dialogue tracks for a video scene were stuttering and dropping out. And while glitch music can be fun, it doesn't really work for dialogue. I immediately suspected a bad video capture and suggested another go. However, when I heard the bad audio coming off the tape (analog) during the second capture session, I suspected another problem. It turned out that the cameraperson had reused an old tape (for the fourth time!). In the DV/HDV world, you should *never* reuse a tape. If you re-record, you risk losing data or getting garbled sound, video, or both. Treat DV/HDV tape as you would film —use it once. The students' entire shoot was ruined by not spending less than $5 for a fresh DV tape. It's funny how people will spend a lot of money on gear, but cheap out on something as critical as new tape.

Tape is quickly going the way of the dinosaur, being replaced by the solid-state memory card. These cards are reusable, but I also suggest that you reformat them regularly and always before a critical project. You also need a way to back up these cards as you fill them, so that you can grab the files off of them, store this material, and then reuse the card. Frankly, the cards used by most recorders are inexpensive (compared to comparable camera cards), so having a lot of them on hand makes sense.

Invest wisely, because the initial upfront cost will usually be far less than having to redo a project completely.

---

## Double-System Recording

Hollywood and TV primarily capture sound on a separate recorder that runs in sync with the camera. This started because the optical sound during the early days of sound film required that the sound be recorded separately from the film. This process is called *double-system* recording. The practice of recording audio to one machine and the visual to the camera continued even as magnetic recording became the norm. Smaller-format cameras, such as 16mm, were the first to marry film and sound together on the film, but it took video (for the most part) to make recording sound and picture to the same device the industry standard.

That said, there are some advantages to recording the audio to another device in addition to the camera. Recorders dedicated to audio are typically higher quality than the equivalent facilities on a camera alone (such as today's HDSLR cameras, with their compromised audio features and quality). For example, you can get external recorders with higher sample rates and bit depths, resulting in a better sound. These recorders may also offer multiple recording channels that allow you to separate and record different mics (and actors) to their own channels. This gives you the most flexibility during post-production. And, of course, using portable external recorders instead of (or in addition to) the camera sound is another way to have redundancy in the field. If one of the audio recordings is somehow compromised, the other can be used instead. Even if you take this route, use the camera audio as a reference for post-sync and as a backup to the primary sound recorder. For one-of-a-kind content, having a backup is the best practice.

Other times, the camera functions as the primary recorder with a secondary recorder as a reserve. Many wedding videographers mic the groom with a wireless mic and use another wired mic connected to a small recorder placed in the groom's pocket. The wireless goes to one channel on the camera; the other camera mic input gets connected to a wired shotgun at the camera position. The pocket recorder is there in the event of a worst-case scenario. Syncing will take a little futzing, but it is better than no usable sound at all. You might try a casual sync reference in this case. With everything running, a well-chosen cough—even if it's yours!—will make it onto *all* the recordings, making initial sync so much easier!

If you record double-system, it makes real sense to monitor in two places: the recorder itself and a return feed from the camera. Even if you will use the recorder for your sound, the best redundancy comes from sending its output to the camera and recording there as a backup. A mixer might have the requisite extra outputs built in. Otherwise, use a simple mic splitter to route your mic or mixer output to two separate places. The camera audio would function as a backup to your primary recorder and be available for use in a pinch. Consider setting the camera audio level a little lower than the external recorder, which helps if you record a little too hot on the main recorder. The camera will have the same audio minus the overloading. This is great in noisy places or when the talent gets a little overzealous and really cooks the recording before you can turn the level down or move the mic.

Recording double-system sound does not need to be as difficult as it might first sound. Today's digital recorders are quite solid in their timing, so drift is minimal (if there is any) even when both the camera and the recorder are running completely wild. It's important that the sample rate at the external recorder match the camera, though, and that is almost always 48 kHz. A common sync reference—the slate—is all you need to post-sync the two tracks. While you can use the typical clichéd Hollywood-style film slate, it's not required. The easiest slate to have around is a single loud hand-clap that gets picked up by the mics and recorded to both the external recorder and the camera(s).

If you can't route the recorder audio to the camera, use the on-camera mic to pick up sound anyway. The good sound goes to the recorder, but the camera picks up enough for sync purposes only. The slate will be prominent on both soundtracks in the NLE/DAW, which makes lining things up fast and easy. You might see some drift over time—usually several minutes—causing you to slip a frame or two on the soundtrack before you match up again. If you're cutting a lot instead of very long takes (such as a concert or other uninterrupted performance), you might never experience any sync drift at all.

It is also possible to link the secondary recorder to the camera using simple LANC on the low end and timecode on the high end. For example, the Edirol R-44 recorder accepts LANC from some Sony cameras. Pressing Start/Stop on the camera automatically starts and stops the audio recorder. Higher-end audio recorders, such as the Deva, accept timecode from cameras that support this feature to maintain sync. As I said earlier, this sync is not necessary because digital recorders are rock solid—provided you match the camera's sample rate of 48 kHz.

## Slate Procedures

The key to using the double-system sound approach is the slate. At the start and/or end of every take, the slate provides a visual and aural mark that facilitates syncing the sound and video during post-production. As you use a secondary recorder—and even when you're relying on a single primary camera for sound recording—follow the slate procedures discussed in this section.

1. Always try to slate both the audio and video, verbally and visually when possible. Also note that even if you are doing a multi-camera shoot, these techniques apply. Fill the frame with the slate. If applicable, fill out the information about the project clearly. Start the video camera(s) and the audio recording device. Wait a moment to check and make sure everything is running correctly. Usually, once everything checks out, the camera operator and sound mixer say "speed." Announce the scene with the clapper open. Slam the clapper down hard and hold it for a second or two before removing it from the shot. If you're using your hands for the slate, they should be in the frame.

2. Match the naming convention used for the video. Create a folder for the digital audio files and name it to match the camera tape name. If the camera uses HDD or memory card acquisition, then follow the same file naming protocol. All audio associated with the tape/HDD/card goes into this folder. Also, name the individual files to match the verbal slates or camera file names, such as Scene 1, Take 2. Taking the time to do this while on set will save you a lot of time looking for material in the audio suite later.

3. Place a line-up tone at the start of the tape and/or initial file on the digital recorder and camera. Use a 1-kHz tone at either –18 dBFS or –20 dBFS and equal to 0 VU. Verbally announce the following information on the tape start and initial file so it gets recorded to the camera and digital audio recorder. Include the following information in your verbal slate and keep written notes with the same information:

- Project name/producer/company.
- Location specifics.
- Date.
- Tape/roll/file number/name. (Match sound files/discs/cards to camera tapes.)
- Recorder specifics (make, model, sampling rate/bit depth).
- Mic used (make, model).
- Mic placement/technique.
- Preamp specifics (if applicable).
- Channel assignments (left boom, right boom −10).
- Any other information or comments you deem necessary.

4. At the start of *every* recording, announce the scene name, its take, the file name (if applicable), and any other information that varies from the initial slate, such as if you swap out a mic or try another technique. Sometimes you can't record the slate first because the action is happening so fast. It's acceptable to put the slate at the end, known as a *tail slate*. If you use a clapper, it's common practice to hold it upside down for the tail slate. On long scenes, I recommend doing both a head and tail slate.

5. Take written notes of audio settings and issues while on location. Log the scenes and takes and your opinion of them, which is useful for other field shoots and also for post-production. If you will do any dialogue replacement, knowing what was used on location can make matching the production sound to the ADR easier. I do paper notes and also often dictate into the camera or double-system recorder, too. Detail the initial slate information and note the recording take info from a moment ago. Be sure to note file names and/or timecode, if applicable. It's prudent to add comments after each recording and indicate any problems along with successes. If possible, back up the files from the audio recorder regularly by offloading to another format, such as a computer, and then burning a CD/DVD.

6. Don't forget to record and document room tone. You may also capture impulse files for use with convolution plug-ins. (I'll discuss this process later in this book.) There might also be opportunities to catch wild lines from talent and even sound effects while on the set. When you do capture room tone or wild lines, note these both with verbal slates and in your written notes.

7. When you return to the edit suite, you will use the slate to sync the camera audio and external recorder audio. There will be a loud spike in the audio recording where the clapper hit. The clapper or handclap shows up predominantly in the visual waveform display of both the camera and the recorder audio. If you started and stopped the two devices simultaneously while on the set, they will be very close in time. If not, you might need to hunt down the correct place. The first frame of video

where the clapper isn't blurry (from movement) corresponds with the audio clapper sound. Sync those two points, and the scene will be in sync. Visually align the claps on the audio tracks using the waveform display. You might need to zoom in a little to be accurate. Generally, leave the video/audio in place and slide the second-recorder audio track in relation to the audio associated with the video. When correct, your audio should look like the example in Figure 8.1.

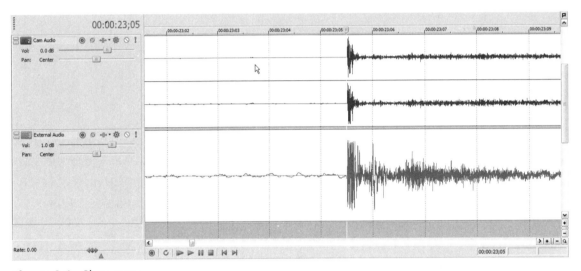

**Figure 8.1** Slate sync.

8. Note that some NLEs force you to edit sound to the project frame rate, 1/30th of a second. A lot of sound can happen in even that short timeframe. This can make it impossible to align double-system sound with camera audio. You might need to switch to a DAW for this, which lets you move sound around freely without being tied to the frame boundaries. Some NLEs, such as Sony Creative Software's Vegas Pro, let you disable this quantizing to frames limitation. If you can turn off this feature, you can slide your external audio sound around to get better sync. This makes working with sound such as this so much easier. There is software called PluralEyes, available from Singular Software (www.singularsoftware.com), that automates the syncing of double-system sound. This can be a real timesaver for you.

9. After you've visually aligned the waveform, listen to the tracks playing together. You'll hear short echoes or repeats if the two tracks are off. As they get closer together, the sound ceases to be two separate images and begins to blend. You might still hear a slight phasey, swirly sound known as *phase sync*—you are there! After lining up the slates, move along the file and watch lips and listen carefully to be sure. A single frame slip is a *lot* of error.

10. Be aware that if the camera was a great distance from the sound source, its audio will be delayed somewhat from what the closer mics picked up and recorded on the

external double-system recorder. Sound travels about 1.1 feet per millisecond, so 50 feet is 50 ms—a time differential that the ear can notice and that will wreak havoc when you try to sync the two tracks. If you slate close to the camera, the recorder slate will be delayed; record close to the recorder mics, and the camera slate will be delayed. The best thing is to temporarily move the mics to the slate near the camera just for the slate and then move them back into position for the actual recording. Otherwise, the situation forces you to use the slates for rough sync and eyeball and ear the correct sync. Time aligning these tracks can be time-consuming, but the increased dialogue quality is usually worth the effort.

## Audio Recorders

While the Zaxcom Deva sees wide use, there are other digital recorders that work well and don't require expensive synchronization. Professional digital recorders will run in sync quite well for extended periods, provided that the recorder's sample rate matches the camera recording. Several units from different manufacturers all function quite well and feature a rich toolset using either solid state memory cards or hard drive storage. A few units offer timecode support for precise camera syncing and/or the Broadcast Wave format (BWF), which helps make aligning things on an NLE/DAW timeline that supports BWF much easier.

Following is a list of some digital recorders you might come across:

- Edirol R1, R4, R44, or R09 (will also LANC sync to some Sony cameras).

- Fostex FR-2.

- Marantz PMD670.

- M-Audio MicroTrack II 24/96.

- Sony PCM-D1.

- Sony HD MD recorders.

- Sound Devices 722 and other 7-Series recorders.

- Tascam HD-P2 (does SMPTE).

- Zaxcom Deva.

- Zoom H4n (very popular with HDLSR users) or H2 (shown in Figure 8.2).

- A laptop with a pro soundcard and suitable recording software can also function as a location field recorder. Though not as rugged as the others mentioned, it's still a viable option for many. With the right soundcard, you could record multiple channels simultaneously, giving you even greater flexibility in post.

**Figure 8.2**  Portable digital recorder.

## Shoot for Sound

Another CYA technique that you should consider is taking extra time to get the audio right without worrying about the video side. For narrative sequences, consider running through the takes normally—camera and audio—and then going back and shooting again without regard to hiding the mic; it can be seen on camera. Good actors will consistently deliver their lines, and you'll get a better recording because you can position the mics closer to their mouths. These separate performances can often substitute for less than stellar recordings made when you are forced to keep the mic farther away. You will have some post sync to do, but the sound quality will be so much better, making it worth the effort. Editing takes like this, along with wild lines, are often easier to do and sound better than many ADR sessions.

Consider capturing the lines wild when there's free time on the set, away from noise and action. I often record on-camera talent (usually amateurs) on location but then bring them to a quieter place to do the lines and/or interview again. This gives me flexibility in post, and I can always place B-roll footage over the top to cover up dialogue edits. You often can grab actors in between camera setups and have them run through their lines on mic. These wild recordings aren't in sync with the camera, but they still serve as another way to get some redundancy and better-quality audio while still on location.

Take a simple VO box on location to get quality audio, too. Again, talent can start/end on camera, but do the rest as voiceover. Instead of a separate studio date, just take a VO box on the set and record using it. There's more on the VO box in Chapter 13, "Voiceover."

Sometimes you might shoot without needing sound, such as a sequence you know will be replaced in post-production by narration, music, or just sound effects. Shooting without sound is called *MOS*. Legend has it that the term MOS comes from the early German movie directors, who would ask for a scene to be shot "Mit out sound," the word "mit" being the German equivalent of the English "with." MOS actually meant *minus optical sound*, but the legend makes for a fun story. I urge you to never truly shoot MOS because you never know what might happen—that is to say, you never know what serendipitous sound moment might find its way onto your track. So if you are not recording sound all the time, you might miss this fortuitous event.

## Quality Control

In addition to headphone monitoring while recording, quality control on location can also be helped by playing back takes and listening for audio issues before wrapping up. With tape-based systems, a little rewind and playback is a good idea. With HDD and solid-state recording systems, playback is even easier. When using an external recorder for capturing sound, playback is fast and easy.

## What Is Wrong with This Scenario?

Picture this: You are making a documentary inside an office and you are currently shooting a talking-head interview with the subject seated. There is a shotgun mic with a windsock on a boom pole pointed at the talent. The output of the mic goes to a mixer, and then the mixer output goes to the camera. The sound recorder/boom operator wears headphones connected to the mixer (see Figure 8.3).

*So, what's the problem?*

Image courtesy of Tony Santona.

**Figure 8.3** What's wrong with this?

First, let's look at the genre. It's a documentary. Therefore, it's acceptable to have the microphone show on camera. If this was a narrative, you wouldn't want the mic appearing. Using a mic on a fishpole boom is probably not the best choice in this case. Also, it is unwise to use a shotgun inside, as room resonances can fool it, resulting in an inferior sound. A hypercardioid would be acceptable, though. A lavaliere clipped to the talent would give a robust "interview" sound and would mean not having to use a boom operator (though a fixed boom could be employed). Many people prefer the sound of the suspended mic over the lav's in-your-face quality, so you may reject this suggestion.

Because the shoot is inside, the use of a windsock where there is typically no wind is also questionable. Take it off when indoors. If the mic would be moving in the shot, then a small foam windscreen is a good idea, even indoors. Windsocks cut down on high frequencies, which can make your recording sound dull and muffled. Outside you have no choice, but inside you do. Remove the windscreen!

The lav should be wired because the subject is seated and not moving. This eliminates worries of wireless interference. If you decide to use the lav but prefer not to see it, consider clipping it farther down than normal and out of the camera's range. It won't sound as strong as if you use the preferred position, though. Better still, mount it under the clothing, using the ideas presented earlier in this book.

Next, there is a mixer. With only one person to record using only one mic, there is no need for this extraneous piece of gear. This adds another layer of complexity and risks having yet another item that could fail or otherwise affect your sound adversely. For this example, it makes far more sense to plug the mic directly into the camera. If you *do* decide a mixer is needed, make sure levels are calibrated between the mixer and the camera, as mentioned earlier.

Notice the sound engineer monitors the output of the mixer, even though the camera is doing the actual sound recording. That's a *big* mistake. There is the opportunity for a mismatch between the mixer and the camera, and by not monitoring at the last stage, you risk not hearing problems on the set while you can still fix them. Audio might sound fine at the mixer, but be totally bad at the camera/recorder. Don't take that chance, and be sure to monitor at the right place in the recording chain. Note that some mixers allow connecting up to the camera in such a way that you can monitor both what the mixer hears and sends and what that sounds like at the camera.

With the tips and techniques from this chapter in mind, you will overcome some of the gremlins that often destroy your best efforts at getting good production sound. In the next few chapters, we'll look at building the audio-post suite in which you'll do most of your work from now on.

# 9 Hearing Sound

There is a tangible problem with talking about audio equipment in this book, especially software. By the time this book hits the streets, some of the information will be outdated. Therefore, I've taken a somewhat generic approach here so you know generally what you need to acquire for serious audio work. There will also be some specific recommendations, which may have been updated after this edition. There are also some standbys and workhorses that have been around for a while and should continue to be available, though the names/companies may change.

You must have a few tools in place before you can begin working your audio post-production magic. Essentially, you need to hear sound, make it, record it, make it *sound* better, and deliver it to the world. You also need a room in which to work. If you already have an NLE and/or DAW in place, you have most of what you need. Building your audio suite around a computer and associated software is the ideal solution today. While many people use external hardware, it is usually dedicated to very specific tasks. Working "inside the box" is the preferred method today, and for budget productions, this is the only way to go.

The next several chapters will cover these topics and more.

## Monitors

Critical video work depends on a color-calibrated video monitor. For critical audio work, you must rely on a high-quality speaker system and a carefully controlled acoustic space. If your work looks and sounds good, you can be reasonably confident that it will translate effectively for your audience.

Proper audio monitoring is a key ingredient to making prudent sound decisions. It amazes me when video editors will invest heavily in TV monitors to make sure their video color is accurate, but they are unwilling to make even a modest investment toward improving the sound playback in that same editing suite. Thankfully, audio costs far less than its video counterparts. A $500 to $1,000 speaker system will serve you well for sound editing, selection, and mixing duties, with the possible exception of a theatrical mix. That said, much theatrical premixing is done in smaller suites and rooms, leaving only the final mix to the large mixing theater.

The goal is to craft a soundtrack that plays back consistently and predictably in a wide variety of listening environments, situations, and end-user equipment options. Unfortunately, I see editors using a built-in computer speaker or some cheap external ones that shipped with their computer to mix their soundtracks. These editors are usually utterly amazed at and disappointed by how bad their project sounds when playing back through a full-range system. All the warts that were obscured or missing show up from their use of the less than adequate speakers placed in the editing suite. A bad sound system doesn't tell the whole story of what's happening with the audio, which a good monitor system reveals. Therefore, you must invest in a quality, accurate, full-range audio monitoring chain if you are serious about making your soundtracks shine. You can't get by with cheap speakers or—gasp!—headphones for this step. If your audio monitoring lies to you, the soundtrack will not translate well to other playback systems.

I prefer bigger speakers primarily because they can reproduce the lower bass frequencies. Small speakers just can't push enough air for my tastes. The addition of a dedicated subwoofer can complement smaller speakers and may be a good choice. However, adding the sub creates other possible problems related to space, placement, and calibration. If set improperly, the sub might fool you into thinking there is more low-end bass in your recording than there really is. When playing back elsewhere, the soundtrack might sound bass-light or otherwise different or worse.

Because your monitor choice needs to reflect what the vast majority of audiences will hear, consider matching your monitors to the final listener. For example, if podcasts are your thing, making the mix sound its best on both average computer speakers and headphones is more important than having it work for an audiophile home theater. Just be sure that this is the right choice. You can never err by making your tracks sound their best in many environments.

Invest in quality speakers designed for critical audio work, such as those used by the music industry. You have two choices. Passive speakers require a separate amplifier for power. Powered speakers (a.k.a. active monitors) come complete with a built-in amplifier. These are an ideal choice because the amp and the speaker have been designed to work together. You will be using these speakers close to computer monitors, so select models that are magnetically shielded so they don't interfere with your screens. If you plan to do surround, you need five matching, full-range monitors (same model, same brand) along with a brand-matched subwoofer. Choose a direct radiator design (sound comes only from the front) and not a dipole one (sound exits both the front and rear of the speaker). Manufacturers such as Genelec, Mackie, Event, KRK, M-Audio, Adam, and Tannoy all make great choices at varying price points. For example, I use the passive Event 20/20s with a Hafler amp for stereo work and an M-Audio 5.1 active system for many surround sound projects, as shown in Figure 9.1.

Having a worst-case speaker available for checking your mix is important, too. I wrote that sentence while sitting in a hotel room with my MP3 player hooked up to a mono

**Figure 9.1**  Various speakers in use.

clock radio. Despite this horrible audio system, I could still understand the vocals and hear the primary elements of the music (though many subtleties were lost). Do your mixes work equally well on the junk as they do on the good stuff?

Many consumers and even many venues lack decent audio systems. Despite a surge in home theaters, the majority of our carefully crafted soundtracks still emanate from crummy little speakers. Your primary high-quality system might not provide the real-world feedback you need to subjectively evaluate your mix. For example, how will the mix sound on a clock radio, a mono TV set, an MP3 player docking station, or a set of typical computer speakers? Don't guess. Be sure to check your work on suitable speakers in addition to the quality full-range system.

## Real-World Reference

Avant Electronics (www.avantelectronics.com) has a terrific solution with their Mix-Cubes Mini Reference Monitors. If you've been in the audio industry for a few years, these cubes look vaguely familiar. Avant engineers set out to update and replace the ubiquitous Auratone 5C, and they've done a terrific job. For many years, the original 5Cs, affectionately nicknamed "Horror-Tones," were the go-to worst-case reference monitor for audio engineers. If you wanted to know how your mix would sound on nasty, cheap consumer gear, you listened through them. If your mix worked on a 5C, you knew you were on the right track.

Unfortunately, "Horror-Tones" have been unavailable for several years, so Avant's MixCubes are a welcome replacement. MixCubes use a single, full-range, 5-1/4-inch driver housed in a glossy, butter-cream 6-1/2-inch cube. They are shielded for use next to TVs and computer screens. Each speaker has a standard recessed microphone thread for mounting on a mic stand, or the base is non-slip, acoustic-isolating neoprene for placing on a surface. Binding posts for amplification connection accept bare wire or banana plugs. Avant recommends powering MixCubes with a good-quality amp rated between 50 and 200 watts using high-quality 12- to 16-gauge wire.

When you first pump your soundtrack through these puppies, you will be disappointed immediately. There will be no deep bass or clear highs, just the midrange. So what's the point, you might ask? These monitors are not meant to sound good. They are meant to reflect the real world of less-than-stellar audio components—an important consideration when making critical soundtrack adjustments. Despite being both bass and high-frequency limited, the MixCubes have a smooth, linear frequency response with no bumps in the critical ranges.

I've been listening to a variety of projects on my MixCubes over the past few months. It took me some time to overcome their shortcomings, as I'm rather accustomed to my regular monitors. Once I realized how much information they revealed, I grew to respect and trust their playback. It's like having a second opinion in the control room when mixing. I'm constantly asking myself: "Sure, it sounds good on the *big* monitors, but what do the MixCubes think?"

Running the MixCubes, indeed any monitors, at low volume also often exposes problems that need addressing. Low volume and limited frequency response means you must work extra hard to get important information, such as voice, to cut through. And because almost all mixes are built around the voice, testing playback in this way is invaluable.

I also performed some mixes using only the MixCubes, and then listened to how well they translated to my main monitors. I was pleasantly surprised. The tweaks employed to make the mix work on the MixCubes made the full-blown experience even better.

The MixCubes were also helpful for checking mono mixes, such as those destined for TV. Cheap TV speakers are notoriously lo-fi, loaded with muddy midrange. It's ideal to test how your mix works in that scenario and see whether a voiceover would cut through a radio spot's busy music mix. When posting indie film, these speakers are invaluable at every turn, including the final mix. And they are beneficial for ensuring some music mixes will hold up, too. If your audio work requires really good speakers to sound good, then you are fooling yourself. Use the MixCubes for the confidence that everybody will hear what's important.

Again, keep in mind that using something like the MixCubes won't sound perfect; their purpose is to provide a worst-case reference to make sure your soundtracks will work in every situation. They won't be your only or main monitors; they are an alternative presentation.

Figure 9.2 shows an example of MixCubes.

**Figure 9.2**   MixCubes.

## Speaker Location

Placing speakers requires having a dedicated listening position. Typically, you will sit at your computer monitor, so make that the primary position. The high-frequency drivers, known as *tweeters*, should be at ear level with nothing in the way between the speakers and your ears. Be sure to isolate speakers from the surface upon which they sit.

I recommend using the Auralex MoPADs (see Figure 9.3). These high-density foam pads help keep the natural resonances of the speakers from traveling through surfaces. Consider using speaker stands instead of setting speakers on your desk or other surface. Stands are designed to minimize resonances and allow height adjustments. Place monitors in the free field away from walls, in the center of the room's shortest wall. Do not place speakers against the wall or in corners, or you risk changing their bass response. Generally, placing speakers from three to five feet away from boundaries is the best. If you use a subwoofer, it can rest on the floor between the stereo speakers.

Stereo speakers should be placed so that they form an equilateral triangle with the back of your head at the listening position forming the third point. They should be the same distance apart as they are from your listening position, angled about 30 degrees in.

Surround sound setup uses the International Telecommunications Union (ITU) Rec. 775 standard specification. With the mixing position in the center of a circle, place the five matching speakers the same distance away from it, preferably about six to eight feet. The center speaker faces you, while the front left and right are the same as the stereo placement mentioned a moment ago. Place the left and right surround speakers between 110 degrees and 135 degrees from the center, also angled

**Figure 9.3**  MoPADs.

30 degrees in. Keep the surrounds at the same height as the front three. It is acceptable (though not preferred) to have the center slightly higher than the other speakers (usually because your computer screen is in the way). Locate the subwoofer slightly to the side of the center, not directly under it. Some experimentation may be necessary for this component to sound right. See Figure 9.4 for an example of stereo and surround setup.

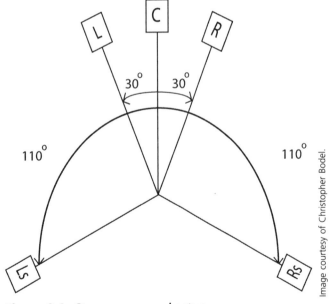

**Figure 9.4**  Stereo surround setup.

Don't forget to make sure your speakers are connected correctly. With passive speakers, make sure red from the amp connects to red on the speaker, likewise with the black lead. If you reverse these, the speakers will be out of phase, causing all kinds of problems. Active monitors will get the feed from the audio interface, usually 1/4-inch mono cable. On the topic of wire, keep the cables as short as possible and use *equal lengths* to all speakers (even if one is closer to the amp or computer output). Invest in high-quality cabling from Mogami or Monster Cable. The heavier and thicker the wire is, the better the cable!

## Speaker Calibration

You also need to calibrate your speakers by setting a reference sound pressure level. While we use sine-wave tones for calibrating electronic equipment, acoustics uses pink noise, which sounds like hiss or a distant waterfall. The standard for speaker calibration is to use –20 dBFS RMS pink noise, such as that available from test CDs or from Bob Katz's website (www.digido.com; click the Downloads link), or to make your own. (Sony Sound Forge generates pink noise, for instance.) There is some merit to band-limiting the pink noise by using a high-pass/low-pass EQ to roll off frequencies below 500 Hz and above 2 kHz for the primary speakers and, if calibrating a surround system, to band-limit the LFE to 20 Hz to 120 Hz. Limiting the frequency response of the pink noise can give you a more accurate reference. You also need a sound pressure level meter, such as the one manufactured by Radio Shack (see Figure 9.5).

**Figure 9.5** SPL meter.

Proper calibration requires independent level control over each speaker. This level control can come from an audio interface, amplifier, or the speaker itself. It's best to make the adjustment at one point, leaving all other settings at a nominal or unity gain setting.

Add the pink noise to your audio software timeline and set the track, bus, and master faders to 0 or unity gain. Check your software's output meters to confirm that the pink noise is playing at –20 dBFS or 0 VU. Peak meters will read substantially higher, as shown in Figure 9.6. A useful tool from Voxengo is the freeware VST plug-in called SPAN (www.voxengo.com), which provides several audio monitoring and analysis tools (see Figure 9.7). Note that pink noise will hover around the –20 dBFS/0 VU mark and will not stay pegged to it exactly.

**Figure 9.6** Peak meter.

Not all meters are created equal, though. Many do not subscribe to the Audio Engineering Society's (AES) AES-17 standard. In short, the standard says that a sine wave test tone with a –20 dBFS peak level should read the same as its RMS level. This calibration standard has been in place for more than 60 years as a means for matching RMS and peak levels in decibels. Unfortunately, some meters may read 3 dB lower (dBFS/RMS) if they don't follow this practice. If you know the pink noise is –20 dBFS RMS, but your meters say otherwise, trust the source, not the non-AES-17 metering.

Turn off all but one of the speakers. Play the file, and you should hear the noise coming from the speaker. With the SPL meter positioned at the listening position, increase the speaker's volume, depending on your setup, until the pink noise reads 83 dB on the SPL

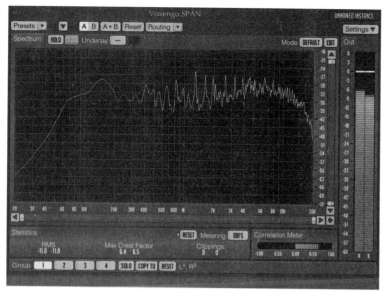

**Figure 9.7** SPAN.

meter using the C-weighted, slow response setting. Repeat this step for each speaker. Note that TV generally uses a standard of 77 to 79 dB, which better reflects the typical TV listening environment; film and music use the 83-dB setting (which translates to 86 dB in stereo using two speakers).

If you are calibrating for surround sound, calibrate the LFE to read 4 dB higher than the other speakers—87 dB—which by the nature of its limited bandwidth effectively makes the LFE 10 dB louder than the satellites.

After you have made these adjustments, note the settings, and then *leave them alone*. Do *not* adjust the levels of your speakers or audio interface; instead, work with your audio staying at the same monitor level. Regularly check the calibration and adjust as needed.

You have just set up a correlation between what your meters show and what your ears hear: −20 dBFS RMS = 0 VU = 86 dB SPL (stereo). Working this way is quite liberating. When you want something to be loud, it will sound loud. You won't struggle to make your dialogue fit either, because it will sound right at comfortable listening levels. Music has long associated *forte* with about 85 dB, and Hollywood has mixed movies since the 1970s using this consistent monitor level, too.

Also, don't forget the Fletcher-Munson Equal Loudness discussion from earlier in this book. A byproduct of this approach is that you won't need to watch meters much. Sure, you'll have to keep an eye on loud peaks, but the average or RMS level will be obvious to your ears. You won't be forced to turn up the volume to make it loud or resort to over- or hyper-compression (a common ailment in the music industry).

Mastering guru Bob Katz details this approach in a pair of articles on his website. I highly recommend you read them at www.digido.com and/or grab a copy of his invaluable book, *Mastering Audio, Second Edition: The Art and the Science* (Focal Press, 2007).

# Ruminations

Another aspect of proper audio monitoring is the room itself. Whether you work from home or an office, edit suites are one-room affairs. That's perfectly acceptable for most audio-post chores. However, you might want a dedicated recording space for doing Foley and/or perhaps an isolation booth for voiceover and ADR sessions. Of course, if you have open mics in the same room as your speakers, you will need to mute the speakers and monitor on headphones. In the home, a spare bedroom, a basement, an attic, or even a garage can function well, though even a corner of a family or living room could suffice in a pinch. A larger space is usually a better choice than a smaller one, especially when room dimensions are similar. For example, a $10 \times 10 \times 8$ bedroom will suffer some unusual acoustic anomalies that will be costly to overcome.

There are two aspects of sound that require treatment. First, soundproofing your audio suite may be necessary. You don't want the noise from the outside world getting into your recordings, and you don't want your soundtracks annoying the neighbors. Unfortunately, soundproofing requires a major investment. The typical wall and ceiling in a home or office is not sufficient for serious work; doors and windows are even worse at stopping sound. Most noise and audio will penetrate these boundaries with only a little attenuation (lowering of volume level). And tacking a few acoustic tiles on the wall will do little to soundproof a space, though they are useful for sound control (discussed in minute). Because sound travels through air, boundaries, and structures, there are three concepts to know about soundproofing: *mass*, *decoupling*, and *airtightness*. Thick, heavy walls reduce sound energy. Walls and floors decoupled from their surroundings reduce structure-borne sound; essentially that calls for a room within a room. Airtight windows and doors reduce airborne sound.

Second, you need to control the sound within the room itself to make it neutral-sounding and somewhat more "dead" with reduced reverberation time (the time it takes for sound to decay by 60 dB in a space, called $RT_{60}$). You need to hear what's coming from the speakers and not have the room itself interfere with the sound. Small, boxy rooms will accentuate certain frequencies and possibly reduce others, resulting in a skewed sound. You might compensate for these problems you hear in the mix, which are really related to the room itself and not the audio. Played elsewhere, these fixes may sound incorrect.

Overall, work to lessen reverb time (called *deadening*) in the room and reduce early reflections—the first surfaces sound strikes after leaving the speaker. Sound travels from the speakers to your ears, but it also bounces off of nearby surfaces, arriving at your ears time-delayed to the original. This delayed sound can smear the direct sound adversely. The out-of-phase sound may be constructive or destructive, but in either case, the room is affecting what you hear. Therefore, when you listen in a different space, your soundtrack might not sound the same. Sound is somewhat slow, moving only about 1.1 feet per millisecond, so eliminating reflecting surfaces within five to ten feet of the monitors creates an initial sound gap. This initial gap is sufficient to let you hear the audio from the speakers before the room takes over and imparts its own attributes to your soundtrack.

To craft this reflection-free zone, use a hand mirror and a helper. Sit at the mixing position and have the helper move around the nearby surfaces of the room with the mirror. When the mirror reveals the front of the speaker, that point is a first reflection point. Just as the mirror reflects light bouncing off the speaker, the surface reflects sound coming from the speaker as well. To combat this, place sound-absorbing and/or diffusing material at the locations revealed by the mirror. It's important to use broadband sound absorbers, typically acoustic tiles of varying thickness that absorb a wider range of frequencies. High frequencies are the easiest to control, but it's no good just eliminating them, because the pesky low-frequency waves will continue to cause problems. Diffusing material disperses sound waves more evenly.

Sometimes reorienting furniture or other surfaces so sound reflects away from your ear will suffice. All you need to remember is that the angle of incidence equals the angle of reflectance (for example, if sound strikes a surface from a 45-degree angle, it will bounce off the surface at the same angle). Therefore, you can either deflect those first reflections away from the listening position or absorb them with acoustic material. Or use a little of both remedies.

Also, place broadband absorption behind and to the sides of speakers. If your room is small, consider corner bass traps to deal with the troublesome low frequencies that build up in small rooms. Diffusers located along the sides (behind the listening position) and at the back of the room help disperse sound more evenly. Furniture such as bookshelves, couches, and other items with solid and uneven surfaces help, too.

If you build a room, splaying the walls and ceiling to reflect sound away from the front listening position is a great idea. Eliminating parallel walls is another good tactic, but not an easy option in finished spaces. If you can't change the walls, break them up with a combination of absorbing and diffusing materials. There are some ready-to-hang solutions provided by several acoustic specialists. (See the sidebar "More on Acoustics" for details.)

Setting up your space for comfort, both physical and aesthetic, is another consideration. Choose furniture that supports your equipment and your body. Invest in a quality desk to accommodate your primary workstation, and don't skimp on your chair. Your butt will be parked in it for many hours. Either take a modular approach, buying furniture as needed, or choose from several all-in-one solutions provided by manufacturers such as Omnirax Studio Furniture (www.omnirax.com) and Raxxess (www.raxxess.com).

Figure 9.8 shows a sample studio floor plan. Though the diagram appears symmetrical, the space is actually open on two sides, and the walls shown are actually splayed

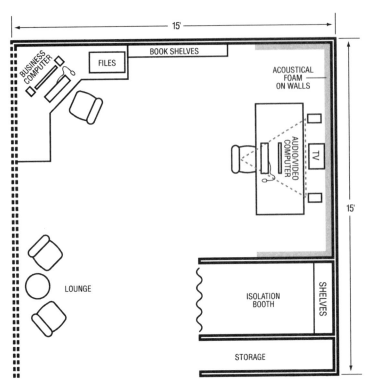

**Figure 9.8** Studio floor plan.

slightly. There is also substantial sound absorbing and diffusing material used strategically to create an acoustically neutral listening space. Figure 9.9 shows the same room as a picture, with some dude blocking part of the view.

**Figure 9.9** The author in his office.

Don't ignore the overall environment, either. You want a comfortable space in which to work. You want light and temperature control. Add personal touches to the space and make sure it reflects your personality and image. Choose a wall paint color that is conducive to working. Be aware that if you are a video editor who does color correction, you might need to go with a neutral color to avoid color casting. Select lighting for task, general, and mood. Finally, your gear may constitute a substantial investment, so insurance and security are must-haves.

---

**More on Acoustics:** Because a full explanation of audio room acoustics is far beyond this book's scope, I urge you to visit Acoustics 101 (www.acoustics101.com) for more information. For soundproofing advice, be sure to check out Jeff Cooper's seminal book, *Building a Recording Studio* (Synergy Group, 1984). The richly detailed *Recording Studio Design, Second Edition* (Focal Press, 2007) by Philip Newell is invaluable. For more on building a solid audio project studio, refer to my other book: *Profiting from Your Music and Sound Project Studio* (Allworth Press, 2001). Also, several companies make solutions for dealing with small-room acoustics. Here are the best:

- Acoustic Sciences Corporation (www.tubetrap.com)

- Acoustics First (www.acousticsfirst.com)

- Auralex Acoustics (www.auralex.com)

- RPG Diffusor Systems (www.rpginc.com)

---

## Audio Interface/Soundcard

The built-in soundcard in your computer simply won't cut it for serious audio work. The built-in models are noisy and low-quality, and they don't have the requisite inputs and outputs for doing serious work. Take a better approach and choose either a USB- or FireWire-based external audio interface. USB is acceptable if you only need stereo in and out. To record multiple tracks at once or to mix surround sound, only a FireWire interface can handle the increased I/O. With level and volume knobs conveniently placed, a well-selected audio interface becomes the central component of your recording and monitoring. Audio interfaces typically have software that makes routing audio to different software inputs and hardware outputs a snap, so you don't need to crawl around plugging and unplugging cables.

Another bonus of using an audio interface is that many come equipped with microphone preamps, phantom power, and even musical instrument inputs to make recording easier. This eliminates your need for a bulky mixer that will probably go unused most of the time. If you will record VOs, ADR, sound effects, and/or Foley, a mic preamp–equipped soundcard is the most prudent investment. A stand-alone preamp may also be handy for certain situations, such as using a tube-based preamp to warm up voice tracks.

Note that some audio software choices, namely Pro Tools, prefer that you use their own hardware. The software won't work with all off-the-shelf hardware resources. Most other software packages let you choose the specific hardware interfaces you want to employ. I prefer the latter method because it allows me to work with different manufacturers. If you decide to use Pro Tools, then you must choose from the approved hardware.

USB choices include several models from Edirol, Mackie, M-Audio, and PreSonus, to name a few. These choices typically include stereo in and out, microphone inputs with phantom power for condenser mics, headphone connections, and more. There are other brands and models, but I'm most familiar with these, and they are solid choices. Always check to make sure you have the latest drivers when you're using USB-based devices.

FireWire choices include models from Apogee, Focusrite, M-Audio, PreSonus, RME, and others. Currently, I use the Focusrite Saffire (see Figures 9.10 and 9.11). FireWire models usually have mic inputs with phantom power, additional line ins, digital I/O, and up to 10 analog outputs, which means you can have both a stereo and a surround system connected at all times. Some models allow recording up to eight mics at once, which is useful for music sessions but is probably overkill if all you do is voice and some sound effects/Foley. Routing software lets you control where everything goes, both input and output. The Saffire has two headphone outs, and both mute and dim switches, which turn off the output and lower the volume by 20 dB, respectively—perfect for phone interruptions or for checking mixes at a lower volume without affecting speaker volume calibration.

**Figure 9.10** Saffire hardware.

Another useful component when monitoring is checking for monaural compatibility. Although you might feel your soundtrack will never play back in mono, you are in for a

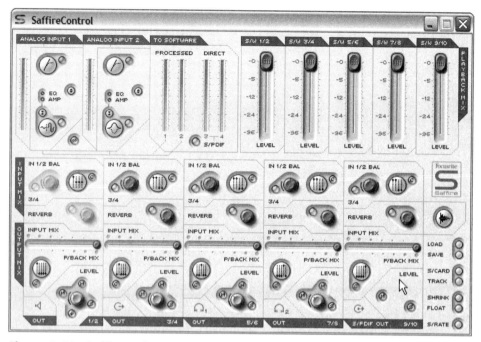

**Figure 9.11**  Saffire software.

shock. Mono is alive and kicking for a variety of reasons. There are plenty of cheap TVs still out there, people incorrectly wire their stereo speakers and inadvertently create mono, and there are other such problems. Frankly, if you sit outside the stereo sweet spot or are farther away from the speakers, the sound tilts more toward mono even when it starts as stereo.

Some stereo effects do not translate well to mono; some sounds completely disappear when stereo gets summed, or downmixed, to mono. For example, if a background sound is placed in stereo and one side is 180 degrees out of phase with the other, you will hear a very wide stereo image, one that almost appears to be outside the speakers. Unfortunately, when you downmix to mono, the two sounds, being exact opposites of one another, will add up to nothing. Zilch. The mono listener will hear absolutely no background sound in this example. If you only monitor in stereo, you would never know this. What if this was dialogue? Ouch. This exact scenario happened to me.

Some audio interfaces have a mono switch, as do some amplifiers; however, most people use a mono switch in their audio software (see Figure 9.12), such as the mono downmix button in Sony Creative Software's Vegas Pro. This way, you can easily make sure that what you are doing will translate to a monaural listener.

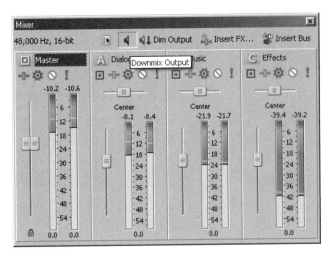

**Figure 9.12**  Mono downmix button.

**RSI:** Repetitive stress injuries (RSIs) are those medical conditions affecting your hands, wrists, arms, neck, shoulders, and back. By overusing and overextending certain muscles, tendons, and nerves, you can suffer from chronic pain or other debilitating symptoms.

Because RSI is caused by many repeated small movements, give your affected body parts something different to do. Put them through larger ranges of motion. Do stretches and other exercises that move them counter to the routine of keyboarding and mousing. Consider regular, vigorous exercise as part of your plan, too, such as taking a power walk at lunch. Keep the room warm. A chilled body is more susceptible to injuries than a warm one. Especially make sure that your fingers, hands, wrists, arms, and shoulders are warm. The human body is primarily water, so be sure to keep yourself hydrated; several glasses of water a day is best. Most importantly, get plenty of extended rest so your body can properly rejuvenate and recover from overuse.

Make sure your computer workstation is set up properly. Position the monitor directly in front of you with the top of the screen at eye level. Position the work surface at the proper height so that your wrists and arms are parallel to the floor. Leave ample room for your knees and legs. Get a good, comfortable chair that easily adjusts to your body. It should have lumbar support and arm rests. Sit up straight in your chair, with your feet flat on the ground. You should feel comfortable at your workstation, not awkward, and you shouldn't strain to reach the keys or mouse. Every half hour, take a break, get up, move around, and work those neck, shoulder, and back muscles, too.

While armrests and wrist rests are fine for relaxing, you shouldn't use them while keyboarding or mousing. Wrist supports, in particular, often create a condition where your wrists are bent back when they should be in line with your arms. Lift your hands up above the keyboard/mouse when you are working. Lightly touch the keys while typing and hold the mouse gently. If you're not typing or mousing, move your arms and hands to different positions instead of leaving them in place.

Try to reduce overall mouse use by learning keyboard shortcuts. Also, cut back on your computer time altogether by finding alternatives, such as using the phone instead of typing emails. I also use the Contour ShuttlePRO v.2 to control some software, which gives my left hand more to do than simply typing. As with a mouse, position the ShuttlePRO comfortably and use it gently without bending your wrist or reaching awkwardly.

Recently, I've started using the Contour Design RollerMouse Free (ergo. contourdesign.com) as a mouse-replacement device. There are two major drawbacks to the traditional mouse. One, you have to reach for it using one side of your body. This asymmetrical repetition can cause muscle tightness and even pain. Two, you have to grip the mouse to move it, and that can lead to various RSIs. With the RollerMouse Free, you don't reach or grip. You use both of your hands equally. Its ergonomic design is comfortable and easy, and it really works.

Figure 9.13 shows my desk setup.

**Figure 9.13**  Desk setup.

In the next chapter, we'll discuss ways to create and record sound in the audio-post suite. Software choices will form the framework around which you will build your studio, so making the right decision in this area is critical to your workflow.

# 10 Making and Recording Sound

You will need to acquire ways to create sound in the audio suite. For example, you may need talent, such as voice actors for narration. You may need props, surfaces, and other materials for Foley. You might bring in specific items for sound effects gathering. Typically, you will use sound effects and music libraries to cover other aspects of your audio needs. However, depending on your skill set, you might also do some or all of this work yourself. If you are musically adept, you may employ synthesizers, samplers, guitars, basses, other string and wind instruments, percussion instruments, and so forth. Synths and samplers may be hardware or computer-based virtual instruments. Both are useful for non-musicians, as sample and musical loop libraries add other colors and textures to your palette, too. You'll find additional information about these subjects in future chapters.

If you want to create sounds outside the computer, then you will need microphones to record acoustic events. Refer to Chapter 6 for more details.

There is no need to get into a discussion about which computer platform is the best. I have a simple theory: Find the computer *software* you want to use, and then buy the platform on which it runs best.

## Computer Hardware Choices

As for computer hardware, buy the biggest and fastest computer you can afford. You want the quickest processor and as many of them as you can afford, the most RAM, the biggest hard drives, and the latest everything that fits your budget. Don't forget to include a CD/DVD burner or two. Make sure you have at least two hard drives—one for the operating system and programs and the other for media. I prefer a mirrored RAID. I also suggest using external hard drives for storing projects, media, and your music and sound effects libraries (see Figure 10.1). They are portable and affordable, and they work well. You can move them from computer to computer and even share them with other people. For example, the director/editor of the indie feature *The Craving Heart* sent me a clone of his hard drive so I could do the sound editing chores for it. We've continued this workflow on subsequent projects.

If your software takes advantage of it, invest in the right graphics card, too. I prefer dual monitors because screen real estate can be at quite a premium on busy projects, so

**Figure 10.1** External hard drives.

buying a video card that supports multiple monitors is a good choice. Once you go dual monitor, you never go back.

## Software Choices

The primary tool you need is multitrack software because it lets you build soundtracks from many diverse elements—several tracks of dialogue, dozens of sound effects and backgrounds, and a few tracks dedicated to music. Having control over the individual elements and groups of similar tracks is the ideal situation. Multitrack software offers power and versatility to record, edit, sweeten, mix, and deliver a final mix. Packaged in an NLE or DAW, your work is nondestructive and therefore doesn't affect the underlying sound files in any way. The software lets you manipulate sound and then plays the results in real time. A dedicated mono, two-track, or stereo recorder/editor is also useful for some sound tasks, such as restoration and noise reduction.

Generally, a DAW is the better choice for complex audio work. The tools are more robust and flexible than the rudimentary tools built into the typical NLE.

Today, most software is optimized for either a Mac or a PC, with a few crossovers still around. New Macs have the advantage of running either Mac or PC software (using emulation software, such as Boot Camp). There are some audio choices in the Linux world as well. Here is a partial list of available audio and video Mac/PC software tools. The asterisks denote NLEs; the rest are DAWs.

- Ableton Live
- Sony Creative Software ACID Pro
- Audacity

- Adobe Audition
- Avid *
- Bias Peak and Deck
- Apple Final Cut Pro Studio *
- Apple GarageBand
- Apple Logic Pro
- Steinberg Nuendo
- Propellerhead Record
- Adobe Premiere Pro *
- Digidesign Pro Tools
- Cockos REAPER
- MAGIX Samplitude
- Cakewalk SONAR
- Adobe Soundbooth
- Sony Creative Software Sound Forge
- Apple Soundtrack Pro
- Mackie Tracktion
- Sony Creative Software Vegas Pro *

Another element that might enter into your decision is compatibility—both with the outside world and with other applications with which you work. Many pro recording studios (and quite a few audio studios and mixing stages) use the ubiquitous Pro Tools. If you will find yourself heavily using outside facilities, it might make sense to join that world. If not, it's acceptable to look at other alternatives. Because digital audio itself is quite portable, moving simple projects from one software platform to another is relatively painless. Industry standards such as Open Media Framework (OMF) and Advanced Authoring Format (AAF) make it easier to share complete project files across multiple software products, retaining edit, volume, and other basic information. There are third-party translation tools, such as AATranslator (www.aatranslator.com.au), which translates project files from one software product into a format another can read. That said, really complicated projects benefit from some built-in compatibility.

For example, notice how Adobe Premiere Pro and Audition, Apple Final Cut Pro and Soundtrack Pro, and Avid and Pro Tools all fit together and complement one another. If you video edit on one of those platforms, it might make sense to use its audio software counterpart, too. Chances are both products take a similar design approach, which means you wouldn't have to learn a whole new interface.

For me, Sony Creative Software's Vegas Pro offers a tremendous advantage because it is a capable NLE and a powerful DAW fully integrated, so you don't have to visit another application. I do use Sony Creative Software's other tools—Sound Forge, Cinescore, and ACID—too, because they complement my Vegas workflow. Figure 10.2 shows a shot of the Sony Creative Software family of applications.

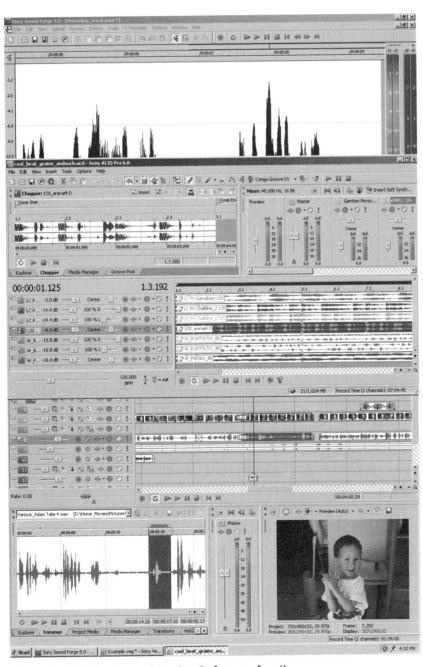

**Figure 10.2**  The Sony Creative Software family.

GarageBand (included with Apple's iLife suite) and Audacity (freeware) are powerful alternatives perfect for the budget conscious. They offer a solid introduction to the world of software-based sound manipulation. You might outgrow them quickly, though, and long for more powerful features. Similarly, both Sony Creative Software ACID and Vegas come in light versions that make moving up to the pro versions quick and easy. The cross-platform and increasingly robust REAPER is also worth exploring.

What should you look for in your audio software? The ability to bring video into the audio timeline is critical, especially when you are working with dialogue, syncing sound effects, and choosing music. The visual reference makes it all easier (unless, of course, your work is audio-only, such as a podcast). You want multitrack support, too, because soundtracks can get rather complicated quickly. For example, while Sony Creative Software Sound Forge has a useful audio toolset, it does not support multitrack work, only mono, stereo, or multichannel files. I use it for cleanup and mastering, but its lack of multitrack facilities makes it the wrong choice for building complete soundtracks. Surround-sound support in your DAW is another must-have if you plan to mix your work in the multichannel format.

No matter which software you choose, they all share common controls. There will be separate tracks for audio and MIDI if applicable. There will be sliders for controlling the relative volume of tracks, buses, audio effects, and masters. Pan pots allow you to place sounds in the stereo field, and a surround-sound pan control allows you to position sounds among the six speakers. You can place audio effects on tracks or buses, as insert sends, and on the master. Meters show levels, though usually these are digital peak reading meters and are only marginally useful for audio-post work.

You want third-party plug-in support for audio effects (and perhaps software-based virtual musical instruments). There are myriad tools available in Audio Units and VST formats (see the next chapter) that can help you clean up and otherwise augment your sound work. Pro Tools uses RTAS and TDM formats. Many effects run natively by using your computer's power. You can also add accelerator cards, such as the Universal Audio UAD, for increased performance. You might not want to be tied to a proprietary effects format and relegated to using only built-in processes. If the software allows you to use audio effects in real time (as opposed to having to render them), that's a timesaver and a far better way to work.

Having a flexible mixer with busing and auxiliary (or send) effects makes grouping (or premixing) similar tracks easier. Every NLE/DAW has volume and pan controls, but a dedicated software mixer interface adds complex routing for handling more sophisticated projects. Track/channel and bus mute and solo buttons are handy when working, too. If effects can be added on the track/channel, bus, auxiliary, and master buses, that's all the better. With more flexibility comes the power to realize your vision for your soundtrack.

Busses, much like their public transportation counterpart, help you route audio to specific destinations. Use busses to group similar sounds and for applying audio effects (see Figure 10.3). Busses allow sharing a single effect with many sounds, which can help the performance of your computer on complex projects. For example, one instance of reverb could be shared by anything from dialogue to thunder. That's efficient and brings a sense of sound continuity to the project.

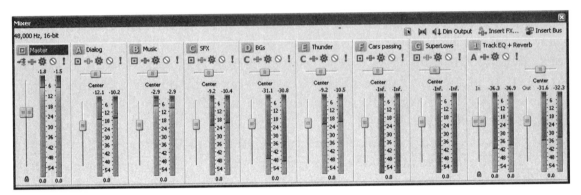

**Figure 10.3** Bussing.

Finally, it helps if your software choice works outside of the constraints of the frame time base. Most NLEs force you to edit audio to the nearest frame, which can be from 1/25 to 1/30 of a second. That's an eternity in the audio world, as a lot of sound can fall between the frames. DAWs don't limit you that way, which is why most NLEs have a separate audio application. The exception is—you guessed it—Sony Creative Software's Vegas Pro; it lets you turn off frame quantization and work on audio like a DAW, not tying you to frame boundaries.

Beyond these key choices, the decision rests with you regarding which features are most important to your workflow. Most software manufacturers offer demos that let you try before you buy. Take advantage of these evaluations and find the right software for your brain. It should match the way you think and work, and if you can't seem to figure it out quickly, it is probably not the best choice for you. Software should mirror your own working methods and not force you into a metaphor and workflow around which you can't wrap your head. Although seeking the advice of others can help, as can reviews, remember that opinions are like noses—everybody has one. In the end, the best decision is the choice that works for you and your specific situation.

Don't take your primary software choice lightly, and don't be tempted to follow the lemmings that tend to support only one software and/or platform brand. There is a reason why there are so many products on the list earlier in this chapter. Each software tool has advantages and disadvantages, and you need to weigh them in relation to the projects you do and the way you prefer to work. I have used almost every product on that list and have subsequently made the best choices for my workflow.

# NLE to DAW

Video editing systems (NLEs), such as Adobe Premiere or Apple Final Cut Pro, are unsuitable for serious sound work. For the most flexibility, you need to get your sound out of a video-editing program and import it into a separate, far more audio capable DAW.

It's no good to simply export the audio with a rendered video file, because you need the extra audio, called *handles*, that exists around the audio/video edits. Therefore, you need another method for getting the sound exported in a format you can use.

Why handles? Think of a single film/video shot. The picture editor would cut right to the start of a dialogue line, such as, "Hey, where are you going?" During production, though, there is more audio before and after that single line. This extra audio gets eliminated to tell the story better, obviously. However, these extra bits—the handles —are useful for dialogue smoothing. A video-editing program does not delete this additional sound; it's still there, but it's trimmed so as not to be heard. You want access to it for the sound work.

Most NLEs support exporting an OMF file. This format exports the audio (no video) and the specific way the audio is arranged on the timeline. It also supports exporting the handles that you need. OMF can include some other elements, such as volume (though generally sound editors ignore most of this and rebuild these settings from scratch). You also want a separate, rendered video file with the current audio in place to use as a guide track and sync reference, too.

Whether you are doing the video work yourself or getting it from someone else, request an OMF with three to five seconds of handles and a rendered video file (with audio) in a video format your DAW can import. Because the OMF includes all the audio in one file, there is a 4-gigabyte limit to the format. Unless your picture department has gone crazy with sound, this shouldn't be a problem.

Depending on the DAW software you use, you may need another program to translate this OMF. Pro Tools users can purchase the DigiTranslator (www.avid.com/US/products/DigiTranslator) to have OMF import capability. It's not an inexpensive purchase, though. Thankfully, there is an alternative for users of Pro Tools and many other DAWs; it's called AATranslator (www.aatranslator.com.au). This software works amazingly well at taking OMFs and converting them to other DAW formats.

Once you bring in the OMF (or its converted equivalent), import the video and its associated audio next. Now you will have a timeline that looks and functions exactly like the video-editing one, with all the audio edits, complete with their handles, in place. The handles are hidden, just like in the NLE, but you can access them in the DAW as needed for J/L cuts and crossfades. Also, you have the video to use for sync and a guide audio track, too. You can then start working on the dialogue and adding the other soundtrack elements, as detailed in the pages of this book.

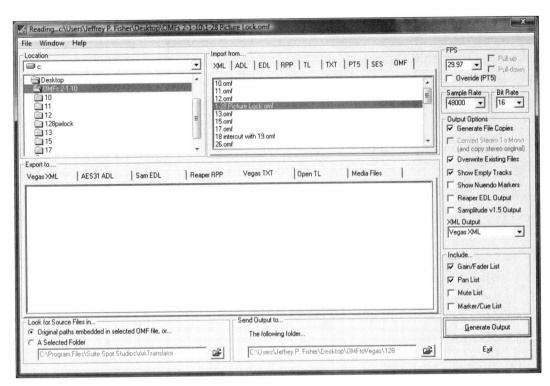

**Figure 10.4** AATranslator.

I suggest you make a copy of every track you import, move these copies to the bottom of your DAW timeline, and mute them. This way, you have a backup of the original import available if needed.

When you finish your work in the DAW, you can render a stereo file of the completed, mixed soundtrack that you or the picture editor can then import back into the video-editing program for the final video delivery.

## Gearing Up

For many of us, nothing starts our hearts racing faster than the latest, greatest audio gizmo. Although some of us can fight off the temptation to buy new gadgets, the rest of us succumb to the allure of what's new. Our emotions take over and convince us that our work will be better when we buy such and such. Thankfully, logic steps in occasionally, or we'd all be swimming in gear.

Virtually everyone has bought equipment that they really didn't need or that didn't work the way they expected. It's okay—we all make mistakes. You were probably caught up in the moment and didn't fully evaluate your needs or follow some basic purchasing guidelines. You just said, "Charge it!" And now your dirty little secret gathers dust in a back closet.

But from now on, you can follow this five-step process and save yourself the heartache of making bad equipment-purchasing decisions.

## Strategy

Develop a game plan that lets you objectively evaluate your needs and wants, industry trends, client demands, and profitability. Before shopping, take a few minutes to examine your situation. What is it you want to do? What equipment will help you accomplish those goals? You don't need everything in place before you get started, either. Experienced world travelers always say this: Pack light. That applies here, too. Why burden yourself or your bank account with excessive stuff you don't/won't need? Instead, pare your needs down to the bone. Quit fretting about stuff you don't have and start focusing on what you can do with the gear you already own (or with a few carefully chosen additional items).

Ask yourself these questions:

- What do you do? (Or what do you *want* to do?)

- What equipment do you already have that lets you do what you do?

- Are there any gaps in your gear list? If no, stop reading this section and move on. If yes, what gear do you really need right now?

- And now the *big* question: Why do you need it?

What's the real reason for this appraisal? Taking time to focus on specifics keeps your emotions in check. You'll evaluate with your logical mind and reduce (or maybe even avoid altogether) impulsive decisions. Also, build some flexibility into your plan that lets you adapt to changing circumstances. You don't want to spend umpteen dollars soundproofing your studio, only to find you have to move in a month.

## Research

After you determine what you need and why, carefully research all the available choices. It's homework time. Start to research the gear possibilities. First, check the industry magazines by looking at ads and reviews. Second, check the Internet for information and reviews. For example, equipment queries are common threads on the ACID, Sound Forge, and Vegas forums I co-host on DMN (www.digitalmedianet. com). Participants are usually a great source for good suggestions and things to definitely avoid.

Third, ask others what equipment they use and why. Specifically target other people who are doing what you do or plan to do. Fourth, equipment manufacturers' websites can be helpful for comparing features, but useless for the unbiased opinions. Finally, stop by your local gear palace and give the gear a test drive. But don't pull out the credit card yet; you're still tire-kicking at this point.

Be reasonably wary of untested technology or trendy items. It's wise to choose either timeless gear or technology with a clear upgrade path. Quality mixers, mics, speakers, and other fundamental components are usually worth the extra investment. Software-based tools offer the flexibility of upgrades and expansion. It doesn't always pay to be the version 1.0 guinea pig, though.

After collecting information and perhaps even trying a few pieces through demos or rentals, you can start to make the best decision. For most of us, that means looking at price versus features. There are often less expensive alternatives to top-of-the-line items that still have 75 to 80 percent of the same feature set. In many cases, the alternative will suffice with the added benefit of a lower price. Your research should reveal these alternatives. If not, you didn't look hard enough.

The web makes comparing prices a snap, too. Don't forget to include shipping in the equation when you evaluate online prices. Also, depending on the retailer and the state in which you live, you might save sales tax when you shop online. Still, buying locally means you get local service when there are problems. That fact might make paying a little more worth it.

## Set Goals

Establish specific guidelines for the gear. You've determined your needs and researched the potentials. Unless you are wealthy, you will need to prioritize. Chances are you'll have to buy some gear now and wait to purchase other things later. It's time to craft a strategy for gear acquisition. You need to decide what you plan to get and when. I've talked with many people about this issue, and the general consensus is that having a detailed action plan of what to get, when to get it, and how to get it reduces buyer's remorse significantly.

If the equipment you're considering allows you to make some money directly through its use, figure out how much you will charge for using it (or how you will recover its cost). For example, suppose you buy a surround-sound system because a new project demands it. If you charge $X for its use, how long will it take to pay for the new gear? Calculating the payback eliminates some of the guesswork from your purchasing timeline.

## Budget

Decide how you will acquire the gear. How are you going to pay for it—with cash or credit, by leasing or renting it, or will you beg, borrow, or steal? Cash is always the ideal way to control your spending. If you only use money you already have, you won't go over budget or get into debt. Start a rainy-day fund, set aside five to ten percent of what you earn from your audio-post work, and earmark it for new purchases. When you've saved enough cash, buy what you need.

I rarely buy any capital items (capital equals expensive, in this case) unless I can pay for them quickly through a single project. In short, if I can get the money I need for something from a single client job, then I'll get it—not before. This method helps keep the gear lust at bay and also helps ensure that I don't spend money on things I might not need (or I might never use).

I never recommend financing your purchases through high-interest credit card debt, either. However, there are alternatives, such as the "same as cash" deals offered by many companies. These are essentially interest-free payment plans. You order the product for something akin to three payments of $29.95. The company takes your credit card number and charges you equal installments spread over time, usually once a month for three months. They bill you the same day each month, too, until the total amount is paid in full. Combine this technique with the grace period on your card, and you get gear or supplies today and easily pay for them over time. You also won't incur finance charges or interest as long as you pay the balance each month.

Similarly, some major retailers, such as Dell, Sony, and Best Buy regularly promote great financing deals on computers, such as no interest for up to 24 months. You get a new box for a low monthly payment with no finance charges, as long as you pay for it in full in 24 months.

You might try leasing gear in certain circumstances. However, unless it is a major capital purchase, not too many equipment dealers will set up lease terms for you. Also, consider renting instead of buying. For example, short-term renting lets me use high-end, high-quality gear at a low price. I've had to rent reel-to-reel recorders to accommodate client demands; there was no reason for me to own that gear. I then charged back the rental fee to the client. Find a local rental house and see what they have available. That way, when you need a fancy mic, preamp, or other cool gear, you can get what you need, use it, and pay a lesser rental charge, which is always a significantly lower cost than buying and maintaining the gear yourself.

Have a garage sale. Scour your home or office for stuff you no longer need or want. Price your things at about 10 to 15 percent of their original purchase price, take out an ad in your local paper, make a few signs, and spend a Saturday earning some easy money. If you prefer, eBay some items instead. Use the proceeds to finance whatever new equipment you need today. That same auction site can be a source for money-saving used gear, too.

## Buy/Pass

After working through these steps, you should have a better idea about whether you should buy the equipment you need. Hopefully, your diligence has paid off and you can now decide what's best for your particular aspirations. One final tip: If your decision means buying the new gizmo, take another 48 hours to mull it over anyway. If you're still hot for it after two days, your decision is sound. If you've cooled a little, perhaps you should reconsider.

If it's a go, grab what you need and move on to the next step in your plan. It's also acceptable to pass this time around and move on without opening your wallet. Every year, step back and reevaluate your situation. Ask those questions from earlier in the chapter again. And only after you've answered them should you consider going shopping.

Always keep in mind that you want both flexibility and access to the best. Almost all the audio software listed earlier has solid standard features. And the third-party support opens up every application to myriad add-on tools. However, the real power comes from how you apply those tools, and that is the subject of the next chapter.

# 11 Make Sound *Sound* Better

Audio effects (FX), sometimes called *processes*, and restoration tools are an important part of audio post-production. You will spend a lot of time cleaning up noisy and otherwise flawed audio tracks. And you will apply unique effects to give your work greater impact. Mixing all the disparate soundtrack elements usually requires digging deep into your toolbox to pull the project together.

You may use hardware equivalents of some or all of the effects mentioned in this chapter. That will be the exception for many, though, because most of us work in the digital domain of the computer—inside the box, so to speak. Therefore, once the sound gets into the computer, that's where it stays. Instead of analog gear, we take advantage of software-based tools to craft the soundtrack effectively.

## Using Effects

You can divide audio FX into several categories. Most NLEs/DAWs include some (or all) of these effects, and there is a vibrant third-party marketplace, too. On the surface, many effects seem designed primarily for music production; however, a few key effects cross over to audio-post.

### Tone

Tonal-based effects (equalization or EQ) affect the frequency content of the audio. EQ can function as a *filter* because of the way it affects certain sound frequencies, leaving others alone. An EQ allows cutting/boosting certain frequencies to either overcome problems or accentuate certain elements. EQs have control over the amount of boost or cut, the frequencies affected, and sometimes the range or width (a.k.a. Q) of the effect. A low-pass/high-cut filter lets low frequencies through and cuts off or reduces higher frequencies. A high-pass/low-cut filter does the opposite. EQ can be shelving, where it cuts/boosts equally starting at a certain frequency (and its shape looks like a shelf) or band-pass, where it affects a narrow, bell-shaped range of frequencies. Band-pass EQ can be wide or narrow (called a *notch filter*). The uppermost example in Figure 11.1 shows a 100-Hz and 12-kHz shelving, several boost/cut examples with different Q, and a 6,500-Hz notch filter. The lower example is a software emulation of a vintage EQ hardware device.

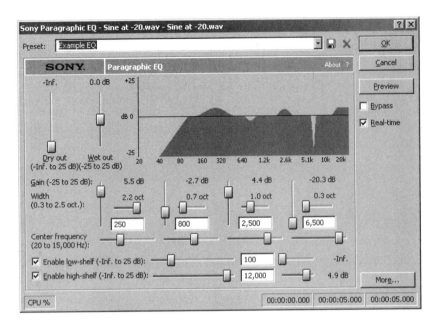

**Figure 11.1**  Software-based EQ examples.

## Time

Time-based effects use additional copies of a sound, typically delayed in time, and combine them in unique ways. Though the terms echo and delay are often used interchangeably (they really refer to the same principle), generally a single, discrete repeat is known as *echo* (hello…hello). This is sometimes called *slapback echo*. Several discrete repeats are known as *delay* (hello…hello…hello…hello…hello). The delayed sounds are usually softer than the original sound and, in the case of echo, ultimately decay away to nothing. The delay effect can also mix in some of the delayed sound and delay it again (and again and again). This delay feedback loop is reminiscent of the twittery sound of John Lennon's vocals on the Beatles song "A Day in the Life."

When the many delayed sounds are spaced very close in time to the original, there is a sense of depth and space. Known as *reverberation* (*reverb* for short), this is the effect of sound decaying in a room. Clap in a large parking garage for a hands-on example of reverb. Singing in the shower is yet another example of reverb in which the hard surfaces in the room support your dulcet tones, making them sound fuller to your ears.

Delay/echo is useful for thickening sounds and for special effects, such as the sound of a public address announcer in a football stadium. Reverb is helpful for giving a sense of space to close-miked studio recordings, for matching ADR to location work, and for thickening and lengthening sounds. For example, I often add reverb to some sound effects (SFX), such as thunder, to make them last longer and sound fuller. See Figure 11.2 for an example of a reverb effect plug-in.

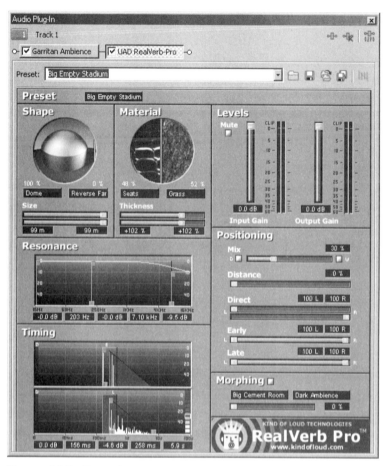

**Figure 11.2**   Reverb.

## Modulation

Modulation-based effects, such as flanging, chorus, phase, and wah are time-based delay effects that include an additional modulation source, such as a low-frequency oscillator, that isn't audible but that still affects the sound in a unique way. Some effects use a moving filter or EQ to accentuate and resonate, too. Although delay time doesn't change from repeat to repeat, modulation effects *do* change over time so they swirl and phase in useful ways. For creating otherworldly sounds, modulation effects such as flangers can't be beat. The effects are more predominant in music production and mixing, but they find their way onto soundtracks, too. For example, I used extreme chorusing to make one actor's lines sound distant and strange because the other actor wasn't really listening. It gave the effect of being inside the character's head and not paying any attention to the outside world.

See Figure 11.3 for an example of a flanger plug-in.

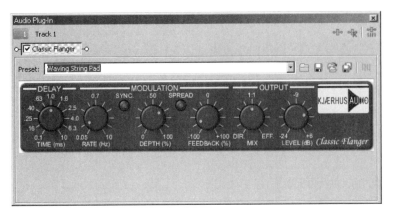

**Figure 11.3** Flanger.

## Dynamics

Dynamics-based effects reduce the dynamic range—the difference between the loudest and the softest parts—of an audio file and/or maximize volume without clipping. The FX are used to smooth dynamics on audio sources; increase punch to certain sounds that have fast attacks, such as drums; decrease overall dynamic range (compression); increase dynamic range (expansion); reduce peaks that can distort recordings; and reduce sibilance (de-essing).

A compressor squeezes the dynamic range by reducing the level of the loudest parts closer to the level of the softest parts. It works kind of like a funnel. With sounds closer in level, the overall volume can be raised, making the file sound louder. Compression can be frequency-dependent and therefore only affect a certain range of frequencies. A de-esser, useful for controlling excessive sibilance, is really just frequency-dependent compression. Some compressors let you divide up the frequency ranges and compress them separately. This multi-band compression can let you raise the level of the bass, for instance, and not compress the midrange.

Limiting is an extreme form of compression that tames loud peaks and can prevent them from ever going past a certain level. Expansion works on the soft parts and makes them even softer, leaving louder sounds intact. This expands the apparent dynamic range to be larger than the original. Expansion is useful for reducing noise on dialogue tracks. An extreme version of expansion is a noise gate, which cuts off any sound having a volume below a certain threshold level.

Figure 11.4 shows a standard and a multi-band compressor.

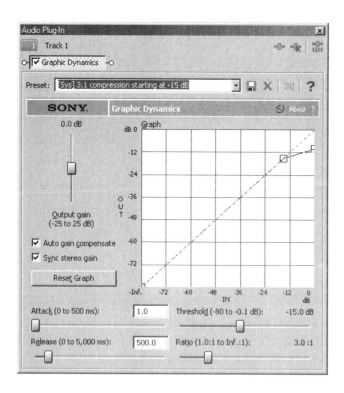

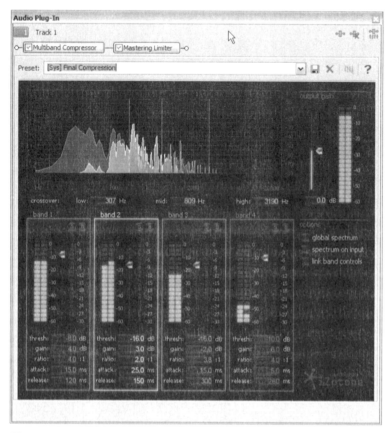

**Figure 11.4**  Compressors.

## Pitch

Pitch-based effects allow you to alter the original frequency of a file. Using pitch-based effects, you can turn people into chipmunks, Darth Vader, and anything in between. Pitch-shifted audio takes on unique characteristics that can be just what a track needs to work. For example, I might duplicate a sound, pitch-shift the duplicated sound down an octave, and mix it back with the original for a deeper, fuller tone. This is an invaluable tool for crashes, explosions, thunder, and other such sound effects.

Figure 11.5 shows an example of a pitch-shift plug-in.

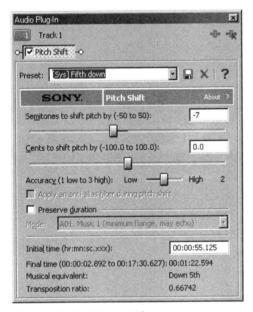

**Figure 11.5** Pitch shift.

## Time Compression/Expansion

Being able to slow down and speed up a sound is another useful tool to have at your disposal. In some cases, you want the pitch to change along with the time shift. Other times, you prefer to have the pitch remain the same while just the speed changes, either faster or slower. An example would be when Jenny yells "Run, Forrest!" in slow motion in the movie *Forrest Gump*. Other sounds besides voice take on a unique texture when you adjust this time base. Many DAWs include this feature as a timeline adjustment rather than as a separate audio FX plug-in.

## Other Effects

There are many other effects, such as distortion, vibrato, and reverse, that fall outside these primary categories. That doesn't mean they are less useful, though. For example, to emulate the sound of an overloaded police radio, distortion can make a clean VO nasty and grungy and can work to fool the listener. Other unique FX enhance and sometimes simply mangle sounds. For my music work, I use granular effects that

**Figure 11.6**   Granulator.

chop up the audio into tiny slices and rearrange them into something completely different and unrecognizable (see Figure 11.6).

## Channel Strips

There are also some effects that combine many of these elements into a single unit. For example, the channel strip effect re-creates the controls found in a typical recording mixer's single channel. The Neve 88RS channel strip from Universal Audio (www .uaudio.com) is one such example (see Figure 11.7). It emulates the famed Neve 88 Series large-format analog console in software. The channel strip plug-in includes a gate/expander, compressor, and EQ section all in one. It's a great tool for audio-post work, and I find it ideal for dialogue tracks and busses.

I'm also fond of iZotope's Alloy, as it integrates several useful functions into a single plug-in. It's also quite efficient, which means you can run multiple instances of the process without bogging down your computer's performance. And unlike the UAD plug-ins, it doesn't require a separate DSP card installed on your computer; it runs natively.

I like having audio FX that do their job as designed. However, I also prefer having some that impart a certain sound to my work. For example, all compressors work in essentially the same way, but something like Universal Audio's digital emulation of the famous Fairchild 670 compressor/limiter has a unique quality that works nicely on certain sounds (see Figure 11.8). Therefore, I have a mix of standard effects, effects that sound cool, effects that make things better, and effects the mangle sounds in uncommon ways. You will find that having many different audio effects at your fingertips helps you both fix problems and arrive at creative sweetening solutions for your projects.

**Figure 11.7** UAD Neve 88RS.

## Restoration Tools

Restoration tools are required for serious audio post-production work. You need them to fix the problems that interfere with quality recordings. Overcoming location gremlins requires a toolbox of fixes. Many of the tools mentioned earlier are useful for restoration, and these will be explored further in coming chapters. However, a dedicated noise-reduction tool is a must-have. I'm fond of the iZotope RX Advanced suite, which includes software for general noise reduction, a de-clicker, a de-clipper, hum removal, and more (see Figure 11.9). Similar tools are available from Adobe, Bias, Sony Creative Software, and Waves (see Figure 11.10).

## Audio Analysis Tools

Closely related to this subject is having solid audio analysis tools. A good spectrum analyzer plug-in lets you see what's really happening with frequency, phase, average loudness, and peaks. Though I encourage you to rely on your ears to make good decisions, there are times when checking under the hood, so to speak, is helpful. Some NLEs/DAWs have built-in tools, and there is a handful of third-party plug-ins, such as the aforementioned SPAN.

**Figure 11.8**   Fairchild 670 emulation.

**Figure 11.9**   iZotope RX Advanced.

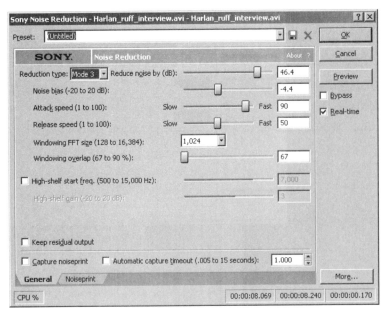

**Figure 11.10**   Sony Noise Reduction.

## Multi-Effects

There are also some multi-effects solutions that cover many different areas at once. The iZotope Ozone 4 mastering plug-in is indispensable for many tasks, especially putting the finishing touches on music tracks and even entire soundtrack mixes (see Figure 11.11). It includes EQ, multi-band compression, a harmonic exciter, a stereo widener, and a loudness maximizer.

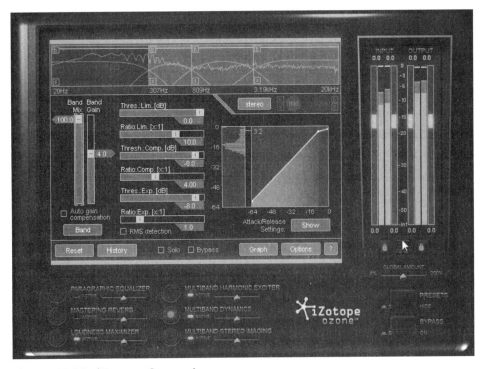

**Figure 11.11**   iZotope Ozone 4.

Another handy tool is a convolution plug-in that uses impulse responses (IR) to model acoustic spaces and electronic equipment. A program such as Sony Creative Software's Acoustic Mirror, included with Sound Forge, allows you to "sample" a space or piece of gear and overlay that on another recording (see Figure 11.12). I've created impulses from some of my favorite spaces and analog gear and now use these IRs with Acoustic Mirror. For example, you could sample the space where your dialogue took place. If you needed to re-record dialogue via ADR or even record Foley, you could then run those studio recordings through the modeled space for a more realistic effect. These tools are also useful for sound design. Acoustic Mirror, in particular, lets you use any WAV file for the impulse, and that can lead you to some interesting sound effects.

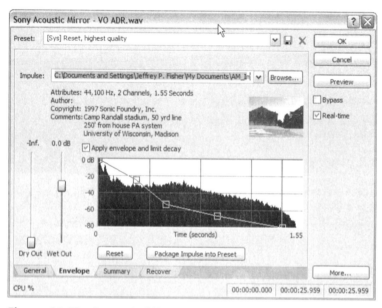

**Figure 11.12** Acoustic Mirror.

**Business Management:** One other software tool you might want to consider is business software for helping you manage your audio post-production facility. StudioSuite 9 from AlterMedia (www.studiosuite.com) is ideal for handling clients, projects, financial matters, equipment, maintenance, and more. A good accounting program, either stand-alone or online, can help you to manage your finances, too.

## Must-Have Plug-Ins

Here's a handy list of what I consider to be mandatory FX for audio post:

■ EQ with detailed control over frequency, gain, and Q

■ Compressor that works transparently

- Compressor that has a specific "sound"

- De-esser

- Noise gate and/or expander (both, really)

- Noise reduction and restoration tools

- Mastering tool

- Versatile reverb with flexible programming options

## Links

And here's a list of some of my favorite resources for FX:

- Digital Fish Phones Fish Fillets (www.digitalfishphones.com)

- iZotope RX, Alloy, Ozone 4, Spectron, and Trash (www.izotope.com)

- Kjaerhus Audio Classic series (www.kjaerhusaudio.com)

- LUXONIX LFX-1310 (www.luxonix.com)

- PSPaudioware (www.pspaudioware.com)

- Sonic Timeworks CompressorX (www.sonictimeworks.com)

- Sony Creative Software (www.sonycreativesoftware.com)

- Universal Audio UAD DSP (www.uaudio.com)

- Voxengo SPAN and more (www.voxengo.com)

- Waves (www.waves.com)

## FX Workflow

You can apply audio FX destructively or nondestructively. A destructive application permanently changes the audio file. A nondestructive application is a real-time application of the desired effect that doesn't alter the original. Working in an NLE or a DAW allows the nondestructive approach. You can therefore constantly tweak settings without committing to the final sound until the project is complete. This is the preferred method for audio-post.

There are exceptions, though, in which permanently fixing an audio file makes sense. For example, I often perform noise reduction tasks in Sony Creative Software's Sound Forge or iZotope RX and save the changes to the file destructively (though I work on a *copy* of the original). I then use the fixed file in the multitrack. Audio FX, especially time-based ones, can eat up processing power on your computer. Therefore, some NLE/DAW software allows you to freeze tracks to free up resources. This is the equivalent of destructive effects processing, but the software usually creates a new file and allows you to unfreeze and rework a track if necessary.

You can apply audio FX to individual sounds, tracks, busses, and even the master output. Generally, you choose what you want to change, select an audio effect, adjust its parameters as needed, adjust the mix of dry (original sound) and wet (effected sound), and preview your work. You can also string multiple effects in a chain and process the audio through this complex effect.

---

**Note:** The specific application of these effects will be explored in subsequent chapters. For example, ways to reduce noise on dialogue recordings will be discussed in Chapters 13 through 15. The audio FX settings to accomplish that task will also be part of the discussion there.

---

## The General State of Generic Advice

When it comes to advice about audio effects settings and related areas, I despise generalities. Some people may say you should always add 4 dB of boost at 160 Hz when using EQ or you should always run your dialogue through a compressor at a 3:1 ratio, with a fast attack, slow release. This kind of advice is akin to telling somebody to always put salt and pepper on her food before tasting it. Consider these words from award-winning sound designer Randy Thom: "The surest way to guarantee nothing interesting will happen is to go into it with the assumption that you know exactly how to do it."

Generic advice is dangerous and often hinders creativity. Instead, use your ears and treat advice such as this as a starting point. If it sounds better, it probably is—but if it doesn't, don't worry that you're not conforming to some rule. And by the way, there are no rules! It's the mix that matters, and therefore your application of any audio effects must work in the context of the whole soundtrack.

Working on a complicated soundtrack requires more than just tools. You need to develop an organized workflow that lets you juggle many different elements, track changes, and generally get the job done. The next chapter delves into this area in detail.

# 12 Audio-Post Workflow Tips

Even what appears to be a simple project on the surface can grow quickly in complexity. Therefore, it's important to find a workflow that supports your particular working style. This can be a daunting task if you've never really tackled a major project before. Don't neglect its importance. Getting organized and developing good practices will save you a lot of headaches later. This chapter profiles some ways to develop an approach that makes sense, is efficient, and feeds your creativity.

## Keeping Organized

Developing an organizational routine and a backup strategy is crucial to efficiency. I'll offer my suggestions here, but use them a guideline and find your own methods that work. Do not throw everything into a single shoebox, because you'll waste a lot of time searching for elements. And if you will hand off your work to another, do that person a favor and have some semblance of order in the project and on the hard drive(s) that she can understand and easily master.

Of course, if your project has a single VO, a handful of sound effects, and a music track, you do not need to be so fastidious. However, if you're working on a project with a few-hundred gigabytes of media, it's prudent to get organized.

Dedicating a hard drive (HDD) to a new project is a good idea. I usually clone all the material provided to me and work on a copy. Back up your changes to the original drive regularly. Don't risk losing your hard work. Back up often and to multiple places. Lose your work, and you sacrifice valuable time and often large sums of money. More important, it's difficult to bring the same creativity and passion to a project the second time around. Consider backing up material to other drives or CDs/DVDs and storing them off site. An online storage resource is also worth the money.

On the hard drive, set up a primary project folder and move all your media into it. Set up additional subfolders to keep related elements together. Here's how the main project folder might lay out in terms of subfolders:

- Raw Video (Capture) or rendered video
- OMFs and translated project files

139

- Stock Video (or Tweaked Video)
- Stills
- Graphics
- Raw VO/Dialogue
- Edit/Restored VO/Dialogue
- ADR
- SFX (Sound Effects)
- BGs (Backgrounds)
- Foley
- Music
- Test Renders
- DVD Builds

If you prefer to use the virtual storage provided via your software's media bins (or the equivalent), organize them in a similar manner to what I suggested here. I organize the HDD first and then often duplicate that organization in my DAW software.

When you are setting up a project, don't be parsimonious with audio tracks. Tracks are cheap in the typical NLE/DAW. Don't mingle music, dialogue, and SFX on the same tracks. Keep them separate, because these elements often need different approaches to EQ, volume, panning, and such. If your software supports it, consider color-coding tracks and/or buses and keeping like sounds together on appropriate tracks. As mentioned earlier, when I'm given a project with sound already in place, I duplicate it on the timeline and move the originals out of the way to the bottom and mute them. They serve as a useful reference and the ultimate fail-safe. Always lock any video in place so it won't be nudged accidentally. Figure 12.1 shows how this might work in an example project using Sony Creative Software's Vegas Pro.

Also, add busses as needed and route all tracks/busses to the master, industry-standard dedicated dialogue, music, and effects buses (DM&E). In essence, your NLE/DAW timeline is your stem, busses serve as premixes, and the final DM&E serves as the final mix.

## Preparing the Project

One of the fortunate events of watching an incomplete project is that it can be inspiring to your audio creativity. There is something magical about seeing a narrative or a documentary for the first time. In some cases, I've had no preconceived notions about what I would see. Sometimes I don't even know the full title, let alone the story or plotline.

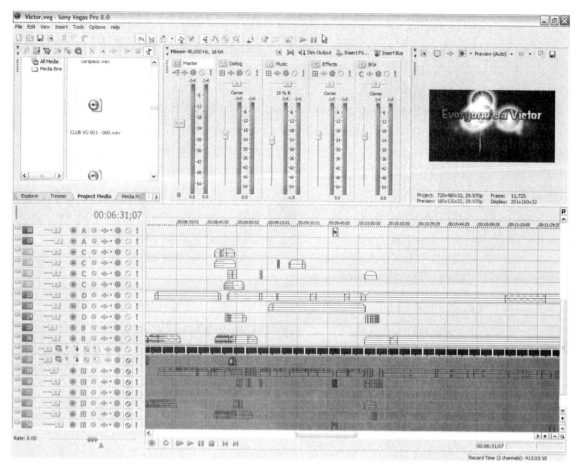

**Figure 12.1**   An example project in Vegas Pro.

When you go to the movies or add a DVD to your Netflix queue, you at least have some idea about what you're getting. I welcome *not* knowing, because that initial viewing can be an amazing and memorable experience.

As mentioned earlier in this book: Prepare for your work by watching the complete project. You will be absorbed in the story too much to focus on audio. Don't cheat yourself out of this initial screening. It's your one and only chance to respond to what you see as an audience would. Once you begin working on a project, you're too close to the material to ever have that first-time, open objectivity again. I encourage you to just go into the film's world and respond emotionally to the events as they unfold. There will be time enough to get down to the trivial and nitpick your way through the sound-track. First, enjoy it. Then, go back and analyze it!

Watch it a second time and really listen to the sound. Even if you recorded all the audio yourself, and especially if you received the audio from another source, take the time to go through everything and *really* listen. There will be mistakes or audio glitches that you didn't hear before.

As mentioned earlier, work on copies of files so you can always return to the originals. Start working on dialogue. Get a rough together (scene by scene) by quickly getting rid of obvious junk, and start bringing in sound effects, backgrounds, and whatever else is needed. Keep music out for now. Take a break, but not before you save and back up your hard work. After resting your ears and your mind, listen to the rough and look for ways to improve it. Get back in and clean things up, and begin to sweeten the soundtrack. Get ready for the mix. Put as much time between finishing your work and the mix as you can. This will bring a fresh perspective when you pull together the final soundtrack.

If somebody else will approve your work, don't waste time getting approval for every little idea you have along the way. Put everything in and screen it periodically for the decision maker. Take notes about their reactions and suggestions. In other words, show, don't tell. Then, fix what they don't like.

One you are organized and have a workflow in place, it's time to get down to the nitty-gritty of doing the specific audio-post chores. Chapter 20, "Mixing" also contains some additional organizational methods specifically related to preparing for the final mix. The next chapter looks at recording voiceovers, and after that the focus is on more voice, with additional dialogue recording and editing.

# 13 Voiceover

To paraphrase an old expression, "If it ain't on the page, it's not on the stage." Story is arguably the most important part of any production, and it is the dialogue—what people say both onscreen and offscreen—that drives the story. But to understand your story, your audience must hear what is being said clearly and without annoying noise or bad sound edits. Dialogue comes from many sources, with production sound being the most predominant. Whether your dialogue encompasses a voiceover narrator, on-camera interviews, cinema verité dialogue, or scripted dialogue, audiences want to understand all that is being said. So, cleaning up and presenting your dialogue at its best has to be the primary focus in post-production.

All you need to remember is this: Build your soundtrack around the dialogue. And then let everything else fall into place around the words. In short, dialogue rules!

From a practical point of view, it's smart to start with the dialogue simply because fixing it is slow and tedious work, and it's usually the most non-creative aspect. Don't get me wrong: All the hard works pays off because dialogue is so important to your production's success, but getting there means long hours of working on a microscopic level—trimming, fixing, cleaning, fading, adjusting, and often whipping the speech into shape.

Why is dialogue so difficult to capture in the first place, and then to present effectively? First of all, we live in a noisy world, and much of that noise gets on our recorded dialogue tracks. Hopefully, the dialogue levels are loud enough to mask the general din. But what about those times when the actors don't speak? Our audience can tune out steady noise, but when those background sounds "jump around," the audience will notice and be distracted from the all-important story. These presence jumps require extensive smoothing.

Second, filmmaking is usually a disjointed process. A two-person dialogue sequence that appears natural in the finished sequence might require several hours or days to shoot. When pieced together in the editing suite, the rough cut exposes all the audio problems—mismatched volume levels and perspectives, hum, hiss, crackles, and more. Cleaning up the sequence to make it all sound seamless and clear is no easy task. But that is exactly what you *must* do so your audience can relax, understand, and experience the story as told through dialogue.

Thirdly, picture (and acting) tends to rule on set. If the shot is perfect and/or the acting superb, then the director is often hesitant to reshoot should the sound crew chime in with an issue. Few sound people have the authority to order a retake because of problems recording the sound. You'll all too often hear the phrase, "We'll fix it in post."

It is these issues that keep a sound editor busy trying to squeeze perfect dialogue from the turnips that come in from the field. The next several chapters will cover various aspects of dialogue that will ultimately contribute to your soundtrack success.

## Scripting Voiceover

Narration is often the easiest type of dialogue to record because you usually have far more control than you do with other types of dialogue. Recording in an acoustically correct studio—away from the elements and noise in the field—leaves far less tweaking to be done in post.

Good voiceover work (VO) starts—not surprisingly—with the script. Write the way people actually talk, and strive for a conversational approach, rather than an omniscient, disembodied announcer. The more believable and real the script, the better the finished recording will sound.

Generally, avoid long streams of compound adjectives, such as, "Using a limited-access telemetric wireless plant-floor terminal and wedge scanner...." That's a hard sentence for anyone to get out correctly, even a professional. Watch out for multiple prepositional phrases; for example, "Make your plans to join us at the BigName Hotel on the historic Riverfront in Savannah, Georgia, over the holiday weekend." Avoid at all costs writing in a passive voice, such as, "Each unit is assigned a unique serial number ID." Change this to active voice, such as, "The software assigns a unique serial ID to each unit." And never begin a sentence with a preposition. Or sentence fragments. Actually those last two "rules" are jokes. It's okay to break the rules a bit if it's reasonably correct and, more importantly, sounds good. Your third-grade teacher may have marked your paper wrong for splitting an infinitive, but c'mon folks—where would we be without: "To boldly go where no one has gone before?"

A terrific way to test your VO scripting prowess is to simply read what you've written out loud. How do the words roll off your tongue? Is it difficult to read the script smoothly? Does it sound right? If you can, record this performance, listen back, and then rewrite as needed to fix any problems you discover. If your project requires precise timing, such as a radio commercial, make sure the copy comfortably fits the time allotted.

Of course, a talented professional voiceover actor should be able to bring almost anything written to life, but your words will shine even brighter if you've taken the time to craft the best script possible in the first place.

To make it easier for VO talent, print your script using an 18-point serif typeface, such as Times Roman. Use regular capitalization, uppercase and lowercase. Spell out everything, including numbers if you want them read a certain way. Use phonetic spelling of difficult, technical language and names. Don't split a sentence or paragraph to the next page, or you'll be dealing with paper-handling noises.

## Casting Voiceover

When you have a solid script, turn your attention to casting the VO. Don't go into casting without a clear idea of what you want. Casting is too important to leave to the useless "I'll know it when I hear it" decision-making procedure.

Ask yourself this question: What (voice) is the best way to convey the information? Document your ideas and be descriptive, but not overly so. Using a celebrity voice as a guideline can help, but don't be so enamored with a particular voice or style that you aren't open to fresh ideas. Be careful in using celebrity references with talent auditioning for you, too. Make sure they realize you want the general tone and feel of the voice and *not* an impersonation of the celebrity. Sometimes you may write the script with a particular person in mind. I often write specifically for the style of my friend, fellow author, and favorite VO, Harlan Hogan (www.harlanhogan.com), literally hearing his voice in my head as I write the words.

With a better understanding of what you're looking for, start collecting demos from suitable VOs either online or through talent agencies. Listen to the demos and eliminate those who you feel don't fit your needs. Contact the most promising candidates either directly or through their agents and set up an audition. Most VOs should have the ability to record a basic audition on their own and send it to you. Many have full-blown studios that can produce high-quality professional work, too. Have candidates email a demo as an MP3 to let you better assess their suitability.

In addition to talent agents and individual talent websites, you might want to use one of the general voice sites, such as Voice123 (www.voice123.com) or Commercial Voices (www.commercialvoices.com). These sites allow you to put out a casting notice and collect auditions from VOs from around the world. One caution: Unlike with agents, there is no way to filter who responds. You will receive auditions from pros and newcomers alike, with prices across the board and usually more auditions than you could ever have time to listen to. A good idea is to listen to a number of demos on these sites and then ask only specific talent to submit an audition—in essence doing the work that a traditional talent agent provides.

Establish some criteria to subjectively judge the audition:

■ Listen to each performance carefully.

■ Check for problems such as excessive mouth noise, including sibilance and popped P's.

■ Is the voice dull or pleasant? Light or heavy? Lacking clarity?

- Is the delivery and tone right for the part the person plays?

- Does the performance meet the needs of the project?

- Does the talent offer immediate new ideas when asked?

- Is there appropriate energy?

- Does the candidate enunciate well? Too much? Slur certain sounds? Have weird mouth noises?

- How's the mic technique?

- Are there good, even volume levels, or is the performance all over the map?

Though this might seem counterintuitive, *a good voice is not enough*. What you really need is a good actor. Actors are storytellers, and VO work is the epitome of storytelling.

I work with a lot of voiceover talent—amateur, semipro, and professional. In almost every case, working with a pro is worth the extra bucks. Pros do a better job, deliver consistent performances, and rarely make mistakes. Want a different read? Many can give you a dozen deliveries, each one unique.

There's no doubt that amateur talent appears to be cheaper on the wallet; the union talent scale (minimum) rate is $333 per hour, plus a more than 14 percent health and welfare contribution and a 10 percent agent's commission. Many top VO pros demand —and get—fees far in excess of that.

However, most amateurs take far more time to get a good and consistent performance. You will probably spend a considerable amount of time coaching them and then cleaning up their work in post. All too often, amateurs and beginners will actually be more expensive. This is a reality based on my experience, but if the amateur is right for your project, don't let my experience stand in your way. Always be open to what's right for your vision. Of course, in many cases you may have to work with the amateur talent, such as when doing documentary, educational, training, and corporate/industrial work.

What about celebrity VOs? Many people—advertisers especially—like to use celebrity talent. The feeling is that the "borrowed interest" of a big name being associated with their product or service adds a celebrity cachet. The fact is that much of the time, the celebrity voice is a hindrance rather than a help. Listeners play a "who is that?" guessing game instead of paying attention to your message. Obviously, celebrities cost a lot more, too. On the other hand, if having a celebrity associated with your projects makes fiscal and image sense, there's nothing wrong with going in that direction.

## Getting the Best Performance

Don't over-direct the pros, and in particular avoid giving line readings. If you've selected the right talent, you already know their capabilities and range. Give them the words and some general guidelines and let them have at it. Tell the VO about the intended audience, the message, and what the results should be. Use action verbs to describe the path to a specific outcome. Talk about how you want to elicit an emotion that resonates with the listener. By all means, let the VO know the words or phrases you want emphasized, where pauses need to be longer or shorter, and whether to end up or down on a line, if that applies.

Most pros would rather work to timings than to video. It might seem easier to show the video and have the VO read along with the visuals, but it's actually harder because the VO must split her attention between the script, the video, and the voice/performance simultaneously—a difficult balancing act for anyone. Show your talent the visuals for mood and for imparting a general sense of what's there, but when the record light goes on, work with timings.

Conversely, don't under-direct the amateurs. They'll usually need a lot of coaching and coaxing to get the VO right. Again, don't read the lines exactly to them, or you'll get a stiff, unnatural performance. I find that VO novices tend to be intimidated by the process, and especially the all-hearing, all-judging cold, hard stare of a microphone. Public speaking is a top fear for humans, and even in a VO booth, that primal instinct rears its ugly head.

Whether they are amateurs or old pros, make your talent comfortable. Provide some water, directions to the restroom, and an overview of how the process will go. Be personable and supportive, and communicate constantly as you run the session. For example, don't walk into the booth, move the mic around, and return to the control room without letting the talent know why you are doing what you're doing. If you don't let them know what you're doing, they might think they did something wrong (and they may have, but that's immaterial) and feel intimidated.

Record *everything* when there's an amateur on mic, because the best performance might very well occur when the pressure's off and the person thinks you aren't recording!

Sometimes the performance just isn't happening. Take a break and try to connect one-on-one with the person. This is not an adversarial confrontation. You are there to make the VO talent sound her best, and she wants to deliver. Sometimes, you can deviate from the exact script and talk about the subject extemporaneously. For example, many amateurs are cast for a project because they have the content knowledge. I interview a lot of CEOs and find that with a script, they freeze up. But when asked to talk about the subject—something they know a lot about—extemporaneously, they sound more confident and relaxed. Their words might not be as precise as a script, but the delivery is far more believable. In some extreme cases, I've had to hide mics and other production elements and just hold a conversation. It's not meant to be surreptitious, but rather to relax the person and get the performance you really need.

Beware of sentence pickups. If the talent makes a mistake, do not just pick it up from the error and move on. Never record just sentence fragments. Often these lines become impossible to edit; they sound strange because the emotion and emphasis are all wrong. You don't want parts of sentences sticking out noticeably. You want a smooth, consistent performance. To get the best result, go back to the nearest full sentence and start again from there. Sometimes going further back to a paragraph start is the best tactic. This approach will both reduce your editing work and make for better-sounding finished VOs.

Both pros and amateurs often suffer from some common ills. Dry mouth is the most universal and is easily fixed with tepid water and often a liberal dose of lip balm. Talent should keep their throat lubricated with water, not too hot or too cold. Apple slices can also do the trick. VOs should avoid dairy, fruit juice, and caffeine before the session. Excessively salty or garlicky meals can exacerbate the condition. For sore throats, Entertainer's Secret Throat Relief (www.entertainers-secret.com) is a must-have, though having a few throat lozenges handy works, too.

Professional VOs should know this next one, but others may not. Clothing, jewelry, and even dentures can create a lot of extraneous and difficult-to-eliminate noise on the recordings. The solutions are natural fabrics and a solid dental adhesive—and leave the bling behind.

Bad mic technique is another issue. You don't want the talent turning away, talking down, or moving closer to or farther away from the mic all the time. You don't want them touching or moving the mic or pop screen, either. You might want to subtly coach a beginner a little on proper technique—staying in one place, talking up toward the mic, and such. Obviously, this is a discussion that would be insulting to a professional. You'd be wise in any event to set up your gear in a way that's comfortable for your talent so they aren't forced into an unnatural position. Some VOs prefer to sit, so have a quiet chair or a stool nearby. Deal with excessive sibilance and spittiness with an appropriate mic choice and a pop/spit screen; handle popped consonants with some coaching or by miking from the side and slightly above.

## Recording VOs

Even though it's far easier to record voice in a studio environment than on a noisy location, it's absolutely critical that you still invest in a solid front end for your recorder. That includes a mic designed for voice recording; a preamp or channel strip that complements the mic choice; a shock mount to reduce the risk of handling and infrasonic noise ruining the recording; a high-quality and effective pop/spit filter; short, high-quality cables; a solid stand with an adjustable boom; a copy stand for the script; comfortable headphones; an armless chair or stool; and a large, easy-to-read timer (or a quiet stopwatch).

## The Recording Environment

VOs are best recorded in an acoustically dead space, quiet with low or no reverb time. Be wary of nearby reflecting surfaces, such as walls and even the copy stand itself. Although you do not need to go to a fancy recording studio to capture quality VO, you can't get professional results in a bathroom or stairwell, either. Choose a room or area in your workspace that is already quiet. Your audio editing suite may suffice, but listen for HVAC noise, fan noises from computers, and outside noise leaking in. If you are capturing VO on location (which is not unheard of for government and corporate projects), search for quiet, dead rooms in which to work.

Large pillows stacked in a corner with the talent talking toward them can work in a pinch, as can a walk-in closet filled with clothes. Hanging heavy, quilted moving blankets from the ceiling and building a tent around the talent and the mic is another inexpensive solution. The Reflexion Filter from sE Electronics (www.seelectronics.com) and the Mic Thing from SM Pro Audio (www.smproaudio.com) are other good ideas, especially when used with other minimal acoustic treatments, such as the tent. There is a similar offering from RealTraps (www.realtraps.com). There are also dedicated booths from companies such as WhisperRoom (www.whisperroom.com) and VocalBooth (www.vocalbooth.com), but they don't come cheap.

## The Porta-Booth

Recording VO isn't always done in a controlled environment, so this next idea works in the audio post-production suite, in less-than-stellar rooms, and on location.

A VO box such as this won't keep the leaf-blower noise outside your window from ruining your tracks, but it will take a lot of the room out of the recording and give you a nice, dry, resonant tone to your recordings. If you record VOs and you can't afford to invest in a sound booth, this little widget can help tremendously. It's inexpensive, portable, and sounds great. If I know I'll be recording VO on location, I use it. For example, on a corporate video, the CEO may start talking on camera but do the majority of his script as a VO narration. I'll use the VO box for that material, giving me far more control over the quality of the sound. I also use this box for some Foley work.

Michael Palin recorded his voiceovers for the BBC travel documentary *Around the World in 80 Days* during the actual production because he wanted to capture the essence and feeling of the moment instead of the hindsight perspective he would have in the studio after he returned from the trip. You may have similar cases where what people say during the production will have greater impact than a recorded VO later, after everything either worked out or failed. This can add more credibility and believability to what you are trying to convey, and is a mainstay in reality programming.

This idea comes from Harlan Hogan, who was inspired by a portable vocal booth built by Douglas Spotted Eagle and mentioned in our book, *The Voice Actor's Guide to Recording at Home and on the Road* (Course Technology PTR, 2008). Douglas realized that for a microphone to sound good and tight, the performer didn't need to be inside a box; the *microphone* did. Because you will often find yourself in less than perfect recording environments, build the Harlan Hogan "Porta-Booth." All you need is a collapsible, pop-up, folding cube wastebasket (such as the ones available from Target), some acoustic foam, a microphone desk stand, and perhaps a little clip-on LED reading light.

Harlan's first attempt with a flimsy mesh cube from the Container Store worked, but sounded only so-so. Then, I pointed out to Mr. H. that the cube needed to be made of a more substantial material to sound right. Another shopping excursion, and he struck gold—a collapsible cube from Target that has a tight sound and is a perfect size at 15×15×15 inches. Despite its relatively light weight, it's very sturdily constructed.

Purchase the acoustic foam from Markertek (www.markertek.com), SONEX (www.sonex-online.com), or Auralex (www.auralex.com). Some music stores may carry the requisite foam, or you can try online sources, such as American Musical Supply (www.americanmusical.com). Get the two-inch-thick foam tiles for the best results. You might need to cut them down a little to fit the container.

The photo in Figure 13.1 tells the story. Pop the container open, arrange the four foam tiles, set your favorite mic inside, and talk. The foam pieces aren't attached to the interior, so you can nest them together to save space when you flatten the box. The whole shebang folds up to a thickness of about four inches. Hogan tightens a nylon strap around the box to compress it even thinner and shoves it in his suitcase. You can also use a compression bag to squeeze all the air out, and it packs up even smaller.

You can get a ready-made version of this booth along with a newer version, called the Porta-Booth Pro, at Harlan's Voiceover Essentials (www.voiceoveressentials.com) website.

Image courtesy of Harlan Hogan.

**Figure 13.1** Porta-Booth.

Harlan also shares this advice. If you still can't find the right room or place to record, try this. One of the best designed acoustic spaces on earth is the modern automobile. So, if all else fails, get in the car, drive to a quiet place, shut the car off, and start recording.

## Engineering Equipment

With the talent accommodated, the audio engineer needs a few items, too. Same-room recording requires headphones for both talent and engineer. A talkback system for communication between the director, engineer, and talent is also useful. This might be as simple as a mic plugged into an unused mixer or audio interface channel and routed to the talent's headphones. A dedicated mixer or a control room monitoring device, such as PreSonus's Central or Monitor Station (www.presonus.com), may have talkback facilities that you can employ. There are also options for remote recording using telephone patches, ISDN, and Source-Connect software available as well.

Typical microphone choices include expensive large-diaphragm condensers, such as the standby Neumann U 87 or U 89. I also like the Blue Mouse (on male) and Dragonfly (on female) (www.bluemic.com). The MXL M3B and Avant CV12 are also good choices. Harlan Hogan uses the Lawson L47 (www.lawsonmicrophones.com) for some spots, but typically grabs the Sennheiser 416 short shotgun.

It might seem strange to use a shotgun microphone in a quiet VO studio, but the reality is the 416 sounds tight and full, perfect for VO work. Recently, I was impressed by a sound-alike from an unlikely source. The MXL 909, a large-diaphragm cardioid condenser, sounded as good (if not better) when compared head to head to the 416. While the 909 won't replace the 416 for field use, I've been using mine for VO work, coupled to a quality preamp, with excellent results. The Oktava MK-012 also works well for a lot of voice recordings; it's a versatile mic. I'm also a recent convert to using ribbon mics for some VO work, and I like many of the models coming from Cascade (www.cascademicrophones.com) for this purpose.

There are variety of all-in-one vocal channels that facilitate VO recording. Many of the audio equipment manufacturers mentioned earlier in this book work well, such as the Focusrite Saffire, the PreSonus FP10, and the Mackie Spike. For some, a tube-based preamp may be just the right companion to a bright-sounding microphone. There are inexpensive choices, pricey ones, and many in between. I like the ART models on the low end; Joemeek oneQ in the middle; and PreSonus Eureka, Universal Audio LA-610 or SOLO/610, Focusrite Producer Pack or Liquid Channel, and the John Hardy or Avalon on the high end. If you will do a lot of VO recording work, invest in a quality preamp—it can make even the cheapest mic sound really good. Couple a boutique mic preamp with a great-sounding mic, and you'll have an unbeatable combination!

It's important to match the mic to the talent, so having a variety of mic choices available is a good idea. If you are the talent, take time to find a microphone that complements your vocal qualities. Listen to as many mics as you can and make educated purchases. When picking mics for the talent, set up two or three possibilities and have the talent run through a part of the script a few times. Listen back to these recordings and make the best choice.

## Mic Placement

Mic placement is important as well. Typically, you should place the mic in its shock mount at the end of a boom on a mic stand. For studio mics, position your talent about four to six inches away from the mic with the pop filter splitting the distance. If you use a short shotgun, eight to ten inches is better. I like the mic slightly higher and pointed down slightly, with the bottom of the pickup element about even with the top lip. It's acceptable to move the mic off to the side slightly, say 10 to 15 degrees off center (as shown in Figure 13.2), to reduce pops and also leave room for the script. A pencil taped on the outside grill of the mic centered over the diaphragm can stop plosives (popped Ps), too. If the talent is too sibilant, try a different mic and/or a tube preamp. A figure-eight or omnidirectional pattern can reduce pops and sibilance, too, but you risk picking up more room and noise.

**Figure 13.2**  Side mic technique.

## Record Flat

Always record flat with no effects—especially *no compression*—because it's almost impossible to reverse or remove it after the fact. Turn off any automatic gain control and set the recording levels manually. Get levels as loud as possible to maximize signal-to-noise ratio, but be careful not to exceed 0 dBFS. Keep the peak range between the –6 to –15 range. You can always turn down a loud recording in the mix, but increasing the volume on a too-soft recording brings up the noise floor substantially. For the recording, set the sampling rate to 48,000 Hz and the bit depth to 24 bits for the best quality and compatibility (if your recording hardware supports these specifications).

### Talent Placement

If the talent needs to yell or scream, move her farther away from the mic and reduce levels accordingly. Whisperers and soft speakers might need to get closer to the mic. Cranking the preamp gain up all the way will be noisy, so close-miking is the better choice.

Don't be afraid to try different placement ideas, distances, mics, and preamp combinations, but listen closely so you don't hear too much room sound. The goal is to capture the voice in a natural way that's upfront, dry, and clean. It should sound natural, without noise, sibilance, and popped consonants. And you don't want it to sound as if the mic was at the other end of the room, either.

You will find extended coverage on fixing voice problems and sweetening performances in Chapter 15, "Editing Dialogue."

## VO Resources

For more detail on recording VO, check out *The Voice Actor's Guide to Recording at Home and on the Road* by Jeffrey P. Fisher and Harlan Hogan. Stop by its companion website (www.audiosmartactors.com), too.

Also, Harlan Hogan's *VO: Tales and Techniques of a Voice-over Actor* (Allworth Press, 2002; www.harlanhogan.com) is a wonderful, practical, and fun book. If you're interested in pursuing this work yourself, or if you just want to learn about the VO world from an insider, grab this resource.

Now that you know how to get good VOs for your soundtrack work, the next chapter explores other studio-based recording: ADR and walla.

# 14 Recording ADR and Walla

Recording automatic dialogue replacement (ADR) and walla is somewhat related to VO narration sessions. With ADR you bring the talent into the studio to re-record lines that were unsatisfactory. The field recordings serve as a guide track for the performer to re-voice what was said, and then the new recording replaces the bad one. Walla entails recording a group of people who add voices for background scenes that contain crowds.

## The Challenges of ADR

It is best not to hold the ADR session(s) just based on spotting notes. As you get into editing the dialogue, you might be able to recover lines that you thought were lost causes. Additionally, you may uncover more lines that need ADR. Therefore, it behooves you to wait a little into the dialogue-editing process before putting together the work destined for ADR.

The challenge of ADR is to match these new recordings to the location recordings as closely as possible. If you will intercut field recordings with these looped lines, it is vital that they match. And that's no easy task. If you only ADR one side of a conversation, for example, it will be very tricky to cut between the location-recorded sound and that from the studio. Of course, if you ADR the whole scene, then you can go for the best sound possible. (Refer to the recording VO discussion in the previous chapter.) Sometimes the only real solution is to ADR *all* the lines if you just can't seem to match them. That certainly beats having every looped line stand out like a sore thumb from its location-recorded counterpart.

Sometimes you may do your ADR wild on location, essentially having the talent do their lines in a quieter place and in a more controlled manner. There's no sync here—they just say their lines, and you record them, hence the term "wild." This approach can work when you know the production dialogue is terribly noisy, such as a street scene in a busy urban area. It's also handy when people speak in a long shot and it's impossible to get the mic close enough to the talent for good-quality sound. Moving to a nearby location and/or bringing the talent close to the mic to record their lines is a good ace in the hole.

Unfortunately, cutting these wild lines to match production dialogue can be tricky. Usually the wild lines sound great, but when intercut with other tracks, they stand out. You may need to wield some post-production magic to make these replaced lines closely approximate the other dialogue. Adding in some room tone and perhaps even extra sound effects/backgrounds can make these wild lines fit. Typically lip sync is off, so wild lines work for long shots, over-the-shoulder, and other framing where tight lip syncing isn't required. That said, occasionally actors are dead-on with their line delivery, and even a wild line may sync fine.

Recording these wild lines (and shooting for sound, as mentioned earlier, in Chapter 5) brings an additional advantage when doing narrative projects. The actors are still on the set and still in the moment. Often you can get a better performance from them this way.

It's important to note that many actors despise doing ADR. The process is rather mechanical and disconnected. They are forced to work line by line and can't play off of other actors. Therefore, it's hard to capture the magic of a performance delivered during the original shoot. If you can avoid the whole issue, I urge you to take that route or use the other techniques mentioned earlier. But if the audio is so bad that nothing short of re-recording will fix it, you might need to convince your talent that ADR is the only way.

## Getting Quality ADR

Using the exact recording chain that was used on location goes a long way toward helping match the quality. Choose the same mic, preamp, and recording device and settings. Hopefully, you took copious notes on the set to facilitate re-creating this setup. If a lavaliere was used, mike up the talent with the same lavaliere and in the same way. Distance and direction are also critical to completing the illusion. So if a boom was used, closely approximating the distance from talent to boom used in the field can help to blend the tracks. This is not a VO session, so much of the discussion in the previous chapter will not necessarily apply. ADR is a re-creation of the location recording setup, and authenticity rules over arguably better equipment choices and technique.

The real problem is not being able to match in the studio how the voice sounded at the location itself. The acoustics in the recording studio will rarely correspond to the location's acoustics. Room tone and presence captured at the location can help put the new recordings in the same space, but that's only half the equation. How the voice swims around that space is tougher to get right.

Adding reverb to or using a convolution plug-in with ADR tracks can impart some of that missing location's quality and sense of space. You need a reverb with plenty of controls for successfully matching an existing space. However, taking a sample and creating an impulse response for use as the modeled space is good workflow for scenes that are dialogue-intensive or ones in which you know ADR will come into play. Playing the test tones needed for creating an IR (*impulse response*) and recording that while still on the set will save you a lot of time in the long run. You will use the same recording chain, which adds to the authenticity, too. As a byproduct, you will build a library of modeled spaces that you can use for future projects. You can also find impulse responses on the web. Figure 14.1 shows an IR in Sony Creative Software's Acoustic Mirror.

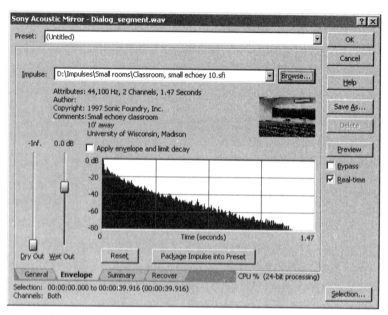

**Figure 14.1**  IR in Acoustic Mirror.

Setting up for ADR requires having a TV monitor so the talent can see their original performance, and headphones so they can hear the bad recording and their new recording simultaneously. You want to monitor similarly and record just the new performance.

Surprisingly, trying to get the best-quality recording in the ADR booth may *not* be the ideal solution. Instead, you are striving to match the location sound, which might mean tweaking to get tracks to sound alike, bad or good. As a rule, though, always record the best sound possible. You can mess with it later in post. Although it can be hard to remove noises from bad field audio, it's relatively easy to add noise to decent studio recordings to make them better fit the scene.

The best approach is to do one dialogue line at a time. Anything longer is actually trickier to pull off and counterproductive. You do not need any special software to do ADR. Your DAW/NLE will usually have the tools needed. Set up your software to play back a loop. Set the loop in/out points around the dialogue line. You might want to give some wiggle room leading up to the loop and just after the line to make it easier on the talent. Essentially, you play the loop repeatedly as the talent recites the line. A few times through is usually all it takes for the talent to lock into the rhythm and match the sync. It's easier if you can loop-record, too, because then you capture every delivered line and you can choose the best one later. If you can't do that, you will need to punch-in record to capture the line.

Alternatively, set up a series of tones that lead up to the record point. Three short tones spaced evenly create a simple rhythmic pattern. Where the fourth tone would be is where the line starts. This "beep, beep, beep, line" system helps the talent anticipate the dialogue to be replaced and often results in a smoother, better recording. Visually, I superimpose two thick white lines over the video, one screen left and the other screen right. When playback starts, the far-left line wipes across the screen to meet the right one. This is called a *streamer*, and it helps as a visual cue to go along with the aural one. Figure 14.2 shows an example streamer used for an ADR session inside Sony Vegas Pro. At the actual edit point there is a single white flash frame, too. That's the talent's cue to begin speaking and when the recording begins. The streamer and beeps take about a second to complete. Extend the loop slightly beyond the line. Once again, run through the loop a few times to get the mechanics down. The focus should then shift to the performance so that it either matches or improves upon the unsatisfactory field recording.

Some performers are quite adept at ADR, and these sessions flow quickly. Others require a lot of time and patience to get something marginally acceptable. They tend

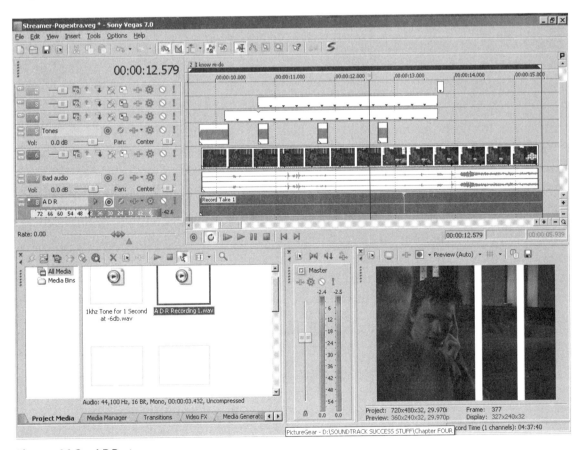

**Figure 14.2** ADR streamer.

to get too distracted by staying in sync, and if they have a poor sense of rhythm, they get easily frustrated. My best advice to these people is to focus on their performance and try to ignore the technology and sync. And record everything, because it's usually when they are relaxed and not paying attention that you finally get the right take.

Dialogue should be dead-on accurate in sync or, if necessary, slightly late. Our brains are accustomed to hearing sound late (think lightning and its delayed thunder), so err on the side of a touch late as opposed to early.

# Walla

Suppose your scene takes place in a crowded restaurant. There are people in the background as your two main characters converse. On the set, all the background actors mime their conversations while your characters deliver their lines according to the eventual situation. In other words, if the scene calls for a loud environment, the actors should voice accordingly, as if they were talking loudly to get above the din. You wouldn't want all that noise on the recording, though—just their dialogue. In post, you can add the suitable restaurant backgrounds. But what about all those other voices?

You could have the on-set talent create this soundtrack element for you either before or after the main dialogue recording. Slip this wild track in as needed. However, circumstances may dictate that you re-create these conversations in a controlled environment. Additionally, you might go out in the field and capture crowd noises at other locations using a portable recording rig.

## Defining Walla

In this business, non-sync vocal sounds are called *walla*. Urban legend says that many years ago, groups of actors were hired for the express purpose of giving voice to background crowds. To make sure what was said didn't sound like real words, these performers would utter the word "walla" in varied intonations to complete the track. And although there might be some merit to this verbal approach, it does not need to be strictly heeded.

Walla recordings involve groups of people recorded simultaneously to create the desired crowd sounds. Recording longer sequences and layering performances can turn a small group into a large crowd. Ten people recorded a few times won't sound like a stadium filled with spectators, though. Often a couple of walla tracks combined with other crowd noises comprised of different close and faraway perspectives and densities add a richness to the experience.

## Recording Walla

For some projects, I've crammed a dozen or more people into the recording booth for walla sessions. Stereo techniques, such as mid-side, can give you added flexibility for the mix, too. Consider doing multiple takes and of a longer duration than you think you'll need. This provides variety and alternative choices as you assemble the entire soundtrack.

While the group is there, considering capturing other sounds that you can add to your personal library—boos, laughs, exclamations (oh!), and so forth. At the session's end, throw a party and record that—you never know when you might need party sounds for another project down the line!

## Handling Walla Challenges

Occasionally, there will be a background performance that is more predominant than intended. In the field, you focused on getting the primary dialogue and you might have missed something voiced by the extras. During the edit, you see lips moving, but the walla track alone doesn't fill in the obviously missing dialogue.

In this case, you might be forced to pull together a wild sync track using the ADR methods discussed earlier. Unfortunately, you won't have the guide track from the performer because he was off-mic or, more likely, silent and just miming words. First, figure out what was said. This might require more lip reading than anything, or if you are lucky, a recording may exist. Second, cast the part. Third, set up an ADR session to record the line. Finally, cut the new dialogue into the walla track.

You certainly do not need perfect sync of every person on camera—the walla should cover most of the general din. However, a carefully chosen foreground character with good sync will make it seem as if everything was recorded as it appears, when the reality of it all is just an illusion. The audience will latch onto the sync dialogue excerpt and ignore the other wild tracks. (Recall the entrainment discussion from earlier in this book.) The film *Ghostbusters* has a perfect example of what I'm describing. Near the end of the film, as the team arrives for the final confrontation, people lining the streets are talking. There is one single sync dialogue point of one crowd speaker during the scene, while all the other voices are just walla. Supporting a single sync point makes the audience feel as though all the voices are in sync, when in reality they are not.

## More Techniques for Effective Walla Recordings

For better continuity, record walla using the same equipment used in the field. You won't be close-miking like a VO, but rather trying to match the visual perspective with your mic placement. If the crowd is small and close, place the mic closer and have the walla group stand packed together. An omni- or bi-directional mic can be helpful here if your recording space is small. If the crowd is farther away in the shot, move the walla performers away from the mic and spread them out some. Of course, the studio where you record might not match the acoustics of the location set, so reverb/convolution can help support the sound, just as they do with ADR.

If your walla requires movement, don't be afraid to have the performers move around the mic. The noises of walking, shuffling, and so forth can really make the track seem more alive. Place an omnidirectional mic in the middle of the room and capture the magic.

Very large crowds, such as at a sporting event, can't be created convincingly in the studio. Although standard small-group walla will work for sweetening a large crowd or when the story takes place in just part of the crowd, the main crowds will come from either a sound effects library or a recording trip to a sporting event to capture the real sound.

As you develop your walla tracks, keep changing perspectives in mind. As the scene changes, so should the sound. For example, the establishing shot of the stadium might feature the roar of a large crowd. A close-up of a main character sitting in the stands would feature small-group walla around the performer, with a more distant (lower-volume) hint of the large crowd, too. These subtle—and not so subtle—sound moments are what make a soundtrack work. The sound is so convincing and real that the audience ignores it and is instead absorbed into the story. And sometimes exaggerating the reality still works when it drives your message in a convincing way.

Some sound effects libraries will feature various walla tracks, and although they are technically sound effects, if they feature voices, they belong with the dialogue and are therefore part of that mix element. If you *do* use pre-recorded walla such as this, make sure your choices reflect the scene properly. If the audience sees the streets of Marrakech but they hear the sounds of New York City street walla, your scene will not work. Always scour your libraries for the correct sounds that are evocative and indicative of the locale and the time period.

ADR and walla are additional techniques that can help you achieve more professional results with the all-important voice component of your soundtracks. The real secret, though, is working with existing production sound. Whether you are making documentary, narrative, or other projects, learning how to properly edit dialogue is a skill you must master. And that topic is the subject of the next chapter.

# 15 Editing Dialogue

Hopefully, you've spent a lot of time and effort grabbing the best dialogue on location. Now you can use post-production techniques to make the voice tracks even better, including fixing less than pristine takes through the aforementioned ADR and a variety of editing and sound-shaping tools, such as dedicated noise reduction. A dialogue editor's primary function is to use whatever means are necessary to make the spoken lines sound smooth and consistent.

Editing dialogue is both an art and a science. Rarely is there a project for which you won't spend time making those voices recorded on location sound better. To a certain extent, dialogue cutting is the constant fight against noise and, to a lesser extent, overcoming other production woes, such as improper mic placement, clothing and prop interference, and bad tonal quality.

## The Importance of Editing Dialogue

When it comes to dialogue, far too many people give up. They've lived and died with the project, and when faced with the prospect of adding even more to their workload, they prefer not to get their hands dirty bringing the dialogue tracks alive. Don't fall into the trap and compromise on the soundtrack! Because you are reading this book, you already understand the power of sound, and you want to learn how to use the sound tools as effectively as you use video tools. So, remember this little observation: Picture editors are lazy.

Wait, hear me out. Every NLE on the market makes it a snap to cut audio and video at the same time. Using some sort of razor tool or keyboard command, you position the cursor where you want to cut, and—bam!—the software cuts the audio and video at the same point. There is nothing wrong with this approach, as the editor is truly cutting for visual and storytelling needs. Audio is the furthest thing from her mind. And that is how it should be, at this point in the project, anyway.

To be fair, picture editors *should* focus on telling the story. If that is you, forget about the audio when you're assembling the picture edit. Tell your story! If you are handling both video and audio chores, I urge you not to cut picture and fix audio at the same time. Your brain won't like it. But once the picture is locked, it's time to turn your attention to your story's audio needs. Take off your picture editor hat and switch to the dialogue editor one. Then and only then, go back and start working on the dialogue. Working on sound is far different from the other editing chores. You need to be in a different state of mind and employ dissimilar tools. Trying to smooth dialogue while cutting picture is a bad idea. Cut the picture. Tell your story. Then, go back and repair the audio.

The real problem with simultaneous picture and sound edits is that what works for the visual rarely works for the audio. Compounding the issue is that when a picture change and audio edit happen at the same time, there is greater attention drawn to the cut. Unfortunately, for seamless dialogue that flows smoothly, the picture-edit point is often not the best place to cut the audio. If there are any small problems in the audio edit, the picture edit accentuates them, drawing too much attention to the audio *faux pas*. If there is any discrepancy in the sound of the subsequent shot, the picture edit magnifies the miscue. This problem is typically a presence change that literally jumps out at the audience. These presence jumps often make the visual editing more noticeable, instead of the seamless presentation that's desired. A dialogue editor works hard to smooth these edits by using a variety of techniques.

Our ear/brain combination is well-tuned to ignoring background noises and concentrating on speech. Therefore, when there is *steady* room noise, humans focus on the dialogue and don't notice the background sound. But when this background sound changes from shot to shot, people notice. The audience may not express that something is wrong, but these irregularities spoil the illusion and interfere with their enjoyment. They don't expect the sound to change in any way from cut to cut within a scene at the same location. However, hiding these audio red flags can be hard work.

## Smoothing Dialogue

The essence of smooth dialogue work is to cut the sound differently from the picture. The best approach to dialogue editing is to ignore the picture edit and essentially re-edit the dialogue so that it makes sense from an audio standpoint. Obviously, you must maintain lip sync and keep talent performances that the editor has deemed noteworthy intact. The primary tools for dialogue smoothing are split edits (a.k.a. J-cuts and L-cuts) and crossfades (JLX). You will also be pressed into stealing lines (and parts thereof) and using room tone/presence/atmos fills in both mundane and creative ways.

It's best to work with *locked* picture (no more visual editing or changes). Note that the whole project does not need to be finished, just full sequences. During the spotting session, where you meet with the director, producer, editor, and others and watch the locked cut, make notes about the dialogue. You will also spot for sound effects and music, but make sure you also focus on the dialogue. As mentioned earlier in this book, a timecode window burn can make taking accurate notes easier and more exact.

As the project plays, determine the problem areas. For example, are there lines missing? Are some lines too noisy, too low in level, and/or too high in level and distorted? Is dialogue split to multiple channels (such as one actor panned left, the other panned right)? Is there a mix of boom and lav? Are there tonal anomalies or phase issues? What other audio gremlins have conspired to ruin the dialogue tracks?

Next, make a judgment call about the quality. Is a particular problem area fixable? Or do you need to ADR lines? After you've gone through the scenes and taken notes, you are prepared to take the next steps.

To make the process of dialogue-smoothing easier, you might find it helpful to checkerboard the voice tracks on adjacent tracks. Also, doing the best job requires you to have access to *all* the sound files, not just the edited or fully rendered ones. If the edits have "handles" (extra audio before and after the visual edit point), your job will be easier. Without these handles, it's tricky to edit dialogue effectively.

Depending on how the production sound was recorded, you may have additional material not included with the picture edit. This could range from alternative takes to multi-track recordings. The former can be mined for replacements to noisy or otherwise bad takes. The latter is handy if there is additional separation between characters. For instance, the picture editor may have used a single mono dialogue track, but the multi-track may have each mic separated on its own. This brings added flexibility to the dialogue-editing process.

Dialogue—and room tone—should be mono. Many camcorders will record in stereo. Or, the location sound recorder may have split tracks (dual mono) between boom and lavaliere or even have given characters their own tracks. As mentioned, some dialogue may come as a multitrack, with individual performers residing on their own tracks. Everything should be converted to its own mono track before you begin the next phase. A single dialogue track from the picture editor may quickly balloon to multiple tracks as you start the necessary work.

Sample-rate differences between camera-recorded audio and external double-system recordings will cause sync drift quickly. This happens when you use audio from an external recorder and you try to align it with a redundant or guide track recorded by the camera. Camera audio always has a 48-kHz sample rate, but other recorders can be different. Exact multiples of the rate will not drift, but 44.1 kHz from a recorder will quickly drift out of sync from the camera's 48 kHz. It's nearly impossible to make edits to bring it all back together. Therefore, it is crucial to make sure any double-system recorder you use employs the same sample rate as the camera. Resampling the 44.1 kHz to 48 kHz will not work to restore sync either, because the time-base is already locked to the lower rate. Using time compression/expansion may help, though. Another egregious error I run into regularly is volume changes made by the picture editor to compensate for level mismatches made in the field. For example, editors may normalize some audio tracks or otherwise boost volume because lines are too soft. This can make it difficult to match shots because the louder, boosted tracks might be noisier than other parts left alone. If one shot was normalized and another was not, their noise floors may be radically different. It is often best to "de-normalize" everything and start over using other means to deal with the volume issues as you build the mix. Rare is the picture editor who adds audio FX, but you should be on the look-out for them and turn them off anyway.

Before you begin working on the dialogue, you should remove any volume, pan, and audio effects that may have been added during the picture edit. Do note that depending on your NLE/DAW of choice, these volume automations and other changes may be hidden from view. Don't forget you are working on a copy of everything done in the picture edit, because you stashed the originals away at the bottom of your timeline and muted them. You can always return to those references as needed.

The only exception to this rule may be when you are both the picture and sound editor. You might have made suitable audio changes as the edit unfolded, and these may continue to be valid as you begin the crucial sound work.

Often picture editors will leave the dialogue to only a track or two. To fix and sweeten these tracks, you will need to split them off from this jumbled mess into a few more manageable tracks. So use them, name them, color-code them, and give them the detailed work they need to shine.

---

**Special Note on Mixing at This Stage:** Often I do a little bit of dialogue mixing as I go along, essentially premixing the key elements. This makes the final mix so much easier and creative. By having the main elements on bus faders already, I can go back to the stems (the timeline) to tweak if the buses won't give me what I need or what the director wants during the mix. In essence, the NLE/DAW timeline holds the stems; buses become premixes, which feed the final DM&E buses; and the master output is the finished stereo (or surround) sound-track mix.

---

# JLX

*Split edits* mean that video and the audio associated with it are cut in different places. The tools you have are J-cuts, L-cuts, and crossfades (JLX). The J-cut makes the audio edit before the picture edit. That brings the next shot's audio in earlier. On the timeline, the two different edit points look like the letter J, hence the name. To perform a J-cut, unlock the audio from the corresponding video on both sides of the edit, if applicable. Shorten the first shot's audio and lengthen the next shot to fill in the gap. This works best when the presence is identical between shots or when the second shot's audio begins earlier. Cut on the exact start of a word to help cover up or mask any small anomalies.

Figure 15.1 shows an example of a J-cut.

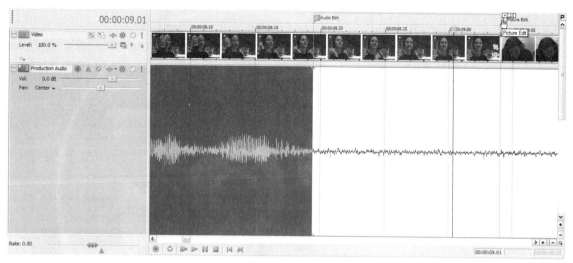

**Figure 15.1**   J-cut.

An L-cut places the audio edit after the picture edit by extending the previous shot's audio into the next shot. The subsequent edit appears like the letter L on the timeline. This is a good choice when there is a pause at the video edit point before the next person begins speaking. With the previous shot's audio covering the pause, there is no audible change in the soundtrack. Then, cut right on the next spoken word—at the start of sentences, especially a consonant—and the edit point will be masked by the speech. Listen carefully so you don't accidentally cut off a breath or part of one. Generally, L-cuts are the most used and most effective dialogue-smoothing trick (see Figure 15.2).

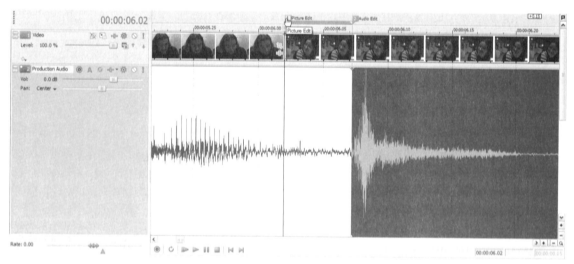

**Figure 15.2**   L-cut.

Sometimes the best solution is to fade out the first shot's audio and simultaneously fade in the second shot's audio. Different crossfade time lengths—how long the two fades overlap—can give different results, as can the shape of the crossfade. Figure 15.3 shows an example of a crossfade. Experiment with both these crossfade times and crossfade types (if your NLE/DAW supports these) for the best results. Crossfades do not have to be very long to sound smooth; often one-third of a second or less can do the trick. I regularly use tiny, quick fades both in and out and minuscule crossfades to cover some edits. Tiny crossfades in addition to the J/L cuts mentioned a moment ago can also turn jumps into smooth edits.

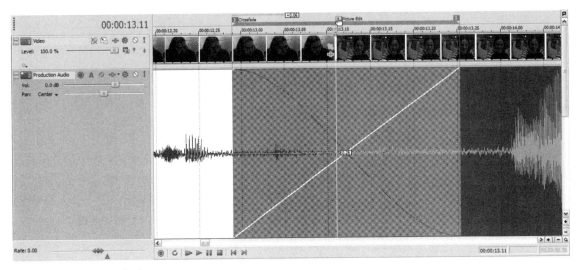

**Figure 15.3** Crossfade.

You've got one more trick up your sleeve for those situations in which the previous three do not work, such as a long pause devoid of dialogue. In this example, you can't go to complete silence. You need to grab the room tone/presence that was recorded on location and use it to fill in these gaps. That ensures there will be no annoying sound jumps, from noise to silence and back. A room-tone segment may be long or short depending on your needs and may be placed within a track or on its own. Be careful not to double up the room tone by having it overlap a dialogue line that already has room tone on it. I often resort to crossfades when pasting in room tone. Placing the room tone on its own track below the dialogue can make positioning and adding fades easier, as shown in Figure 15.4. Once again, adjust the duration and shape of the fades to get the smoothest result. It should sound natural and smooth with no noticeable increases or decreases in noise.

When you need to cut out parts of a dialogue track, such as to remove a distracting noise, use room tone to fill in the blank section. For example, I often have to remove actor breathing, clothing rustles, microphone thumps, set/crew noise, and other nasties that find their way onto the dialogue tracks. Slicing them out entirely creates a break in the presence. Grabbing a little room tone and mixing that into the gap works very well. If no room tone was captured, you might be able to steal it from the production tracks

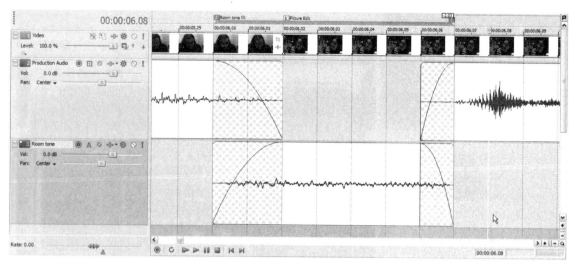

**Figure 15.4**  Room-tone fill.

by looking in between words, during pauses, and so forth. This search may result in shorter pieces that need to be butted against one another to lengthen the overall time. This creates a repeating loop that can sound bad if it's too short with an obvious repeat. Crossfades between shorter room-tone pieces can smooth this, though.

Do not confuse room tone with backgrounds. As previously mentioned, room tone is the "sound" of the location where the dialogue was recorded. On the other hand, backgrounds are built as part of the sound effects process. Although a carefully constructed sound effects background track can hide some problems with dialogue, this may not be the right solution. Equally, music can mask dialogue anomalies, too. Problems arise when the director decides to lose the music and/or sound effects backgrounds, and your soundtrack remains with badly edited dialogue. You were depending on the music and effects to hide the mistakes, and now that they are gone, your work suffers. You should always smooth the dialogue and make it as good as possible. Then the other soundtrack elements can only enhance the project as a whole.

You can use the same process to find and replace missing words and even parts of speech. It's especially easy to find a new consonant elsewhere in the recordings and splice it onto the head or tail of a word. Consonants are gender-neutral, which means a male letter S could be made to fit a missing female S, for instance. Try it, and you'll be surprised.

Wylie Stateman, supervising sound editor on *Memoirs of a Geisha*, had a difficult time because the actors did not speak English well. The dialogue editors worked hard to build the track using words, fragments, and even syllables. Stateman reported in *Millimeter* that, "The dialogue is made up of syllables that were gathered from multiple sources during production. There is rarely an intact line from a single take. It was about placement and rhythms and examining and re-examining and polishing each performance."

## Other Smoothing Techniques

If a dialogue track is intermittently noisy, you might need to add a steady noise and/or background sound to cover up the edit. In other words, you have to mess up the sound a lot more to make it flow throughout a single scene. Wind, rain, and other water sounds often interfere with dialogue tracks. If you can't get rid of these noises entirely, you have to keep the noises and often augment them to fool the audience. For example, picture a conversation in a park, late summer near twilight. There is a lone cricket on one side of the conversation, while on the other, recorded a few minutes later, there is a chorus of crickets. To smooth these edits, you would need to put the cricket chorus room tone onto the actor's track with the single lone noisemaker.

Adding background ambiences that fit the locations gives you a neutral filler to help smooth dialogue, too. You are essentially building your own room tone in an effort to match what occurred on location. Again, remember how the ear/brain tunes out steady noise so it can focus on human speech. Use that point to your advantage.

Related to this would be those occasions when a sound or noise gets on one side of a conversation but is missing from the other. For example, suppose a distant car-by is on the close-up dialogue from one actor, and a second actor's shot doesn't have the car on it. When cut together, the car-by comes out of nowhere, ends abruptly on some dialogue, and is missing completely in other cuts.

If you can't remove the noise with editing and/or appropriate noise reduction, you will have to mask it, or cover it up, using a sound effect. This technique falls into the discussion of sound effects, and therefore should be part of your effects mix. However, you might need to hear whether it works while editing and smoothing the dialogue. Go ahead and add the sound effect, keeping it separate from the dialogue and well-documented in your notes and on the timeline. You might want to remember to revisit this as you work on the sound effects later.

Positioning this effect means having it fit in with the already existing car sounds. You might need to start the sound effect well before the part where it's most noticeable on the dialogue track and extend it past the noisy dialogue so it sounds smooth and unobtrusive.

Figure 15.5 shows an example of a sound effects fill.

Matching dialogue from different locations is another difficult task. Many indie filmmakers will shoot part of a scene in one space and the rest elsewhere. I've worked on projects where two people are conversing, and each side of the conversation was shot in a different location at a different time. That means two different room tones and a difficult matching job. In this case smoothing each dialogue separately and then adding room tone from both might work. ADR is always a possibility, but costly. You might need to rely on a sound effects background (and/or music) to unify the scene.

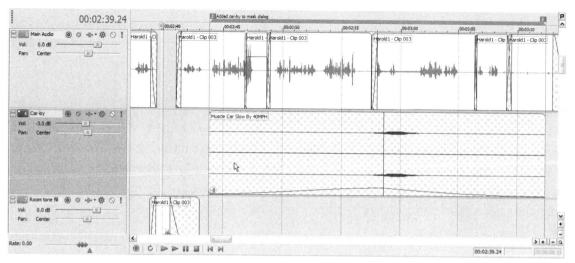

**Figure 15.5** Sound effects fill.

Worse still is matching a close mic with a far mic or matching two different mics entirely. A character wearing a lav while another is on a boom can be tricky to fit together. One will have a tight, warm sound (the lav), while the other will be more open and roomy (the boom). Trying to make the boom match the lav is very time consuming and sometimes nearly impossible. Instead, mess with the lav track (by using EQ and perhaps reverb) to make it more boom-like.

## Close Your Eyes and Hear

The best way to test your dialogue edits is to close your eyes and listen to the playback. It's too easy to anticipate an edit when you can see it coming up on the timeline. Problems really stand out when you take your eyes out of the equation. Visuals can hide some problems, which is fine for the viewing audience, but not for you, because it's your name on the credits!

Switching speakers, location in the listening room, or even lowering or boosting the volume can also give you a new perspective and let you subjectively evaluate your work. Resting your ears is another tactic, and while a long lunch can freshen your perception, I find the best rest for tired ears is a night's sleep. What sounded great at 5:00 p.m. one day often sounds less spectacular at 9:00 the next morning. I can't begin to tell you how many major changes I've made to a project I thought was "there" after I had a chance to step away and really hear it again. So, close those eyes and listen. If the edits can pass that test, you are on the right track. If it sucks with your eyes closed, you need to get back to work.

Although I said earlier that I despise headphones for critical audio tasks, there is some merit to listening to some soundtrack elements through decent cans. Depending on your monitoring situation, you might miss some of those pesky little noises that can be on your recordings. Headphones quickly expose these pops, smacks, clicks, and other glitches, enabling you to deal with them using the techniques discussed later in this chapter. Headphones are also required where your work will disturb others, such as in an office or a classroom situation. Of course, a good monitoring system with properly calibrated monitors and a consistent monitoring level will expose these issues, too.

## Dialogue and Phase

Another problem that you might run into with dialogue is phase. When two mics are near one another, they interact in constructive and destructive ways. This situation creates an acoustic comb filter that sounds tinny, hollow and swishy/swirly or phase-y. This will be pronounced in mono, which is where dialogue ends up either in a dedicated center channel in surround or in the phantom center of a stereo mix.

One fix for this is to carefully intercut the mics and/or use volume automation changes to make sure only one mic is on at a time. Figure 15.6 shows volume correction for out-of-phase mics. By eliminating one mic, the phase issue goes away. The tracks will be less noisy because there won't be the noise from both mics on simultaneously. The downside to this is that if the dialogue goes back and forth, or if there are overlaps between characters speaking, it can take a lot of effort to clean this up. Use those JLX techniques, room-tone fill, and volume to make the segment sound smooth.

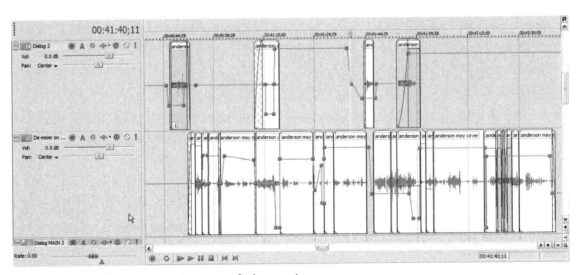

**Figure 15.6**  Volume-correcting out-of-phase mics.

Depending on your software, you may be able to invert the phase of one mic in relation to the other. This may help to overcome the problem. More often than not, though, mics are not exactly 180 degrees out of phase. Employing a software tool such as the Little Labs IBP Phase Alignment Tool (www.uaudio.com) provides more control over minute phase adjustments.

You might also receive "stereo" dialogue on audio tracks that are not true stereo. This can be either two mics routed to separate camera channels (two-track/twin-track/dual-mono) or out-of-phase audio.

You can't depend on the fact that your soundtrack will always play in stereo or surround. There are plenty of mono listeners out there (not to mention incorrectly wired, out-of-phase speakers) that will make your soundtrack not work. Plus, voices belong in the center, not panned to stereo left/right. Always check mono compatibility on everything you do!

For example, I worked on the soundtrack to an indie film in which all dialogue was recorded directly to the camera. The finished recordings appeared as stereo on the time-line, but when summed together—adding the left and right together to form a monaural signal—all the dialogue disappeared. The problem in this case arose from using a single mic on the set that terminated in an XLR plug. The camera only accepted a 1/8-inch mini. The person who created the adapter cable wired it incorrectly, leaving the sound in the left and right channels exactly 180 degrees out of phase. Essentially, that meant that when the left channel was at maximum compression (positive amplitude), the right channel was at maximum rarefaction (negative amplitude), which added up to no sound. And while the dialogue in "stereo" or two-channel sounded fine (if a little too stereo-wide), the mono file left only sound effects and music, with no dialogue. The fix was to choose only one channel, either left or right, and eliminate the other channel. This made the dialogue mono, as it should be, and it was completely mono compatible. Whew!

In another case, I received audio that appeared as stereo but had been treated to some plug-in to get rid of noise, according to the client. Instead, this process created a phase issue such that, when in mono, the dialogue disappeared altogether. In this case I went back to the original audio and ran my own noise reduction techniques to solve the compatibility issue.

Sound Forge includes a handy phase meter that illustrates the mono compatibility of a stereo file. You want the meter to be in the middle or leaning toward the right. Mono-compatibility issues show when the meter is at the far-left −1.0 range, as Figure 15.7 illustrates. The file playing here is the badly wired cable audio example mentioned a moment ago, completely out of phase and having no mono compatibility at all.

Another common dialogue issue comes from routing different mics to different channels at the recorder or camera. This is a very good procedure in the field, but it has a downside in the editing suite. If two actors wear lavalieres, and you record their audio separately to the left and right camera channels, they will show up as hard-panned stereo on the timeline—one voice will come from the left speaker and the other voice will come from the right. While the Beatles often put vocals on one side and instruments on the other with their early stereo records, it's not the correct approach for today's modern soundtracks. We want the dialogue anchored to the middle of the screen so that no matter where the audience sits in a room, the voice comes from the screen itself and not the sides (as in hard-panned stereo).

You need to convert these stereo files to mono and/or split them off to separate tracks and pan them back to the center where they belong. The added benefit to this approach

**Figure 15.7**  Phase meter.

is that you remove the unused channels from their respective recordings, which can cut down on noise and phase issues, resulting in a better product in the end.

Figures 15.8 and 15.9 show before-and-after examples of split audio.

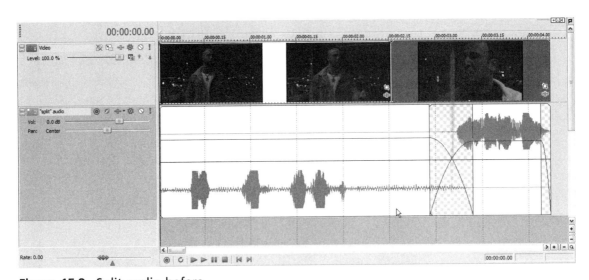

**Figure 15.8**  Split audio before.

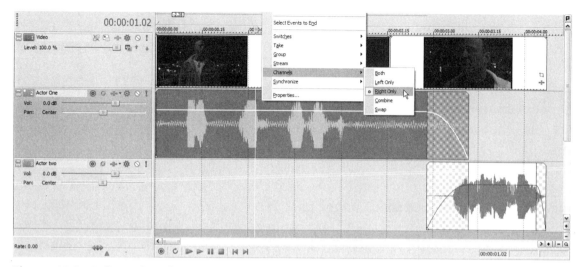

**Figure 15.9**  Split audio after.

**Special Note about Sound Effects from Production:** You might run into certain sound effects, such as clothing rustles and other prop sounds, along with more noticeable sounds, such as doors closing and so forth, that work their way onto your dialogue tracks. Usually, you will replace these later with suitable sound effects of better quality. However, some of these field recording sounds may make it all the way to the final mix. If you can, you might want to separate these sounds from the dialogue tracks to their own timeline track(s). That gives you greater control over them when you start to pull together the sound effects for the final mix.

This is especially important for a foreign-language dub because all original dialogue gets muted and kept out of the new language mix. That means any sound effects that are part of the original dialogue will be muted, too. These will be missing from the mix, resulting in an inferior final soundtrack.

Also keep in mind that production sound effects—those recorded during the original shoot—will have room tone on them. However, a foreign-language dub will remove all room tone from the original language dialogue track. Therefore, production sound effects that fit in nicely with the original dialog (and its room tone) may now stand out as being noisier or different from other sound effects and/or the newly recorded foreign-language track.

# Fixing Common Dialogue Ills

Noise—it's all around us. And it gets into every single one of our video recordings. Don't you often wish there was some magic switch in your DAW/NLE that could just turn off all that noise? Well, there may not be a single switch, but there are myriad tools you can use to reduce noise in your recordings and make your audio shine.

Our ears, along with our brains, are rather adept at ignoring the noise around us. It's called the *party effect*. You're in a crowded room where everybody is talking, yet you can still focus on the conversation you are having and ignore all that's going on around you. If your conversation gets boring, you can turn off that person and try to listen to other conversations nearby. Even now, as you're reading, you're focused on your inner voice and—hopefully—ignoring the other sounds around you. Take a minute to listen to your room. Perhaps there's air-conditioning noise, a computer fan, music playing, a distant conversation, traffic, and other environmental sounds. You were able to ignore these sounds. Of course, now that I've pointed them out to you, you're hearing them rather strongly. Try to focus back on the page. Your ear and brain combination works rather well, doesn't it? Unfortunately, microphones don't discriminate like our ears do. They pick up everything. And that's the problem we face in field recording. No matter how hard you try, you are going to record some unwanted noises.

What you want to do is reduce this interference as much as possible in the field while you still can. And then, the tricks you'll learn here will go a long way toward making your audio even better.

Generally, it is easier to mess up good, clean sound than to fix bad sound. For example, some people do not like the deep, resonant, in-your-face quality of a lavaliere microphone on talent. Using a shotgun on a boom can open up the sound a little and put more "room" on the recording. However, bad boom work has its own problems. For me, I'd still reach for the body mic and then add some room to the recording in post via a reverb plug-in. This will make the dry lav sound fit better in the mix.

How do you define noise? I have a simple definition: Noise is everything that you don't want that gets onto your recordings. For example, when recording a voice, you don't want air-conditioning fan noise on the track. Of course, if you're recording an air-conditioner sound effect, you don't want extraneous voices on the recording either. Therefore, focus on getting the wanted sounds, and work very hard to reduce or eliminate the unwanted noises in the field while you can.

Some noises survive to the post process; the following sections discuss some common ones and their solutions. Some, such as popped plosives, might not be the usual noises you think about. They are nevertheless bothersome and therefore need some work. We'll also look at the most common noises—hum, background sounds, and excessive echo—and examine ways to reduce or eliminate their destructive influence.

Also note that these same techniques apply to restoring "old" audio, not just salvaging "new" audio that was recorded with problems.

---

**Special Note on Workflow:** You can apply some of the fixes using real-time plug-ins placed on the track or bus level. However, you might prefer to do your clean-up work outside of the multitrack DAW/NLE environment, using a dedicated mono/stereo audio editor. Alternatively, you might choose to apply certain effects destructively to your audio files. With either of these last two approaches, you make permanent changes to the files. Therefore, make sure you work on *copies* of the files to protect the originals from permanent damage. Update the DAW/NLE timeline with these new, updated files when completed. Be aware that should you make edits in the audio offline, you risk losing lip sync when you bring that audio back to the DAW/NLE. You can't simply cut out a noise. You must use mute instead to keep the time base correct.

## DC Offset

When you work in a mono or two-track audio editing software application, always run a DC offset utility to make sure that the zero crossing is correctly aligned. Sometimes a waveform gets misaligned because DC current gets added during the digitizing process. When you make edits or perform other effect work, this misalignment can cause clicks, pops, or glitches. Run the DC offset utility to prevent this from happening.

Also, when editing in this manner, *always* make edits and/or apply effects with both ends of your selections at a zero crossing—where the waveform crosses the center line. If you don't do this, you risk getting audible glitches. DAWs and NLEs compensate for this by placing short fade-ins/fade-outs at edit points, but an editor such as Sound Forge does not.

## Sibilance

Many people have natural sibilance—the excessive S sound that can positively hiss and sizzle in some recordings. Female voices and children tend to suffer from this malady, but male voices are not immune. Some microphones may accentuate this noise. Usually, a swap to a different mic and/or preamp can lessen or eliminate sibilance in a recording. If it is too late for that, you need to employ a post fix to correct the issue.

At first it might seem prudent to just reduce the S sounds using an equalization filter that can zero in on the troublesome frequencies. This can work in some instances, but may result in a dull-sounding recording if the EQ fix is too strong. What would work for killing the sibilance will also affect the rest of the sound file.

What if you could turn down the sibilance only when it's present and leave the rest of the audio unaffected? Frequency-dependent compression, more commonly called *de-essing*, does just that. As noted earlier, compression reduces the volume of loud sounds, creating a steadier, more even level. Frequency-dependent compression only pulls down the volume of sounds that fall within a specified frequency range. It's like a dynamic EQ, reducing certain sounds—such as sibilance—and leaving the other sounds alone.

Settings for a plug-in de-esser vary by manufacturer, but the key to making this work is finding the right frequency to compress. A de-esser that lets you sweep through frequencies like an EQ and evaluate the results is best. You should also be able to adjust the threshold for certain sounds and determine how much the S sounds should be pulled back. Too much de-essing will sound unnatural, as if a pillow were being placed and removed from in front of the speaker's mouth. Or it could sound much worse—try dialing in some extreme de-essing sounds, and you'll hear what I mean.

The freeware Spitfish de-esser from DigitalFishPhones (www.digitalfishphones.com) has a unique tool that I find very helpful when setting up the plug-in on dialogue. You can listen to what is being cut out instead of what's left. Figure 15.10 shows a shot of the Spitfish de-esser. Enable the Listen feature and check for the loudest sibilance, adjusting the controls as needed. Once again, the frequency setting is the most critical and will change from person to person. You should only hear the annoying S energy. If you hear other sounds or parts of words, you need to back off on the settings. Turn off the Listen function, and then you can check the final file, minus the sibilance, and tweak settings again as needed.

**Figure 15.10** Spitfish de-esser.

You can apply de-essing either on a file basis or in real time if your NLE/DAW supports this. I often set up a de-esser on a track and move any dialogue for a particular person that needs fixing to that track. Rarely will one setting be ideal for more than a single person, so you may have several instances of de-essing in place to deal with different people and/or situations. If it's a one-shot problem, I may just fix that segment offline using a copy of the original media and replace the sibilant file with the new fix on the timeline.

## Popped P's (and B's and T's)

Close on the heels of sibilance are annoying pops that can occur on certain plosive consonant sounds, most notably P's, B's, and T's. The issue stems from air slamming into the microphone's diaphragm with such force that it creates an undesirable pop or clunk on the recording. This problem is more common on VOs or handheld interviews when the microphone is closer to the mouth. Lavaliere and boom work rarely suffers from this problem.

Once again, address the issue from the start by placing a suitable pop filter between the actor's lips and the mic. Additionally, some mics are more poppy than others, so swapping out a different model might work, as can moving the mic to the side slightly to reduce the effects of wind hitting the mic diaphragm dead-on. A final measure would be to tape a pencil to the front of the microphone to diffuse the air and reduce the popped consonants.

Despite your efforts, you might still have some pops to eliminate. There are actually several techniques you can use. Your first possibility is to simply edit the pop right out or mute it, which is usually quite effective on words that start with a P, for example. The pop is quite easy to spot in the waveform display because it doesn't look like the surrounding waveform. Instead of cutting out the pop, a well-placed fade-in or a brief volume dip that starts before the plosive can work and sometimes sound smoother, too. Figure 15.11 shows how lowering the volume on just the popped P can work.

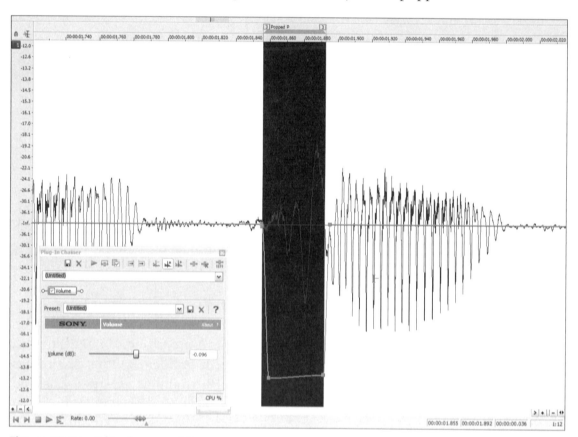

**Figure 15.11**   Edited popped P.

Select the pop, being careful to get only the nasty part, and delete it, mute it, or use volume automation to reduce it in level substantially. Some DAWs have a Pencil tool to literally redraw the sound and make it right. Be aware that if you grab too much of the plosive, you might eliminate the consonant altogether, resulting in an "opped" P, for example. Let your ears be the judge.

You can also use multi-band compression, similar to the fix for sibilance. With plosives, though, the sound is low-frequency, and a low-frequency shelf EQ works better than the more precise EQ setting used for de-essing. Figure 15.12 shows a multi-band being used to reduce plosives. Even just a high-pass EQ might be all that's needed to reduce the plosives, eliminating the need to use the compressor section.

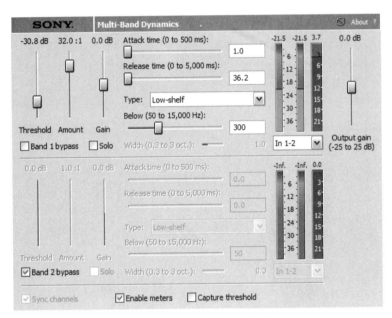

**Figure 15.12**   A multi-band to reduce plosives.

Yet another tool that can work in some cases is a click and crackle removal tool, such as those designed to eliminate noise from vinyl recordings. There's more detail about using this later in this chapter; it can be a versatile tool.

## Mouth Noises (Breaths, Lip Smacks, and Other Vocal Garbage)

Some people have noisy mouths, and mics are all too good at picking that up. Close-up microphone work, such as interviews and voiceovers, is more prone to mouth noises, such as excessive breathing, lip smacks, and tongue/teeth problems. Other recordings are susceptible to these undesirables, too. Therefore, this is almost always a post fix; there's little you can do on set to preempt it.

Breaths can be either eliminated completely or reduced in volume. I'm not talking about deleting every breath. Rather, consider addressing those annoying sharp intakes that feel out of place at the starts of sentences and loud catch breaths (gasps!) that talent sometimes needs to finish a long or difficult sentence. These are the breaths that stick out the most. Take care of those, and your tracks may work better.

Lip smacks come from opening the mouth loudly before speaking. Like plosives, they are easy to spot on the waveform display and even simpler to select and delete or mute (see Figure 15.13). Other noises can often be spotted by their sharp waveform displays and can be similarly treated.

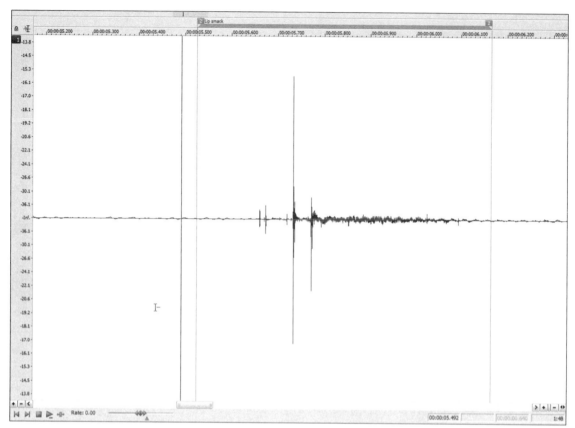

**Figure 15.13** Lip smack.

---

**Special Note about Edits and Room Tone:** Be aware that when you eliminate breaths, lip smacks, and other noises from a location dialogue track, you are also deleting room tone. You most certainly will need to fill in the missing room tone to make the edits convincing. On a studio VO recording, the room tone will be virtually nonexistent, so you usually can get away without the room-tone fill.

---

An automatic way to eliminate some of these sounds, especially on quiet studio recordings, is to use a noise gate. Put simply, a noise gate looks at a specific volume level, called a *threshold*. Any sounds above this setting are let through (the gate is open), and sounds falling below the level are turned off (the gate is closed). Additionally, you can set how quickly a gate opens (attack) and how quickly/slowly it closes (release). Figure 15.14 shows the typical noise-gate controls.

To set a noise gate threshold, start with it fully open. Play the file and raise the threshold until the voice sounds fine but the noise goes away between phrases or during silent

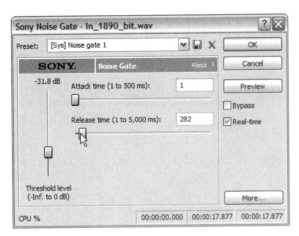

**Figure 15.14**  Noise gate.

passages. You can also look at the meters for the lowest-level sound, set the threshold a little below that, and tweak as needed. Adjust the attack and release controls to smooth the opening and closing of the gate.

If you set this correctly, you can grab many low-level breaths, lip smacks, and other noises and eliminate them. However, if you set it incorrectly, you risk chopping off words or parts of words (such as turning a word like "stop" into "tah" because both the s and p are far lower in level than the middle "tah.") *Always* check how the gate affects every word and back off on the threshold or extend the release time to make sure you don't eliminate what needs to be kept.

A noise gate will be ineffective against tracks filled with steady noise, such as traffic; use other noise reduction tools to overcome those types of sounds (discussed in the section on using dedicated noise reduction later in this chapter). Remember, a gate only mutes noise when other sounds are absent. This noise continues when the talent speaks. Hopefully, the sound of the voice will cover up the noise sufficiently. When it doesn't you will hear the noise gate working, cutting in and out in a noticeable and annoying manner. This often draws more attention to the noise, because it is constantly coming in and out. Audiences are more oblivious to steady noise than to the staccato artifacts of noise gates. Adjust the controls to make it sound smooth or stop using the gate completely and resort to other techniques, such as using an expander instead (explained in the next section). However, a noise gate can be very effective on otherwise quiet recordings. Applying a noise gate to eliminate people not speaking, but who still have their mic on, can quickly make noisy tracks sound cleaner. For example, Person A is on mic and speaking while Person B is off mic and not speaking. The A dialogue will bleed slightly into the B mic. Gate the B mic and keep the A dialogue off of it. (This also can help overcome some phase issues between multiple mics, as mentioned earlier.) You can often gate bleed caused by too loud of headphones used during VO and ADR recordings, too.

## Expansion

Expansion is often a better choice than a noise gate for dealing with low-level, undesirable noise. An expander is essentially a noise gate that doesn't close and instead turns down quiet sounds, making them even quieter. Figure 15.15 shows an expander at work as part of a full channel-strip plug-in. The figure shows about 12 dB of expansion, which means that the quiet parts are being turned down a further 12 dB, making them even lower in volume. Functionally, expansion is the opposite of compression (which turns down loud sounds). However, using expanders is not a substitute for good, clean dialogue editing. It's best to smooth dialogue first using the aforementioned techniques. Then, late in the dialogue-editing stage, or even the mixing stage, use expansion to further reduce noise in the dialogue channels.

Setting the threshold for the expander can be tricky because it can lower the volume of the good audio as well. And if you are not careful, there might be a rush of noise that pops in when the dialogue cuts back in, too. You are counting on the dialogue itself covering up or masking these noise jumps. It doesn't always work that way, though. When it does, an expander can make the final dialogue even quieter after all your smoothing and other noise reduction is finished. It's the icing on the cake!

**Figure 15.15** Expander working.

Note that expansion will affect room tone, so you might need to apply it across multiple tracks (or even on the bus level) to be truly effective. Expansion can work well on noisy tracks but really shines on dialogue recorded on a quiet set and/or location, which is a rarity these days. Expansion can actually make the dialogue smooth and whisper-quiet with minimum effort. When that happens, rejoice in how a digital tool can make your work easier—because without its help, you will be doing all the expansion and dialogue smoothing manually.

A carefully drawn volume automation envelope can also work for removing extraneous noise between words, phrases, and sentences. Although it is not automatic like an expander or gate—you have to physically add this—taking this approach might be better when you require a simple, quick fix. Volume automation level adjustments also can reduce loud breaths when you don't want to eliminate them completely.

## Too Much Reverb

Excessive reverb, resulting from sound swimming around a large room and being picked up by the microphone, makes the voice sound distant and indistinct. Next time, move the mic closer to the subject. Expansion can also help reduce this excessive reverb. This fix won't be perfect, but it works reasonably well when other methods are unavailable.

Start with EQ and find the room resonance, essentially the "sound" of the room itself. Use a parametric EQ to boost one of the parametric band gains up 15 dB, set its Q or width to one octave, and set a starting frequency of 100 Hz. Play the file, sweep the frequency slowly, and listen. Try to find where the sound of the room sits. This resonance will usually sound considerably louder as you reach it while sweeping the frequency. Ignore any distortion or clipping as you perform this task. When you find the pesky frequency where most of the room reverb sits, pull down the gain slider all the way and tighten the width a little. Do note that it is usually low to mid frequencies in the 400- to 1,200-Hz range that are the real culprits. This notch filter can help take some of the room out of the recording, which effectively makes the voice track seem a bit closer.

You might want to bump speech intelligibility a bit, because this often get lost in the reverb. (This is explained later in this chapter, in its own section.) A little warmth in the 150-Hz range for males and the 300-Hz range for females can make the voice sound fuller, too. Don't boost these frequencies if this is where the room lies, obviously. Next, use expansion with a 2:1 or 3:1 ratio, adjusting the threshold until the reverb tail disappears at the ends of words and phrases.

Another really cool tool that works wonders on this phenomenon is the SPL Transient Designer, available as a Universal Audio plug-in (see Figure 15.16). It lets you reshape the sound, pulling reverb down considerably while bumping the attack up a bit to make the voice sound crisper and less mushy. It works surprisingly well for many reverb-y situations.

**Figure 15.16**   SPL Transient Designer.

## Rumble and Hiss

Two of the most annoying noises, extreme low-frequency rumble and high-frequency electronic hiss, are easily handled.

A low-cut/high-pass filter will take care of the low-frequency garbage, and a high-cut/ low-pass filter will reduce the high-end hiss. Many field recorders, mixers, and some microphones have a high-pass/low-cut filter that you can employ while on location. This is almost always a good idea. You can, of course, also use these filters in post.

For dialogue, set the high-pass around 80 Hz and try to move it higher in frequency if you can. Listen to the voice carefully and make sure you are not thinning it out. What you should hear is something akin to lifting a heavy curtain away from the background noise. The filter should not affect the vocal quality at all. If it does, lower the frequency of the filter and reevaluate the tonal quality. For the low-pass, start around 12 kHz. Don't dip below 10 kHz, but you can set it higher than 12 kHz if needed. You can see these cut filters in place in the upper-right corner of Figure 15.15.

These EQ fixes affect both dialogue and room tone, so if you apply them to one track, you must apply them to the others. Similarly, if you apply them to one mic, you need to apply them to a second mic used in the same scene. Often you can just put these filters on the bus level and run all dialogue, including room tone, through them.

**Special Note on Runaway Woofers:** If you glance over and see your woofers moving in and out excessively during a quiet section of dialogue, you have some extreme low-frequency sounds that you can't hear but that are still present on the recording. You might say, "I can't hear it so...so what, right?" WRONG! This sub- or infra-sonic information takes up space in your mix and can prevent you from getting suitable levels later. Why? Because these unheard low frequencies still affect the dynamic range, putting constraints on the overall volume. Your woofer is trying to play them, hence the crazy vibrating, but they don't contribute to the overall enjoyment of the piece.

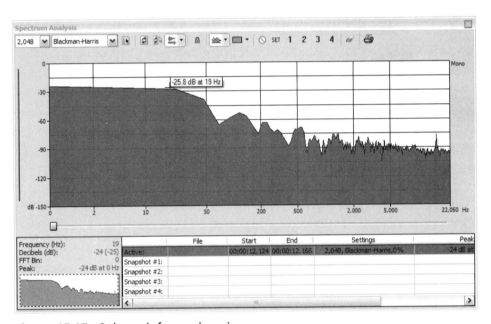

**Figure 15.17** Sub- or infra-sonic noise.

Use a Spectrum Analysis tool to see these anomalies that you can't otherwise hear. Figure 15.17 shows an example of subsonic noise. Notice the excessive low-frequency content that's below the range of human hearing (20 Hz). Remove subsonic information with an aggressive high-pass/low-cut filter. You might need to use multiple EQs or several offline passes with different settings to eliminate these troublesome frequencies altogether.

## Tonal Fixes

There might be instances in which there is an annoying quality to a particular voice track. This may be something in the talent's vocal quality, an on-set noise, or the artifacts of poor or improper mic techniques. For example, a lavaliere hidden under many layers of clothing may sound muffled and dull. You might then reach for EQ to boost some of the missing brightness.

However, be very aware that if you EQ one mic of dialogue, you *might* make it harder to edit another mic from the same place. The EQ differences make blending the mics and the room tone difficult.

That said, EQ may in some cases make smoothing dialogue between multiple mics *easier*, because using EQ can help you compensate for problems with one mic versus another. The only way to tell is to try the fixes and compare them. If the EQ fixes sound better, then you are on the right track.

Also note that on some dialogue, your need to use radical EQ to fix problems can sometimes be successfully disguised with room tone or perhaps a sound effects background. Always keep the whole mix in mind as you make adjustments.

By the way, it is often better to cut EQ than to boost; it sounds more natural. So, if you find yourself needing to bump up 3 to 4 kHz to overcome a muffled lav, you might try cutting around 650 Hz to eliminate the mud instead. Figure 15.18 shows an example of an EQ fix with both high- and low-pass filters, a cut in the "mud range" (where things sound dull), and a slight boost for speech intelligibility.

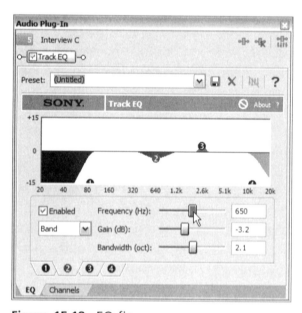

**Figure 15.18**   EQ fix.

Also, changing EQ can change volume levels, so keep an eye on meters to make sure you are not clipping. Even extensive cutting with EQ can result in a louder file. I know that doesn't make sense, but it is nevertheless quite true. Watch those levels post EQ!

## Better Speech Intelligibility

Having trouble understanding a line? Try an EQ boost around 2.5 kHz, which brings out consonants, making the words a little easier to understand. You may need to adjust the frequency and the Q width for the best results. It's not a miracle cure, but it can help in some circumstances.

If the dialogue competes with another sound element, such as music, removing a few dBs at 2.5 kHz from the competing track (music) can help the voice cut through better. This might be something you do at the mixing stage, though.

Is the voice a little thin-sounding? For males, boost EQ about 2 to 4 dB at 160 Hz. Try adding about 2 to 4 dB at 320 Hz for females. These are general guidelines, so let your ears be the judge of whether the EQ makes the voice fuller.

For dull voice recordings, cut at 640 Hz and/or boost a bit around 3 to 4 kHz and perhaps again between 10 and 12 kHz. You should avoid boosting in the 5- to 9-kHz range, because this is typically where sibilance resides.

## EQ One File with Another

Some EQ plug-ins let you save the EQ properties from one file and apply them to another. This can be very useful when you are trying to match the quality of one recording with another. For example, you might have an on-camera line that is very crisp and then a slightly off-camera line that is dull. This typically results from a changing mic perspective, where the mic was moved radically for the second shot. Grabbing the EQ of the first shot's audio and then applying it to the second shot's audio can make the dialogue edit together more smoothly. For example, iZotope Ozone 4 has this functionality, letting you grab a snapshot of the EQ curve from one file and then apply that same snapshot to another. It's a very handy tool that takes the guesswork and time-consuming nature out of using EQ manually.

## Clicks, Glitches, and Pop Removal

Clicks, short pops, and other glitches are another aggravation from both studio- and field-recorded dialogue tracks. They may manifest themselves as digital glitches, drop-out pops from wireless mics, or even mouth noises, such as the tongue striking the roof of the mouth, resulting in an odd click. Since they happen *during* a word or phrase, you can't simply edit them out as you did with other noises. Use a plug-in that helps remove clicks or crackles, such as Waves X-Click, Sony Noise Reduction Click and Crackle Remover, or iZotope RX, shown in Figure 15.19, which includes a de-clicker.

These tools were primarily designed for vinyl restoration—to remove the annoying clicks, crackles, and pops inherent in those analog discs. However, these same tools work wonders on other ticks, digital glitches, and often nasty mouth noises. They also work on crackle caused by faulty connecting cables and even some mic-handling noises, too.

It might seem quite strange to apply vinyl-restoration tools to voice, but if you really focus on the noise you are trying to eliminate, you'll find the plug-in choice makes

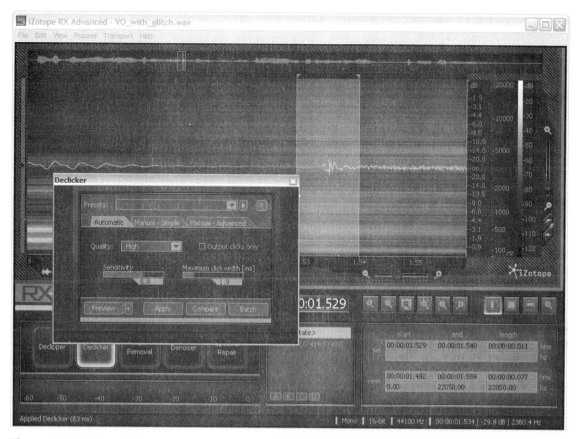

**Figure 15.19**  De-clicker.

perfect sense. Listen to the noise. What's there? Now choose the best tool based on what you hear, regardless of its original design intentions.

If you can, choose a click and crackle tool that enables you to monitor what's being cut out rather than just what's left. This listen-or-monitor-output feature is critical. Engage it and then adjust the controls and listen for odd and seemingly random clicks. If you hear whole words that are recognizable or even parts of words, you are trying to do too much click/crackle removal. Back off a little; you just want to capture the clicks/ crackles.

Refresh your perspective by turning off the listening feature and alternate bypassing and activating the plug-in to hear the before and after results. If it sounds better, it probably is. If it's worse, you're on the wrong track. When you apply the effect, you'll see obviously visible glitches disappear from the waveform display without changing the voice quality at all. Though some of these de-clicker effects function in real time, I typically apply them offline, saving the fixed file to a new name and updating the DAW/NLE timeline accordingly.

To a certain extent, a click/crackle removal tool can also reduce the annoying compressor distortion in recordings made with automatic gain control (AGC) and with some mixer/recorder/camera limiters, too. AGC works by boosting the volume until the sound crosses a threshold. The AGC also pulls down the volume to prevent overloading past digital zero. The limiters just pull down the volume on excessive peaks to avoid distortion. Unfortunately, the downside of AGC/limiters is that they sometimes make a kind of harsh sucking sound as the circuit pulls the level down too quickly. Apply the click/crackle tool to take the hard edge off this unpleasant artifact. And while the post-fixed audio will never be as good as a properly set manual level, it can make the AGC/limiter recording more tolerable.

## Repairing Clipped Peaks (Distortion)

When digital audio goes beyond 0 dBFS, the waveform gets squared at the top as if somebody clipped off the top of the waveform with scissors. This is even called *clipping* or *clipped peaks*, and the result is a very nasty, harsh distortion. Just as it is impossible to make a silk purse out of a sow's ear, it is nearly impossible to fix badly distorted audio. That's because there is no detail left to recover; it was cut off. A visual equivalent is over-exposed white in the video world. Although you can bring the level of the white down and darken it, you won't recover any detail from the image. It will always be a white blob. In audio, you can lower the volume of the clipped peak, but as with the visual example, you won't recover any detail and instead will be left with distorted audio, as shown in Figure 15.20.

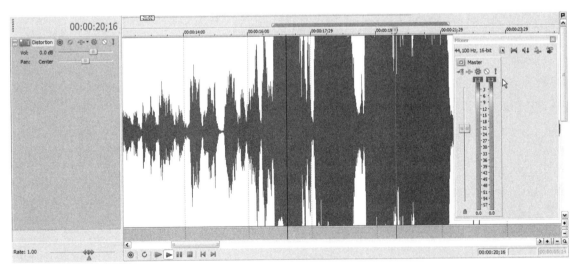

**Figure 15.20**   Distortion.

With this distorted dialogue, your best approach is to re-record it via ADR. But what if that is impossible? It'll never be perfect, but you can sometimes make listening to the lines more tolerable for your audience. Make sure you actually need the section where there is clipped peak distortion. This may be a lip smack, cough, or other noise problem that can be eliminated altogether. Can you replace the distorted lines with alternate takes or steal words—even parts of words—from other places?

Is it only a short, passing clip? Thankfully, these occasional and brief clipped peaks can be recovered in a way that doesn't sound too bad. Some audio editing software includes a Pencil tool that lets you literally draw the peak out. Figure 15.21 shows an example of redrawing a waveform to remove a brief clipped peak. When using the Pencil, try to match the shape of the waveform directly adjacent to the clipped one. Remember that audio can clip both at the top and the bottom of the waveform display. Play back the results to make sure everything sounds good.

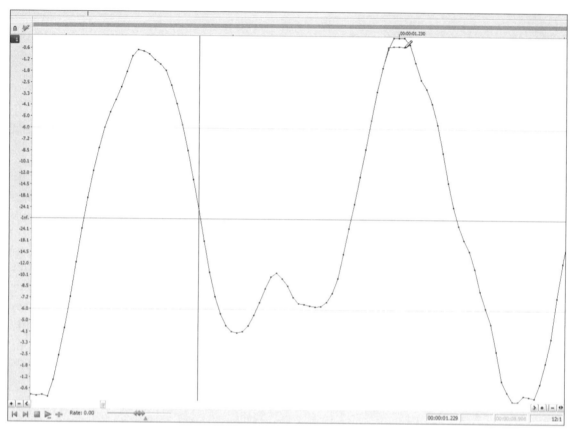

**Figure 15.21**   Pencil-drawn clips.

Apply a little EQ to help take the edge off the harsh sound of mild distortion (see Figure 15.22). Try a sharp notch filter around 1,000 Hz. Apply another notch around 7 kHz too, if it sounds better. If not, don't. Keep these notches narrow, because they will affect the surrounding good speech, too. You might also have good luck applying some click/crackle remover (as mentioned earlier) to soften some of the hard sounds of the distortion. This works surprisingly well *after* applying the EQ first.

It is quite tricky—if not impossible—to make fixing long sequences of horribly distorted dialogue sound convincing. You need a dedicated clipped-peak restoration tool, such as iZotope RX, which includes a Declipper. Essentially, you indicate the threshold where the clipping occurs and then apply a makeup gain, because the fixing

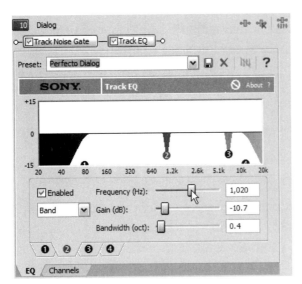

**Figure 15.22** EQ for clipping.

process pulls the level down; you need to boost the overall level back up. There may be more or fewer parameters, but generally you just tweak until it sounds better. Consign yourself to knowing that it will never be as good as well-recorded dialogue; these fixes are marginal at best.

Often, applying two (or more) passes of the Declipper with different parameter settings can result in a better-sounding file. Using the EQ and click/crackle fixes from earlier can also make the final file sound its best. Figure 15.23 shows the result of two passes of Declipper processing (after using both EQ and click/crackle remover) on the horribly distorted file shown in Figure 15.20. But trust me, it doesn't sound as good as it looks in the picture.

## Hum

The noise from 50- to 60-Hz electrical hum is truly the most annoying sound to utterly ruin your recordings. It is also one of the hardest problems to fix. You might say that using EQ to notch out the errant frequency is all it takes—and sometimes that is true. Unfortunately, more times than not, EQ alone won't work. The real issue is that there is not just 60-cycle hum. There are also multiples of that hum frequency, called *harmonics*, including 120 Hz, 180 Hz, 240 Hz, 300 Hz, and so on. To combat this, use an EQ that allows for very narrow notches and can address the fundamental and harmonic frequencies at the same time. Once again, a plug-in such as iZotope RX has such a Hum Removal tool (see Figure 15.24).

Also, in Figure 15.24, notice the banding in the spectrogram display that clearly shows the pattern of harmonics in a voice track that has hum on it.

As you make adjustments, be careful when the hum harmonics enter the realm of voice, making it sound funny. Back off on those higher harmonics as needed. This might

**Figure 15.23**   Declipper.

result in a compromise between eliminating the hum and maintaining an acceptable vocal quality.

Another tool that can work on hum is one you might not consider: chorus. Guitarists use this effect to make their guitars sound richer. Why would you use it on a voice track with hum? The plug-in essentially works by delaying the sound slightly and adding it back on top of itself. It's the delay time that matters, so zero out/turn off any other parameters. Set the delay to 8.33 ms (milliseconds) and you'll hear the result. You might try reversing the phase of the chorus to hear whether the result sounds better. See Figure 15.25 for an example of using a basic chorus plug-in to remove hum. Alternatively, duplicate the track on an NLE/DAW timeline and offset one copy by the same amount (if your DAW/NLE supports this fine adjustment) instead of using the Chorus tool.

Neither method is better; they both work. Unfortunately, there might be some leftover artifacts—a kind of robotic, metal sound—that you will have to accept. Adjust the level between the original (dry) sound and the effect (wet) until you reach the best overall result with good hum removal and less noticeable artifacts.

If these tricks don't work for you, try a dedicated noise reduction tool. It might be the best bet for getting rid of annoying hum. Figure 15.26 shows the positive results of

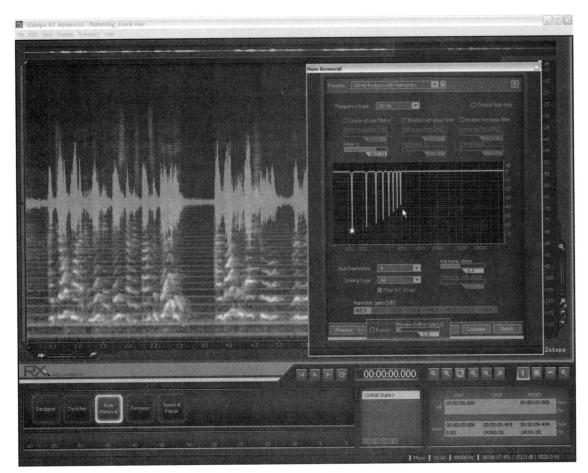

**Figure 15.24**   Hum removal.

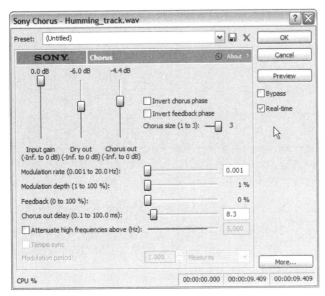

**Figure 15.25**   Chorus hum tool.

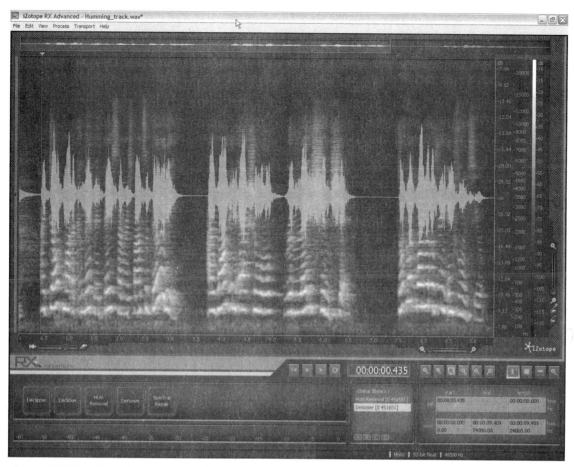

**Figure 15.26**   After hum removal.

applying the harmonic notch EQ first and then using dedicated noise reduction on the file shown in Figure 15.24. Especially notice how the banding was reduced significantly and the noise is now missing from between the phrases. Best of all, it sounds much, much better.

## Time Compression/Expansion

Occasionally, needs arise for changing the time base or duration of a voice file. You may do this with voiceovers or ADR (to get a line or parts of one to fit better). Rarely, if ever, will you apply time compression or expansion to dialogue because of the obvious loss of lip sync. Exceptions would include speeding up or slowing down voice to match undercranked/overcranked special effects—in other words, fast or slow motion.

A time stretch plug-in allow you to change the duration, usually as a percentage of the original (see Figure 15.27). Various algorithms or modes help to minimize the artifacts caused by the stretching/shrinking. These are necessary because the plug-in alters pitch (to keep it the same) while changing the duration. A shift of five to eight percent is hardly noticeable, but beyond that, the trick draws attention to itself.

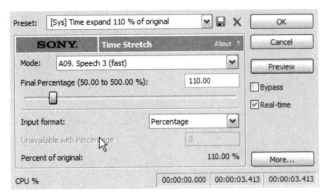

**Figure 15.27**   Time stretch.

Generally, I prefer tighter or looser sound editing rather than resorting to this fix. Need a second? Cut out three one-thirds of a second by shortening pauses and/or grabbing dead space between phrases and even between words. Add silence (or room tone) in a similar manner (lengthen pauses) to stretch time and therefore extend the duration.

## Pitch Shift

A pitch shift plug-in lets you change the apparent gender and/or age of a voice or create evil bad guys or singing furry creatures in the extreme. Pitch shifting also can alter voices in unique ways for various alien and otherworldly effects. One solid use of pitch shifting is to double certain bass sound effects an octave lower and mix them with the originals for a heavier sound.

Figure 15.28 shows an example of pitch shifting. You usually get the option to preserve duration when changing the pitch, which is a requirement for lip sync. Much like time stretching/expansion, shifting pitch sounds better in smaller increments (less than a musical third up or down). Most settings use musical terms for the pitch shift amount, typically in semitones (white key to black key on a piano) and fractions thereof.

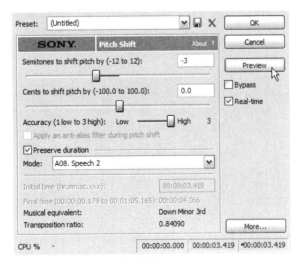

**Figure 15.28**   Pitch shift.

## Volume

When working on dialogue, you will have myriad volume inconsistencies to deal with. I only mention that here to keep this section complete. The fix for volume is very simple no matter what NLE/DAW you use. There is usually a slider, knob, or other control that you can adjust to boost or cut volume. You want to even things out as much as possible now, but understand that the final volume balance comes at the mixing stage. Get the dialogue smooth and consistent and strive to match volume to the screen action. (People shouting should be louder than people whispering.)

Depending on your software, there might be other ways and places to make volume adjustments. For example, Sony Creative Software Vegas Pro lets you lower the volume of every clip event on the timeline individually, as well as the track as a whole. You can implement more volume changes at the bus and master levels, too. Every NLE/DAW supports some way to change volume over time, usually with an envelope/breakpoint automation system that is invaluable. Many allow an automation mode that lets you adjust volume (and other parameters, such as pan) as the project plays and then records these changes in real time. Some sound mixers even use an external mixer-like control surface loaded with knobs, buttons, faders, and switches that let you change settings on the fly and record them into the software.

It's important to note that you should start from scratch with volume when you begin working with the dialogue. I mentioned this before, but it bears repeating. Picture editors often play with volume so they can hear things better. You need to use volume to make the dialogue work as a whole, so strip off what they did and work your magic instead. You will be working with room tone and other processing, so you don't want inconsistent volume changes to send you down the wrong road.

For example, for one film I worked on, the editor boosted the volume on one side of a two-person conversation. I spent a long time trying to get inconsistent room tone (one was louder than the other) to work. When I later discovered the volume boost the editor did, I realized stripping that off would have saved me a bunch of time and aggravation. I ended up redoing my work. Yuck.

Another volume issue you might see is normalization added by the picture editor. You may use this tool, too—it's handy—but it's somewhat dangerous in how it works. Normalization looks at the loudest peak in a file and raises it to be its loudest (based on what you say you want that to be, typically –0.3). It then maintains the ratio of the dynamic range of the other elements of a file. In other words, if the loudest peak gets raised 3 dB, the whole file—even the softest parts—goes up 3 dB. This is no miracle. It's nothing more than a smart volume boost—one that avoids clipping by staying just under 0 dBFS.

Normalization doesn't necessarily make a file louder either, because peaks don't contribute to loudness. Our ears respond to average levels instead. So raising levels based on the peaks can have minimal impact on the final file. This is unless the file gets boosted 15 dB—it will be louder then, of course. The problem with normalization is that if you have a single loud peak, say from a cough, but the rest of the file is low in level, the normalization might only raise the volume slightly. You need to either eliminate the peak from the process or choose some other volume adjustment. Also, on low-level sounds, using normalization will boost equally not only the dialogue you want, but also the noise surrounding it. And that can be counterproductive.

I use normalization sparingly and instead prefer to simply raise or lower the volume of files on the timeline, letting my ears and the way elements fit together in the overall mix be the guiding factors for the exact settings.

## Compression

As mentioned earlier, compression reduces the dynamic range and can help smooth volume levels, making them more consistent. A little light compression on the dialogue will tame swings in volume, but I prefer to manually tweak the volume with envelopes. It's tedious but better overall. I typically avoid compression during the dialogue cleanup and smoothing phase because it can adversely affect room tone and other elements. Leave compression for the mix stage so you adjust not only individual voices, but also whole sections, room tone, and other elements together.

That said, dynamics processing is very important to soundtrack work, so learning about the tools and working with them to gain experience is very important. A compressor has several interactive sections. Multi-band compression differs only slightly in that it allows you to compress different frequency bands independently. For example, you could compress the bass and make it louder than the midrange, where the voice resides.

### Threshold

When an audio signal reaches a specific threshold level set by the compressor, the effect kicks in. Usually this signal is reduced in level depending on the ratio setting (see the following section). Any signal below the threshold setting is unaffected, while all signals above the threshold are compressed.

There are two different kinds of compression, which are known as *hard knee* and *soft knee*. With hard-knee compression, the signal is affected immediately when it exceeds the threshold. Soft-knee compression affects the signal slowly and gently. These options are usually in addition to the attack control, discussed in a moment.

### Ratio

Ratio settings determine how the output is compressed. Ratios can be set at unity (1:1) up to infinity to one. In other words, at a 1:1 ratio, a 1-dB signal change results in a 1-dB output (no or unity gain). At other ratios, the output is reduced by relative amounts. At 4:1, a 4-dB increase in input level results in only a 1-dB output level gain. Any ratio above 10:1 is not compression, but limiting. With heavy limiting, no matter how much the input level increases, the output is restricted (limited) to only a small range. This is useful for controlling the wide sweeps in dynamics produced by some sounds. At extreme settings, the limiting takes on a special sonic quality.

### Attack

This is the time it takes before signals above the threshold setting start being compressed. It's possible to let a small amount of a signal get past the compressor before it starts working. The times range from microseconds, to fractions of a second, to even a few seconds or more. To a certain extent, attack can control how punchy a sound is. A slower attack can let the initial transient of a sound through before clamping down, making something like a snare drum hit have an exaggerated attack.

### Release

This control determines how long it takes for the compressor to return to unity gain after the audio signal has dropped below the threshold. Again, you can vary the time from very short to very long. Short times act on the signal, constantly producing some unnatural staccato effects known as *pumping* and *breathing*, whereas long times tend to sound smoother and more forgiving.

### Output

Because compression reduces volume (called *gain reduction*), you can add level back into the signal that is often lost during the other processing steps.

## Dedicated Noise Reduction

After you've tried many of the fixes outlined in this chapter, you might still need help with really noisy dialogue. This is where a dedicated noise reduction tool is invaluable. If you are serious about making your soundtrack—especially dialogue—sound its best, then you really need to invest in such a tool.

Though each noise reduction software program has unique controls, they all work by a similar principle. You provide the software with a sample of just the noise, and the software analyzes that and applies its fix.

Although noise reduction plug-ins can work wonders, they don't work miracles. I read a quote recently from Marc Berger that puts this in perspective: "These things work best when you need them least." The tools do excel at reducing steady noise on sources that already have a decent signal-to-noise ratio. If your dialogue is buried in the mud, it'll never come out squeaky clean. Never! The top example in Figure 15.29 is very noisy compared to the dialogue. Noise reduction will only be marginally effective here and will be full of undesirable residual artifacts. The bottom example is from a recording in a relatively quiet room. Applying noise reduction here will virtually eliminate all of the low-level noise from this file and leave a natural-sounding voice, too. Some added expansion after this process can result in almost studio-quality sound from field recordings.

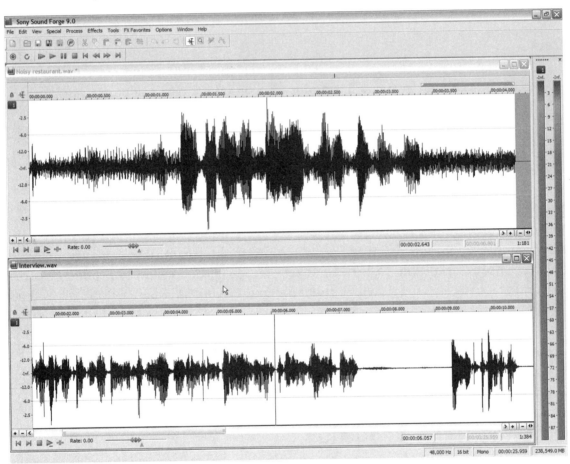

**Figure 15.29**  Noise examples.

With extreme noise reduction, there are always consequences. When the noise sits in the same frequency area as the voice, using noise reduction also adversely affects the voice quality. You can't just attack the noise without hurting the voice, too. For example, one of my students claimed to have discovered the miracle of noise reduction. He had some horribly noisy recordings, and he showed me how he got 100 dB of NR with just a simple slider move in the plug-in interface. The resulting sound was a watery, swirly, robotic, and metallic mess—the result of too much noise reduction being applied. He would have been better off applying smaller amounts of the noise reduction process, rather than trying to get the whole shebang at once. This is good advice. Work in sections and do a little noise reduction here and there until you get the best sound. Noise reduction is always a compromise between residual noise and other undesirable artifacts caused by the process itself.

On particularly noisy dialogue, you might have to get aggressive to make the dialogue work. Unfortunately, those artifacts might ruin the final result. On some news, documentary, and reality programs, this may be acceptable. Don't forget that with these genres, you can always use subtitles for sequences that are difficult to understand. This might be better than trying to kill the noise and leaving nasty-sounding dialogue in place.

In a narrative story, heavily processed voices would never work for the audience. You would need to find the best compromise between noise and good vocal quality. When confronted with this situation, consider disguising noise reduction artifacts with other soundtrack elements, such as room tone/presence; adding sound effects and background ambiences; and even adding music. Of course, don't use these other elements as a crutch; just know that they might work in the overall soundtrack mix. I've had a few instances in which the voice sounded really thin after working on the noise, but once it sat in the overall mix with other sound elements, it worked. Of course, you need to be sure that you can use these other elements. For example, a director may decide to axe the music for a scene, and you were using the music to cover up your bad-sounding dialogue tracks. Ouch!

Here are the steps to using a dedicated noise reduction tool. The example below is a single-person interview with some A/C noise and general din in the background. The voice masks this noise well, so it is most noticeable during the gaps between speech phrases and sentences. If you cut out the noise in the gaps only (by using a noise gate, for instance), the noise will rush back in during the speech. This choppy, on/off quality of noise never sounds good and actually draws more attention to itself than leaving all the noise in place.

Before using the noise reduction process, be sure the file is edited and in presentable form. Let noise reduction be the last step. After editing, consider using gentle high- and low-pass filters on the sound (from Figure 15.18) at 80 to 100 Hz and 10 to 12 kHz, respectively. This process will quickly eliminate rumble in the low end and hiss in the top. Already the track may begin to sound better. It's acceptable to tweak other EQ bands based on circumstances, too.

Open your chosen noise reduction plug-in—iZotope RX Advanced in this example. Make a selection of just the noise (see Figure 15.30). Search for and select a representative sample of *only* the background noise that you need to eliminate. Some noise reduction plug-ins want a tiny slice, while others work better on a longer sample. (Refer to the documentation to be sure.) Be very careful with your selection. Avoid including the end of a word, breath, or part of an intermittent sound or other one-time noise in the sample slice. Get the best representative sample of the general noise in the scene.

Depending on the software you use, capture the noise print of the selection. In this example, click the Train button. The plug-in analyzes the noise and develops a method to combat it. The iZotope RX solution includes three algorithms, and I find that the

**Figure 15.30** Noise sample selection.

C (offline) method is the best. It doesn't function in real time, but the extra processing time is well worth the wait, and the resulting file sounds great and will be less noisy.

Select the entire file and adjust the noise reduction amount and smoothing controls for the best results. You might find that taking multiple noise-print samples from different parts of the file and applying smaller amounts of noise reduction—say, 6 to 10 dB— during each processing step will give you a cleaner and better-sounding file.

If you have trouble adjusting the controls or you hear too many artifacts, activate the Output Noise Only check box. See Figure 15.31. Many other noise reduction plug-ins have a similar noise-only monitor or "listen" feature. This lets you preview only what is being reduced and not what's left. You should hear just the background noise. If you hear speech or even parts of speech when this feature is on, it will translate into more artifacts on the output. Adjust the controls for the best compromise between reducing noise and minimizing its impact on the program material. Make sure you uncheck the Output Noise Only check box; otherwise, when you process the file, you will only have noise left.

After noise reduction, you might need to perform a little manual cleanup, such as eliminating a breath, lip smack, or other one-time noise. These sounds are often more

**Figure 15.31**   Tweaking noise settings.

noticeable after you apply the noise reduction and therefore they require your attention. Also, consider applying an expander or even a noise gate to further reduce the noise. Figure 15.32 shows the before (top) and after (bottom) results of using EQ, noise reduction, and gating on the file. Notice how not only the general background noise was eliminated, but also several other ticks, pops, breaths, and such were removed. Because the noise reduction process eliminates noise both during and in between speaking, a gate or expander will now work well without drawing attention to itself (unlike before). Your dialogue will sound very quiet and clean, ready for the mix.

The Sony Noise Reduction program is another alternative that works similarly (see Figure 15.33, shown running inside Sony Creative Software Sound Forge). You still capture the noise print, but this program prefers a shorter slice—usually less than one-third of a second. The controls differ slightly, too. The most useful are Reduction Type, Reduce Noise By (dB), and Noise Bias. Reset the plug-in by choosing the Default for Fast Computers preset. Set the Reduction Type to Mode 3. Of the three modes, Mode 3 does the least amount of noise reduction, but it has fewer residual artifacts. Mode 0 is very aggressive with reducing noise, but you will notice more unusual swishing sounds in the output.

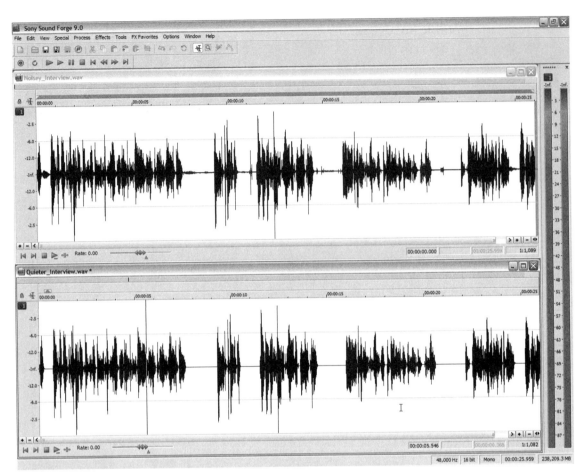

**Figure 15.32**  Before (top) and after noise reduction.

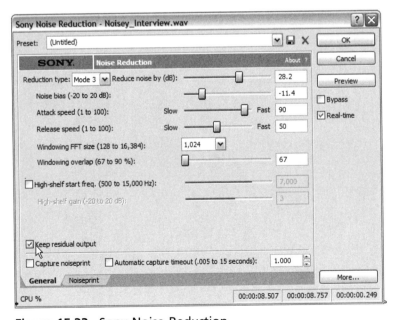

**Figure 15.33**  Sony Noise Reduction.

It is perfectly acceptable to tweak the Reduce Noise By (dB) and Noise Bias sliders while you preview. Check the Keep Residual Output check box to monitor what you are cutting out, as mentioned earlier. As the noise reduction amount increases, so will the artifacts. Back off on the amount and/or adjust the Noise Bias, typically to the left, for best results. When you are satisfied, uncheck the Keep Residual Output option and then click OK to process the file. You will easily see and hear the results of your hard work in the waveform display.

## Special Voice Effects

Occasionally, you might need to treat the voice in some special way. Up until now, the focus has been on fixing problems. However, there are opportunities for creating more realism and achieving unusual effects, called *futzing*. Many of these effects would be applied at the mix stage, but it's helpful to know about them now as you work on the dialogue.

---

**Note on Voice Effects:** Rather than print these effects—that is to say, permanently change the files—move a sound or sounds to their own track(s) and add the effect there. In other words, add these effects nondestructively so you can change them later as the soundtrack takes more shape. This workflow lets you preview effects in context, but still makes it easier to make adjustments to these initial settings in the final mix.

Mark the track with a good name and even color-code it in some way to remind you that the track is special and reserved for a particular effect. It might be better to add the effect at the bus level if several tracks use that effect, or use an assignable effect send. This is often a better use of computer resources, as many audio effects hog computer processing power.

---

### Simulating a Telephone Line

If one side of a conversation takes place on a telephone, it's important to re-create the telltale limited sound quality of a typical phone. For this, an EQ adjustment that limits the frequency response between 500 Hz and 3.5 kHz is all it takes. This is known as a *band-pass filter* because it only lets certain frequency bands through. Sometimes some strong compression (10:1 with medium attack and release) can complete the illusion. I've even added some distortion to the voice to make it sound more realistic; see Figure 15.34.

If you are alternating characters so they are heard sometimes on the phone and sometimes normally, move all dialogue that needs the phone treatment to its own track or bus and treat it through the same effects chain.

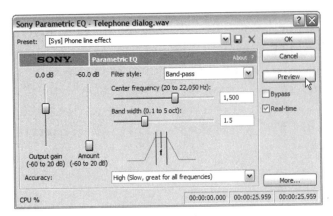

**Figure 15.34**  Telephone simulation.

## Simulating Rooms and Spaces

If you record in a quiet studio location or if you use lavalieres, you might need to add artificial reverb to dialogue to make it match the space. This is often a critical ingredient to getting ADR lines to match production dialogue. Reverb and convolution reverb are the tools of choice for creating spaces around voices. Again, these are usually added during the mix, but occasionally you might need to use them as you work on dialogue. For example, an off-camera actor may sing in the shower, and you might need to simulate this effect for a director/producer to prove it can be done. You might test other scenarios before the mix, too. Always apply this effect after you finish all edits, cleanup, and other fixes.

## Delay…Delay…Delay

What would Gary Cooper's soliloquy as Lou Gehrig from *Pride of the Yankees* be without the simulation of the Yankee stadium PA echo (see Figure 15.35)? Shot in the studio with rear-screen projection, the scene works better with the addition of artificial delay. It's a simple slapback echo (single-repeat) effect in that landmark film, but you might want to add a little feedback to the delay to re-create a more convincing sound.

## Reversing Dialogue

Reversing dialogue can give you an unusual language that is handy for walla when you need to hide or disguise recognizable words or put your actors in a foreign locale.

The always clever David Lynch used the reverse effect in *Twin Peaks* by having his actor learn to *speak* his lines backwards and then filming that. By reversing the film and playing it back that way, the words came out right but with an unusual quality.

The specific effect used in the old horror movie *Poltergeist* is easy to achieve. Simply reverse the dialogue and add a short reverb to it while it is reversed. Then, reverse the

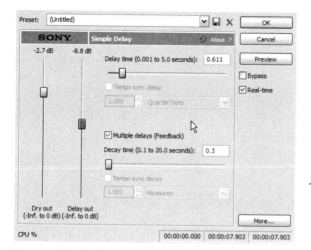

**Figure 15.35**   PA announcer effect.

dialogue so it is back to its normal direction, and the reverb will now come first—preverb!

## Flanging, Chorusing, and Phasing

Oh my! These effects are perfect for creating ghosts and otherworldly sounds. When you are searching for certain unusual effects, try these. There will be more on sound design techniques in the chapters ahead, which address sound effects, backgrounds, Foley, and more.

In this book, several chapters addressed the challenges and offered solutions to working with the most important component of soundtrack success: dialogue. Dialogue is crucial to delivering your project's message, and that means you need to present it well. The techniques discussed here will go a long way toward making your dialogue sound its best. It can be a lot of work editing and cleaning up dialogue, but the effort is always worth it in the end.

The next chapter addresses the reality side of your soundtracks, and that means sound effects.

# 16 Sound Effects

Imagine a simple film sequence with just minimal production dialogue, a car pulling up and idling, car doors opening and closing, a few footsteps as someone runs around the car and back, some minor prop sounds, such as clothing rustles, and then the car pulls away. Simple enough, right? Not really. In a scene such as this, nearly every sound gets added during post-production just to make it all sound natural.

Many sound effects get recorded on location as part of the dialogue recordings. Usually these are not high enough quality to make it to the finished mix. They serve as useful starting points and can help you with synchronization, but rarely more. Once you jettison these inferior sounds, there's only the dialogue remaining. That means everything else gets created or replaced in the audio-post suite. Everything! Sometimes nothing from the original production remains, such as when you're using ADR to replace the dialogue. The whole soundtrack gets rebuilt from scratch in post-production. This is also true of animated films, where no real "production sound" exists. Of course, recording dialogue in a recording studio in advance of animation is normal. Everything else gets built one sound at a time in the audio-post suite.

Even the most mundane scene, as described in the first paragraph of this chapter, can require hours of meticulous soundtrack work. The result is a natural feel to the scene, almost as if you pointed a microphone at the scene and recorded it live. You know that is not possible, so a lot of effort goes into making every scene's soundtrack work.

This audio-post work is another one of those unsung aspects of filmmaking. Nobody leaves the theater humming your sound effects. But their complete absence breaks down the illusion and leaves your audience with the feeling that something isn't quite right. Most people won't be able to express specifically what's off with what they are watching, though; it just won't "work" for them.

Sound effects help the audience believe the artificial world. When obvious sounds are missing, the audience feels a sense of unreality. Therefore, adding the right level of reality to a scene is the primary focus of sound effects work. Because when it's done right, nobody notices—at least not consciously. The scene seems perfectly normal to the casual viewer. This proper application of sound effects makes the scene more realistic and believable, and consequently makes a stronger impact.

There is an adage in the sound-design world: "See a dog. Hear a dog." This is the mantra that many of us who cut sound effects live by. If the audience sees a canine flapping its jaws, they expect to hear a bark in the soundtrack. It's a good rule, generally, as most sound effects work is rather obvious and even mundane—a character opens a door, and we cut in the sound of the door. Exciting, eh? Of course it is, especially when you search for just the right door sound to underline and support the scene. Is the door squeaky? Loud? Soft? What quality or timbre will make the best door opening ever?

But just because some of the sound effects work you do is blatant and obvious, that doesn't mean you should choose any old sound, throw it on the timeline, and call it a day. You will make careful choices and select specific sound elements that serve to enhance elements of the story—its setting, time period, place, characters, narrative drama, and more.

## Oodles of Sounds

When most people think about sound effects, they're the big, beautiful, and unforgettable sounds of something akin to the light sabers and spaceships from one of the six *Star Wars* movies. Ben Burtt did a masterful job of creating the aural universe for these beloved films. His real contribution to the world of sound is better known as *sound design*. And while many sound effects are created through sound design, many more are real-world recorded sounds, frequently mundane in nature, whose purpose is to provide the bed of reality around which a narrative revolves.

The full sound effects mix (SFX) is composed of many layers of different sounds. There are all those hard effects, such as the aforementioned door opening, that breathe reality into a scene. Other soft effects are not as obvious as the front-and-center hard effects, but they nevertheless contribute to building a cohesive sonic whole. Sound effects on their own sound kind of dry and in your face, so layering them with backgrounds or ambience helps fill out what's missing and allows the hard and soft sound effects to fit better into an environment. Then there are all those highly specific sounds the purveyors of Foley add. Without these additional layers, the soundtrack seems thin.

Take footsteps, for instance. They are a filmic convention. In real life, we pay little attention to footsteps around us. But in a film, their absence contributes to a sense of unreality and makes a scene feel empty and wrong. Audiences may not pinpoint precisely what's wrong, but they do notice. Adding the footfalls and often other subtle sounds to the soundtrack imparts a sense of realism that works, almost subliminally, on the audience so they buy what you are doing. Once Foley is in place, it seems that almost any scene comes to life.

---

**Music and Sound Effects:** I've worked on musicals and plenty of other films where there are musical sequences with no dialogue. Sometimes these sequences have sound effects, and sometimes they don't. A strictly musical number—

characters singing—usually is devoid of most sound effects. There are exceptions, of course. However, sequences that are just music—such as in the boy-loses-girl-sits-alone-in-a-park kinds of scenes usually dominated by heart-wrenching, emotional music—can usually work better with some additional sound effects to sweeten the track and bring some realism. Without the effects, the narrative slips into music-video mode. Personally, I never feel that works as well as good music and good sound design working together. Of course, whatever serves the project is the best choice. It can be a hard battle. If the director has been listening to only the music and watching the images in the edit suite, the new layer of sound effects can be distracting. These new sonic accoutrements need to be subtle and subservient to the music, but experience shows that some background ambience and perhaps a little Foley can make the track come alive with both realism and emotion. Others may disagree, so I'll get off my soapbox now.

## Spotting Sound Effects

Building the sound effects tracks is a major undertaking. Even apparently simple projects can require hours of effort and dozens of sounds. For a jam-packed action feature, the sheer volume of work is huge. The best way to manage all this is to start with a spotting session. Get together with the director, the producer, and all the sound crew and go through the film. Carefully document the running time and onscreen action and then list the primary sounds and backgrounds that should go with what you see.

Spotting sound effects this way can save a lot of time. Do it. It avoids misunderstandings and can often save a lot of work. You could waste hours adding effects to a scene, only to have them all muted in favor of a "Let's just have the music here" comment from the director. Been there, done that...too often.

Another huge timewaster is simply not asking your clients their specific vision for the project on which you are collaborating. Don't assume you know, and don't assume they know, either. I'm not talking specifics yet. Rather, I'm talking about defining the overall feel of a piece, its emotional impact on its eventual audience. I find the best question to ask is: "What is your vision of the soundtrack, and how do you expect it to impact the audience?" This line of questioning helps your client see the big picture before getting mired in the minutiae. Details are important, obviously, but without the overall vision established, the details are irrelevant. Together, you can arrive at the ideal focus for your creative contribution.

For a recent film soundtrack, we decided on dark, gritty, and heavy. This simple definition of the vision meant using sound effects and backgrounds that were dark, muffled, bass-dominant, distorted, loud, and abrasive—not bright or cheerful. Establishing this upfront saved a lot of headaches because we were focused on the same vision from the start. This approach also resulted in a more cohesive soundtrack that better delivered its message and emotional appeal to the audience.

---

**Note:** As mentioned earlier in the book, don't jump right in and start working on the project. Watch it once by yourself and record your initial impressions. As you begin working on the material, you will be too close to it, and you will lose some of the freshness that comes from seeing it for the first time. Your notes from the first viewing will be invaluable and will help strengthen your work.

---

Usually, you can effectively spot a project by going through it a few times and noting the kinds of sounds you need. These sound notes should detail the video action accurately and list all the necessary and possible sound elements to go with each video shot and/or action. It's important to be specific and indicate time (using timecode values), what happens onscreen, and then possible sound and background ideas. These spotting notes are best used to capture initial impressions and to provide a general direction. You could create a form with a word processor or even a simple spreadsheet. It might look like Table 16.1.

**Table 16.1** Sound Notes

| Time (in Seconds) | Video | Main Sound Effects | BGs |
| --- | --- | --- | --- |
| 08 | Pan of city | Crane lifting away | City |
| 12 | | Giant radars turning | Industrial |
| 18 | | Cars moving away from rocket | Distant |
| 20 | | Rocket engine starts | Spaceport |
| 21 | Brian enters shot | Footsteps | |
| 25 | | Rocket takes off | |
| 30 | CU of Brian | Sound filtered through him? | |
| 34 | MS Brian at terminal | Touches computer, starts moving away | |
| 36 | | Sparks rain down | |
| 38 | | Lights blinking, activity increases | |
| 44–50 | LS pan of city cont'd | Rocket going overhead | |

You will add more detail to this document and then create a sound map that serves as the roadmap of sorts for building the sound effects layers. The sound map should have highly organized detail of the video shots and action with accurate timings and then be matched to the primary sound categories—SFX, Foley, BGs, dialogue/VO, and music—and also be populated with actual sounds to use. Including the dialogue and even music cues can give you a complete picture of the whole soundtrack. See Table 16.2.

**Table 16.2** Sound Map

| Time | Video | Dialogue | SFX A | SFX B | Foley | Backgrounds | Music |
|------|-------|----------|-------|-------|-------|-------------|-------|
| 08 | Pan of city | (PA)14, 13, 11, 10 ... | Crane lifting away | Giant radars turning | Distant footsteps | Spaceport | Main theme |

The more detail you include in the map, the better off you'll be. This document allows you to work through scenes and decide on all the sounds and where to place them. As you start to gather the necessary sounds—either by recording them or getting them from libraries—the map is invaluable. Using a highly detailed map also makes it easier for a large sound crew to collaborate and divvy up the work. Of course, as you start building the soundtrack, there may be other sounds necessary to complete the work, and ideas that seemed to make sense on paper don't always sound right when the audio and video are matched up. That's why you should treat the map as only a specific direction to take. As on any map, you may want or need to take a different route to get to your final destination.

One other document that can be useful is a schedule. It's helpful to establish the delivery date (when the soundtrack's final mix is due) and then work backward and indicate the major milestones along the way. For example, you need time for dialogue work, sound effects and Foley, premixes, and the final mix itself. Your schedule may be days, weeks, months, or sometimes just hours!

Include time for gathering sound effects from existing sources. It can take quite a lot more time than you may initially think to find the right sounds and add them to the workflow. Also, consider setting aside a day or two in your post-production schedule to record on location for the specific purpose of gathering sound effects, backgrounds, and other one-of-a-kind effects. Obviously, a more extensive project may require a lot more time to procure the basic sound elements you need.

## Hunting and Gathering

With spotting notes and a richly detailed sound map in hand, you can begin to pull together the sounds you need. Coming up with the sound palette can be very time consuming. It takes time to find, audition, select, and organize all the sounds. There are the literal sounds you need to dig up, such as cars going by, footsteps, doors closing, and so forth. Authenticity is as important as consistency. The sounds you choose must match the screen action and be used throughout the single project.

There are also the non-literal sound design elements that are equally difficult to find, record, tweak, and even create from scratch. This can be the most creative aspect of the whole soundtrack process. On this quest, you will constantly refer to your notes and the conversations you had with the director and others involved.

Good organizational habits can really help here. You need to develop a way to categorize and group what could be hundreds of sounds. A shoebox with everything lumped together is probably not the best approach for anything more than the simplest project. Consider creating folders that relate to specific scenes or locations. Refer to Chapter 12 for some additional organizational tips. For example, everything you need for the big car chase could go in a single folder dedicated to that. Or all the sounds associated with the main character's house could be kept together. You might want to separate your hard effects from your Foley and backgrounds, too. This might seem like overkill, but once you realize you have a thousand assets or more for a particular project, you will be glad you took the time to organize them all.

Consider using some software to help you manage your sound effects collections as a whole and by project. It can take time to organize and apply keywords to all your material, but ultimately you will save time. Database-building is a great job for interns and part-time employees. Your DAW software may even include some of these organizational tools. For example, Sony Creative Software's Vegas Pro includes a robust Media Manager (see Figure 16.1) that makes searching for and organizing all types of media—not just sound—quick and easy.

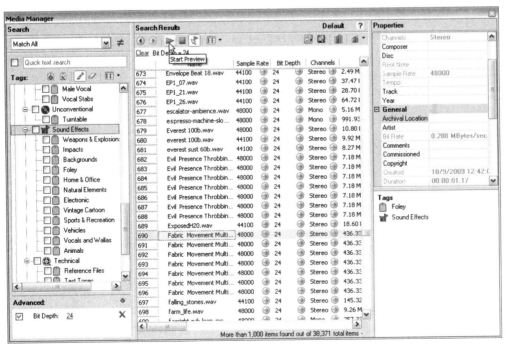

**Figure 16.1** Sony Vegas Pro's built-in Media Manager.

Soundminer (www.soundminer.com) is an asset-manager software application that can make searching for sound effects easier, too. Most major suppliers of sound effects (such as the Hollywood Edge) make their offerings compatible with Soundminer. This means you can use the Soundminer application to manage, search, process, and present the sounds you need for your project. Keyword searches are especially useful as you audition possible SFX. Another option is BaseHead (www.baseheadinc.com), but it isn't as universally supported as Soundminer.

> **Note:** Sound effects titles are often insufficient when you're searching for suitable material. Associated keywords, stored as metadata with some file formats, can help make your search more effective. Using software to read these extra keywords can make you far more efficient.

The Juicer 3 application from Digital Juice (www.digitaljuice.com; see Figure 16.2) makes keyword-searching their extensive four-volume sound effects library a breeze. What's special about this application is that you can build a batch list of sounds as you find them and then export them all at once, even to separate folders. I usually start here for my initial sound search, especially for many general-purpose sounds.

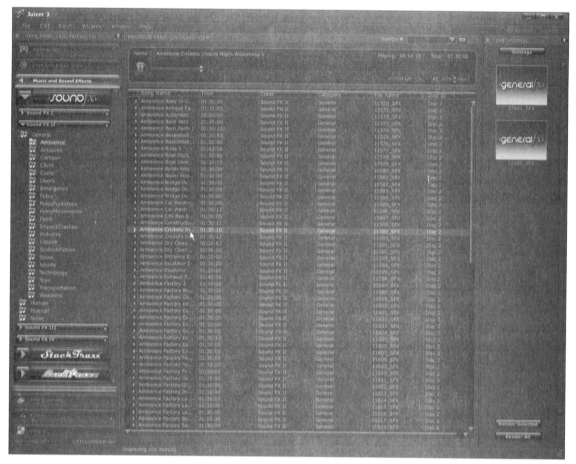

**Figure 16.2**  Digital Juice's Juicer 3 software.

After that, I start hitting all my other sound collections. This includes all the other libraries that I own, along with my personal sound recordings. These are stored on a dedicated external hard drive. Typically, I copy the sounds into the project folder I'm working on and don't link to the media drive. Audio files are small, and HDD space is cheap. Making these copies is an additional backup that brings peace of mind. A feature-length project can result in a sound palette approaching a gigabyte or more of sounds, though. Figure 16.3 shows a listing of just some of the more than 1,000 sounds used for a recent project.

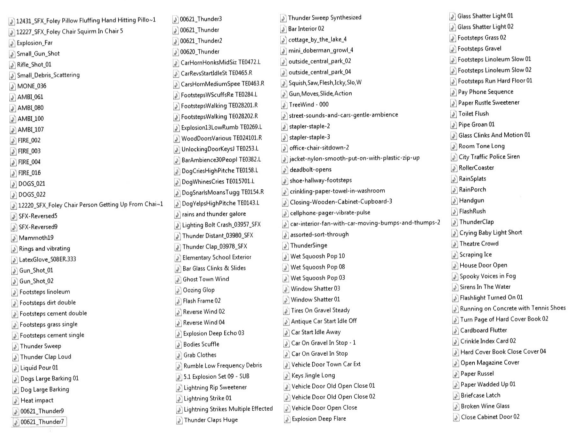

**Figure 16.3** A partial list of the SFX used for a recent film project.

After exhausting all of my library sounds, I turn to my software-based musical synthesizers and samplers to uncover or create more sounds. Though more suited to music, they can be used for sound design, too. You can use them to mangle existing sounds in unique ways or to build from scratch. For example, UltimateSoundBank has a soft synth called X-treme FX (see Figure 16.4) that is ideal for sound design. Instead of being a musical instrument, it is loaded with sound effects that you can layer, filter, add audio effects to, and use other synth controls with. It really excels at making unusual sound-design elements, too. If I need cars, thunder, and restaurant ambiences, I use libraries or my own recordings. But when I want otherworldly screams, this is a go-to tool.

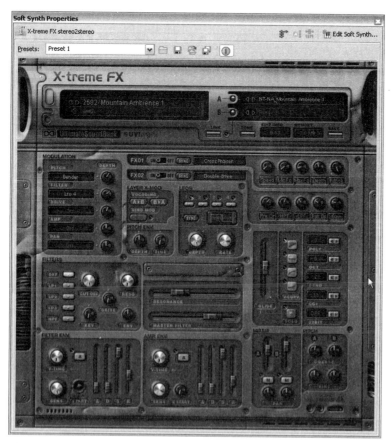

**Figure 16.4**   USB's X-treme FX software synthesizer sound design tool.

To get sounds out of this software, you need a MIDI-capable DAW. I record these MIDI performances using Sony Creative Software ACID Pro 7 (if you consider holding down a key for 20 to 30 seconds to be a real performance). Once recorded as MIDI data, they can be rendered to 24-bit/48-kHz WAV audio files and exported for use in the soundtrack project. I never mix MIDI performances with digital audio when building soundtracks. I prefer to keep these MIDI files separate and just export the audio for use in the project instead. This workflow applies to sound effects and musical work, too.

If I can't find or create (with synths/samplers) the sound effects needed, it's time to hit the road and go out into the field to record. For sound effects work, a portable recorder is ideal, such as the Zoom H4n (www.samsontech.com), the M-Audio MicroTrack 24/96 (www.m-audio.com), or a similar recorder. Add in a couple of different mics—a short shotgun, an inexpensive large-diaphragm condenser, and a pair of inexpensive binaural mics from Core Sound (www.core-sound.com)—for versatility in getting what you need. The four-channel Zoom H2 recorder works great for surround-sound recordings of ambiences and some sound effects.

You can also create your own sound effects using just your mouth. It's easy to emulate a lot of sounds—cartoon effects and even a few dramatic ones—by recording your voice. Use your audio software to mangle and manipulate these sounds even further. For instance, the voice of WALL-E started its life from the utterances of sound designer Ben Burtt.

And after all this, there is still Foley to record, too. But we'll talk about that more in Chapter 17, "Foley and Backgrounds."

---

**Everybody Loves Wilhelm:** The "Wilhelm Scream" may be the best-known sound effect, having been used in hundreds of feature films and television programs (and countless student films, I'm sure). The scream originated in 1951 and became part of the Warner Bros. sound-effects archive, where it was reused for many films. Years later, Ben Burtt, sound designer for the *Star Wars* films, began slipping it into all the films on which he worked. It became a sort of an homage or in-joke, and numerous other films snuck in a Wilhelm Scream or two. A well-placed Wilhelm, such as at the end of Gary Rydstrom's Pixar short *Lifted*, is a thing of beauty (not to mention very funny to those sound people in the know). But overuse can be annoying and distracting, such as in the UK sci-fi program *Primeval*, which uses it at least once (if not more) in every episode!

I have my own Wilhelm Scream that I try to use on every project. It's a sound effect called Suburban Neighborhood—a mono recording of the typical ambience one might find in such a place, complete with dogs barking and birds chirping. I try to sneak this sound into every project I can. Much like Hitchcock and his well-known cameos, a sound dude or dudette needs a sonic cameo.

Some sounds have become sound clichés, such as the lone cricket when somebody tells a bad joke and the misuse of the red-tailed hawk screeching. Some sounds are so recognizable that using them in your work is strictly verboten. The light saber sound from *Star Wars*, for instance, is permanently etched into our mind's ear.

Check out FilmSound on the web (www.filmsound.org/cliché) for more sound clichés and Hollywood Lost and Found (hollywoodlostandfound.net/wilhelm) for the complete history of the Wilhelm Scream.

---

Once you build your sound palette, the actual work of adding effects to the timeline and placing them in sync with onscreen action is relatively straightforward. It's finding the right sounds and/or combinations of sounds that takes time, effort, and creative prowess. After all this hunting and gathering of sound effects, you usually end up with more than you need. It's often good practice to build a larger sound pool from which to draw and then whittle your choices down as the work progresses. And inevitably, you will need to revisit your collections and find new or alternate sounds, either because initial choices don't work or because the project calls for another approach.

# Your Sound Effects Library

If you are serious about audio-post, you need to invest money in building a comprehensive and versatile sound effects library. An assortment of basic sounds will help cover a variety of sound situations. As you work on more projects and add sounds from a variety of sources, your personal collection will grow.

Have your library where you can get to it quickly. Many collections come on CDs/DVDs, some are downloads, plus you may be recording your own sounds for the collection. Rather than having to grab a disc every time a sound is required, dump all of your sounds to a dedicated hard drive. External FireWire or USB hard drives are ideal for storage. In a larger facility, a storage area network (SAN) that all workstations can access makes sense, as does using a database program to catalog all those assets.

Where can you find the sounds you need?

- Production tracks

- Sound effects collections

- Sound effects websites

- Ones you've created on your own

---

**A Cautionary Note:** Avoid the temptation to search for and use free sound effects that you might find on the web. You will not know the sound's pedigree, and you risk infringing on a copyright. Many so-called "free" sound effects have been stolen from another source. Don't risk it; buy from legitimate sources. Sounds from motion picture and television soundtracks are also off limits. And although an argument can be made that nobody will know that the car sound you used came from a specific source, *you* will know. Don't steal—period!

Also, be aware that a sound effects CD purchased in a retail store or borrowed from the library may *not* grant you a license to use the effects for commercial purposes. They are for personal use—in home videos, for example—and the license may not extend to other projects destined for public performance and mass distribution. Read the license carefully. As a rule, the reason you pay more for legitimate SFX is because you are buying both the quality and the license.

---

## Production Tracks

Though your primary goal during production should be to capture clean voice— dialogue, interviews, and so on—you may also capture sound effects that are suitable for building the soundtrack. Particularly listen for sounds of props, clothing, and even footsteps that can survive to the final mix, as a whole or as part of a layer. These sounds are handy as sync references, too, even if you will replace them with better-quality sounds later.

Unfortunately, most production effects are off-mic, noisy, and therefore unsuitable for quality work. Various ambient sounds, such as traffic, wind, rain, and so forth, sound very garbled and indistinct—like white noise. Trashing these elements and rebuilding them with better sounds is almost always the better choice. Occasionally, the sound mixer on set may take the time to specifically record these elements. When that happens, these sounds captured during production may work.

An exception to using production sound is when those sounds are from a particular location or are one of a kind and specific. For example, for a video about a printing press, the factory floor was quite noisy. Still, I had to use the sound of the machine; I couldn't just use some other factory sounds, as the sound was very distinctive.

Another aspect to keep in mind applies to alternate language projects. Any production sounds you use for effects will have the room tone from the location where they were recorded. These sounds may fit in well with the original dialogue and its room tone. However, once you dump the original dialogue tracks and their respective room tone and replace them with the alternate language, these production sound effects may stand out too much. They will be noisy compared to other sound effects. Therefore, with few exceptions, replacing production sound effects with cleaner, higher-quality ones is always best when a foreign-language dub is planned. If your project will not be dubbed, then keeping these sounds in the project may be acceptable.

---

**Genuine Ingenuity:** Harley-Davidson tried unsuccessfully to copyright the distinctive signature rumble of their hogs. But that frivolous anecdote brings up an important point. Sometimes viewers may recognize the specific sounds that you use. You won't get away with using the sound of a Vespa zooming along the road when the visuals clearly show a Harley. All the Harley owners out there will know the sound is wrong, and they'll complain. That very fact makes it more difficult for the sound designer. You can't just throw down any old sound; it has to match in the real world. You have to be reasonably authentic to the sound source. If you're doing sci-fi or animation, you can often get away with a lot more, as there is no real-life reference for the audience.

---

## Sound Effects Collections

Buying sound effects is much like buying stock photography or stock video footage. You don't buy the clip, just the right to use it. You can purchase these licenses to use sound effects from a variety of sources. Notice I used the word "license." You do not buy the sound effects; you rent them, non-exclusively, for use in your production. In some (rare) cases, you pay a fee for each use. In the vast majority of cases, you purchase a buy-out license, where you pay one fee to use the sound and then can continue to use the sound in all of your productions, non-exclusively, without paying another fee. This is known as *royalty-free*.

There are several companies that sell commercial sound effects collections on CD or DVD, by download, and even on HDD. The push today is to offer single effects and collections as downloads instead of as physical products. Buying a collection of sounds is handy for several reasons. You usually get access to hard-to-acquire sounds, such as weaponry and explosions, certain cars and other machinery, exotic animals, and locales. For example, if the project demands a Marrakech open-air market, it's often less expensive to buy a sound than it is to fly to Africa with a mic and recorder.

These sounds may also work as temporary placeholders while you record or otherwise create or acquire the final sounds. Modifying an existing effect and layering several effects together to create something new are two ways to get more from commercially bought sounds. And although some sound editors may not admit it, many commercial sounds make it all the way to the final mix, too.

The real downside to these non-exclusive, royalty-free sounds is that you run the risk of hearing them someplace else, as the entire world can access the same resources. A particularly distinctive sound may get overused (think: the Wilhelm Scream), while a garden-variety effect, such as a door slam, won't be as noticeable. A way around this is to combine, mix, stack, and otherwise customize the sounds you license to make them your own. A single sound effect rarely makes a complete soundtrack. The more layers you add—subtle and not so subtle—the better your ultimate resulting soundtrack mix.

## Sound Effects Websites

There are several legitimate websites from which you can download sounds as needed, too. (See the "A Cautionary Note" sidebar earlier in this chapter.) Some of these sites offer free sound effects (via Creative Commons licensing), but most are pay sites. What's especially nice about the download approach is that you can search by keyword, audition the results, and only download (and pay for) the sounds you need.

Here are some links to the popular websites for audio sound effects downloads:

- Audio Network (www.audionetwork.com)
- Big Fish Audio (www.bigfishaudio.com)

- Blastwave FX (www.blastwavefx.com)

- Digital Juice Sound Effects (www.digitaljuice.com)

- FreeSFX (www.freesfx.co.uk)

- The Freesound Project (www.freesound.org)

- Fresh Music (www.freshmusic.com)

- The Hollywood Edge (www.hollywoodedge.com)

- iStockphoto (www.istockphoto.com)

- Pro Sound Effects (www.prosoundeffects.com)

- Sonomic (www.sonomic.com)

- SoundDogs.com (www.sounddogs.com)

- The Sound Effects Library (www.sound-effects-library.com)

- Sound Ideas (www.sound-ideas.com)

- Soundsnap (www.soundsnap.com)

## Roll Your Own

Creating your own sounds helps personalize your projects. Instead of settling for less-than-stellar production sound or purchased sounds that almost work, you can go and grab whatever you need, exactly in the way you need it.

For one project I needed the sound of two characters kissing. I didn't have the right sound in-house, so I started searching. Most kiss sound effects are comic in nature and were unsuitable for this particular narrative. After about an hour, I found a few candidates from Sonomic. After paying for the kiss and downloading the file, I put it in the film…and the next day, the director told me he didn't like my choice and to just use the (production) kiss instead. In hindsight, my wife and a mic would have worked for the kiss. It would've been faster and cheaper (and more fun!) to simply record some real kisses, timed and matched to the picture. Duh!

Most professionals prefer to gather their own sound effects. In many cases, the project almost demands it. For *Master and Commander*, there were few commercially available sounds authentic to that era. The sound team had to find old boats and period weaponry to lend an authentic feel to the film.

When recording your own sound effects, it often makes sense to get multiple perspectives. Don't just stick the mic in one position. Experiment with different mic positions and distances. For example, in recording the vintage weapons for *Letters from Iwo Jima*, mics were placed all around the guns and at close and long distances. This gave the sound editors more choices in post to match onscreen action, as well as to build layers.

For instance, if you need to record a car or truck, you would want to get both inside and outside perspectives of the following:

- Start, idle, rev, shutoff

- Pull up, stop, and pull away slowly

- Pull up, stop, and pull away quickly

- Reverse away

- Driving perspectives, such as driving toward, driving away, left to right, right to left (both slowly and quickly), and so on

- Doors opening and closing

- Windows up and down

- Trunk opening and closing

- And more…

Using different mics and mic preamps can add some color, too. Capturing in true stereo—even surround—can give you more bang for your recording buck, too. As an aside, some sounds are so loud that you need to make careful mic choices and often pad them down with in-line level attenuators. The Heil PR 40 worked well for capturing mortar fire for *Letters*, as it could withstand the high SPLs (*sound pressure levels*).

Sometimes it's not the sound itself that is important, but how it sounds at a particular location. Laurent Kossayan reported in *Mix* that the sound team on *Public Enemies* went to the Warner Bros. NY Street backlot to record gun sounds for the movie. "We put up something like 20 mics—distant, closeup, overhead—and spent a half day shooting the guns. We wanted to get that city slap and that feeling."

If your project has a car chase, using the same wheel squeal applied over and over will quickly "tire" your audience (think: original *Dukes of Hazzard* TV show). Take the time to acquire a variety of sounds from multiple perspectives; that will help keep the soundtrack fresh.

Going out into the field and bringing sound-producing objects into the studio are the primary ways to gather the required sounds. A portable recording rig—even the same rig you use to get dialogue—is sufficient for effects gathering. Go record what you need, bring it back to your studio, edit and tweak it, clean it up, and otherwise transform the raw sounds into what you need.

A combination of purchased and custom sounds can be a good compromise, as some sounds are difficult, impossible, dangerous, or too expensive to acquire. However, the main benefit to getting custom sounds is how it lets you build your own sound effects library that you can use in the future—and even license to others if you so choose.

In the next chapter, we'll explore Foley and a variety of other ideas for using sound effects successfully in your projects.

# 17 Foley and Backgrounds

There are two aspects of every soundtrack that you should not forget about or abandon: the Foley and background sounds (BGs). These two crucial sound elements add layers of reality that really bring scenes alive for your audience.

Foley, in particular, adds a dimension to the sound environment that heightens the audience's awareness that what they are watching feels more natural and therefore more real. This is not a conscious act on the part of the audience; rather, Foley sounds work on an almost subliminal level or aspect.

Background sounds, a.k.a. *environments* and/or *ambiences*, anchor the sense of space and place that is equally crucial for providing the proper setting for all other sound elements to populate. Don't confuse backgrounds with room tone. You build BGs intentionally and add them in post, while room tone is the sound (wanted or unwanted) that sneaks onto field dialogue recordings (and gets used for smoothing dialogue).

The careful marriage of detailed specificity (Foley) to indistinctness or ambiguity (BGs) contributes to the success of the overall effects mix.

## Foley

One of my students spent two hours going through every sound effects CD we had in the computer lab. Then he asked me whether I knew of any sounds of a person spitting. I told him no, and he complained about wasting the whole lab period. I said, "Why don't you take a garbage can into the recording booth and record yourself spitting into it?" That took him less than five minutes. You see, some sounds are simply easier to perform and record "live" than to find as preexisting sound effects.

And that's where Foley comes in. Foley sounds are all those very specific and subtle sounds that can't be represented by traditional sound effects or aren't in the original production (such as when shooting MOS—that is, without sound). Foley sounds include footsteps, prop handling, clothing rustles, body sounds, and similar sounds that are too particular to be covered by libraries.

It can be somewhat simple to find suitable ambience background recordings, such as a cityscape background. It's an equally easy matter to track down recordings of many hard effects, such as explosions. And other sounds, such as those used in sci-fi and fantasy films, remain the sound designer's domain. Foley, however, adds another layer of detail and realism to scenes that no other single sound element can do. The Foley recordings provide mostly mundane sounds and present them in a straightforward way and in sync with onscreen action. But don't be fooled by the apparently unglamorous nature of footsteps and clothing noise. When you add Foley (such as these examples) effectively to a scene, it simply breathes and becomes more alive and believable.

Foley is both an art and a science. The art comes from the performance and being able to use various materials to match the onscreen imagery. The science comes from the recording techniques you use, which are quite simple but still effective.

In a *Mix* magazine article describing his work on *The Bourne Ultimatum*, Foley artist Dan O'Connell said: "We're adding the cherry on the sundae that the effects editors make. Most of what you hear is many layers that all play together, and each little bit of detail heightens what the audience is going to take in as their reality. The more that [Foley] can provide, the more [the audience is] in the film and excited by it."

On the recent movie *Nine*, dancers were brought in to "dance" the numbers on the Foley stage and they were recorded to be mixed in the film. Supervising sound editor Wylie Stateman reported that, "Foley was…very important to this film. It's not about covering everything; it's really about finding the dramatic punctuation, finding just the moment for a bit of movement to help with the perception of reality."

You record Foley sounds in a studio while watching the film and performing the sounds in sync with the picture. This is similar to ADR recordings mentioned earlier in the book. The Foley performers are sometimes known as *Foley walkers* (so named because a large part of what they do is adding footsteps to the soundtrack), but more likely today are called *Foley artists*. Foley itself gets its name from the man who invented the technique, Jack Foley, who began the process in early film sound.

## Recording Foley

Getting Foley recorded is very similar to ADR sessions. (Refer to Chapter 14 for details.) You need a way to watch the film and record the Foley performances at the same time. Generally, this means importing the video into the DAW and sending that video image to a large monitor or projection screen. Then you bring in the props, set up the mics, and record while watching the screen. I prefer to set up a loop-recording scenario that records multiple takes, one after the other, while matching the screen action. Then you can select the best takes later or make other edits as needed.

And just like ADR, it's best to work Foley in short pieces. This is not a live radio play, where you do it all in one pass. Take it a sound at a time and record multiple takes until you get it right before moving on to the next layer.

Multitrack recording brings an advantage for complex scenes. It allows you to record numerous passes of single performances and then layer them to represent a larger number of people or denser screen action.

The key to good Foley is capturing an upfront, clean, low- or no-noise sound. Generally, mics with tight patterns (hypercardioids or even shotguns, such as a Sennheiser 416) are the best choice used in a room with a dry, low-reverb time character. Most Foley recordings are mono, too, with few exceptions. Foley is about capturing the sound correctly (so it works with the onscreen thing making the sound) with the right perspective, capturing the performance, and getting it in sync with the picture. It is not about the mix at this point. Leave the ultimate levels and any effects, such as reverb, to the mix and just focus on capturing a clean, dry, accurate sound.

If you are in a good recording environment, such as a recording studio, you can often keep the mic farther away from the sound you are trying to capture. If the acoustics in your recording space are less than stellar, you may need to close-mike a lot of your Foley. You can always add a little artificial reverb to these sounds later during the mix if needed. I find that using the portable voiceover booth mentioned in Chapter 13 works great for many Foley recordings at my studio.

Figure 17.1 shows the Foley recording of the unscrewing of a light bulb. Because the timing and perspective of the onscreen action was so specific, it was easier to create this sound via Foley than to find a prerecorded library sound effect. Notice the DAW on one monitor (Sony Creative Software's Vegas Pro set to Loop Record) and the full-screen video on the second monitor. This makes it easy to perform along with the video to match the sync of the action. The Loop Record function means that multiple takes are captured automatically. You can then choose the best take later. The mic is a large-diaphragm cardioid condenser, necessary to pick up the rather low-level volume caused by turning the light bulb. The speakers are muted, of course, and the Foley artist is wearing headphones (and a nice sweater, I might add).

Big Foley studios are jam-packed with myriad noise-producing items. Central to the room are walking surfaces, often called *pits*. These surfaces are made of concrete, wood, dirt, gravel, and other surfaces and are accompanied by a diverse range of footwear. Additionally, the Foley stage will have all manner of fabrics and related clothing hardware (for example, snaps, buttons, and zippers), tools, household items, weaponry, doors, drawers, latches, and much more.

## Footsteps

When people walk or run onscreen, it's important to include the sound their feet make. In real life, most of us don't pay attention to such sounds. But when footsteps are missing in a film or video, the scene is less believable for the audience. Therefore, one of the primary goals with Foley is to add the missing detail—for example, footsteps. As mentioned in the previous section, a professional Foley studio contains several different

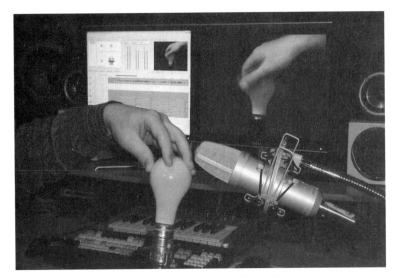

**Figure 17.1** Recording Foley in the edit suite.

surfaces for use. You may need to cobble together something simpler for your work. I've found that single floor tiles in wood and stone, along with a small rug, can work well without taking up a lot of storage space. You can even place the wood tile over a makeshift box (just a couple of woodblocks) for a more hollow sound. Throw in a few shoes, and you are good to go.

## Clothing

Collect old clothing or visit the local Goodwill and grab some pieces in different fabrics, such as cotton, polyester, wool, leather, and such. Choose different sizes and weights for more versatility. Some paper products can stand in for clothing, too. Make sure what you add to your collection has snaps, buttons, Velcro, zippers, and such.

## Props

Foley artists are always on the lookout for stuff—junk, really!—that makes noise. And they balance their search between ordinary and unique sound-making items. You'd be surprised by how many commonplace household items can (and do) work for Foley. You don't always need the full item as it appears onscreen, either; you can accomplish a lot with bits and pieces of this and that, along with various scraps of cloth.

Always be on the lookout for things that make noise. You may have much of what you need around your house, and you can press it into service as needed. The lamp in Figure 17.1 came from my wife's office, for example. Foley artists are consummate collectors of noise-producing stuff. To add that extra-special layer of detail to your projects, you need to build your own sound-producing collection, too. The best part is that all the sounds you create are unique to your projects and free from any licensing fees.

**Note:** Take a virtual tour of the Warner Bros. Foley stage at wbpostproduction. warnerbros.com/QTVR/foley_360.html.

Don't think that every Foley sound needs to be the literal, real-world equivalent of what the audience sees onscreen. You can get creative and use whatever you want to represent the sound. It's all about what the sound *is* (for example, a click) and not what's actually making it in the recording studio (for example, a light switch). Here are a few ideas I've used for recent projects:

- Fruits and vegetables make for realistic-sounding punches, gore, and bones breaking.

- Throwing birdseed or kitty litter into a box sounds like debris.

- Wrapping and removing masking tape from fingers emulates thumbing through papers.

- Moving old CD cases, thread spools, plastic cutlery, and various pieces of metal and plastic junk in a small, corrugated box reproduces rummaging through a box.

- Sliding the top off a toilet tank can simulate removing the top of a stone-covered vault (as used in *Raiders of the Lost Ark*).

- Old lighting gel (or other cellophane plastic) can make fire-crackling noises.

- Try slowly twirling a lavaliere in space to simulate wind noise.

- Substitute a manual staple gun for gun-handling noises.

- And, of course, for horse hooves, take a note from Monty Python and bang together two coconut shell halves!

Don't neglect the power of your own body, including your voice, to create some needed sounds. Using your own body to produce noise can be a fun diversion when you're stuck looking for a sound, and the exercise can generate some interesting audio, too. Remember, you can always manipulate a recording using other audio effects to make it better or different (or to disguise the fact that your mouth created the sound).

You can get a boatload of Foley-based sound effects "recipes" at Epic Sound (epicsound.com/sfx/).

## Foley Sound Effects

I mention this because many sound effects libraries include Foley-like sounds. These recordings can often work for some scenes, and this approach is worth considering if you can't record your own Foley well. I've resorted to the libraries many times or used them as sweeteners for my own Foley work. Similarly, as you record a lot of your own Foley and build a collection, you may be able to reuse some recordings for other projects. You will have more success with clothing and prop sounds. Footsteps will require extensive editing to match the action (been there, done that!). That said, recording Foley can be a lot of fun and always gives you control over the exact sound so that you deliver what best serves the soundtrack and project as a whole.

Figure 17.2 shows why editing a preexisting Foley walk to make it fit another scene is more work than simply recording new Foley in the first place. This much editing takes time, and the end result lacks the nuance of a real performance that is so crucial to effective Foley. That doesn't mean you won't edit some Foley performances—you will! Just determine the actual effort required and make the more efficient choice.

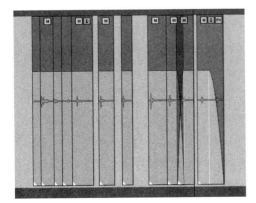

**Figure 17.2** Editing preexisting Foley is often inefficient.

### Software-Based Foley

A variation on recording Foley is to use a software-based sampler or even a synthesizer. You can load a bunch of sounds into a sampler, map them to various keys, and then use a piano keyboard to "play" the Foley as you watch the screen action. (Try it with footsteps!) I use the X-treme FX soft synth mentioned in Chapter 16 for some Foley work, though any sampler that lets you load in your own recordings will work. These performances can be captured as MIDI data (if your DAW supports it) and can remain that way until the mix or can be quickly rendered out to digital audio files and cut into the soundtrack.

My workflow is to capture these performances as MIDI, edit them a bit, and then export to an audio file and use that for the mix. You don't need great keyboard skills to do this; two- and four-finger performances are usually all that's required. A basic USB-based piano keyboard controller is an inexpensive hardware addition as well. This method is less messy than a typical Foley session, can be as much fun, and will still generate the sounds you want.

## Backgrounds

When you need to evoke a sense of space, place, and even time period, the background ambiences or environments you choose can serve those purposes effectively. The right background sound anchors other effects and gives them a framework in which to live and breathe. Sound effects (and Foley) sound dry and naked on their own. But when you surround these highly detailed sounds with more indistinct backgrounds, the soundtrack comes together into a more cohesive whole.

Background ambiences can be subtle, such as a light wind outside in a barren land, a cacophonous bustling cityscape, and everything in between. Authenticity is important, especially when you're aiming to represent a specific locale or time period. When speaking about his work on the movie *127 Hours*, supervising sound editor Glenn Freemantle told *Mix*, "We went to Utah, set up mics all over the canyon where [the story] takes place, and then [recorded] 24 hours a day for two days."

That said, moving beyond the obvious and choosing other sounds for the backgrounds can help tell the story better, too. For example, I've layered deep bass drone sounds with realistic environment sounds to give them a heavier, darker feel. If it serves the story, then whatever works is the best choice.

It's also rare that a single recording fulfills the needs for a scene's environment. Layering several recordings together often provides a richer depth that better supports the imagery. You may start with a single recording of a cityscape and then add traffic layers, car horns, crowds, industrial sounds (such as a jackhammer), distant sirens, and more. All of these individual elements let you build the environment you need to support the narrative. Crafting the right BG immerses your audience in the scene and helps make the scene more realistic and therefore more effective. Of course, setting up the BGs in an exaggerated or unusual way can take your audience on a different journey, too.

To a lesser extent, the use of background sounds can also help disguise noisy dialogue tracks. For example, if there is traffic noise during a dialogue sequence, adding in some carefully controlled traffic sounds can help mask the issue. For one film, an actor's line was stepped on by a passing car—the only vehicle noise during the whole shoot. The edit of the actor's line chopped off the start and end of the truck-by, so it sounded horrible. There was no suitable room tone, so the solution was to add a full car-by onto the soundtrack, positioned in a way to coincide with the noise still remaining on the dialogue track. Figure 17.3 shows a piece of the timeline illustrating this technique. Adding some other traffic noises in the background before and after this part made the scene as a whole work better (so that there wasn't just the single truck passing).

## Gathering BGs

There are many sound-library resources available that contain recordings suitable for building backgrounds. When you need specific time periods and exotic locales, the commercial offerings are a lifesaver. Most of these are stereo recordings, with a few even available in 5.1 surround sound. Either format gives you flexibility. (See the "Super-Size Your Stereo Backgrounds" section later in this chapter.)

As with Foley, the real power comes from capturing your own ambiences and using them in your projects. A stereo recorder and a stereo mic (or a matched stereo pair) is

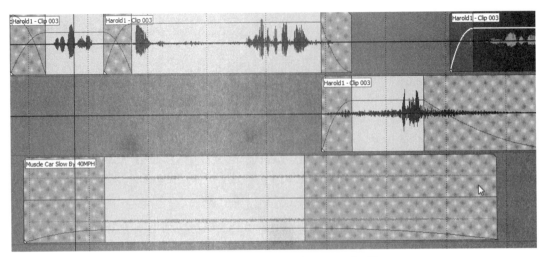

**Figure 17.3** Masking dialogue noise with a similar sound effect.

ideal for going out into the field and gathering the sounds you need. I addressed these subjects earlier in the book, so refer back to those chapters. Proper wind protection is a must, too.

If you are the production sound mixer on the project, take some time during lulls in shooting to gather background sounds from the actual shooting locations. For outside shoots, capture what's in the nearby area. For inside shoots, capture the sound of the space, as well as the sound out any windows or doors. These well-chosen environmental sounds can really sweeten scenes with an additional layer of reality. If you are not recording on the set, ask the sound crew to gather some of these sounds for you instead. Be specific with your request, or you'll just get more room tone and not well-recorded and focused background sounds that you can really use.

The greatest obstacle to recording your own background ambiences is noise. Trying to capture specific sounds without other elements interfering is difficult. For instance, trying to record my local coffee shop was impossible because of the music playing (and they wouldn't shut it off for me while I recorded for a few minutes). Standing on a street corner trying to get the traffic often results in picking up voices, too—including the voices of people who stop and ask you what you are doing.

> **Note:** Be careful using the Zoom H4n stereo recorder in public, as the device looks like a Taser and can bring unwanted attention from individuals and law enforcement.

The secret is to record a lot of extra takes and to do longer recordings that you can edit into usable pieces. Environmental sounds tend to change over time in both subtle and not-so-subtle ways, so capturing longer segments provides you with more choices. Also, make sure you match distances and perspectives that go with the scenes on which you are working. And just like sound effects gathering, recording multiple per-spectives of the same environment allows you to layer the separate recordings into a broader picture that also has sonic depth. Think foreground, middle ground, and dis-tant action and plan your recordings accordingly.

Another tactic is to visit locations early in the morning, before most of the world wakes up and makes it their day's work to ruin your recordings. Weekends can be quieter in some areas, while weekdays are quieter for others. Of course, if you need the sound of a crowded park, it doesn't make sense to record there when the place is deserted.

## Super-Size Your Stereo Backgrounds

Sound effects, especially backgrounds, offer opportunities to use stereo (and surround) in interesting ways. Because dialogue typically stays anchored in mono, in the phantom center in stereo, or in the dedicated center channel with surround, you can and should expand your mix with wide stereo ambiances. This serves two purposes. One, you cre-ate a bigger soundscape around the dialogue, and two, by pushing sounds way out to the stereo extremes, you leave a big hole in the middle for the dialogue to sit. This can make it easier to combine dense soundtrack elements with that all-important and crit-ical dialogue.

There are electronic stereo wideners packaged as audio effects plug-ins that do a terrific job of making things sound bigger and wider. I often use the effect from iZotope Ozone 4, as shown in Figure 17.4, on a bus dedicated to ambiences and other BGs.

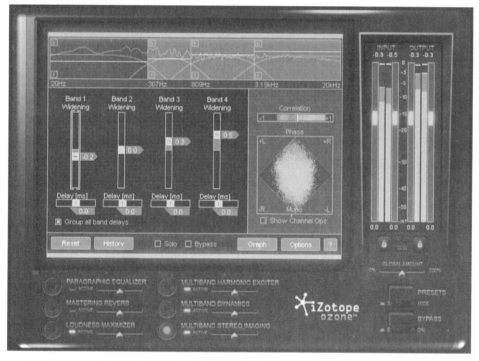

**Figure 17.4**  iZotope Ozone 4's stereo widener.

What other favorite tricks are there for super-wide stereo backgrounds? Use either stereo or mono recordings of similar spaces and then hard pan one left and the other right. Or use different pieces from the same, longer recording. As an example, I recorded a three-minute restaurant BG. I placed the first minute on one track and the third minute in the same place on another track, and then I panned the first track hard left and the second track hard right. This creates a wider stereo than the single track alone.

Another approach is to duplicate a BG sound to another track and offset it by half its length and then hard pan the two tracks. Because the left and right channels are different in time (but from the same place), the effect is a very wide stereo, leaving a nice hole in the middle for the dialogue. Figure 17.5 shows this in action. What's especially important about either of these two approaches is that they sum to mono well.

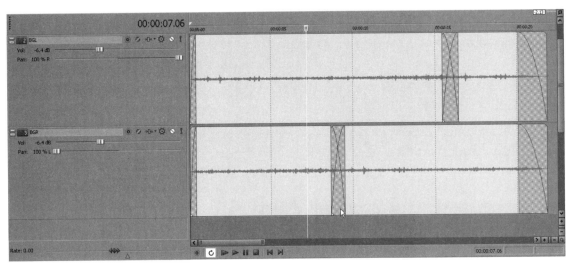

**Figure 17.5** Layering and panning recordings to create wider stereo BGs.

Take the same sound, duplicate it, and hard pan the results. Place a chorus effect on one side. Substituting a pitch shift and adjusting the cents (not semitones) on one side can work, too. Or try using a high-pass filter on one side and a low-pass on the other. These effects don't always translate well into mono, though, so be careful to check your results.

With the same sound on two channels, invert the phase on one channel. This works in stereo, but it doesn't sum to mono at all. (They cancel each other out, leaving *no* sound in their wake.) It is a gorgeous, huge, super-wide stereo effect, though. But I caution you not to do it, as the mono-summing issue is a big deal. If you can adjust the phase in other increments, such as by using the Little Labs Phase Alignment Tool shown in Figure 17.6, then experiment with that. Once again, check for mono compatibility, to be sure.

Adding reverb (or short delay) to a stereo recording in such a way that the left channel's reverb goes to the right side only and vice versa can also widen any BG's stereo picture.

**Figure 17.6**  Little Labs Phase Alignment Tool.

## Surround BGs

The approaches discussed here also work in surround sound. For example, I may use one of these stereo tricks for the front L/R channels and then send the tracks to a stereo reverb panned only to the rear surround-sound channels. Simply placing some ambiences in the front and others in the rear also works. These techniques literally immerse your audience in the environment. It's a strong surround-sound effect, so use it sparingly. *Das Boot* takes this approach during the sequences when the U-boat is running silent. You really feel as if you are on the sub as creaks, groans, and other sounds come from all directions.

The next chapter looks at ways to use sound effects for greater impact. When you combine the Foley and BGs with these hard effects, your soundtrack really transforms into something special.

# 18 Sound Effects in Use

There are both creative and technical aspects to working with sound effects. On the creative side, it's all about finding and/or creating the right sound for the project. The technical aspects revolve around placing the effects on the DAW timeline and making sure they are in sync with the visuals. Additionally, there are ways to treat sounds—and some of this falls into the realm of mixing—to make them work in the soundtrack. What follows are several important points to consider—some creative and others technical—as you work on the sound effects side of your soundtrack.

No soundtrack happens accidentally. Crafting a soundtrack is a conscious, deliberate process. And it's hard work: 3 percent inspiration and 97 percent perspiration. When I show project timelines to other people, the level of detail often shocks them. A first-time project generally has a VO, a couple of SFX, a BG, and maybe music—8 to 10 tracks, tops. For a similar project, I may have 60 to 80 tracks!

## Write Once, Use Many Times

Building the sound palette for a particular project can take a lot of time and effort, as does getting everything to sound right on the timeline. However, once some of this material is in place, it's a simple matter to reuse it as needed. For example, suppose several scenes take place in the same location. You will need to build a suitable BG and other effects for that specific locale. Thankfully, once those layers are finished, you can copy and paste them to every scene that takes place in that location. You can then tweak this as needed by adding a few other subtle sounds or necessary obvious sounds to sweeten things somewhat. That's certainly easier than building from scratch every time. This not only saves effort but also adds audio unity to the project by giving each location its own consistent sonic mark.

## Play to the Emotions

A lot of sound effects live in the literal world with the sole function of supporting obvious onscreen action. However, there are often opportunities to select sounds and sweeten them to make them more effective. It's a constant battle between using sounds that are authentic and realistic and knowing what sounds best serve the drama. In these cases, choose sounds that reinforce the emotion of the scene in a special way that is less literal and more subjective. Sounds won't usually have the same emotional effect as music, but that doesn't mean you can't also include sounds that better strengthen the project's message.

---

**Note:** Remember this: Every sound choice you make is an opportunity to support, complement, augment, and enhance the story.

---

# The Long Road

One issue of working with sound effects is that tracks never seem to sound complete until they are, in fact, complete. If you work only on backgrounds, you may find the lack of hard sync effects makes you feel as if you are making very little progress. If you work on just the obvious sync sound effects, the lack of backgrounds to form a foundation makes these effects seem too prominent, too in-your-face, naked, and bare. After the backgrounds join the effects, the individual sounds seem to sit better in the mix.

If you decide to do effects first, you might want to temp in a quick background or two to give your effects placement some perspective. For example, you might be working on a city street scene. Drop in a simple, all-encompassing city traffic background temporarily and build your sync sound effects. You can then return to the backgrounds and make them better, but this first step can help keep you focused on the entire mix of elements.

Progress can be slow. It's not backbreaking work, but it can be very detailed and tedious work. Don't be fooled when you plow through things quickly. For one project I spent two days working on the effects to reach Minute 16. I went to bed feeling rather stoked about getting so many minutes done in two days. (Of course, 8 of those 16 minutes were musical numbers requiring little or no intervention on my part.) The next day, it took me 8 full hours to get to Minute 17. Ouch.

I find that reviewing the previous day's work before moving forward is a solid approach. You return to the project with fresh ears, which usually results in you having to make a few tweaks, and then you are ready to move forward, picking up where you left off. This also helps ensure that your audio work remains consistent as the project progresses.

# Sound Saves Money

Always remember that sound can overcome some production woes, especially on low-budget productions. Two actors in an ersatz foxhole can be made to seem in the thick of combat with the judicious application of quality war-based sound effects. If you don't have the money to spend on the visuals, spend what you do have on the sound. I mean, what really sells the most fantastic visual effect? The computer software used to make and render it? ITSS!*

---

*It's the sound, stupid!

## Movie Physics

Sound effects almost always defy physics. A lightning bolt seen off in the distance typically has its SFX in sync rather than the delay you would expect in real life (one Mississippi, two Mississippi…). A deeper rumble that follows the initial crash and sustains for some time can add to the reality and be more like real life without losing the sync convention.

The same idea applies to explosions. You see an explosion onscreen and hear it immediately, even if the thing exploding is a half-mile (or more) away from the camera. There would be a delay to the sound if you were really there, but audiences expect sound to be in sync with the picture—even if that defies the physical world.

Don't get me started on sound in space! The last 10 minutes of the original *Star Wars* would have been a nearly silent movie! Kubrick did follow the rules of physics in *2001*, though.

## Think Cause and Effect

An actor clicks a switch. Although it would be acceptable to add the sound of the click, it might be better to add the sound of what the switch turned on (or off), too. Think of the movie convention of a giant warehouse, and somebody throws the switch to the lights (which is usually some obnoxiously large electrical switch from the 1940s). The switch makes its obvious clunk sound, and as the camera cuts to the lights going on, the audience hears a *whoompf*. Now, lights don't *whoompf* in real life—but they do on many soundtracks.

Seriously, get in the habit of thinking of cause and effect. Here is the cause of the sound—the literal—and here is the effect of the sound—sometimes literal, sometimes unseen, sometimes neither. Say a character fires a gun—the cause. The effect might be a ricochet, striking a surface, and even the secondary sound of the shell casing ejecting and hitting the floor.

## Remember the "See a Dog, Hear a Dog" Adage

If the audience sees a sound-producing something on the screen, they expect to hear it, too—especially if there is action involved. You can often ignore static objects, but when there's movement, there needs to be sound. This sound doesn't necessarily need to be dominant, but it does need to be on the track. For example, I was working on a dramatic scene that had a truck whiz by behind the actor during a close-up. Ironically, the truck-by was not picked up on the production dialogue track; it was barely audible. In post, I added a full truck-by and carefully mixed it low in the track. The effort seemed innocuous at the time, but it actually made the scene more real and therefore more effective.

## Finding the Sync

When working with sound effects on the DAW timeline, you need to be cognizant of synchronization. Obviously the fun, creative part of this work is finding the right sounds and seeing how they work with the visuals. But first you need to place these audio clips on the timeline in sync with the picture. And placing the clips in the right place can be tricky sometimes.

One method is to watch the film in real time and either pause or insert a marker where the sound should go. The second method is to go through frame by frame and find the right place. In reality, a combination of the two approaches works best. You will find yourself alternating playing in real time and scrubbing through in slower speeds or frame by frame to get all the sounds in place.

What can make finding sync points so difficult is that the action in many film/video frames is blurry. As an example, it's hard to see where the foot hits the floor because of this motion blur. Furthermore, some elements go offscreen or out of frame, making it even more challenging to find the right sync point. Despite all this fuzziness, there is usually a frame with little or no blur. That frame is usually the right point. With the footstep example, watch the blur of the leg/foot and note the frame where the blur disappears. That non-blurry frame is usually the footfall. Drag the sound effect in place and then go back a couple of seconds and play the sequence in real time to be sure. Tweak as needed.

Watch out for entrainment here, as you may be fooled into thinking something is in sync when it's not. Even sound pros fall for this. What's the best tactic in this case? Either bring in another person to watch and ask her if the scene is in sync or take a day away from the scene and return to it with fresh ears and a clear mind. As with many of these skills, you will get better at recognizing the right sync points as you expand your work experience.

## Sync the Foreground

Related to the previous comments, you need to selectively add sounds to support those most obvious elements. If obvious action happens onscreen, such as a car going by, it is best to put the sound effect in place even if it is not on the production track. Sometimes these are background sound effects, as mentioned earlier in the truck example. More often, these are predominant foreground elements. Although you don't have to (and probably shouldn't) match sound to every single bit of action you see onscreen, you do need to cover the most noticeable ones. When you provide sync sound for these elements, the whole track seems in sync. These foreground elements may not be in the physical foreground of screen action; they are just the most noticeable elements that scream for some kind of sound treatment.

In Figure 18.1, notice the bus and taxi. These are the primary foreground elements in the shot that need distinct sound treatment. In fact, as the bus moves across the scene, any sound the taxi might make would be masked by it. You could feature the bus and ignore the taxi. What about the other cars in the far-right background and behind the bus? These can be safely ignored as well or just covered by a general cityscape background. The same goes for any people in this shot. By providing sound for the obvious foreground, dominant elements, everything else feels in sync, too.

01:33:22:18

**Figure 18.1** Sync the foreground, and other elements seem in sync, too.

> **Note:** Remember the concept of *entrainment* discussed earlier in this book. As humans, we like to make order from chaos, so we want the sound and picture to be in sync. Keep this in mind as you work on your sounds. If your audience can latch on to a few obvious sync moments, then they will see sync in everything (even if it's an illusion—for example, background sounds that aren't really in sync).

## Don't Mistake Clip Edges for Sound Starts

Be careful when lining up sound effects. Sometimes the sound itself doesn't really start at the beginning of the actual audio file. If this is the case, when you line up the edge of the audio clip to correspond with a visual event, the sound effect may end up being late. Although accurate, dead-on sync is the basic rule, there are times when it works better to be a smidge early on the SFX than to be late. Zoom in and see where the effect actually starts and either move or trim accordingly to be in sync with the visual.

Some DAWs support a snap offset feature where you can designate within the file clip where to snap. Figure 18.2 illustrates both of these points. In the figure, the snap offset is being moved to correspond to the start of the gunshot, which doesn't begin until about a half-second into the sound file itself. The marker indicates where the effect should be to work with the visual.

## Be Authentic

Use caution when adding prerecorded sound effects by making sure that the choices you include fit the scene. If you have a small classroom filling up with students, you wouldn't add the crowd at a baseball game because it is too big and doesn't match the vibe or perspective of the scene. Instead, you'd try using something like a small cafe

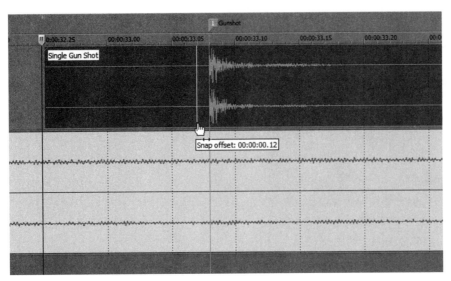

**Figure 18.2** Snap offset can make it easier to place some SFX in sync.

crowd or students in a hallway to better suit the scene. Also, if you show high school students hanging outside, you can't get away with the sound of elementary school children at recess. The sounds have to reasonably match what the visuals tell you.

That said, the sounds you choose often work because you *say* they work. Things do not always need to be literal. In fact, many real sounds do not actually sound good when recorded. A soft sound, such as a pillow fluff, actually sounds rather rough. That means you need to substitute a different sound that is more "soft" in this example. I've used many stand-in sounds to represent other sounds—not because I'm lazy, but because they sound better or right for the scene. On their own, they may not work, but in the mix and accompanied by the visual, the sound choice may be ideal.

## Make 'Em Your Own

Make sure you personalize and customize your sound effects, especially backgrounds. I often hear projects in which someone just threw a few canned backgrounds on the track and called it a day. Instead, ask yourself how you can sweeten these mostly canned effects. For example, perhaps you have a distant recording of a restaurant. Add some close-miked voice, perhaps some glasses clinking, and balance them in the background mix. Record these wild or as Foley to make the scene more interesting.

## Get Real during Pauses

When characters are talking, it's best to push back the effects in the mix. Sometimes you will do this with volume, but more often this is more effective with less density (in other words, fewer sound effects). To keep the city example going, you may reduce the traffic effects to a simple, not too overpowering general city background din. An effects track with less going on often works well when there is heavy dialogue. However, when characters are not talking, that's an ideal moment to push up the scene realism. Again, this isn't strictly a volume thing. Adding density—meaning more sound effects when the dialogue pauses—can make the scene feel more dynamic and alive.

## Use Layers

Think foreground, middle ground, and background sounds as you plan the effects soundtrack. Picture a scene with rain. In the background, you might place distant thunder rumbles. In the middle, consider the swishy white noise of rain. Make this really wide stereo, too. For the foreground, perhaps include the sound of the rain striking a nearby surface. These layers together provide more depth, resulting in a more complete, more real illusion.

Another way to look at layers is that rarely does a single sound effect work on its own. Many apparent single sound effects are really an amalgam of different layers and recordings. Each layer adds detail(s) that enhance what the audience hears. Stacking several recordings together to create a final sound is a common approach. This is a mainstay in sci-fi/fantasy work, but even building realistic tracks requires this approach. The sound designers on *The Hunt for Red October* reportedly combined seven sounds, from bubbles to animal sounds, to create the underwater torpedo sound effect.

Combining disparate sounds and using various processing (for example, pitch shifting) to add fullness or a different quality to the pieces is just one path to crafting the right sound for a particular instance.

## Watch Out for "Noise" Sounds

Rain, wind, water, and other similar sounds just become noise on a soundtrack. If you feature them too much, they lose their effectiveness and clutter the soundtrack. You have to be careful. As mentioned in the earlier discussion on layers, consider combining some close-up sounds with the general "wash" of the noise elements for variety and to make things clearer. Make these noise elements really wide stereo, too. Keeping a sound such as rain out of the dialogue area means it will sound like rain and not just a noisy dialogue recording!

With rain, try combining different perspectives—close, far, and in between—push it out to the far edges of the stereo, boost the high frequencies, cut the lows, carve out the middle mud for dialogue to sit in, and add a little thunder, too.

Similar to that notion is to be careful of unseen noise elements that make it seem as if the soundtrack is bad instead of creative. For example, for a scene that took place in an alley, I considered putting the sound of a window air conditioner humming and rattling away. The problem was the audience never saw said A/C unit. Therefore, the sound effect was more like really noisy on-location sound. Once I eliminated the extra noise, the dialogue actually sounded better.

## Beware of "Temp" Video

Though it is good practice to begin the real hard work of sound effects after the picture is locked, there are times when you may work with temp video. For example, in today's CGI (computer-generated images—in other words, visual effects) world, you may have rough placeholders slugged into the video, awaiting the final visuals. Though the timing is correct, the final video may *look* different from the placeholder. When working with the sound, you may find it inspiring and easier to work with what you see. But if what you see changes, the sound may need to change, too.

For example, I've had several projects in which certain sequences in the final video were different from what I'd been given. In one case, there were no sync changes to conform (thankfully), but there was an entirely new opening title sequence that screamed for SFX work. On another project, a special effects shot had been finished, and that made me realize I had to redo all the sound effects work for that scene because what I'd done before didn't really work with the new, improved visual. (I'd been working with raw footage of an actor against a green screen.)

## It's What the Sound Sounds Like, Not What It's Called

As you search for sounds, there is a tendency to look for the name of a sound. For example, you need the sound of a light switch turned off. So you search for "light switch." The better approach is to search for the kind of sound the switch makes—and that's a click. In other words, listen for what the sound *is*, and not the thing that makes the noise. Search for "click," and you will be presented with myriad possibilities that can work for your light switch.

The expanded keyword searches offered by some websites that sell sounds, along with the extensive capabilities of the Soundminer (store.soundminer.com) or BaseHead (www.baseheadinc.com) software, work on this principle, too. You have to name the file something, but it is the keywords associated with a given sound that make it easier to identify exactly what you need.

So don't be as literal when you search for sounds; instead, widen your search. For instance, I've used explosions and echoes from explosions to represent thunder. Adding some reverb with a long pre-delay can thicken up and lengthen the explosion-as-thunder, too. Pitch-shifting a copy of the sound an octave lower and mixing that with the original can add some special low-frequency "oomph" to the sound, too.

## And Then There's Sound Design

What is the sound of an illicit drug coursing through the veins of an unfortunate addict? What do you do when a sound doesn't exist? Coming up with these kinds of sounds usually starts in the physical world, and they are composed of many elements. Don't think of the literal nature of the sound; instead, think of a stylized version of what something might sound like and then build it up from pieces, or use electronic manipulations. I mostly rely on synthesizers and samplers for these kinds of sounds, but other approaches, such as stacking and combining sounds in unusual ways, work, too. Applying reverse, pitch shifts, and all manner of audio effects is the path to realizing these sounds. For me, it's a journey of discovery by starting with an often mundane real-world recording and then mangling it in many ways until I arrive at something interesting.

What are some of the ways you can craft the sounds you need? Whether you start with a mundane sound or with something more unusual, fire up the DAW and experiment with the sound to see where it takes you and what you can make of it. Try these ideas:

- Edit.

- Stack.

- Combine.

- Double.

- Reverse.

- Chop up.

- EQ.

- Slow it down or speed it up.

- Shift the pitch up or down.

- Use filters in a synthesizer/sampler and then mangle the sound using the synth or sampler tools.

- Bit-crush.

- Granular-ize.

- Add flange, chorus, wah, delay, reverb.

- Mangle.

- Distort.

- Convolve.

- World-ize.

- Don't accept the first thing that pops into your head. Work to find the right sound.

Personally, I like working on a sound file in Sony Creative Software's Sound Forge Pro, where applying effects and tweaking *ad infinitum* is easier. I also like the visual nature of working this way, where you can see the physical changes to the waveform as you make them.

Using convolution (as mentioned in the list) is another path to take for sound design. Convolution is a way to multiply the frequency content of two sounds via FFT (*Fast Fourier Transform*). Essentially, one sound—the impulse response (IR)—affects another sound. You don't hear the IR, just its result on the other sound. Figure 18.3 shows the Sony Acoustic Mirror plug-in, which works as a terrific convolution-based sound-design tool. Convolution was mentioned earlier in this book as a way to sample ambiences (reverb) and apply them to sounds. Generally, you can use *any* sound as the IR, and you can therefore craft many unique sound-design ideas, too.

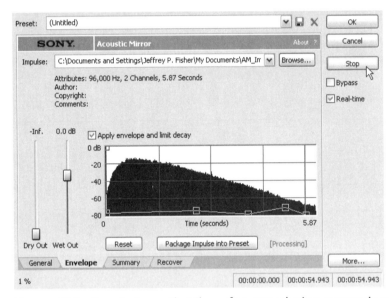

**Figure 18.3** Sony's Acoustic Mirror for convolution processing.

Also, keep your ears open for unusual-sounding things that you come across in your life. Work to capture these sounds to use either for a current project or for the future. Travel with a small recorder so you can record these happy accidents. Build your own library of sounds that provide the raw material you need for all your work.

## Use the Non-Surround LFE

One area worth addressing is low-frequency enhancement—or LFE, for short. The LFE is an integral part of surround sound—it's the .1 in 5.1. However, just because your project is destined for lowly stereo (or even mono), that doesn't mean you shouldn't pay some extra attention to the extreme low-frequency elements of your soundtrack. After all, the original name for the LFE was the "Baby Boom" channel. These effects might include explosions, crashes, airplanes, thunder, punches, impacts, or other such sounds. Typically, these LFE sounds are enhancements to other sounds, not functioning as the *only* low-frequency sound.

For example, you might have a crash of thunder and then enhance that with a deep, resonant sound that has its frequency content limited to the extreme low end (low pass below 120–80 Hz). In addition to limiting its frequency content with a low-pass filter, consider shifting the pitch down an octave. This will leave only the very low bass rumble to shake the audience.

Compression can help here, too. Apply just a little compression to smooth things out and tame extreme peaks—use a 3:1 ratio with a medium fast attack and medium release and a −12 to −20 dB threshold. Of course, like all suggested settings, use these as starting points only and tweak them to taste. If your ears tell you it is right, it is (provided you can trust your ears, monitors, and room!).

With non-surround projects, I often tap the signal from certain sound effects, route them to a bus, add a low-pass filter and a pitch-shift plug-in set for one octave lower to that bus, and then add in this heavy bass rumble at key points. These LFE sounds are a good final mix sweetener that provides some extra low-end power when needed. These same sounds can go to the dedicated LFE in a surround sound project, too.

You have to make sure these low-frequency effects are tight and controlled. If they are too flabby, they may sound mushy or boomy (but not in a good way). Watch the levels. At certain listening levels, low frequencies need to be higher in volume than higher-frequency sounds to be perceived as the same loudness. If they are too loud, they may "rattle" cheaper consumer speakers and TV sets.

## Worldizing

Today's sound effects editor has countless digital tools to alter, enhance, and mangle audio tracks to create new sounds, stylized versions of familiar sounds, and environments for these sounds to exist.

Many sound effects, especially those purchased commercially, sound rather dry and upfront. You need to work with them to get them to sit better in the mix. Tools such as volume, stereo (and surround) panning, delay/echo, reverb, and convolution all help to make these sounds fit the space represented by the visuals.

However, despite having the latest, greatest digital gizmos, there's often nothing better than recording in a real space to bring the sound effects to life. For example, the sound crew on *The Green Mile* reportedly loved the sound of the film's location so much that they returned there to record all of the film's Foley. Gary Rydstrom mentioned on a *Monsters, Inc.* special feature how he recorded hitting a milk jug in a parking garage for the sound of a plastic-bat-wielding child hitting a monster.

Similarly, Walter Murch and George Lucas played back the music used in *American Graffiti* outside and re-recorded the sound for use in the film. Essentially, they played the music through a speaker and picked up the sound using another microphone. George moved the speaker around while Walter, some distance away, moved the mic. This gave a special quality to the sound that they could use as needed. Orson

Welles did a similar thing by playing back the soundtrack to *Touch of Evil* through a speaker at one end of an alley and placing the mic at the other and then recording the result. This "atmospheric" track could then be mixed in as needed. This approach is called *worldizing*, and it still happens today (see Figure 18.4).

**Figure 18.4** A simple approach to worldizing.

Image courtesy of Tony Santona.

## Include Some Ear Candy

Ear candy, for me, is all the little bits of business that support, enhance, or augment the big picture. Your sound work will be stronger if you truly take additional time and effort to sweeten every scene with some extra sounds that work to make things more realistic and better. Some of these sounds can come from recordings and sound libraries, and some are more suited to extra Foley work. These sounds can heighten drama or add comical effect. For instance, something as simple as a chair squeak while an actor shifts uncomfortably in his chair can work wonders to liven up a scene. Be careful with these kinds of adornments, though. Restraint is the measure of the day.

Some of this work is, frankly, for my own amusement—a direct response to endless hours spent in dark rooms cutting audio. For example, a door to a coffee shop kept opening and closing in a scene, so I added a little bell chime to each opening and closing. The director thought that had been recorded on location, but in reality, it was fabricated in the audio edit suite to make the scene more real. These little sound moments add to the feel, making the soundtrack come alive and work better. The absence of these sounds makes the piece dull, lifeless, and less believable. When they are in place and balanced well in the mix, these sounds make a huge difference in your audience's perception.

## Use Perspective Shifts

As the scene shifts, the sound perspective should change, too. Sometimes these changes may be minor, such as a volume dip or a tonal change. Other times, you need to resort to different recordings that mirror the perspective shift. Drastic changes require equally drastic alterations in sound. That's why you can never have too many background sounds recorded—or built—to match varying perspectives. You want traffic that is distant, close, filtered, from above/below, and more. Sweetening these basic tracks with particular and often in-sync "business" completes the illusion.

## Pre- and Post-Lap

Sometimes the sound for Scene B begins well before Scene A ends. This is known as a *pre-lap*. The incoming sound may be dialogue, but more often it is the new scene's effects mix. Extending the sounds from B into C would be a post-lap, but it is more rare. You don't need to do anything technically special beyond aligning the various sounds accordingly to match the visuals. I mention it because it is a creative decision that may work for some projects. In particular, going from a quiet scene to a louder one can get added emphasis with a pre-lap and can even jar the audience (in a good way!).

## Beware the Exit-Sign Effect

Even if you don't do surround-sound work, this phenomenon is still worth mentioning, as it applies to stereo soundtracks, too. Be careful with hard-panning sound effects to the extreme left or right. You don't want this kind of sound movement to make your audience turn away from the screen toward the source of the sound and be left watching the theater's exit sign. Brief off-screen sounds are fine, but work quickly to move them into the field of vision.

## Throw in the Kitchen Sink

It's generally a good idea to provide a thorough amount of sound effects and backgrounds that reinforce each and every scene and then sort it all out later. I call this the "kitchen sink" approach. It's often difficult to get at the essence of each scene— how it works dramatically in relation to the sound until all the elements are together. I'm not suggesting that you put off all decisions until the final mix, but often this is what you must do or nearly do. It's hard to make a decision about a background, for instance, until you have the music (if any) in place.

If it's in the foreground or dominates part of a scene in any way, it needs sound. And just because you may lose some sound elements as the project moves along, that doesn't mean you shouldn't provide sound support for the most obvious screen elements. A lot of time it's the subtle, more Foley-ish sounds that really bring a scene alive. The door slam, the gunshot, the car horn—those are the easy and obvious visuals that need sounds. However, all those little sounds, including footsteps, clothing rustles, and so forth, are the sounds that bring a scene to life, even when they get buried under louder, more obvious sound elements. As I said before, it's when these sounds are missing completely that their absence gets noticed.

When all the sound elements are finished, you can start working through the project and deciding what to feature most. You can't feature everything, as we've discussed, or the soundtrack just degenerates into a jumbled mess. "Actually, a lot of mixing is about removing things," reported dialogue mixer Andy Nelson in *Mix* magazine. "You're always going into the game fully loaded, and then you start saying, 'What *don't* we need?'"

It's important to step back, strip away all the unnecessary sound elements, and find the root of the soundtrack to find the message (and emotion!) of the piece that you are trying to convey via sound. And this is not an easy process. As audio professionals, we often become enamored of our own work, and it's painful to cut out the bits we worked so hard to include. But that is the creative process—working and reworking the audio to best support the story.

When you're working with some directors, they aren't always sure what they want at this stage, either, so I find it better to give them a few options. If I have an idea for something, rather than ask whether I should do it, I generally just go ahead and include the sound and then discuss it later.

Also, as a soundtrack comes together, it often provides a new, fresh perspective for directors and editors who have lived with the crummy production sound (and maybe a few temp sound effects) for so long. When your soundtrack joins the picture cut, even as a rough mix, it may re-energize them and restart their creative juices. The sound may help them better see the possibilities of a scene or of the movie as a whole. This kind of collaboration is invaluable. Embrace it and expect it. (It may mean more work for you, though.)

## Never Close the Door to Creativity

Don't rely too much on the way things should be or—worse—the way "we've always done it 'round here." Instead, use your tools to make the sound come together as it should in the service of the project. The soundtrack as a whole must work, and only when expanding your approach—and your creativity—can you discover the right way.

When you've acquired a significant amount of knowledge in a particular area, there is a tendency to rest on your laurels and take a similar approach to any new work that comes your way. This is a dangerous notion. You suffocate your creativity when you resort to the same old fixes for the same old problems. For example, students and other would-be pros often ask me what EQ settings and such I use. And my reply is simple: whatever makes the track work. I never want to resort to canned settings; instead, I rely on my ears to make the right choices to drive and support the story. In fact, I don't care what anything sounds like on its own as long as the mix as a whole works. Individual sounds can be rather thorny when soloed, but in the context of the entire DM&E mix, this thorny sound may fit in perfectly. In short, every problem is unique, and every solution to said problem is equally distinctive.

There are no shortcuts and no easy fixes. I have a client who is always looking for the easy fix: What will make my audio better, less noisy, and perfect? And the answer to that question is simply this: hard work and even harder-won skill. Acquire good sound to begin with and then use your skill and audio tools to make it shine. There is no magic button for fixing audio—it takes effort to craft a seamless soundtrack that makes an impact on your audience. It is the raw skill that really matters, not the tools.

As Albert Einstein once said (and I suspect he may have dabbled in audio-post in his spare time): "Imagination is more important than knowledge. For knowledge is limited to all we now know and understand, while imagination embraces the entire world, and all there ever will be to know and understand."

## Futzing Around

Sometimes you need to make sounds take on a specific quality. For instance, you need the music to sound as if it's coming from a clock radio or a voice from a mobile phone. Adding such an effect to the sound is known as *futzing*. EQs and other filters are the measure of the day to simulate these real-world audio events.

## Premixing, Freezing, and Printing Audio Effects

When your timeline starts to get overcrowded and messy, you may want to freeze or premix some effects tracks. For example, you may want to premix the BGs and reduce your track count and screen real estate accordingly. It's best to do a stereo premix, but *don't* delete the originals. Mute them (or make them inactive, depending on your DAW) and move them to the bottom of your timeline. Inevitably, you will want to go back and tweak these, and that will render your premix worthless.

Alternatively, you could also group and bus similar tracks for greater control and to temporarily keep them out of the way, as shown in Figure 18.5. Others prefer to work in separate sessions and then merge the pieces later. I don't care for this approach because I like to be able to check all elements regularly to hear how the whole sound-track progresses. You should discover which method works for you and plan accordingly.

This same idea extends to "printing" effects (that is, making them a permanent part of a sound). Printing effects or premixing/freezing tracks is usually done to free up resources, in case your computer can't keep up. I rarely print effects; instead, I separate those tracks needing an effect on their own, or, if there are multiple sounds, I group them to a bus and apply the effect there. If needed, the effect can be bypassed when working to free up computer processing power. The exception to my no-printing rule is when I'm building sound-design elements. The effects on these sounds are permanent, so it makes sense to have just the finished version on the timeline and not to roll any audio effects in real time.

**Figure 18.5** Group bussing submixes of soundtrack elements.

Doing a little bit of premixing as you go, including having main elements grouped and on bus faders, means a final mix can be even easier. Keep everything! That way, you can easily go back to the pieces and stems (the whole timeline!) and tweak as needed to get closer to your creative vision.

> **Note:** Computer- and video-game soundtracks carry specific technical considerations you must handle. That said, the aesthetics and such as detailed here remain wholly applicable. You still need to build a convincing environment from which the story unfolds. Sometimes realism is the goal, with exaggeration and hyper-reality often in the fray. Occasionally, counterpoint is called for, too.

## Getting Notes

It makes sense to regularly play your work in progress for the other creative members of the team, such as the director, producer, and others. It's rare to hold these playback sessions in person. More often, you send a mix (I use FTP) and wait to receive notes. These memos tend to only point out what's wrong and nitpick, so don't take them too personally. Instead, get down to work fixing the issues and move forward. There's more about this topic in Chapter 20, "Mixing."

**Note:** Never throw out anything! If a director says to lose a particular sound, don't lose it. Instead, mute the sound and move on. Creative people change their minds, so the director might say, "Let's have that sound back in." If that happens, all you need to do is unmute it. This applies to every change suggested along the way. Keep everything in case you need it again later.

## A Few Short Case Studies in Sound-Effects Work

At this point, it might be useful to share a few solutions to some past projects. The idea is to provide some insight into how you might approach a scene. I know it's kind of hard to describe the sound work in print, but it still should offer some applicable insight.

### Cars in Motion

The scene shows a character waiting in vain for another person while cars whiz by in front of her. It's shown in a series of overlapping dissolves to signify the long waiting time. Some of the car sounds were on the production tracks, but they were low quality. I decided to sync up new car-bys for every car that went by. I carefully selected stereo bys with cars moving quickly from left to right or right to left to match screen action and actual cars (small cars, midsize cars, SUVs, and so on). Using several tracks, I checkerboarded these various car-bys in glorious, very wide stereo. It was time consuming, but the effect was very realistic, if a little exaggerated.

Next, I grouped the tracks and bussed them to a single audio bus. On this bus I added a flanger (essentially a short time delay with modulation) followed by a stereo multi-tap delay. This added an otherworldly sound to the whizzing cars. The extreme stereo was there, almost disorienting, with a weird quality to boot. I started the scene with normal sounds and then gradually added the effects as the time the character waited grew longer. It was a novel approach. To make things a little heavier (the cars were high-pitched swishy noises), I faded in a dark drone underneath to fill in the bass a bit.

### Dream Phone

A character is awoken by a cell-phone ring. I thought it would be cool if the first ring was off in the distance, like you might hear as you come out of a dream. So, the first ring went heavy into reverb, about half as much reverb for the second ring, and then normal dry and up front for the final ring before the character wakes to answer the call. It's a subtle thing that many people notice and comment on how it sounds like waking from a dream.

### Screams

Screams were needed for the final scene, and there really were no good screams from the production. I decided to go very stylized with sound design and create heavily effected screams layered together. Using pitch shifts, EQ, delays, and modulation, the final effect became both eerie and quite dramatic. The source material was a combination of some sound effects I had and a lot of sound-design tweaking with audio effects and my trusty X-treme FX soft-synth module.

## Killer Drug

And what about the sound of an illicit drug coursing through the veins of an unfortunate addict, mentioned earlier in this chapter? My solution, shown in Figure 18.6, was to use a lot of squishy fruit-based Foley, some heavily filtered underwater sounds, some low explosion tails, a knife stab, and a few other bits and pieces. It makes the audience squirm. Yay!

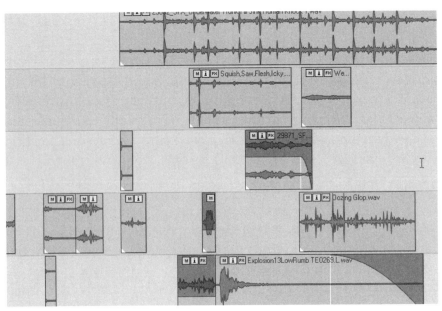

**Figure 18.6** Several SFX layered together create the sound of killer drugs.

In the next chapter, we visit the emotional aspect to the soundtrack—and that means the all-important music contribution.

# 19  Music

**M**usic affects how the audience interprets what they see. It underscores the emotion of your work. Therefore, it's a vital component to nearly every project and should never be an afterthought, something thrown in at the last minute. As filmmaker David Lynch says, "When music marries to a scene, the whole is greater than the sum of the parts."

Music is so important to narrative storytelling that many directors take over the reins either by working with a close collaborator—such as Alfred Hitchcock with Bernard Herrmann, David Lynch with Angelo Badalamenti, or the Coen Brothers with Carter Burwell—or by doing it themselves, such as John Carpenter and Robert Rodriguez. Sharing your musical vision and building a relationship with a composer can result in far more effective music. For those so inclined, because of either skill or budget restrictions, the DIY path can yield some excellent results, too.

Music comes in two flavors: source and underscore. Source is music that appears onscreen or from within the story; it's diegetic. Examples include a band playing during a wedding scene, a musical number, or the radio that wakes up Bill Murray's character in *Groundhog Day*. Underscore is the traditional, non-diegetic music with which we are all familiar. We don't expect the camera to pan over and reveal the orchestra playing offscreen (though Mel Brooks did just this with *High Anxiety*). A music video or other event work, such as a concert, obviously is a special variation of source music.

How does music work? Composer Aaron Copland provided the most succinct answer to this question: "Original music creates a convincing atmosphere of time and place. Original music provides a neutral background filler and helps bridge scenes. Original music creates a sense of continuity. Original music helps build to dramatic finality."

To those words I would add these three primary approaches to using music:

- The music simply mirrors the screen action, supports and complements the emotions, ideas, and messages, and doesn't detract from them.

- The music enhances the subtext or underlying message instead of what is actually happening. This technique can help portray a character's mindset, which may be contrary to the action.

255

- The music plays against either the first or the second idea above. For example, during a scene with extreme violence, a toy piano might play a children's lullaby.

Music works best when it mirrors or augments the raw emotion of a scene. But music can carry emotional baggage, too—especially popular or iconic music. Advertisers often choose existing songs to hock their wares. Unfortunately, many popular songs can be rather divisive. One person's favorite tune is another person's breakup song. The former buys the product while the latter avoids it—all because of the music.

Wagner's *Ride of the Valkyries* was used to great effect in *Apocalypse Now*. But when *Watchmen* co-opted the iconic music, the result was laughable at best. Even as an homage to *Apocalypse*, it failed miserably. *Ride* is music forever etched in many minds and associated with Coppola's Vietnam epic; by including it in another film, it pales by comparison.

Personally, I feel too many producers opt for overpowering music. I'm definitely from the less-is-more school of music composition. The ideal score is usually quite simple. Almost elegantly so. It is often subtle and sometimes bold; organic, yet intricate; atmospheric, but vivid. I try to strike a balance between simplicity and depth. Sometimes it's in the writing; other times it's the choice of instruments and sounds and how they're orchestrated.

Sometimes there is a feeling that a scene requires a lot of instrumentation for its music score. What I find is that less is often more. Sometimes just an atmospheric pad without a melody works nicely. Mark Snow did this to great effect with *The X-Files*. I prefer some beats, so for me, just a decent drum beat can fit nicely. Both approaches stay out of the way of dialogue while supporting the emotion and then make mixing the elements easier. As Dave West, lead mixer on *The X-Files*, recently said in a *Mix* interview, "Music is king. And truly, music can add more to a picture in any case than a gunshot ever will."

## Music Fundamentals

For films and TV, the music supervisor is the primary overseer of the music. Typical duties include working with the composer on original music, finding other music (source music and songs), and clearing rights. Additionally, this person may lead the music spotting session, administer the music budget, supervise the final music mix, file music cue sheets, work on the soundtrack album, and more.

Before you start searching for music, step back and ask yourself the following questions. Your answers to these queries will provide better insight into what you are trying to do with the music.

### Why Are You Using Music?

If your best answer to this is either, "Everybody uses music," or, "We have to have music; that's all," you may need to think a little more seriously about your project.

What is the point of having music? What does it add to the narrative drama or message? Be candid about your answer and really delve into the real, honest reasons why you feel music needs to be part of the overall soundtrack. For commercial projects, music becomes a brand identity and so requires even more careful selection.

## What Emotional Response Do You Desire?

Because music is all about emotion, answering this question can clue you in on the stylistic direction you should take with the score. "I want the audience to sob" might mean you probably won't opt for '80s techno. Also, define the range of emotions you want to convey and how the music may need to change tone with the dramatic arc of the story.

## What Is the Message?

This answer targets specifically what it is you want to say or convey with the project. Music can help certain elements really stick in the minds of the audience and can make the project's message more memorable. What are these important points? And how can music enhance them?

## Who Is Your Audience?

When you know specifically who your target audience is, it can help you better choose the right music to appeal to them. Use this information to make both stylistic and instrumentation decisions. For example, if you are putting together an educational piece aimed at high school students, your music selection will be different from that of the same video aimed at their parents.

## What Style Is Appropriate to the Audience?

This helps you further define your target and what appeals to them. The information helps clarify the ideal musical decision. This answer, along with the next, may be the most crucial path to effective music selection.

## What Style Is Appropriate to the Message?

This is often a very difficult decision. One musical direction may have wide appeal for your audience but may fail to support the message satisfactorily. Or you may find the right fit in supporting the message musically but forfeit some audience appeal. You must put careful thought into finding the right balance for *both* the audience and the message, with serving the story taking some precedence.

## Where Will You Put the Music (or Not)?

Answering this query takes the bulk of the spotting session as you go through the project and make these important decisions. This is the real nitty-gritty, and it's where most people begin. Instead, I urge you to answer the previous questions *before* you tackle these technical tidbits.

When you reach this step, you'll want to make concrete decisions about the following:

- Choose the musical style (or styles, if the project calls for distinct approaches).

- Consider thinking in colors. If your project visually has dark colors, use darker-sounding instruments (cello, for example). If the colors are brighter, choose brighter instruments (such as the flute).

- Decide on the basic instrumentation. What is the best way to represent the style? The budget may constrain this decision. For instance, you may desire an orchestra, but your wallet can only spring for a string quartet.

- Keep other soundtrack elements in mind. If you have a female voiceover, you may want to avoid alto saxophone, as it is in the same range as the female voice, and that can make it difficult to mix them together effectively.

- Detail all musical start and stop points and whether the music will be source, underscore, or song. Where the music begins and/or ends provides the most effective way to impact your audience. It's also important to find those instances where the music needs to sync with the screen action (called a *hit point*). Too many of these hits can quickly become cartoon-like and is actually called "Mickey-Mousing" in the trade. That can work for animation and some comedies, but dramatic films often suffer when the music mimics every little piece of screen action.

- Although it is perfectly acceptable to point to the screen and say, "Start the music there when the bad guy enters," there is a better way. Add a timecode window burn to the video so you can write down more specific timings and other details. Sometimes these spotting notes can become quite detailed, depending on the project's complexity and workflow needs.

> **Note:** Silence can often be more powerful than having music playing. Silence can also work when you do bring in the music later, because it will make a bigger impact.

With your answers to these questions and the specific spotting notes, you have the roadmap you need to find, commission, and otherwise create best the musical score for your project.

Searching for the right music can be time consuming. Plan on going through a lot of ideas before you decide. Answering these questions and then discovering the right style of music helps you eliminate choices. As you narrow choices down, you can zero in on a few ideas. If you know you want orchestra, it doesn't make sense to be looking in rock. Think thematically and repeat themes and ideas, too. And remember that while the right music can make a good production better, no music can make the worst idea palatable.

# Getting the Music

Music is generally added to the project during or after the picture-editing phase. This is known as *post-scoring*. That is not always the rule, though. Obviously, a musical or a music video needs the music completed in advance (*pre-score*). It's interesting to note that composer Angelo Badalamenti and filmmaker David Lynch often worked on the music before principal photography. This helped them discuss characters, define themes, and so forth. Lynch sometimes even played this music on the set for his actors.

There are several options for securing the right music for your needs. First, I hope it's quite obvious that you can't buy a popular music CD or download any ol' file and drop it in your project. The copyright holders of such songs may not be pleased with your actions. Buying a CD or download does *not* give you the right to use it in your film/video/TV show/podcast. You need permission, and such permission often carries a price tag.

Licensing a song—which is essentially "renting" the song—for a particular use can be a complicated endeavor. The process requires contacting the copyright holder(s)—there may be several—and getting their go-ahead, including paying any fees they may demand.

With existing music, there are really two licenses: the song itself and the actual recording of the song, presumably by a particular artist. A musical artist or band can re-record, or cover, any song and offer it for sale. All they need to do is pay the statutory mechanical rate to the song's publisher(s) and writer(s). This is around 9 cents per song, per unit as of this writing (2011).

However, to marry visuals to the music (as in a film) requires a different *synchronization* license. These "sync rights" apply whether you use the actual recording by an artist or you re-record or cover the song. To use the actual recording by an artist requires yet another license, called the *master use*.

Sync rights and master-use licensing can be expensive, depending on the song, the artist, and the eventual use. Some songs may cost a lot of money; others will cost less. For example, you may license some music for a project that only screens at film festivals. If you sell the project, you may need to purchase another license (or worse, remove the music completely). Many TV shows trade artists the use of their song for an advertising plug at the show's conclusion, as in, "Tonight's episode featured music from...."

Don't let these seemingly insurmountable legal obstacles dissuade you from ever using popular music. Just know that you must clear the rights before use. The license may or may not be possible. For example, you'll never get permission to use an actual Beatles recording, but they have licensed covers for certain movies. Fiona Apple covered "Across the Universe" in the movie *Pleasantville*. Howie Day and several other artists covered a lot of Lennon/McCartney songs for *I Am Sam*.

There is some music in the public domain, which essentially means the copyright has expired or there is no copyright in place. Because of the ever-changing copyright laws, it is hard to set a specific date before which something is in the public domain. It is probably safe to say that most, if not all, work before 1900 is in the public domain. Another gotcha to public domain is that although Mozart's musical work is indeed available to all to use without royalty, a particular arrangement or recording of his work—say, by a modern orchestra—can still be copyrighted.

What about fair use? Part of the copyright rules allows for the fair use of copyrighted material, including music. Your use of the material must pass four tests. If it doesn't pass all four tests, then you can't claim fair use. The test questions are:

- What is the purpose and character of the use? Is it nonprofit, commercial, educational, news, criticism?

- What is the nature of the work to be used? Is it a fact or is it an imaginative piece (music is!)?

- How much of the work will you use? A small amount compared to the whole? A chorus from a song is a substantial amount of the whole.

- What effect would this use have on the market for the original? Does the use compete with the original or otherwise take away from its potential sales? Or is using it just an attempt to avoid paying the industry-standard royalties?

Here are two places to consult when deciding to clear existing music and music tracks:

- www.clearance.com

- www.harryfox.com

However, the best way to avoid all this is to purchase music that's already cleared for sync use and/or to commission original music for your projects.

---

**Beware of Temp Tracks:** One surefire way to set yourself up for disappointment is to place some music that you like into a project temporarily, called a *temp track*. If this music is a popular song or other copyrighted piece, you may not be able to license it. Therefore, you risk becoming rather accustomed to these tracks. When you are forced to replace this temp track, you may never find the right music that lives up to the previous choice. You won't be able to see or hear the project the same way when your second-choice score is in place. Do yourself a favor and don't go down this road. Don't temp in something that may stifle your own or a composer's musical creativity.

That said, I know that a picture editor may need to cut a scene to a musical beat. If you can't find the right music first, take a different tactic. Temp in a simple metronome or a basic drum beat with the right tempo. This pulse will help the edit timing, but the simple music will (usually) not cause unfounded adoration. Make sure you note the metronome/drum track's tempo in beats per minute (BPM). Give this value to your composer or use it when searching for other music. Once you acquire the right music, it'll slip right into the scene, line up with the cutting, and make everybody happy.

## Library (a.k.a. Production or Stock) Music

Many companies offer music cleared for use in your projects. Called *library*, *stock*, or *production music* in the trade, there is a wide range of material available. Unlike popular music, these tracks are written specifically for video and related uses and are priced to include the licensing you need. In years past, library music was low quality, mostly electronic-sounding, and generally scorned. Today, the quality and variety has skyrocketed. You can get fully orchestral recordings along with popular (and retro) styles and genres and even songs from indie bands.

These cuts are often called *buy-out* or *royalty-free* music. This means that once you pay the fee, you can use the music however you want for as long as you want without paying any additional fees. (There is a small catch; see the upcoming "Performance Rights" sidebar.) Of course, the typical library track or CD collection costs far more than a commercial equivalent—$20+ per track, and a whole collection could be $100 or more.

Not all library music is created equal, though. There are different business models out there. Read the fine print. Although you may be able to buy the license for certain uses, it might not cover *every* situation, such as use in a motion picture released in a theater. If you are unsure, ask the music supplier for specifics *before* paying any licensing fees. When you know your intended use (and potential future use), you can select the right licensing for your situation.

One major drawback to using stock music is its lack of exclusivity. These companies can offer some amazing music to sweeten your projects at rates that are affordable for even the humblest budget. However, you may not control its other uses. For example, you may select a track for your dramatic movie, only to hear the same music on a late-night commercial for Al's Body Shop—or worse. That's the risk you take. You give up some exclusivity, but at a price far less than licensing other music. Some libraries offer some exclusivity across industries and genres, but you pay a premium for these services, so that may appeal to you instead.

Another shortcoming to stock music is that the music itself is fixed. Some companies provide alternate timings and an occasional variation, but generally the instrumentation and arrangement are mostly set. Don't like the saxophone solo? You're outta luck!

Digital Juice offers a variation that gives you multitrack stems—the musical equivalent of Photoshop layers—that allow you to remix the music. You could easily leave out a part you don't want. Similarly, SmartSound Sonicfire Pro is another product that lets you program many variations instead of being stuck with the same basic track.

VASST's TrakPaks include musical phrases that fit together to generate more variations. All of these solutions give you more choices and greater control than a standard stock music clip.

Here is a very short list of quality music library sources:

- Digital Juice (www.digitaljuice.com).

- FirstCom Music (www.firstcom.com).

- Freeplay Music (www.freeplaymusic.com). Read their license carefully.

- Fresh Music (www.freshmusic.com).

- Killer Tracks (www.killertracks.com).

- Megatrax (www.megatrax.com).

- Music Bakery (www.musicbakery.com).

- Omnimusic (www.omnimusic.com).

- SmartSound (www.smartsound.com).

- Twisted Tracks (www.twistedtracks.com).

- VASST TrakPaks (www.vasst.com).

- VideoHelper (www.videohelper.com).

---

**Performance Rights:** When a song is performed in public, such as at a venue or even via radio or TV, it is subject to another licensing fee. Called *performance rights*, these monies are collected by three well-known performance rights organizations (PROs)—ASCAP, BMI, and SESAC. Songwriters and publishers belong to one or more of these organizations and rely on them to collect these royalties on their behalf.

These royalties are paid by the owner of the entity making this public performance available (restaurants, clubs and other venues, radio and TV stations, and so forth). Interestingly, movie theaters are exempt from paying performance royalties. However, if that same film plays on TV, the station pays the appropriate fee for the music performance.

All music earns performance royalties, even so-called royalty-free library/ production/stock music. (Read the licensing!) For those of us who write for music libraries (your author included; see Figure 19.1), performance royalties are the primary source of revenue for the composer.

TV stations and networks demand that producers supply *cue sheets*—detailed descriptions of the music titles used, timing, writers, publishers, and PRO

**Figure 19.1** Dark New Age Fresh Music library.

affiliation. These cue sheets are then used by ASCAP/BMI/SESAC to determine and pay performance royalties to music publishers and writers. The royalties are on a sliding scale based on audience reach, with networks paying more than tiny cable/satellite channels.

You should keep detailed notes of all the music you use with your projects in case you do sell it in the future and are then required to supply proper cue sheets.

## Indie Artists

Securing the rights to lesser-known (or up-and-coming) original music might be easier than you think. Pump Audio is one such place to license songs (www.pumpaudio.com, now owned by Getty Images). Contacting musical artists directly is another option. Many digital download sites showcase up-and-coming musical talent. You may find that many songwriters and bands would be honored to have their music featured in a project. How do you do this? Ask. They might say yes!

Stan Harrington did just this when he asked Katy J if he could use some of her songs in his movie *The Craving Heart*. He had heard her music in another indie film and started a friendship with the LA-based singer-songwriter. (See the "Case Study: Scoring *The Craving Heart*" section later in this chapter.)

Be aware that not all indie artists can give you permission to use their music. They may have a publishing or record contract that controls their work. If they do indeed control their copyright and master-use licensing, then you can work out a deal. The best deal is that they retain all their rights and get a big, juicy screen credit, copies of the finished project, and perhaps a back-end deal (in the event of project revenue).

## Creative Commons

Some musicians and composers offer their music under the Creative Commons umbrella. You may be able to use their work in your projects with something as simple as an attribution: Music by so-and-so. One website, the Freesound Project (www .freesound.org), offers an amazing collection of musical samples, ambiences, sound effects, and other sound bits using the CC Sampling Plus licensing scheme. For more on Creative Commons, visit creativecommons.org/licenses.

## DIY Music

Another possibility is to compose your own music. "*What?!*" I can hear you screaming. "I'm not a musician or composer. I can't write my own music." Guess what? You *can* compose your own music with a little help from technology.

Sony Creative Software's ACID and Apple's GarageBand are popular software products that can help you create music scores quickly—and require minimal musical skill. These programs (and several others that support these features) essentially let you choose and combine prerecorded music and sound snippets, called *loops*, to create your own original, royalty-free music. Working this way is both flexible and unique, and it's surprisingly easy to learn—not to mention downright fun. Best of all, you can achieve some amazing results that help you support your work without the other hassles of licensing music. You can even license your own compositions made using these programs for other people to use.

ACID and GarageBand use what are known as *loops*. A music loop is a prerecorded, usually short, snippet of a musical performance that repeats flawlessly. Loops come as CD-quality sound files, usually in .wav format. A single loop might be a drum beat, a bass guitar riff, a piano part, or something else. By selecting and arranging different musical loops, you create new songs. Purchased loops are royalty free, and the finished compositions you create from them belong to you.

Buying these loops is easy, and there is a huge inventory available in a variety of styles—rock, orchestral, hip-hop, techno, ethnic/world, electronica, ambient, and nearly everything in between and out on the extreme fringe.

It's a lot easier than you might think to assemble custom scores for your projects. You don't need to be a fabulous musician to do it, either. Although it does help to have an affinity for music, actual skills are not required. If you have a rudimentary understanding of music; musical instruments; a decent sense of rhythm; and an ear for sounds, harmony, and what sounds good together, you have what it takes.

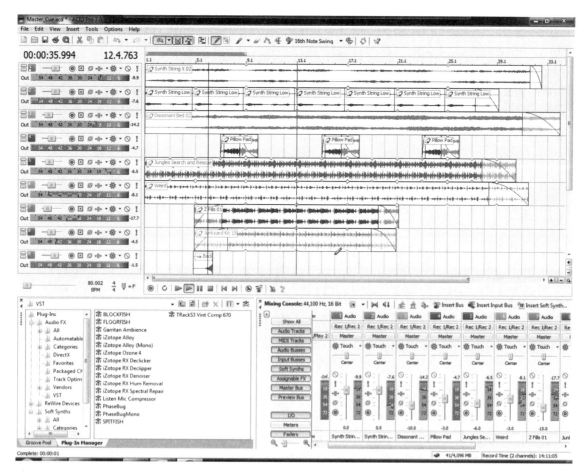

**Figure 19.2** ACID Pro in action.

That said, working with these programs is a snap. Just audition a sound, paint it across the timeline grid, and make music. What makes these programs special is how they automatically match the tempo and musical key of any loops you use. You can combine almost anything in the software, and it will work together well. Warning: Playing with these programs can be a lot of fun, so don't blame me if you waste a day fiddling around creating music scores!

Here are a few ideas to make your DIY approach more efficient and effective.

■ Some musical styles appear easier; others you have to work at. To get the essence of a style, listen to a lot of music in the genre you are trying to emulate. Dissect the commonalities and then choose loops that emulate these basic ideas. It's acceptable to simply capture the "flavor" of a style without overdoing it.

■ Don't try to write the complete song. In most cases, simple themes and musical interludes work well to support and enhance images and emotion. You don't have to create a stand-alone composition.

■ Don't overwrite! The composer in me may balk at a simple, unsophisticated underscore, but the filmmaker in me knows it is right for the scene. To many DIY composers overwrite in an attempt to create songs that stand on their own. Instead, write only what's needed to augment the emotion of the scene. If you use music for mood and emotion and you don't worry about it being a "good" composition, you'll be scoring your own movies in no time. (Opening-title music and other important themes require a more professional or musically literate approach, though.)

- Ostinato is a useful tool. This is a repeating musical figure, such as a bass line or a drum beat, that works to underscore a moment. Repeating it makes it a kind of motif or theme, too. John Carpenter used this approach to great effect for *They Live*.

- A simple pad or bed, which is an ambient musical texture with little evolving action, can also be quite effective. These are typically melody-less musical sequences. Maurice Jarre used a single sustaining synthesizer chord repeatedly in *Witness*.

## Hire a Composer

When only a custom score composed specifically for your project will do, you need to secure the services of a competent music composer. This composer should be able to not only write the music, but also record and deliver the finished score.

Where would you find such a person? I suggest checking out a site such as ACIDplanet (www.acidplanet.com), which can reveal some hungry film composers who are looking for a real gig, a credit, and perhaps a little money to score your project. I discovered several gems with just a quick perusal of the Cinematic/Soundtrack genre on the site. You should listen to what's there and then contact these artists directly.

Another option is to get in touch with college music departments, where you might find talented young composers looking for experience. Ask the instructors to recommend a few possibilities. Some filmmakers have even found suitable candidates via Craigslist. If you are looking for and have the budget for an established professional, check the listings at IMDb (www.imdb.com).

Because working with a composer is a collaborative art, you need to "click," so I suggest holding an interview where you discuss ideas and then decide whether the relationship can flourish for the project. Don't just listen to the writer's music demo; you need to establish a solid working relationship, too. Communication is key. Can you work together to realize the right ideas? You want to solve any technical issues, too. And finally, you need to know that the composer can deliver what you need on time and on budget.

Don't wait until the last minute to bring in a composer. The earlier you can involve the composer in the project, the better the resulting music will be. All too often a composer is brought in at the last minute and given far too stringent of guidelines for coming up with the score. Start early and give the composer some space and creative freedom. You won't regret it.

After you choose a composer, you should hold a spotting session where you screen the work together and determine all the individual music cues, lengths, styles, and other specifics. As the work comes in, test it with picture, discuss, and then finalize the music. The composer should then deliver a finished, recorded score, ready to take your project to the next level.

One method for working with a composer is to request a music package made up of several different cuts of music, often in different styles, timings, and instrumentation. This music may be used for characters, situations, emotions/moods, or more. Rather than being written specifically to picture, these tracks are freeform, freestanding tunes. Essentially, it's a custom music library with different pieces that you can use to fit the moods and emotions of scenes within the project. This approach is best for an ongoing series. Composer Brian Tarquin delivers his music for the daytime drama *All My Children* as "songs" that can be easily slipped in, because there isn't time to score to picture.

A cost-effective approach is to suggest developing a main theme or two and then either creating additional music from those themes or perhaps filling in other musical needs with stock music or DIY tracks. This would give you the original stamp you crave while being a little lighter on the budget.

Instead of creating, finding, or otherwise acquiring all the music for your project, consider developing a longer, more involved theme that, through built-in variations, can be conformed into much more music and molded into a custom score.

In this case, you ask your composer to write and record a "master cue" that you can rearrange for maximum use. (See the upcoming "The Master Cue" sidebar.) This is a fully orchestrated, long musical theme or tone poem used throughout your project. By stripping away the pieces of the master cue and creating alternate mixes of varied tempos, lengths, and styles, much more music is available from the single musical composition. Furthermore, all the music follows the same basic thematic element, but with enough variety to be interesting in different situations.

Additionally, asking for stems (the primary music parts, such as drums, bass, keyboard, and guitars, on their own) allows you to remix the music as needed. A two- to three-minute piece can easily be repurposed into a bevy of thematically and sonically connected music segments for use in different situations.

## Music Budget

As discussed earlier in this chapter, music fees have a large range. Licensing popular music can be extremely expensive, while the DIY approach brings music that's nearly free. When it comes to hiring a composer, there is no better resource than the Film & TV Music Salary and Rate Survey (see filmmusic.myshopify.com and scroll to the survey) conducted each year by The Film Music Store. It's an accurate and dependable way to find the going rates for music in a variety of settings and markets.

Typical payment schedules are done as a package deal, where the composer not only writes the music but also delivers the final recording. Payment terms are usually in thirds—one-third up front, one-third upon approval of demos or another milestone, and the final third upon delivery of the recorded music. Composers keep all rights to their music, of course.

For more information on the business side of music for films, TV, and advertising, see my other book, *Cash Tracks: Compose, Produce, and Sell Your Original Soundtrack Music and Jingles* (Course Technology PTR, 2005).

---

**The Master Cue:** The idea here is to ask your composer to create a theme and then either compose variations on that theme or build some variations into that single composition. From these raw materials you can craft many alternate mixes for use in your project.

This idea comes from Jan Hammer, who applied this technique on TV's *Miami Vice*. "What I do is use some piece of music more than once. It's not that I repeat them, but I record a lot more parts to each piece of music, so the variations are built in. Then I mix each cue differently to produce different cues. I flesh [the music] out to the extreme and then take things away. I might have 20 tracks on the master cue but only use three of them for a particular scene. So I spend more time on these master cues, which are them dissected into individual cues."

Technology gives your composer several methods for building these alternate versions. You can change tempo, key, length, and instrumentation/orchestration to make the music fit better. Because all or most of the music comes from this single idea, your musical score ties together with symmetry and has thematic unity.

If you DIY using something akin to ACID, you can quickly mute tracks, change the tempo and key, and otherwise create a lot of music from some basic building blocks. It's cost-effective and creative at the same time.

---

# Editing Music

Whether you use library music, create your own, hire a composer, or do any combination of these, one skill you need to master is being able to edit music. Rare is the project—including those I score myself—in which I don't conform the music in some way to better match the visuals, enhance the drama, or support the message. Instead of selecting a music track that almost works, make any music track do what you want by editing it to fit your precise needs.

You do not need to be highly musically inclined to edit music well. If you can count to four, you can learn to edit music in ways that keep the beat, make musical sense, and match your project.

Look for natural endings already within the music. These make good stopping or starting points. If your goal is to shorten a musical segment, consider working backwards. Find a suitable ending and then back-time to make any edits necessary before that ending to make it sound right. The ending may be the actual song ending, or it may be elsewhere in the tune. Similarly, you may want to make rises in music correspond to onscreen action—in other words, a hit point. For example, you might have the big musical crescendo match a dramatic climax. Sync the crescendo to the video and then move backward and perform any needed edits to make the music fit.

If you need to force an ending in the middle of the music, look for a natural stopping point. Start with any transition point from one section to another—a chorus to another verse, for instance. However, these edits sometimes sound a bit abrupt, so smooth them out with a short fade-out.

In some cases, adding a touch of reverb to the last note(s) and letting the reverb tail decay naturally can make these endings work better. It's important to find a reverb sound that matches the song for this to be effective. Make a short selection that includes the last note (or so). Be sure the selection includes space for the reverb to decay. This should sound natural, as if the song ends and the last notes hang in the air for a brief moment before decaying away to silence.

It's important not to break the beat/pulse of the music, or the edits will be noticeable. You can do this with straight cuts on the beat or by using crossfades with some music. Edits also need to make sense. Technically, you can make edits almost anywhere, but they do still need to make musical sense. Although you could make an edit to end the national anthem at "and the home," you would leave your audience hanging if it didn't end naturally at "of the brave."

Generally, music comes in two rhythmic flavors: 4/4 (1-2-3-4) time or 3/4 (1-2-3) waltz time. This is known as the *time signature* or *meter*, and it is helpful for finding edit points. A song such as "Edelweiss" from *The Sound of Music* is an example of 3/4, while "Do-Re-Mi" from the same show is 4/4. The Beatles' "Drive My Car" from *Rubber Soul* is 4/4, but the next track, "Norwegian Wood," is 3/4 time. There are, of course, exceptions to these (for example, Pink Floyd's "Money" is 7/4 time), but the majority of Western music falls into one of these two patterns.

Play the song once to get a feel for its rhythm. Play it a second time and tap your fingers along with the rhythm. Once you find the meter (start with 4/4 and adjust if it doesn't seem to work), you can easily count out the beats and then make your edits on those beats. It's typically the 1, known as the *downbeat*, that matters most. Find the 1, and you are on your way. For example:

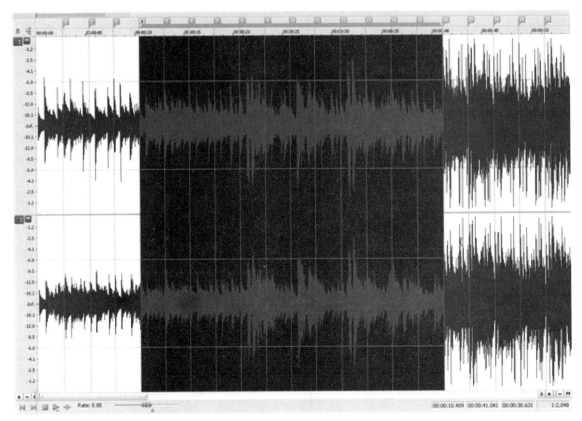

**Figure 19.3** Editing music.

| 1 | 2 | 3 | 1 | 2 | 3 | 1 | 2 | 3 | 1 | 2 | 3 |
|---|---|---|---|---|---|---|---|---|---|---|---|
| E | – | del | weiss | | | E | – | del | weiss | | |

Each one of these 1-2-3-4 or 1-2-3 repeating patterns is known as a *measure*. That's the musical equivalent of a sentence when writing. Editing measures, based on the downbeat, allows you to make edits that sound right, don't break the musical beat, and make musical sense.

## Further Music Studies

Here's a surefire way to learn how best to use music with your projects: Study other music scores. Rather than listen to the music alone, you will gain more insight when you listen to the music along with the picture and note how the abstract nature of music supports the emotional reality of the imagery. The following sections provide some suggestions.

### Opening Titles/Show Theme

An opening title sequence acts as an overture for a film or TV show and helps set the mood. The style as expressed in the instrumentation, themes, and motifs should prepare the audience for what they are about to see. Two films that exemplify these concepts well are *North by Northwest* (Bernard Herrmann) and the original *Halloween* (John Carpenter). A unique feature of *North by Northwest* is that you can isolate the score while watching the DVD. Listen to how Herrmann revisits the main title theme in unique ways as the film progresses toward its climax.

## Motif and Leitmotif

Motifs are reoccurring musical elements meant to enhance specific dramatic moments. One of the most infamous motifs is the shark's theme from *Jaws* (John Williams). Who would have thought that two cello notes could be so frightening? Leitmotif differs only in that it applies to a specific character, such as "Lara's Theme" from *Dr. Zhivago* (Maurice Jarre), the many character themes from the *Star Wars* universe, or the repeating trumpet figure from *Patton* (Jerry Goldsmith). Simple thematic elements can be very evocative and effective.

## POV

Music can also help support point of view or subtext. *Badlands* prominently features Carl Orff's mallet music designed to teach children how to play music. This profound musical choice complements and reflects the main character's naiveté. Contrast that film with the simple, childlike approach taken for *To Kill a Mockingbird* (Elmer Bernstein).

## Building Tension and Foreshadowing

*Psycho* (Bernard Herrmann) provides a strong example of this crucial dramatic tool. Check out the scene just after Janet Leigh's character drives away following a brief encounter with a police officer. Play this scene without its soundtrack, and you'll see the intercutting of three shots: A close-up of Janet Leigh, her view out the front window, and her view of the rearview mirror as she's followed by the police car. Nothing actually happens in the scene. Now crank up the music and be amazed at how Herrmann's score creates a sense of uneasiness, dread, paranoia, and other strong emotions.

## Diegetic to Non-Diegetic and Back

*Amadeus* (Mozart/Sir Neville Marriner) uses Mozart's music both as source music and as dramatic underscore. While the entire movie moves back and forth with this technique, the sequence near the movie's end is especially effective. As Mozart dictates his "Requiem" to Salieri, we hear the music in his head (diegetic) as if the orchestra were there in his bedroom. When Mozart reviews Salieri's work, the scene cuts away to Mozart's wife desperately trying to get back to her husband by carriage. The exact same music as heard before now transforms to dramatic underscore (non-diegetic) to the scene.

## Music as Sound Effect

Often music crosses the line from score into the realm of sound design and sound effects. Commercials often blur this line. Near the climax of *Terminator 2* (Brad

Fiedel), notice that the atonal, pure sound design of the music takes the place of most of the sound effects in the sequence where the T-1000 reassembles itself after being blown apart. Also, during the legendary shower sequence in *Psycho* (Bernard Herrmann), the score's shrieking violins provide a unique tonal color that sounds like a cross between screaming and bird calls.

### Offbeat, Atonal Music

There are few examples of unusual approaches, as many scores today are loaded with either pop songs or traditional orchestral scores. The original *Planet of the Apes* (Jerry Goldsmith) has a wonderful interlude during the first part of the film, where the three astronauts cross the desert looking for life. There is a great deal of percussion, piano stabs, and atonal horn parts that bring an eerie and otherworldly feel to the sequence. By far my favorite is the percussion-driven fight sequences from *Crouching Tiger, Hidden Dragon* (Tan Dun), which are often interspersed with a plaintive cello melody.

### Electronic Music

Composers often employ electronic synthesizers and samplers to either emulate traditional instruments or craft new sounds or colors. *Witness* (Maurice Jarre) adds a new twist by taking a traditional score and using only electronic instruments. It was the vision of the film's director, Peter Weir, to have something both familiar and slightly cold and askew. I suggest watching the "Building the Barn" sequence to hear how this beautiful musical moment sounds slightly off, as the synthesizers used do not quite sound like the real instruments they purport to imitate.

### Firewood

Filmmaker David Lynch often relied on his composer, Angelo Badalamenti, to record what they call "firewood." They used the orchestra to craft drones, dark pads, and otherworldly and non-melodious sounds that Lynch used to sweeten scenes. A film such as *Mulholland Drive* seems to have an almost horror-movie soundtrack at times. Using dark-sounding drones and deep noise samples can give a scene a sense of heaviness, darkness, and foreboding that can enhance the drama.

## Case Study: Scoring *The Craving Heart*

Many movie directors find inspiration in music, but few have the artistic relationship shared by award-winning filmmaker Stan Harrington and singer/songwriter Katy J.

"I went to a screening of the film, *Tangy G*, that a friend of mine was in," recalls Stan Harrington. "The film featured music by an unknown singer-songwriter, Katy J. She was also at the screening, so we started talking about her music and a film I was working on. She gave me her *Stand Still* CD, and I told her I'd be in touch."

Four years went by. While editing his first guerrilla feature, *Bred in the Bone*, Harrington remembered Katy's music and decided to call. "Fortunately, the number still worked, and after hearing about the movie, Katy offered a few tracks to the film." That music made an impact on *Bred* and Harrington. It was the start of an artistic collaboration.

"Katy and I were talking one day, when she mentioned something that had happened to her," relates Harrington. "She told me how one night she stopped her car in the pouring rain because there was a confused lady standing in the middle of the road. This inspired me for the opening sequence of *The Craving Heart*, and I decided to build the story around that image and to use her music exclusively to tell the tale."

Katy also gave Stan some new songs that she'd recorded in her home studio, which Stan loved and also incorporated into the script and ultimately the final film. "There's no doubt that Katy J's music was my muse for *The Craving Heart*. It's so emotional that you can't help being affected by it."

Image courtesy of Katy J.

**Figure 19.4**  Katy J.

Katy feels the muse is a two-way street. "Stan pulls elements from my songs that complement his writing. This allows the music to fit beautifully. I loved how Stan wove the lyrical content from my songs into the dialogue and plot of *Craving*. "Wake Up" is about being with a lover who is married, the same as in *Craving*. We inspire one another and build ideas around each other's creativity."

"I sent Stan some rough mixes—experiments, really, with minimal production—such as "Just for Today" and "Wake Up," which he liked so much he placed them in the film. They were unmastered roughs, but apparently he liked the raw quality a lot."

Katy J has contributed to seven indie films so far. "I have a lot of music, so I'm always interested in getting it out there. Providing songs for independent films is just one more way to stand out from the crowd." Her music hasn't gone unnoticed. ABC picked up the track "Can't Look Down" from her *Stand Still* CD for the *Men in Trees* drama.

The Long Beach Action on Film Festival honored Katy with a nomination for Best Score for *Craving*. CBS's Todd David Schwartz added, "The soundtrack...is easily among the very best original music ever to be heard in any independent film. Her soulful, haunting, utterly sublime tunes elevate the entire production."

For more details, see www.katyj.com or www.xristosproductions.com.

With all the soundtrack elements in place, now is the time to turn your attention over to the final mix and deliver the finished, complete soundtrack. That's the subject of the next chapter.

# 20 Mixing

The final mix (a.k.a. the *dub*) is the final step that involves combining all the disparate sound elements into a completed whole. Every project is unique, and that makes it hard to write about mixing because there are few rules. Yes, there are some technical considerations, and there are some guidelines that are worth heeding.

What makes for the best mix? The easy answer is this: Whatever serves the project! You can't mix to some preset formula or fill-in-the-blanks approach. It's about working with the material in such a way that meets the needs of the project. That thought in no way diminishes the crucial importance of the mix, though. If anything, it shows the real power the final mix possesses. Depending on how carefully you've built the individual elements, you can combine them in infinite, distinct ways to arrive at the final decision.

I've said it before, and it bears repeating: It's the mix that matters. All of the detailed work that you've brought to the soundtrack so far is for nothing if you can't find a way to combine these stems into a coherent whole that delivers your message and makes an impact on your audience. You can't emphasize everything—you have to choose. It's about balancing and blending everything into a seamless, natural, complete picture.

Mixing is about finding the final "voice" for the project and shaping the sound into a specific mood, time, place, and space.

Addison Teague, supervising sound editor on *TRON: Legacy*, told *Audio Media* magazine, "It's one thing to make things coexist, but when you get into the mix, each thing needs to have its moment. If sound effects coexist too much with music, then they can't really have their moment…their punch."

## Housekeeping

Before you get deeply into the creative aspects of mixing your project, it's a sound idea to prepare for the process and take care of a few technical issues. This includes cleaning up and organizing the timeline. It's also important to design an approval process. Here are some general tips to make sure you start the process right.

275

## Listen to What's There

This might seem like an unusual point, because you've been working on the project for some time and are reasonably familiar with everything already. The problem is you've probably been micromanaging the sound details. You need to refamiliarize yourself with the project as a whole. Scott Millan, sound re-recording mixer on *Salt*, told StudioDaily.com that, "The first thing we would do [is] put the dialogue and sound effects up [and] go through the reel with the music one time, without stopping, to hear what we have. That gives me an overview of the reel. And then we go back to the top and start working on segments."

After listening to this "all faders up" mix, go back and listen to elements on their own—such as a pass of just Foley—to reveal any missing elements or other issues. You might listen track by track, too. These steps can help set the stage for other housecleaning chores mentioned in a moment.

Generally, get everything sounding its best. Listen for extraneous noises that may still be on tracks. Clean up any bad elements that remain. This might be slates, extraneous noises, and other unwanted elements that need to be removed. You can physically erase these components by editing, trimming, and deleting them. If tracks are not playing, either mute them or use a noise gate. For low-level interference, a noise gate can shut off unused tracks and channels. Automated mutes and/or volume are yet another way to reel in the noise.

## Don't Mix Alone

The decision-makers need to be present—in person—during the final mix of soundtrack elements. Mixing a project by sending work-in-process files or DVDs just isn't the same thing. That can work early on, but not once you really get into the mix proper. The difficulty with sending files/DVDs is that the director may have an inferior sound system and might not hear everything as intended. I once discovered that a director was listening on laptop speakers! Arghhhh... Also, back-and-forth changes don't come in a methodical way, but instead occur willy-nilly. It's also difficult to argue your point in these remote review situations.

Therefore, I urge you to consider putting together the final mix with the decision-makers in the room with you. On a simple project this may not be necessary, but the more complex the program—especially long-form documentary and feature-length indie films—the more important it is to do the final mix with VIPs involved. Also, know that you can't mix a two-hour movie in two hours; it could take days or even weeks. Plan and budget accordingly to accommodate the final mix needs.

When working with other people, one of your first tasks is to uncover the decision-maker. This is simple, right? If one person walks into the room, he's the one to please. Unfortunately, that often is not the case. This may be only the point person, not the real decision-maker. There might be higher-ups with whom you never have contact. Your point person might have to get supervisory approval before proceeding. Be prepared for this situation.

Alternatively, you might have a group of people in the room. Again, you must find out who is going to actually place a stamp of approval on your work. It is rare that approval is by consensus. Once you know the decision-maker, subtly shift your focus to making sure this person understands the suggestions you make and that he or she is happy with the mix at its conclusion.

Here are some additional suggestions:

- Think before you speak.

- Narrate as you proceed with the mix. Don't just sit there silently clicking your mouse as you make mix adjustments. Give your decision-maker an idea of what's happening. Often, you need to show what you mean with a playback. Let the decision-maker know what you're doing while you do it and then audition the result.

- Sometimes people may insist on another approach. In those cases, do an A/B comparison—their way and then your way—and then let them choose the right direction.

- Be authoritative and in charge when it's appropriate, but also know when to fold and back down.

- Take ownership of mistakes and then fix them.

## Premix/Predub

A final mix can seem a daunting task with dozens or even hundreds of individual audio tracks (and thousands of individual sound clips). One way to deal with all this complexity is to combine like elements and sounds into a smaller number of tracks. This method means you might premix or predub just the effects or just the Foley, for instance. These premixes may be discrete or simply routed to bus faders. Grouping like sounds together to one bus fader enables you to adjust the level of them all in relation to other elements.

If you have a lot of effects tracks, you may want to premix these before the final mix, too. You can often combine many BGs and Foley tracks respectively, so there is less to worry about during the final dub. Reducing the BG and Foley tracks down to just a few stereo premixes makes handling them easier when all the other sounds are present. You can do the same with other soundtrack elements—music being an obvious example, as that's usually mixed by the composer or other engineer and delivered as a stereo file.

I often do a bit of premixing along the way while doing the other sound work, mostly fitting backgrounds and sound effects together. I prefer clip-based automation (fades, volume levels, and so on) over any track-based automation at this stage. For example, my dialogue tracks are usually near final state when the mix starts. The mix may still require some minor tweaks, but usually the extra time taken during the dialogue-editing process gets everything sounding smooth and right. I may even do a lot of noise reduction on the dialogue before the mix, too.

---

**Note:** Even when premixing any soundtrack element, keep the unmixed tracks on the timeline. (Move them to the bottom and mute or hide them.) This way, if a premix doesn't quite work, you can easily return to the original unmixed tracks if needed.

---

## Track Optimization

Timelines can get rather messy when you're working on finding, editing, and syncing all the sounds. To make the mix flow smoothly, consider cleaning up the DAW. You can reduce tracks, group like sound elements together, color-code important pieces, and more. Keep sound "families" on their own tracks—in other words, don't mix dialogue and sound effects on the same track. Use different tracks and checkerboard sounds across the timeline.

Case in point: I often find lone sounds on a track—90 minutes of track with one half-second of sound on it. These sounds can often be moved to another track before the mix to eliminate the extraneous track. Similarly, I often find sounds on the wrong track, such as a bit of Foley that was inadvertently put on a nearby BG track and so forth. In the heat of sound editing, it's easy to overlook these issues. In preparation for the final mix, it's the right time to address these inconsistencies.

Ironically, I'm often quite parsimonious with tracks early on and find that even after organizing everything, the track count actually grows to accommodate having to isolate certain sounds and/or treat them with unique audio effects, noise reduction, levels, and panning so they better work in the whole mix. In my experience, the typical indie film project ends up being between 85 and 100 active tracks. Because I keep originals and unmixed tracks (hidden or muted), the actual track count can be far higher.

Related to this is checkerboarding tracks so that you can better mix sounds together. During the dialogue edit, you may lump characters together. Now is the time to separate them to their own track(s). Put main characters on their own tracks, and keep lesser characters separate. Keep ADR and VO separated, too. If you have certain lines that call for a certain audio effect (such as a telephone call), move those to their own track, too.

Consider color-coding tracks so that related elements show the same (for example, all dialogue tracks in green, Foley in blue, music in brown, and so on). This makes it a snap to see all the related tracks and how they differ from one another. It's also a good idea to group and/or bus like sounds together so you have a master fader for each primary sound element.

At minimum, set up three busses for your DM&E (dialogue, music, and effects). These should feed the master fader for the final output. Then you can create extra busses as needed for the other soundtrack elements. It's also a good idea to order the tracks to appear on the timeline in a consistent way. These are the most common assignments, top to bottom:

**Track layout:**

- Dialogue (including room tone).

- ADR.

- Effects dialogue (such as a telephone line effect).

- Voiceover.

- Production SFX.

- Foley SFX.

- Hard SFX. (This may be many, many tracks.)

- Soft SFX (ditto).

- Effects SFX (sound effects with audio effects applied—in other words, futzing).

- Backgrounds.

- LFE effects. I use a special channel for super low bass effects, even when doing a stereo-only mix. For surround, this is a dedicated channel—the .1 in 5.1 surround.

- Source music.

- Underscore music.

- Pre- or sub-mixes.

- Everything else (original files, the unmixed parts of a premix, and so on).

**Bus layout:**

- Master volume.

- Dialogue.

- Music.

- Effects.

- Other effects busses.

- Audio effects busses (such as reverb).

Essentially, you would route all dialogue tracks to the dialogue bus, all music to the music bus, and all effects tracks to the effects bus. You may want more busses, such as a separate Foley and BG bus, to group them together and then send those bus outputs to the main effects bus, as shown in Figure 20.1. This setup allows you to produce a stereo master file and the separate DM&E stems (if needed).

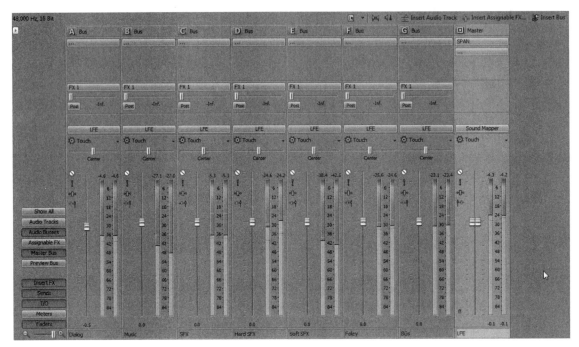

**Figure 20.1** Bus layout.

Having the main elements on bus faders means a final mix can be even easier. You can go back to the pieces (on the timeline) to tweak if the busses won't give you what you need. I also prefer to add analog-style VU meters to my master bus to help keep an eye on average levels. Monitoring both averages and peaks helps you check the crest factor—the difference between the RMS or average level and the peaks. Alternatively, I use Voxengo's free SPAN plug-in (www.voxengo.com/product/span), which shows spectrum analysis, peak levels, and RMS. It's a prudent tool (see Figure 20.2).

Finally, some DAWs allow saving screen sets, which are a particular arrangement of windows. I use several different layouts depending on what I'm doing. During this phase, as you prepare for the final mix, is an ideal time to program these layouts to suit your tastes. Also, consider hiding any unnecessary interface items to reduce screen clutter.

## Audio Effects Optimization

Final mixing often requires a lot of audio effects to bring the soundtrack together. Generally, EQ, compression, and noise-reducing plug-ins are the most used processes. Reverb and delay are also often called for in a particular mix.

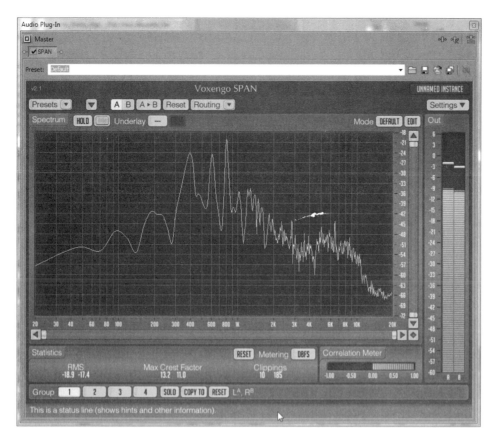

**Figure 20.2**  SPAN.

Before the mix I put an EQ and noise gate plug-in on every track. I keep the EQ disabled until needed to save wear and tear on the computer processor. I do usually set up the noise gate to make sure tracks are shutting down when not in use. You could automate turning Mute on and off, but the gate makes this function far easier.

Another good idea is to use a high-pass EQ filter on material that lacks bass. Often subsonic or infrasonic information sneaks onto recordings, and this takes up space in a mix. Eliminating these frequencies can make everything sound cleaner and better. Dialogue and Foley often benefit from an 80- to 100-Hz low-cut filter. This reduces noise without affecting the quality. Similarly, a low-pass filter helps for bass-heavy sounds. I often put an aggressive 120-Hz low-pass on my LFE channel sounds.

If you need reverb and/or delay, set them up as an assignable effects send so that you can route whatever tracks that need these effects easily. You don't want to have 20 reverbs running, as that will grind your computer system to a halt.

For some audio effects, it's easier to move a sound or sounds to their own isolated tracks and add the effect there (for example, a phone-line futz effect). I prefer real-time effects to "print" effects. This way, you can tweak the effect parameters while you mix. Printing makes the effect permanent and a pain to change. It's a good idea to mark an effects-only track with a relevant name and color as a reminder that the track is special and reserved for a particular effect. You may do this at the bus level if several tracks use an effect, or as an effects send/assignable effect. Choose the method that makes sense for efficiency and your workflow.

The dialogue bus usually gets an expander, which can help reduce the noise of already smoothed and quiet dialogue tracks substantially. An expander doesn't cut off noise like a gate; it's gentler. By pulling down background noise 10 to 12 dB, you get a much smoother and more natural sound. Settings are usually quite mild—just a bit of expansion to make already quiet things a bit quieter. Adjusting the expander controls is critical. If you are not careful, there may be a rush of noise that pops up when the dialogue cuts back in. You are counting on the dialogue itself to cover up or mask these noise jumps. Expansion doesn't suffer from the same unusual, swirly artifacts as other noise-reduction processes, and if you've smoothed your dialogue effectively, a bit of expansion works wonders. If you haven't smoothed your dialogue, expansion won't work. (And why are you mixing already, anyway? Get back to work!)

Put a limiter on the master bus, again set very conservatively, to grab a peak level and pull it down to an acceptable range. I usually limit to $-1.0$ dBFS. If your mix is destined for a specific market, their deliverables may require a different setting. For instance, PBS requires that no peaks exceed $-3$ dBFS on HD material.

Settings for this require a slow to medium attack to let fast transients through without unnecessarily clamping down on them, followed by a fast release to make things a little more punchy. Listen for pumping or breathing—this should be effective but subtle—and adjust as needed.

Don't rely on only the limiter to tame all your peaks. Instead, balance the mix to reach your target most, if not all, of the time. The limiter keeps you honest for when a sound exceeds the target or when you need to hit a specific limit target. The aforementioned Span can help you meet RMS levels (again, if required).

## Monitor Optimization

If you haven't calibrated your monitor system lately, prior to the mix is the ideal time to take care of that important step. Whether you are working in stereo or surround, proper calibration is crucial so that you can judge your mix decisions accurately.

As you already know, I'm a *big* proponent of mixing by using a consistent, fixed monitor gain. I calibrate my speakers so that $-20$ dBFS pink noise reads 83 dB SPL (C-weighted) per speaker using a sound-level meter. It is truly a liberating way to work. Loud will be loud, and soft will sound right. You won't be reaching for the limiter or volume maximizer, and you will create mixes that take advantage of the full dynamic range. Refer to Chapter 9 for details on this procedure.

Remember the Fletcher-Munson curves. Make critical adjustments at the proper listening levels so you can trust your ears and know your decisions are valid.

You might also want a way to check the mono compatibility of the mix. Some DAWs support this function, so you should learn how it works for your particular software. In Vegas Pro, for instance, it's just a single Downmix button. It's important to make sure your mix is 100 percent mono compatible, and checking it is the only way to be sure. It's equally important to check phase, as out-of-phase mixes are not mono compatible, either.

It's also a good idea to be able to check your mixes at lower listening levels than the standard, calibrated level. You need to be able to do this without disturbing your calibrated level. Again, some DAWs include a Dim button that can turn down the level for this purpose. My Saffire audio interface includes this feature on the external hardware.

If you are really new to this whole process, you may find it helpful to listen to your mix in different places and using different systems. This need not be as formal as the main mixing environment. For instance, you could check the mix in a home theater, at a friend's house, in the car, on headphones, and more. When learning this way, listen to your mixes on different speaker systems and in different rooms. Listen at quiet levels and loud ones. Take notes. Adjust your mixes based on what you discover with these tests. Once you learn how things can sound different, you will know how to make your mixes work not only in the audio suite, but across multiple platforms, too.

The way the soundtrack plays in a theater can be a bit surprising after working in the smaller confines of the typical edit/audio-post suite. The subtle things sometimes get buried in the ambient noise of the theater itself—especially with a full crowd, large theaters have the additional element of excessive reverberation. This can muddy up a wet mix and hurt speech intelligibility. Although most of the work you do will be destined for the DVD or the web—and you should build mixes accordingly—you still need to be cognizant of how your tracks work—or don't!—in a large theater venue.

One way to simulate a larger space is by using a reverb on the master bus to audition your mix. This is not ideal, but it can expose glaring errors that you can address. The only way to mix for a theater is by doing a proper theater mix in the proper mixing environment. Because most of your work is destined for the web and DVDs, mix for the living room, and most of that will translate to the theater. The experience you gain can help assure you that what's working in the small mix suite will translate to the theater as well.

---

**External Audio-Level Hardware:** There's no doubt that watching volume levels is important. The digital audio world has a top limit—0 dBFS—that you can't exceed. But screen real estate is often at a premium when working in your DAW. Sure, you can pop the mixer over to a secondary monitor, but that's often filled with audio effects, video preview, and more.

How about moving the audio-level meters "out of the box," so to speak? I use the American Audio dB-Display (www.adjaudio.com) LED level meters by running a redundant audio signal from the computer audio interface to the dB-Display. The main mix goes directly to the monitor speakers, as recommended by American Audio. As long as you make sure that the levels coming from the main volume are the same as those going to the dB-Display, the system works. Now I have hardware meters that display just below my video monitors (see Figure 20.3) so I can always keep an eye on peak levels.

**Figure 20.3** External level meters.

### Have a Reference Mix

You might find it helpful to listen to an existing soundtrack mix that is in a similar vein to your project. This mix is something you can use to refer to before you begin. You might even check it occasionally to hear how your mix stacks up. I actually ask directors for a film or two that captures how they want their soundtrack to sound. I make it a point to watch their choices and listen to what they mean. If the director doesn't offer a suggestion, I always fall back on David Lynch films as my reference. (For music-only mixing projects, I use Steely Dan's *Aja*.)

## Mix Secrets

With everything prepped and ready to roll, it's time to turn your attention to the fun and highly creative task of balancing your sounds into a cohesive whole. All that careful dialogue editing, sound design, sound effects layering, background building, Foley, music, and more needs to find its place in the mix and help you support the project's message and make a lasting impact on your audience.

As mentioned earlier in this chapter, every mix is different. What follows are several hints, ideas, pointers, and a few specific techniques to help you work through the material and arrive at the best possible soundtrack.

## Think WHOLE Mix, Not Individual Pieces

In his book, *The Element: How Finding Your Passion Changes Everything* (Viking Adult, 2009), Sir Ken Robinson discusses the differences between Western and Eastern thought. To paraphrase: Westerners generally bring a more rational and logical mind to their work (in this case, the mix). They tend to focus on specifics and end up micro-managing everything. Contrarily, the Eastern mind tends to look at relationships between the disparate elements, and that process leads to a more macro or holistic view. As Robinson says, "If we keep our focus too tight, we miss the rest of the world swirling around us." So, the lesson is: Work toward a view of the soundtrack as it relates to the story as a whole. Don't miss the forest for the trees.

Related to this thought is the frequent tendency to present every sound at its pristine best. You figure that if everything sounds perfect on its own, then the finished mix will be brilliant, too. Unfortunately, it doesn't really work that way. A sound on its own needs to sound its best—that's obvious. But once you layer in another sound, these two sounds begin to interact. The sum is a synergy that may have an unpredictable result.

Therefore, it's critical to monitor individual (and groups of) sounds as they relate to the complete mix. If you solo something and adjust it, make sure you compare these changes to the rest of the mix. Often the tweaks don't sound right when you introduce the other sound elements. It's equally important to note that sometimes you may need to adjust a sound in an extreme way to hear it properly among other sounds. This newly adjusted piece may sound wrong on its own but work perfectly in the context of the mix as a whole.

I simply don't care what a single sound sounds like, because it's the entire mix that matters. Keep focused on the whole, and your mixes will turn out far better.

## Dialogue Still Rules

Dialogue is the main component or element around which the whole soundtrack revolves. Everything else is subservient to it. SFX, BGs, and music all serve to support the words. You should balance the elements in a mix in such a way that makes speech intelligibility the number-one priority. Dialogue is the primary focus, and every other sound should be layered around it. There are exceptions, to be sure. Action movies feature SFX and music more than dialogue in moments of high action, but once all the cacophony settles, dialogue still takes precedence.

Sequences without dialogue that feature music take the lead briefly, but if the music contains lyrics, the sung vocal takes the place of the spoken word. So the same rules apply.

Don't be tempted to push music or effects too high and thereby obliterate speech intelligibility. This happens all too easily because you are especially familiar with what's being said. You understand the dialogue completely and may bury it under other sounds too low in volume in the mix. The first-time listener doesn't have the benefit of knowing the whole script and will struggle to hear what's said. Couple this with the reverberant nature of large theaters and other playback venues, which tend to obscure words even more. When in doubt, push the vocals forward and back off the volume of other elements.

In the surround world, there is the added benefit of a dedicated center channel, with its primary function to host your dialogue. By keeping effects and music out of the dedicated center channel, you have more control over the balance of speech versus sounds. In stereo, the phantom center doesn't work quite as well as the dedicated center in surround. And in mono, it's even more difficult.

---

**Why Center the Dialogue?** Picture this: Two people talking on a park bench presented in three shots—a two-shot of both people and individual close-ups. In the two-shot, you might be tempted to pan the voices hard left and right to match the screen positions of the actors. But what happens when the story cuts to the close-up? You'd need to pan the dialogue back to the center to match the new screen view. And so on, back and forth. If you do this, the actor's speech will "jump" around the speakers, and that will distract the audience. If your project is destined for a podcast or radio spot, any kind of extreme hard panning (left/right placement) such as this is very distracting for the listener.

Although an occasional "off-camera" voice can be placed in a far left or right speaker (even surrounds in a 5.1 mix), you need to get the dialogue quickly back to the center channel, or phantom center in stereo. This way, the dialogue continues to emanate from the screen itself, no matter where someone sits in relation to it.

---

## Look beyond the Obvious

Mixing is far more than just reeling in volume and positioning sounds in the stereo or surround field. It is about fitting the pieces together into a puzzle that makes sense. The audience needs to hear dialogue, experience the reality of the effects, and feel the emotion of the music. If your mix is a jumbled mess without focus or intelligibility, your audience will tune out. Finding this voice requires a lot of effort and often a lot of hard choices as you jettison beloved sounds in favor of only those sounds that best serve the project's needs.

## Find a Place for Everything

A mix is a dynamic, fluid, and organic entity requiring both subtle and overt changes throughout the project. Sometimes there are big swings in volume and sound density. Other times, it might be something as simple as lowering the volume of the music slightly, just so a brief sound effect can be heard. Your mission is to make sure every sound that's important to the story gets heard at the right moment. It's about supporting what's onscreen but also foreshadowing events to come or reminding the audience of what came before or is still happening.

Just as a picture editor says, "Look at this now," with each shot selected and presented, your job with the soundtrack mix is to echo that approach, as if to say, "And listen to this right now, too." Make sure your mix has a distinct focus on what is important at every moment, and make sure your audience knows what that focus is and how what they hear drives the story.

## Fill the Entire Audible Frequency Range

It might be a tad late to consider this technique once you start mixing. That said, the idea is to make sure you use the whole range of frequencies to their best effect. If there is a lot of midrange taken up by dialogue and other sounds, it can be easier to add in and balance both bass- and treble-dominant sounds because they don't compete with these mids. At any given point, you can examine the central sounds and where they sit and then make choices to envelop and complement those primary sounds with other elements that don't interfere with them directly. You should have made many of these choices during sound effects editing and music spotting. With the right blend of sounds already filling a wider range of frequencies, the mix can come together faster, easier, and better.

## Watch Time

You can't have the explosion, the scream, and the big musical crescendo all happen simultaneously. They need space to be heard; otherwise, the result is white noise. You have to listen for this kind of overlap and buildup. Separating these three events in time—scream (beat), explosion (beat, beat), music—can make all the difference. You might need to do some of this during editing; however, even the mix can present opportunities for shifting sounds in time slightly so they don't compete as much for attention.

## Use Volume

One way that you can fit sounds together is with volume. A loud sound covers up or masks a soft sound. That's an obvious point, yet it is worth qualifying further. A mix is usually quite dynamic, with sound levels rising and falling based on what's happening. A formerly loud sound fades away when a new soft sound gets louder and overtakes it. This constant juggling of levels and focus makes for a balanced and vibrant mix.

Generally, we can only hear two to three sounds individually at once, with the third either rising to replace one of the first two or falling away, leaving the remainder to shine. Once you move beyond two to three sounds, the mix starts to sound cluttered with an indistinct quality—essentially noise, a cacophony. Don't force your audience to pay attention to more than two to three distinct sounds at any given moment.

Other sounds can still support these primary elements (BGs, Foley, and so forth), but these secondary sounds don't command attention; they work almost subliminally. Of course, if you need to disorient your audience, feel free to let the floodgates open. But when you want to carefully direct their concentration, choose to highlight only a couple of sounds simultaneously, letting the other sounds simmer and murmur in the background.

---

**A Few Good dB:** You might be astonished by how little changes can have a big impact on a track and in a mix. Sometimes the difference between a sound effect or a background sitting in a track or sticking out can be a minuscule volume adjustment. Don't become frustrated when it seems as if you can't find the right balance. Keep fiddling with volume (and tweaking the other suggestions here) until you find the right fit. It's there, really—you just need to find it.

Consider this advice from award-winning music recording and mixing engineer Ed Cherney (Rolling Stones, Eric Clapton, and Bonnie Raitt). Although he mentions vocals and song here, just substitute dialogue and your soundtrack mix for those words: "Listen to what's there, see where the song is, [and] eliminate things to find the heart of the song. Placing the vocal is the hardest thing to do. I start dry, not using any effects or EQ. See where the vocal frequency is and try to carve out a space in the mix. Listen to the vocal on a lot of different speakers, too. Don't give up on the song. I get in there and dig and get everything out of it I possibly can. I mixed Bonnie Raitt's 'Thing Called Love' three different times to finally find the pocket and emotion in it. Ultimately, mixing is about heart, not equipment. Nobody leaves a session dancing to what kind of gear you used."

---

Volume helps you avoid stepping on or masking important sounds. It also helps you control important sounds by using level changes to bring them out of the background din or send them away. Dynamically mixing sounds as they rise and fall allows you to smoothly direct attention to what's important. All these level adjustments with fades and crossfades between sounds are the tools to use. There's a reason why all those knobs and faders move in your DAW software—so you can present the right sounds at the right time and in the right way. So move them!

## Use Frequency

Volume is only one way to fit different sounds together. Because many sounds share some of the same frequencies, reducing these interfering frequencies from one sound can help it sit better and balance with another. For instance, you could cut the EQ in a music track where consonants sit (around 2,500 Hz). This effectively carves out a hole in the music track for the dialogue to live in. Staying in the consonant region makes the speech more intelligible. This EQ cut can make the music sound little funny on its own, though. You are relying on the dialogue to fill in what's missing in this case. This means you may need to automate the EQ so it's working only during speech and then goes back to normal so that the music sounds fine on its own.

Multiband compression is another tool you can use to get sounds to fit together. Because multiband compression allows separate compression controls for different frequency bands, it functions as a sort of dynamic volume and EQ tool all in one. Following the aforementioned dialogue-versus-music dance, set up the dialogue with a multiband compressor set at 200 Hz and 2,500 Hz and gentle ratios in the 2:1 or 3:1 range, thresholds resulting in between 3 and 10 dB of gain reduction, and fast attacks and rather slow releases (one second or more). Experiment to find the right settings, with the idea of reducing the dynamic range of certain frequencies and therefore being able to make them louder in relation to other sounds. This can help you pop speech intelligibility out from a busy mix or a dense music track.

These techniques extend beyond just music and dialogue and can be used whenever you have two or more sound elements competing against one another.

## Use S-p-a-c-e

There isn't a lot of physical room for sound in the typical stereo mix. Surround sound does offer some additional spatial advantages, but stereo is tight. The stereo sound field is the space between the speakers and extending back behind them. You can place your sounds anywhere in this zone, left to right, front to back, and top to bottom. As discussed already, it's customary to keep the dialogue in the center between the two stereo speakers so that no matter where someone sits in relation to the screen, the speech comes from one place. However, other sounds, usually as reflected in the onscreen action, can come from anywhere in the sound field as needed.

The biggest problem you will face with your mix is center buildup and overlap—that is, too many sounds competing for attention in the center of the stereo field. Consequently, when you can move sounds away from the center either by panning them or because they are stereo recordings already, you free up space in the center for dialogue and other important sounds. My goal is to make both my BGs and my music mix super-wide stereo (as discussed in Chapter 17) so that there is a bigger hole in the center for SFX and especially dialogue to be heard clearly.

You also want to avoid hard-panning single sounds to one side only. This can pull the audience's attention away from the screen as they "look" toward the source of the sound—too far left or right. It's the aforementioned "exit sign" effect. Similarly, you want to avoid a lot of dynamic panning of primary sounds, or you risk turning your project into a tennis match, with audience members' heads turning back and forth.

This doesn't mean you avoid panning altogether—quite the contrary. Moving sounds around, left to right, is an effective way to find a home for them. Use restraint and your best judgment when you reach for the pan pot, though.

---

**Note:** If you want a voice or other sound to be off-camera or offscreen, panning to either the left or the right side alone usually is not enough. Add some reverb or a short delay along with the panning to create the illusion. You may need to EQ this sound to thin it out somewhat so it sounds more off-mic and distant, too.

---

You can also simulate sounds being more forward in the mix or farther away. Volume does this, and you can use reverb and delay to create space around sounds in the mix. A wetter sound—one with reverb or delay applied to it—will sound farther away than a dry sound devoid of audio effects. A combination of pan and reverb can help you create more depth in your mix, and by changing these effects, you can bring elements forward or send them farther away toward the back.

To summarize:

- Horizontal space is conveyed using stereo and stereo panning effects.

- Front-to-back space is conveyed using volume (softer sounds are farther away) and also audio effects, as a dry sound appears closer than a wet sound, such as one swimming in reverb.

- Vertical space is conveyed using low (bottom) and high (top) frequencies. This isn't quite as distinct as the other two, but higher frequencies do feel as if they come from the upper part of the screen, and bass notes do feel closer to the ground.

## Embrace Dynamics and Contrast

Using the dynamic range is another effective method for structuring the mix. You can't be soft all the time, nor can you be loud for 90 straight minutes. You want to use dynamics to help focus attention and bring the audience into the story and its message. There needs to be some air to breathe after loud sequences. Sometimes you want to drift into near silence, with just a light wind background ambience. Often, the quietest part in a drama is just before the loudest part. Think of a horror movie, as the soundtrack slows to just a whisper and then the bad guy jumps out with crashing sound effects and a big musical hit. Contrast extends beyond mere volume to include density (fewer or more sounds) and frequency (such as more bass).

## Apply Appropriate Effects

Audio effects give you more tools to use in your pursuit of the right mix. You can process audio in ways that allow for better balance and more impact. Although you can process offline, I prefer to use as many real-time audio effects as my system can handle. This allows continuous tweaking as the mix evolves.

- EQ is the go-to tool for dealing with tonal issues and some special effects.

- Compression can smooth the dynamics of various sounds or groups of sounds.

- If you need to tame peaks or make some things louder without hitting the top of the scale, a limiter is the right tool.

- Sometimes you need to reduce some sibilance, so reach for a de-esser to tame those sizzling S sounds.

- Ducking—essentially using either a volume control or a compressor with a side chain that allows you to control the level of one thing with another thing—can help move some sounds out of the way so others can be heard.

- Noise gates cut off annoying background noise altogether.

- An expander makes low-level noise even quieter without shutting down completely, and that often sounds more natural and smoother.

- Adding reverb can give a sense of space, help match locations, and provide some air around dry, in-your-face lavaliere dialogue.

- Delay can simulate certain acoustic anomalies, such as the PA announcements in a ballpark.

- Doppler effects help simulate this real-world phenomenon, making some sound effects more realistic. You can replicate this with pitch and panning or a dedicated plug-in.

- Pitch changes can provide new textures for some sounds, as can adjusting the time base (slowing down/speeding up without changing pitch).

- Other effects come into play on an as-needed basis, such as distortion to futz a police radio scanner.

- Experiment with your plug-ins to really hear what they do. You'll start to discover your own bag of tricks.

---

Note: If you need an extreme setting for a given plug-in (for example, compression), it can often sound better if you don't push it too hard. Use two compressors, one after the other, in moderation rather than hitting one really hard.

---

## Use Automation

Many DAW parameters, such as volume, pan, and audio effects settings, can be changed over time—in other words, automated. Learn the way your DAW handles this automation and how to apply it to your projects. I do a lot of clip-based automation (fades in/out, volume, and mute) and a lot less track-based automation (some volume and pan). The busses get a healthy dose of automation, though—especially levels and pan. Effects automation is often a 50/50 split. Sometimes I automate an effect parameter, and other times I just move a sound to its own track with the effect applied and then use fades to bring the effected sound in and out. You need to decide on the best workflow for your projects.

### Don't Watch the Screen

Listen. And mix with your ears, not your eyes. If you watch the timeline too much, you may anticipate soundtrack elements as they approach. You will slip into micromanaging mode and miss the macro picture. If you have to stare at anything, watch the onscreen action and really listen to the sound. If that doesn't work, try closing your eyes and really focus on the sound that's there, and then make the changes you need.

### Trust Your Ears

Let your ears adjust the controls. Too many novices try to choose the "right" settings—whatever those may be. Instead, listen to what's happening and then make adjustments. If what you do makes the mix work better, it's probably right, even if it doesn't conform to some rule, recommended setting, or other generality.

If your changes make the track worse, you are on the wrong path—even if you're doing what you think should be done or what somebody else told you to do (and that includes me!). All projects are different and require unique approaches. Therefore, your techniques should differ accordingly.

One thing remains the same: Let your ears be the judge. And if you don't trust 'em, bring in a few other pairs *you do* trust!

### Tired Ears = Bad Mix

Time is the best thing you can bring to your mixes. That means taking time away from the mix so you can return to the work with fresh ears. I've made what I thought were good decisions at 6:00 p.m., only to return the next morning to discover that what I did was all wrong. Give yourself the time to find the right soundtrack mix.

Take frequent breaks during a mixing session. Walk away. Come back. Tweak. Take a few longer stretches away, too. These breaks refresh your perspective in ways that result in better work overall.

Another tactic is to work out of order. I generally work on the opening 10 minutes or so, then the closing 10 minutes, and then the middle. I can then return to the opening/closing with a fresher outlook and often make them stronger. The opening sets the stage for the project, so you need to make it good to capture the audience's attention. And the closing is what they remember most, so your sound mix there needs to be the strongest.

## Quality Control

As you complete your project, make sure your soundtrack meets these criteria:

- Is there a balanced, coherent, and original feel to the whole mix? Does it support the message and mood well?

- Is the dialogue smooth? Free from presence jumps and gaps? Remember the J-cuts, L-cuts, crossfades, and production presence/room tone. It should sound natural and even, with nothing popping out.

- Can we understand the words? Remember, dialogue rules! Watch the mix and adjust volume levels and placement carefully. Remember, voice should be in the center of the stereo field most of the time. (A *brief* off-mic/off-camera line is okay, though.)

- Are you using background audio effectively? Remember to build layered BGs for each location (ambience, crowd walla, effects, and so on). Don't forget to manipulate the mix for changing onscreen perspectives of these BGs.

- Are your sound effects consistent and appropriate for the time/place/setting of the story? And are you leaving room for appropriate sound effects? Remember not to have effects step on important dialogue and vice versa.

- Are you missing any elements?

- Have you created a dynamic, ever-changing mix?

- Did you audition your work in progress and the final mix on different speakers? Watch for volume jumps, distortion, digital clipping, and other inconsistencies. Take notes and fix what doesn't sound good.

- Have you played your project for others? And have they offered their honest opinion? Did you follow their advice?

Very few people are adept at offering criticism. People tend to say things akin to, "I liked it," or, "It sounded great," or, "It had a good beat, and you can dance to it." The problem with these expressions is that they lack focus and are too broad, too ambiguous. Useful constructive criticism comes from specificity. After all, you want real, detailed help so you can improve the mix. Push people to offer precise suggestions and eschew the worthless, imprecise platitudes.

For example, here are some of my notes given to a colleague about her project. Note the specifics (and the time-code values), which make it easier to go back and address these issues head on. These suggestions are very specific and either offer solutions or provide some talking points for further discussion as the sound editing and mix moves along.

---

**Note:**
> Wow! This is really coming together quite nicely. You are on the right track. I have a few minor suggestions, as I didn't find any big problems. The weakest link is probably the 3:16 dialogue. This needs to be addressed.

:52 Dialing phone seemed out of sync.

1:38 Street crowd should be different from restaurant crowd.

2:39 Need some bed linen rustles.

3:16 That dialogue needs work…noise reduction? ADR?

3:48 Market scene is pretty decent, though dialogue gets stepped on a bit. Maybe dip the crowd walla a bit or push it wider in stereo, out to the edges.

5:15 A bit more cloth.

5:44 Date-montage sequence. Personally, I like a bit of reality over just music alone, but that's the director's choice. (I hope reality wins over only music!)

5:40 Fade to dialogue here is a bit rough; maybe sneak it in as music ends. Dialogue levels—especially noise levels—are a bit mismatched. Perhaps some noise reduction and aggressive EQ and then bring in your own BG sounds to cover/complement what's there.

7:45 Dialogue is hard-panned. Move it back to the center; it's distracting. Also, the BG sound in this scene sounds "loopy." If it's a short recording, it repeats too much. Look for another recording.

8:40 Needs some footsteps here and at 9:10. Also, the sit down in chair needs a sound.

9:50 "How 'bout that drink?" The lip sync is off.

10:00 Same comment as 5:44.

12:00 Checkout sequence works really well!

12:27 Need more footsteps, dragging luggage, and street work. Dialogue with taxi driver sounds strange. Also, you are missing the opening of the envelope sound.

---

## Surround-Sound Issues

Although virtually everything mentioned so far in this chapter applies to surround-sound mixing, there are a few special circumstances to address here.

The standard 5.1 surround-sound system uses a front left/right stereo pair, dedicated center channel, left/right stereo surrounds, and a low-frequency enhancement channel (LCR, LsRs, and LFE). The center anchors dialogue to the screen, surrounds immerse and envelop the audience, and the LFE provides extra bass for greater impact.

Working in surround requires having a computer audio interface that supports six discrete output channels. You need five identical, high-quality, full-range speakers and one matching subwoofer. Self-powered speakers (a.k.a. active monitors) are the best choice and easily connect to the audio interface outputs. Avoid cheap computer speakers, as they are more suited to gaming and not serious surround mixing projects.

Follow the International Telecommunications Union ITU Rec. 775 recommendations for speaker placement. Form a circle around the mixing position with the five main speakers. Face the center toward the listener. Set the distance between the front left/right speakers equal to the distance to the mix position, forming an equilateral triangle, and angle them in 30 degrees. Place the surround speakers 110 degrees to 135 degrees from the center, also angled in. Set the subwoofer on the floor in the front, slightly to one side of the center speaker.

The center channel is intended to anchor dialogue to the movie-theater screen. It doesn't matter where the audience sits in the theater; the dialogue always appears to originate from the screen itself. This convention extends to TV as well.

Overusing the surrounds can lessen their immersive effect when you need it most. For example, a dialogue-driven scene can work fine in just the center, with perhaps a little L/R stereo support. When the big action scene kicks in, grab the audience's attention by turning on the full 5.1 experience.

Tracks can be assigned to only the low-frequency effects (LFE) channel to provide added weight and power to deep bass sounds. Note that the LFE is in addition to your mix's existing bass content. It's there to enhance the bass, not be the *only* bass. And much like the surrounds, overuse diminishes its impact when you need it.

A strong phantom center image exists between the two stereo front speakers, which can be reinforced with the center channel. However, the phantom images formed between the L/Ls and R/Rs pairs are not so pronounced or distinct. Similarly, the phantom center formed between the Ls/Rs speakers is also difficult for listeners to pinpoint exactly.

Always create a separate stereo mix of all your 5.1 surround mixes. Having two separate mixes is the only surefire way to be sure that the audience hears what you intended.

If a DVD player is not 5.1 capable, it automatically downmixes or combines the surround sound to L/R stereo and in some cases to single-channel mono. This downmix process completely ignores any LFE content, and anything assigned to it is not heard.

Don't pan sounds around in a manner that forces the audience to look away from the screen to follow the sound.

## Export and Encode Options

Once you've finished your sound mix, turn your attention to delivering your sonic masterpiece to the world. This section explains how to export the files to return to the video NLE for the final project render and how to encode them into the common Dolby AC-3 format (for both stereo and surround mixes).

## Render the Final Mix

When you are finished with the final mix, you need to compile it to a single stereo file. This process is often called *export* or *render*, and all you need to do is select this option in your DAW and choose the correct settings (16-bit/48-kHz interleaved stereo, .wav or .aiff). Your software will then create the single stereo file. Pro Tools users use the Bounce to Disk option.

In either case, the result is a single stereo file that can join the video to complete the project. Generally, while you work on the sound, the picture department puts the final touches on the video, such as visual effects, titles, and color correction. All they need is the stereo file to drop into their software and render the completed video with your soundtrack in place. If your work is not video, then the final audio file may be all that's needed (though a podcast may choose MP3 as the output format).

With surround-sound projects, you may export the individual six channels that comprise your surround-sound mix, or you may create either a single multi-channel file or even the final AC-3 stream. The Dolby Digital AC-3 format supports both stereo and surround-sound projects and is the audio format for DTV, DVD, and Blu-ray.

---

**Digital Audio Formats:** There are both lossless and lossy file formats for digital audio. Lossless means the file is either uncompressed, full quality or designed in a way that doesn't lose any information (by using greater data-encoding efficiencies). Conversely, lossy formats are those that use psychoacoustic masking to throw out audio information and therefore reduce file size (if not quality).

**Lossless**

PCM (uncompressed): .wav, .aiff

FLAC (lossless): .flac

Apple Lossless: .m4a

**Lossy**

MP3: .mp3

AAC: .aac, .mp4, .m4a

AAC w/Fairplay DRM: .m4p

Dolby AC-3: .ac3

Ogg Vorbis: .ogg

Windows Media Audio: .wma

Real Audio: .ra

Occasionally, you may need the DM&E stems separated, which requires a different render option. You can render busses separately, or you may need to export three separate mixes, one at a time, by muting what's not needed. The result will be three separate stereo files.

Exporting a DM&E 5.1 mix to its separate stems requires three separate passes, too. For example, to render the dialogue stem, mute all music and effects tracks and busses. Render the six channels of the dialogue. Mute the dialogue tracks/busses, unmute the music, and render the music. Do the same for the effects (muting dialogue and music for the render). When you're finished, there will be 18 separate mono files ready for the next step. For example, you could record an alternate-language dialogue track and join the M&E tracks for a new mix suitable for international delivery. Keeping the stems gives you control over the final balance of the new dialogue against the music and effects.

## Dolby Digital AC-3 Metadata

If you are exporting directly to AC-3, you need to understand the Dolby AC-3 options. The metadata that can be included with the AC-3 data stream ensures that your encode sounds its best.

The Dolby AC-3 format supports both stereo and 5.1 mixes. When choosing the stereo-only option, there are fewer settings available because most of the metadata settings relate to downmix options. The decoder uses downmix metadata settings when it converts a surround mix to stereo during playback.

> Note:  There are many helpful PDF publications available free from Dolby (www.dolby.com) in their document library.

As mentioned before, it's a good idea to have a separate stereo mix and not rely on the downmix of a surround-sound-only mix. But because you can't control what the audience does, program the AC-3 metadata settings for the best encode. The following is a list of the several settings available and how to program them.

- Use the audio coding mode to select the encode format: stereo 2/0 or surround 3/2.

- Enable LFE on or off with this setting.

- Sample Rate sets the sample rate for the encode. Choose 48 kHz.

- The data rate indicates the average data rate of the encoded file. Lower rates will reduce quality significantly but can save space. The minimum for 5.1 should be 384 kbps, but 448 kbps is the better choice.

- Dialogue Normalization (Dialnorm) is a crucial setting, as it applies a level shift to maintain consistent volume levels. The −31 dBFS setting indicates the average A-weighted level of dialogue. Using a formula, the encoder changes the volume based on the setting you indicate. For example, $31 + (−27) = 4$ dB level shift—your audio will be turned down 4 dB. This setting is so important that it's discussed in greater detail later in this chapter.

- Stereo downmix preferences direct the way an encoder handles the downmix.
    - Lo/Ro adds the center channel to the front L/R and the surrounds to their respective front channels.
    - Lt/Rt adds the center channel to the front L/R. It sums the surround channels to mono, adds them to both front L/R channels, the right 90 degrees out of phase.

- Center Mix Level sets the level reduction the decoder should apply when downmixing to stereo. The standard is −3 dB. This means that during the downmix, the center channel gets added to both the L/R front. Reducing the volume by 3 dB helps maintain the original balance.

- Surround Mix Level sets the level for the surround channels when added to the L/R front during a stereo downmix. Again, −3 dB is standard. You can set this higher or to none if the mix balance works.

- LFE Low-Pass Filter makes sure that frequencies above the cutoff point of the LFE channel are filtered out.

- 90-Degree Phase Shift applies a 90-degree phase shift to the right channel that is used by the decoder when downmixing from a 5.1 mix to a stereo Lt/Rt downmix.

- 3-dB Attenuation reduces the level of the surrounds before encoding. This is not a downmix option. This setting compensates for film surrounds that are often 3 dB louder. Television mixes often employ this level drop because viewers often sit closer to the surrounds than they should.

- The six Dynamic Range Compression (DRC) profiles determine how much soft sounds are boosted and loud sounds are turned down, but only if listeners select DRC mode during playback. It works in conjunction with the Dialog Normalization setting. Many stereo-only playback devices automatically engage DRC when downmixing, so set this carefully. This subject is discussed in detail later in this chapter, too.

## Dialogue Normalization

The Dialogue Normalization, or Dialnorm, setting indicates the dialogue level based on the A-weighted average level over time. The AC-3 decoder uses the setting to adjust, or normalize, the audio output to a specific level. The point of dialogue normalization is to maintain consistent volume levels among different sources, such as TV and DVD.

The Dialogue Normalization settings range from −1 to −31 dB in 1-dB increments. The −31 setting indicates no level shift to the encoder. When the decoder sees an AC-3 stream with the −31 Dialnorm setting, it applies no level shift to the material. The −31 dBFS indicates the average A-weighted level of the dialogue over time. That is 31 dB below 0 dB digital full-scale. The formula is as follows:

$$31 + (\text{Dialnorm setting}) = \text{level shift}$$

The point of the Dialnorm is to maintain consistent volume levels and to feed the DRC profiles to help the listener have a more enjoyable experience.

The only way to set this is to measure your average level of dialogue and then choose the correct setting in the AC-3 encoder. General guidelines for dialogue normalization are:

- Motion pictures: −27

- News/documentary: −15

- Music concert: −10 to −12

- Sports: −22

- Television shows: −18 to −20

## Dynamic-Range Compression

The Dolby AC-3 encoder allows specific settings to control the dynamic range of the material, too. Dynamic range is the difference between the loudest and the softest parts of the mix. There are times when a viewer/listener prefers the largest dynamic range, such as when watching a Hollywood blockbuster in a home theater. However, there are times when a reduced dynamic range is desired, such as for late-night viewing.

Properly setting the dynamic range compression, or DRC, metadata tells the decoder to reduce the dynamic range of material based upon preset choices indicated when encoding. The listener can then decide whether to apply the DRC during playback. This feature may be called "Midnight mode" or something like that. For instance, one of my consumer surround systems calls it "Night mode."

Line-mode profile is used by two-channel set-top players and both stereo and 5.1 digital television. This compression profile can boost low-level and cut high-level signals. This effectively squeezes, or compresses, the dynamic range. The compression is scalable, depending on the mode profile chosen and the Dialnorm setting.

The DRC profiles determine how much low-level signals are boosted and high-level signals are cut. There are six profiles from which to choose:

- Film Light

- Film Standard

- Music Light

- Music Standard

- Speech

- None

Though you can indicate a DRC profile in the metadata, it only applies if the consumer chooses DRC mode during playback. Otherwise, only the Dialnorm setting applies. However, many stereo-only devices automatically engage DRC when downmixing.

Each DRC profile has different preset properties that cannot be adjusted. Consult the documentation on the Dolby website for details. Once again, the right settings are project-driven. Therefore, I suggest that you experiment with the DRC modes and the Dialnorm settings. Do some test encodes and evaluate them. Then, choose the best setting for your surround-sound mix based on these tests.

With the files exported and/or encoded properly, your work is done. It's time to celebrate!

## Final Thoughts

So, how do you become proficient and ultimately a much-sought-after expert in the field of sound design and sound supervision? It's an easy three-step process.

1.  Do the soundtrack for a film.

2.  Make mistakes and then learn from them.

3.  Repeat Steps 1 and 2.

Congratulations on making this journey. Now it's time to apply all that you've learned to making your own projects better. I hope you will return to this book when you need some inspiration or help solving an issue.

Don't let your education stop here, though. Stay informed by visiting and participating in my Fish(er)Tales blog, www.jeffreypfisher.com, and by following me on Twitter @JeffreyPFisher. I look forward to hearing your soundtrack success stories!

Jeffrey P. Fisher

May 2011

# Index

AAF (Advanced Authoring Format), 115
AATranslator, 115, 119, 120
accelerator cards, adding, 117
ACID, 116, 117, 121, 264
ACIDplanet, 266
acoustic
    anomalies, post-production fixes, 44–45
    audio rooms, 107
    comb filters, 172
    energy, 19
    instruments, 19
acquiring
    backgrounds, 231–233
    music, 259–268
    sound effects, 213–219
    sounds, 113
"Across the Universe," 259
action, matching, 34
actors, 1
    voiceovers, 144. *See also* voiceovers
"A Day in the Life," 126
ADCs (analog-to-digital converters), 22
adding
    accelerator cards, 117
    busses, 140
    fades, 169
    noise, post-production, 47
    pink noise, 101
    reverberation, 156, 234
Adobe Premiere Pro and Audition, 115
ADR (automatic dialogue replacement), 1, 33, 40, 89
    editing, 165
    Foley, 226–227
    quality control, 156–159
    recording, 155–156
Advanced Authoring Format. *See* AAF
AES (Audio Engineering Society), 102
aesthetics, audio, 7–17
AGC (Automatic Gain Control), 63, 189, 190
agents, voiceover actors, 145
airtightness, 104
*All My Children,* 267
alternative takes, 166
*Amadeus,* 10, 271
ambiences, 225, 246

backgrounds, 232. *See also* backgrounds
*American Graffiti,* 247
American Musical Supply, 150
amplitude, 19, 22
analog sound, 21
analog-to-digital converters. *See* ADCs
analysis
    audio tools, 132–134
    music, 16
*Apocalypse Now,* 256
Apple
    Final Cut Pro and Soundtrack Pro, 115
    iLife, 117
Apple, Fiona, 259
applying FX (audio effects), 125–135
armrests, 110
*Around the World in 80 Days,* 149
artifacts, noise reduction plug-ins, 199
artists, Foley, 2, 226. *See also* Foley
ART models, 151
atmos, 40
atonal music, 272
attaching microphones, 67. *See also* lavalieres
attacks, compression, 199
attenuation, 3-dB, 298
Audacity, 117
audience, music, 257
audio. *See also* sounds
    aesthetics, 7–17
    analysis tools, 132–134
    cameras, 166
    effects. *See* FX
    interfaces/soundcards, 107–111
    monitoring, 95–97
    recorders, 91–92
    separate recorders, 74–75
    slate procedures, 88
    split, 175
Audio Engineering Society. *See* AES
*Audio Media* magazine, 275
Audio-Technica
    2020, 54
    AT822/825, 80
    AT831, 65
    AT899, 65
auditions, voiceovers, 145
Auralex, 150
    MoPADs, 99, 100
Auratone 5C, 97
authenticity, 157, 214, 241–242

automatic dialogue replacement. *See* ADR
Automatic Gain Control. *See* AGC
automation
    using, 291–292
    volume, 172
Avalon, 151
Avant
    CV12 microphones, 151
    Electronics, 97
Avid, 115
avoiding
    built-in microphones, 59–60
    noise, 46

baby booms, 25
backgrounds, 225, 230–235
    Foley. *See* Foley
    gathering, 231–233
    noise reduction tools, 201
    recording, 78–79
    sounds, 1–2, 34
    super-sizing stereo, 233–235
    surround, 235
backups, 139
Badalamenti, Angelo, 255, 259, 272
*Badlands,* 271
balance, mixing, 292. *See also* mixing
band-pass filters, 205
BaseHead, 215
Beatles, The, 259, 269
beats, 270
beeps, 158
Berger, Marc, 199
Bernstein, Elmer, 271
Best Buy, 123
bidirectional microphones, 56
bit depth, 22
blankets, 47
Blue Mouse microphones, 151
bonus features, DVDs, 15
booms
    booming from above/below, 59
    channels, 25
    operators, 40
    positioning boom poles, 69
boosting signals, 62–64
Boot Camp, 114
Bordwell, David, 9
*Bourne Ultimatum, The,* 226
breathing, removing, 169, 180–182, 199

*Bred in the Bone,* 272
broadband absorption, 105
broadcast loops, 67
Broadcast Wave format. *See* BWF
B-roll footage, 92
Brooks, Mel, 9, 255
budgets
    equipment purchases, 122–123
    music, 267–268
*Building a Recording Studio,* 107
built-in microphones, avoiding, 59–60
bumpers, 15
burnishing tools, 78
Burtt, Ben, 2, 210, 218
Burwell, Carter, 255
business management, 135
busses, 118
    layouts, 280
buy-out music, 261
BWF (Broadcast Wave format), 91

cables, 76–77, 107
calibrating
    mixers, 72
    monitors, 282
    speakers, 101–104
camcorders, 85
    recording in stereo, 166
cameras, 85
    audio, 166
"Can't Look Down," 274
capacitors, 51, 52
capturing
    frequencies, 22
    lines wild, 92
    room tone, 40–41
car-by, 15
cardioid microphones, 54
Carpenter, John, 255, 266, 271
cars in motion case study, 253
Cascade microphones, 151
case studies, 253–254
*Cash Tracks: Compose, Produce, and
    Sell Your Original Sound-
    track Music and
    Jingles,* 268
*Castaway,* 16
casting voiceovers, 145–146
cause and effect, 11, 239
cell-phone ring case study, 253
centering speakers, 100. *See also*
    locations
channels
    camera mic, 85
    sound, 24–25
    strips, FX (audio effects), 131–132
checklists, 14
    production sound, 48–49
chorus, 127, 207
Chorus tool, 193, 194
CinemaScope, 23
Cinerama, 23
Cinescore, 116
clappers, 89, 90
clicks, corrections, 188–190
clipping, 128
    peak corrections, 190–192

clips
    edges, 241
    microphones, 78
clothing
    Foley, 228
    rustles, removing, 169
clown noses. *See* foam windscreens
cochleas, 21
Coen Brothers (Joel & Ethan), 255
collections, sound effects, 220–221
combining elements, 2–3
Commercial Voices, 145
communication, 30, 34
compatibility, 30
competing sounds, 289
components of sound, 19–21
composers, 11
    hiring, 266–267
compression, 19
    attacks, 199
    corrections, 198–199
    DRC (Dynamic Range
        Compression), 298
    dynamic-range, 299–300
    hyper-compression, 103
    multi-band, popped P's (and B's
        and T's) corrections, 180
    output, 199
    time, 195–196
compressors, 128, 129
computers, 113–114. *See also* equip-
    ment; hardware; software
condenser microphones, 52–53
configuring noise gate thresholds, 181
connectors, 76–77, 107, 219
consistency, 12–13, 214
Contour
    Design RollerMouse, 111
    ShuttlePRO v.2, 111
controlling noise, 12
*Conversation, The,* 5
conversion
    ADCs (analog-to-digital
        converters), 22
    DACs (digital-to-analog
        converters), 22
    DAW formats, 119
convolution, 246
    plug-ins, 156
Cooper, Jeff, 107
Copland, Aaron, 255
Coppola, Francis Ford, 256
copyrights, 219, 259
Core Sound, 81, 218
corrections
    better speech intelligibility,
        187–188
    clicks, 188–190
    compression, 198–199
    DC offset utilities, 177
    dialogue, editing, 176–200
    distortion, 190–192
    EQ properties, 188
    expansion, 183–184
    glitches, 188–190
    hum, 192–195
    mouth noises, 180–182
    pitch shift, 196

popped P's (and B's and T's),
    178–180
pop removal, 188–190
reverberation, 184–185
rumble and hiss, 185–186
sibilance, 177–178
time compression/expansion,
    195–196
tonal fixes, 186–187
volume, 173, 197–198
Craigslist, hiring composers, 266
*Craving Heart, The,* 263
    case study, 272–274
creating
    sound effects, 222–224
    sounds, 113
Creative Commons licenses,
    221–222, 264
creativity, 250–251
crew noise, removing, 169
crossfades, 14, 165
    editing, 167–169
*Crouching Tiger, Hidden
    Dragon,* 272
crowds. *See* walla
customizing sound effects, 242
cutting, 164. *See also* editing
    dialogue, 169

DACs (digital-to-analog
    converters), 22
*Das Boot,* 5, 235
databases, 219. *See also* libraries
DAW, 114, 117, 140
    NLEs (nonlinear editing systems)
        to, 119–120
Day, Howie, 259
dB (decibel), 19, 288
    3-dB attenuation, 298
dBFS (decibel full-scale standard), 72
DC (direct current), 52
    DC offset utilities, 177
deadening for sound, 47, 104
dead rooms, 149
decibel. *See* dB
decibel full-scale standard. *See* dBFS
de-clickers, 189
Declipper tool, 191, 192
    hum removal, 193
decoupling, 104
dedicating
    dedicated noise reduction,
        199–205
    dedicated surround
        microphones, 81
    hard drives, 139
de-essing, 177
defining walla, 159
delay, 126, 206
delegation, workflow, 28–29
Dell computers, 123
demos, voiceovers, 145
design, sound, 2, 244–246
designers, sound, 28
desk setups, 111
devices, monitoring, 151
dialogue, 1, 49

ADR (automatic dialogue replacement), 33, 40, 89. *See also* ADR
  cutting, 169
  editing, 164–208
    corrections, 176–200
    crossfades (JLX), 167–169
    dedicated noise reduction, 199–205
    importance of, 164–165
    listening, 171–172
    phases, 172–175
    smoothing, 165–167, 170–171
    special voice effects, 205–207
  focus on capturing top-quality, 39
  matching, 170
  mixing, 285–286
  noise, masking, 232
  normalization, 298, 299
  production, 33
  rules, 7
  voiceovers. *See* voiceovers
dialogue, music, and effects. *See* DM&E
diegetic sounds, 9, 271
digital download sites, 263
DigitalFishPhones, 178
Digital Juice, 16, 215, 261
digital recorders, 91. *See also* recorders
digital sound, 22–23
digital-to-analog converters. *See* DACs
digital video. *See* DV
DigiTranslator, 119
Dim buttons, 283
direct current. *See* DC
directional microphones, 43, 49
Direct Sound HP-25 Extreme Isolation Headphones, 40
distances, microphones, 42–43, 49, 58–59
distant miking, post-production fixes, 45
distortion, 86
  corrections, 190–192
  post-production fixes, 44
DIY (do it yourself) music, 264–266
DM&E (dialogue, music, and effects), 3, 140, 279
DMN (www.digitalmedianet.com), 121
documents, 212. *See also* notes
Dolby, 23. *See also* surround sound
  Digital AC-3 metadata, 297–298
*Don Juan,* 23
double-system, 74
  recording, 86–88
Dourdan, Gary, 67
downbeat, 269
downmixing, 300
DPA Microphones, 66
DPA WINDPAC. Omnidirectional mics, 47, 61
Dragonfly microphones, 151
DRC (Dynamic Range Compression), 298, 299–300
drums, 128

*Dr. Zhivago,* 271
dubbing mixers, 28. *See also* mixing
*Dukes of Hazzard,* 223
Dun, Tan, 272
DV (digital video), 22
  tape, 86
DVDs
  bonus features, 15
  education, 4–5
dynamic microphones, 51–52
Dynamic Range Compression. *See* DRC
dynamic ranges, 290
dynamics-based effects, FX (audio effects), 128–129

Eagle, Douglas Spotted, 149
eardrums, 21
ears
  ear candy, 248
  mixing with, 292
echoes, 126
edges, clips, 241
Edirol R-44 field recorder/mixer, 75, 88
editing. *See also* corrections
  dialogue, 164–208
    corrections, 176–200
    crossfades (JLX), 167–169
    dedicated noise reduction, 199–205
    importance of, 164–165
    listening, 171–172
    phases, 172–175
    smoothing, 165–167, 170–171
    special voice effects, 205–207
  music, 268–270
  NLEs. *See* NLEs (nonlinear editing systems)
  popped P's, 179
  visuals, 30
education, DVDs, 4–5
effects
  audio, optimizing, 280–282
  cause and effect, 239
  exit sign, 249
  FX (audio effects), 125–137
  PA announcer, 207
  party, 176
  positioning, 170
  printed, 45
  sound, 33–34, 139, 209–224
    acquiring, 213–219
    creating, 222–224
    fills, 171
    layering, 243
    libraries, 216, 219–224
    music as, 210–211, 271–272
    printing, 251–252
    recording, 78–79
    spotting, 211–213
    websites, 221–222
    working with, 237–254
  sounds, 2
  special voice, 205–207
  stereo, 109
  using appropriate, 290–291

Einstein, Albert, 13
electronic music, 272
Electro-Voice
  EV635a, 52, 54, 61
  N/D767a, 61
elements
  combining, 2–3
  narrative, 9–11
  soundtracks, 11–13
emotions, 31
  manipulating, 237–238
  responses to music, 257
emulation software, 114, 125
encode options, mixing, 295–300
energy, acoustic, 19
engineering equipment, 151–152
Entertainer's Secret Throat Relief, 148
entertainment, 11
environments, 225
EQ (equalization), 125
  clipping, 192
  properties, corrections, 188
  sibilance, 177–178
  tonal fixes, 186–187
equal lengths, 100
equipment
  engineering, 151–152
  financing, 123
  recording, 149
  selecting, 120–124
errors, quantization, 22
Etymotic ER-6.I, 40
Evolvers, 16
exit sign effect, 249
expansion, 128
  corrections, 183–184
  time, 195–196
exporting
  OMF (Open Media Framework), 119
  options, mixing, 295–300
external
  audio-level hardware, 283
  FireWires, 219
  hard drives, 114
extras talking. *See* walla

fades, 14, 168
  adding, 169
Fairchild 670 compressor/limiter, 131, 133
*Fantasia,* 23
FFT (Fast Fourier Transform), 246
figure/ground (Gestalt theory of), 10
files
  naming, 88
  reformatting, 36
  WAV., 19
fills, room tone, 170
*Film Art: An Introduction,* 9
FilmSound.org, 5, 218
filters, 125
  acoustic comb, 172
  band-pass, 205
  high-pass, 234
  notch, 184

final
  dubs, 28
  mixes, rendering, 296–297
financing equipment, 123
FireWire, 107, 108
  external, 219
firewood, 272
Fisher, Jeffrey P., 153
fixes. *See also* corrections
  fixing and sweetening, 11–12
  post-production, 44–45
flanging, 127, 207
flat recording, 152
Fletcher-Munson equal loudness
    contours, 20, 103, 282
foam pads, 99, 150
foam windscreens, 47
focus, 10
Focusrite
  Producer Pack, 151
  Saffire, 151
folders, 36
  managing, 139
Foley, 225–230
  artists, 2, 11
  clothing, 228
  footsteps, 227–228
  props, 228–229
  recording, 226–227
  software, 230
Foley, Jack, 226
foregrounds, 240–241. *See also*
    backgrounds
foreign-language dubs, 175
foreshadowing, 271
formatting, 30
  folders, 139
  noise gate thresholds, 181
  technical issues, 36
*Forrest Gump*, 130
Fowler, Mick, 67
Fox, Jorja, 67
Freemantle, Glenn, 231
free sound effects, 219
Freesound Project, 264
freeware, 117
freezing, 251
frequencies, 19, 22
  EQ (equalization), 125
  harmonics, 192
  mixing, 288–289
  ranges, 105
  sibilance, 177–178
functions, Listen, 178
fundamentals of music, 256–258
furry zeppelins, 47
futzing, 205, 251
FX (audio effects), 125–137
  advice concerning, 137
  audio analysis tools, 132–134
  channel strips, 131–132
  dynamics-based effects, 128–129
  links, 136
  modulation, 127–128
  multi-effects, 134–135
  pitch, 130
  plug-ins, 135–136
  restoration tools, 132

time, 126–127
time compression/expansion, 130
tone, 125–126
workflow, 136–137


gain reduction, 199
GarageBand, 117, 264
gates, noise, 128, 181, 182
gathering
  backgrounds, 231–233
  sound effects, 213–219
Getty Images, 263
*Ghostbusters*, 160
glitches, corrections, 188–190
goal setting, purchasing equipment,
    122
Gold Line GL14 sine wave generator,
    72
Goldsmith, Jerry, 271, 272
gradient microphones, 54
*Green Mile, The*, 247
*Groundhog Day*, 9, 255


*Halloween*, 271. *See also* John
    Carpenter
Hammer, Jan, 268
handles, 119, 166
hanging, 59
hard drives, 114, 219
  dedicating, 139
hard knees, 199
hardware
  external audio-level, 283
  Saffire, 108
  selecting, 113–114
Harley-Davidson, 220
harmonics, 192
Harrington, Stan, 263, 272–274
headphones, 15, 49, 55
  splitters, 78
hearing, 10
  perception of sound, 21–22
  ranges, 19
  sound, 95–111
Heil PR-40, 54, 223
Helgenberger, Marg, 67
Herrmann, Bernard, 5, 255, 271, 272
Hertz. *See* Hz
*High Anxiety*, 9, 255
high-density foam pads, 99
high-pass filters, 234
hiring composers, 266–267
hiss, corrections, 185–186
history of the Wilhelm scream, 218
Hitchcock, Alfred, 9, 218, 255
Hogan, Harlan, 145, 149, 150, 153
hollow sounds, 172
Hollywood Lost and Found, 218
Holman, Tomlinson, 4
Holophone, 79, 81
Horror-Tones, MixCubes Mini
    Reference Monitors, 97–99
hum, removing, 192–195
*Hunt for Red October, The*, 243
hunting for sound effects, 213–219
HVAC noise, 149

hypercardioid microphones, 54
hyper-compression, 103
Hz (Hertz), 13, 19


iLife, 117
IMDb (Internet Movie Database), 266
importance of editing dialogue,
    164–165
impulse response, 246. *See* IR
indie (music) artists, 263–264
infra-sonic noise, 186
input channels, cameras, 85
instruments, acoustic, 19
intelligibility, speech, 187–188
interfaces, 107–111
International Telecommunications
    Union. *See* ITU
Inverse Square rule, 43, 58
IR (impulse response), 157
ITU (International Telecommunica-
    tions Union), 99, 295
iZotope
  Alloy, 131
  Ozone 4, 134, 188, 233
  RX Advanced, 133, 201


Jarre, Maurice, 266, 271, 272
*Jaws*, 271
*Jazz Singer, The*, 23
J-cuts, 167, 168, 293
Joemeek oneQ, 151
John Hardy, 151
Jolson, Al, 23
Juicer 3 application, 215


Katy J, 263, 272–274
Katz, Bob, 101, 103
Keene, Sherman, 9
keyboard shortcuts, 110
keywords, searching, 215
kHz (kilohertz), 19, 22
  sample rates, 166
killer drug case study, 254
kilohertz. *See* kHz
kitchen sink approach, 249–250
Kossayan, Laurent, 223


LANC, 88
"Lara's Theme," 271
lavalieres, 61, 64, 94
  TRAM, 67
laws. *See also* rules
  copyrights, 259
  Inverse Square, 43, 58
Lawson 147 microphones, 151
layering
  recordings, 234
  sound effects, 243
layouts
  busses, 280
  tracks, 279
LCRS (left-center-right and single
    mono surround), 23, 24
L-cuts, 167, 168, 293

left-center-right and single mono surround. *See* LCRS
left/right. *See* LR
Leigh, Janet, 271
leitmotifs, 271
length of time, crossfades, 168
Lennon, John, 126, 259
Letterman, David, 54
*Letters from Iwo Jima,* 222
levels, 71–74
   mic, 62
   SPLs (sound pressure levels), 223
   threshold, 128, 181
LFE (low-frequency enhancement), 25
   non-surround, 246–247
   surround-sound issues, 295
libraries, sound effects, 39, 216, 219–224. *See also* sound effects
library music, 261–263
licenses
   Creative Commons, 221–222, 264
   songs, 259
   sound effects, 220–221
*Lifted,* 218
limiting, 128
lines
   levels, 62
   microphones, 54
line-up tones, 88
links, FX (audio effects), 136
Linux operating systems, 114
lip smack corrections, 180–182
Liquid Channel, 151
Listen function, 178
listening, 10
   dialogue, editing, 171–172
   optimizing, 13
   to what's there, 276
listen-or-monitor-output feature, 189
Little Labs IBP Phase Alignment Tool, 173, 235
live one-of-a-kind content, 45
lobar microphones, 54
locations, 39–49
   audio monitoring, 104–107
   listening to, 40
   mistakes made in the field, 41–43
   sound
      field kits, 77–78
      kits, 71–83
   speakers, 99–101
   studio floorplans, 106
logarithmic, 20
loops, 264
   ADR (automatic dialogue replacement), 157
   broadcast, 67
   delay feedback, 126
loudness, 20, 22. *See also* sound; volume
low-frequency enhancement. *See* LFE
LR (left/right), 24
Lucas, George, 247. *See also Star Wars*
Lynch, David, 206, 255, 259

Mackie Sprite, 151
Macs, 114. *See also* computers
maintenance, microphones, 60
managing
   business management, 135
   files, 36
   folders, 139
   sound effects, 214
   workflow, 28–29, 139–140
*Manchurian Candidate,* 15
manipulating emotions, 237–238
maps, sound, 31, 213
Markertek, 47, 150
Marriner, Sir Neville, 271
masking dialogue noise, 232
mass, 104
Massenburg, George, 8
*Master and Commander,* 222
master cues, 268
*Mastering Audio, Second Edition: The Art and the Science,* 104
master-use licensing, 259
matching
   action, 34
   dialogue, 170
M-Audio MicroTrack 24/96, 81, 217
maximum
   compression, 19
   rarefaction, 174
McCartney, Paul, 259
measures, 270
Media Manager (Sony Vegas Pro), 214
meetings, 29, 30
*Memoirs of a Geisha,* 170
*Men in Trees,* 274
message of music, 257
metadata, Dolby Digital AC-3, 297–298
meter (music), 269
meters, 71–74
   peak, 101
   phase, 174, 175
*Miami Vice,* 268
microphones, 51–69
   bidirectional, 56
   built-in, avoiding, 59–60
   cardioid, 54
   changing positions too many times, 42
   clips, 78
   condenser, 52–53
   distances, 42–43, 49, 58–59
   distant miking, post-production fixes, 45
   dynamic, 51–52
   Foley, recording, 227
   gradient, 54
   hypercardioid, 54
   levels, 62
   line, 54
   lobar, 54
   maintenance, 60
   number of, 57–58
   omnidirectional, 53, 80
   out-of-phase, 172
   pickup patterns, 53–57
   placement options, 66–69, 152

popped P's (and B's and T's), 178–180
removing thumps, 169
ribbon, 53
rules, 57–61
selecting, 48, 57, 64–66, 151
shotgun, 55, 62
signals, boosting, 62–64
storage, 60–61
super-cardioid, 54
types of, 51, 61–62
unidirectional, 54
using the wrong one, 41–42
voiceovers, 148
Microphone University, 66
Mic Thing, 149
MIDI (Musical Instrument Digital Interface), 117, 217
   Foley, 230
Millan, Scott, 276
*Millimeter,* 170
minus optical sound. *See* MOS
mistakes made in the field, 41–43
MixCubes Mini Reference Monitors, 97–99
mixers, 28, 71–74
mixing, 8–9, 275–300
   with decision-makers, 276–277
   dialogue, 285–286
   Dolby Digital AC-3 metadata, 297–298
   downmixing, 300
   editing, 167
   encode/export options, 295–300
   monitors, 98
   quality control, 292–294
   reference mixes, 284
   rendering final mixes, 296–297
   starting, 275–284
   surround-sound issues, 294–295
   tips, 284–292
   with your ears, 292
*Mix* magazine, 213, 226, 231
modulation, FX (audio effects), 127–128
Mogami Cable, 76
monitoring
   audio, 95–97
   devices, 151
   double-system recording, 87
   errors, 42
   MixCubes Mini Reference Monitors, 97–99
monitors
   optimizing, 282–284
   positioning, 110
Monitor Station, 151
monoaural channels, 24
mono downmix buttons, 110
Monster Cable, 76
*Monsters, Inc.,* 5, 15, 247
Monty Python, 229
mood, 29, 31
MOS (minus optical sound), 93
motifs, 271
mouse, 110
mouth noise corrections, 180–182
movies, history of sound, 23

Mozart, 260
mud range, 187
*Mulholland Drive,* 272
multi-band compression, 128
    popped P's (and B's and T's)
        corrections, 180
multichannels, 24
multi-effects, FX (audio effects),
        134–135
multitrack recordings, 166
Murch, Walter, 10, 247
Murray, Bill, 9, 255
music, 2, 34
    acquiring, 259–268
    analyzing, 16
    budgets, 267–268
    diegetic, 9
    editing, 268–270
    fundamentals of, 256–258
    as sound effects, 210–211,
        271–272
    supervisors, 29
MXL M3B microphones, 151

naming
    conventions, 88
    sound, 244
narrative elements, 9–11. *See*
        voiceovers
narrators, 1
natural sounds, 39
Neumann 47/87/89, 53, 151
Neve 88RS channel strip, 131, 132
Newell, Phillip, 107
*Nine,* 226
NLEs (nonlinear editing systems), 27,
        33, 90, 114, 140
    to DAWs, 119–120
noise. *See also* sound
    avoidance, 46
    controlling, 12
    dedicated reduction, 199–205
    dialogue, masking, 232
    eliminating, 243
    gates, 128
    hum, removing, 192–195
    HVAC, 149
    infra-sonic, 186
    mouth noise corrections, 180–182
    pink, 282
    post-production, 176
        adding, 47
        fixes, 44
    reduction, 8
    removing, 169
    settings, optimizing, 203
    signal-to-noise ratios, 43, 58, 199
    sources, 48
    sub-sonic, 186
    technical issues, 45–48
    vinyl restoration, 188
    walla. *See* walla
    wind, 47–48
non-diegetic sounds, 9, 271
nonlinear editing systems. *See* NLEs
non-surround LFE (low-frequency
        enhancement), 246–247

normalization, 167, 168, 198
    dialogue, 298, 299
*North by Northwest,* 5, 271
notch filters, 125, 184
notes, 252–253
    audio settings, 89
    sound, 212
    spotting sessions, 31
*NYPD Blue,* 15

O'Connell, Dan, 226
offbeat, atonal music, 272
off-camera voices, 286
Oktava MK-012, 55, 151
OMF (Open Media Framework), 115
    exporting, 119
omnidirectional microphones, 53, 80
*127 Hours,* 231
on-location sound crews, 39
opening titles, music, 270–271
Open Media Framework. *See* OMF
operating systems, 114
operators, using the wrong
        microphone, 41–42
optimizing
    audio effects, 280–282
    listening, 13
    monitors, 282–284
    noise settings, 203
    sound, 125–137
    sound effects, 247–248
    speech intelligibility, 187–188
    tracks, 278–280
    voiceovers, 146–148
    walla, 160–161
ossicles, 21
out-of-phase microphones, 172
output, compression, 199

PA announcer effects, 207
Palin, Michael, 149
panning, 289
    recordings, 234
party effects, 176
*Patton,* 271
pauses, 242–243
PCs (personal computers), 114. *See
        also* computers
peak program meter. *See* PPM
peaks
    clipping corrections, 190–192
    meters, 101
    reducing, 128
Pencil tool, 179
perception, sound, 21–22
perceptive shifts, using, 248–249
performances
    rights, 262
    voiceovers, 146–148
personal computers. *See* PCs
personalizing
    environments, 31
    sound effects, 242
phantom power, 52
phases, 127, 207
    dialogue, editing, 172–175

synchronization, 90
physics, 239
pickup patterns, microphones, 53–57
pictures
    editorial *versus* sound editorial,
        27–28
    lock, 27, 30, 165
pink noise, 101, 282
pinna, 21
pitch, 22
    FX (audio effects), 130
    shift, 196, 234
pits, 227
Pixar, 16
placement
    options, microphones, 66–69, 152
    talent, 153
*Planet of the Apes,* 272
planning, 7–8
    projects, 29–36
*Pleasantville,* 259
plosives, reducing, 180
plug-ins
    audio analysis tools, 132–134
    convolution, 156
    flangers, 128
    FX (audio effects), 135–136
    noise reduction, 199
    SPAN, 101
    time stretch, 195–196
    UAD, 131
PluralEyes, 90
polar patterns. *See* pickup patterns
*Poltergeist,* 206
popped P's (and B's and T's)
        corrections, 178–180
pop removal corrections, 188–190
portable digital recorders, 92. *See also*
        recorders
portable mixers, 71. *See also* mixers
Porta-Booth, 149–151
positioning
    boom poles, 69
    effects, 170
    monitors, 110
    speakers, 99–101
    studio floorplans, 106
post-lap, 249
post-production. *See also* production
    fixes, 44–45
    FX (audio effects), 125–137
    noise, 47, 176
    voiceovers. *See* voiceovers
    workflow, 139–142
*Practical Techniques for the
        Recording Engineer,* 9
preamps, 62
predubbing, 277–278
pre-lap, 249
premixing, 3, 140, 251, 277–278
preparing projects, 140–142
pre-score, 259
PreSonus
    Central, 151
    Eureka, 151
    FP10, 151
pressure-zone microphones. *See*
        PZMs

Primeval, 218
printing sound effects, 45, 251–252
procedures
    slate, 88–91
    soundproofing, 104
processes, 125. *See also* FX (audio effects)
processing mid-side, 82
production
    compatibility, 30
    dialogue, 33
    music, 261–263
    saving money, 238
    sound
        checklists, 48–49
        mixers, 28, 40
    technical issues, 39–41
    tracks, 219–220
professional voiceovers, 148. *See also* voiceovers
*Profiting from Your Music and Sound Project Studio*, 107
projects
    preparing, 140–142
    reviewing, 238
    starting, 29–36
    timelines, 37
properties, EQ (equalization) corrections, 188
props, Foley, 228–229
Pro Tools, 108, 115, 119
*Psycho*, 271, 272
*Public Enemies*, 223
Pump Audio, 263
pumping, 199
purchasing
    equipment, 120–124
    sound effects, 34, 220–221
PZMs (pressure-zone microphones), 56

quality control, 93
    ADR (automatic dialogue replacement), 156–159
    checking, 42
    mixing, 292–294
quantization errors, 22
quiet scenes, 15–16
quilted blankets, 47

*Raiders of the Lost Ark*, 229
ranges
    DRC (Dynamic Range Compression), 298
    dynamic, 128, 290
    filling, 287
    frequencies, 105
    hearing, 19
    mud, 187
rarefaction, 19
ratios
    compression, 198–199
    signal-to-noise, 43, 58, 199
reading scripts, 29
REAPER, 117
recorders

audio, 91–92
technical issues, 93–94
Zoom H4n stereo, 232
recording
    ADR (automatic dialogue replacement), 155–156
    double-system, 86–88
    equipment, 149
    flat, 152
    Foley, 226–227
    layering, 234
    panning, 234
    separate audio recorders, 74–75
    slate procedures, 88–91
    sound, 113–124
    sound effects, 78–79
    split tracks, 85
    in stereo, 58, 166
    stereo in the field, 79–83
    vinyl restoration, 188
    voiceovers, 147, 148–153
    walla, 159–160
*Recording Studio Design, Second Edition*, 107
reducing
    gain, 199
    noise, 8
    noise, dedicated noise reduction, 199–205
    peaks, 128
    plosives, 180
reference mixes, 284
reflection-free zones, 105
Reflexion Filter, 149
reformatting files, 36. *See also* formatting
releases, compression, 199
removing. *See also* corrections
    hum, 192–195
    pop removal, 188–190
    sibilance, 177–178
rendering final mixes, 296–297
repeats, 126, 270
repetitive stress injuries. *See* RSIs
"Requiem," 271
re-recording mixers, 28, 29
researching equipment purchases, 121–122
resonance, rooms, 184
resources, voiceovers, 153
restoration
    tools, FX (audio effects), 125–137
    vinyl, 188
reverberation, 126, 246
    adding, 156, 234
    corrections, 184–185
reversing dialogue, 206–207
reviewing projects, 238
ribbon microphones, 53
*Ride of the Valkyries*, 256
rights, performances, 262
Robinson, Sir Ken, 285
Rode NT4, 80
Rodriguez, Robert, 255
rooms. *See also* locations
    dead, 149
    resonance, 184
    simulating, 206

soundproofing, 104
studio floorplans, 106
tone, 40–41, 49, 166, 169
rough cuts, screening, 30
routing software, 108
royalty-free
    music, 34, 261. *See also* music
    sound effects, 220–221
RSIs (repetitive stress injuries), 109
RTAS formats, 117
*Rubber Soul*, 269
rules
    dialogue, 7
    microphones, 57–61
rumble, corrections, 185–186
Rycote Softie, 47
Rydstrom, Gary, 15, 218

Saffire
    hardware, 108
    software, 109
*Salt*, 276
sample-rates, 166
sampling, 22
Sanken COS-11, 65
SANs (storage area networks), 219
scenes
    completing, 31
    quiet, 15–16
Schwartz, David, 274
scooping, 59, 69
scores, 255. *See also* music
scouting locations, 43
screams case study, 253–254
screening rough cuts, 30
scripts
    reading, 29
    voiceovers, 144–145
searching keywords, 215
"see a dog, hear a dog," 239
selecting
    equipment, 120–124
    hardware, 113–114
    microphones, 48, 57, 64–66, 151
    monitors, 96
    software, 114–118
    speakers, 96
Sennheiser 416 microphones, 53, 55, 151
sensitivity of omnidirectional microphones, 54
separate audio recorders, 74–75
sessions, spotting, 30–33
    music, 257–258
set noise, removing, 169
settings
    noise, optimizing, 203
    noise gate thresholds, 181
setups
    desks, 111
    stereo surround, 100
shift, pitch, 196, 234
shooting for sound, 46–47, 92–93
*Shop Around the Corner, The*, 4
shortcuts, keyboard, 110
shotgun microphones, 55, 62
show themes, music, 270–271

shuffling, 160
Shure SM57/SM58, 52, 61
sibilance, 177–178
signals, boosting, 62–64
signal-to-noise ratios, 43, 58, 199
    technical issues, 59
simulating
    rooms and spaces, 206
    telephone lines, 205–206
Singular Software, 90
slapback echoes, 126
slate procedures, 88–91
small-room acoustics, 107
smoothing dialogue, 165–167,
    170–171
soft knees, 199
software
    emulation, 125
    Foley, 230
    Saffire, 109
    selecting, 114–118
    Sony. *See* Sony
SOLO/610, 151
SONEX, 150
songs, licensing, 259. *See also* music
Sonnenschein, David, 11, 31
Sony
    computers, 123
    Creative Software
        ACID, 116, 117, 121
        Acoustic Mirror, 135, 157
        Sound Forge, 2, 101, 116, 121,
            174, 245
        Vegas Pro, 90, 116, 121, 140,
            214
    ECMs, 65
    MDR-7506, 40
    Noise Reduction, 134, 203, 204
sore throats, 148
sound
    analog, 21
    backgrounds, 1–2, 34. *See also*
        background sounds
    channels, 24–25
    components of, 19–21
    deadening for, 47, 104
    design, 2, 244–246
    designers, 28, 210
    diegetic, 9
    digital, 22–23
    double-system recording. *See*
        double-system
    editorial, picture editorial *versus*,
        27–28
    editors, 28
    effects, 2, 33–34, 139, 209–224
        acquiring, 213–219
        creating, 222–224
        fills, 171
        Foley. *See* Foley
        layering, 243
        libraries, 216, 219–224
        music as, 210–211, 271–272
        printing, 251–252
        recording, 78–79
        spotting, 211–213
        websites, 221–222
        working with, 237–254

Foley, 225–230. *See also* Foley
    hearing, 95–111
    kits, locations, 71–83
    maps, 31, 213
    microphones. *See* microphones
    naming, 244
    non-diegetic, 9
    notes, 212
    optimizing, 125–137
    overview of, 19–25
    perception, 21–22
    production checklists, 48–49
    recording, 113–124
    separate audio recorders, 74–75
    shooting for, 46–47, 92–93
    starting, 241
    synchronization, 23
    thickening, 127
    transitions, 14–15
soundcards, 107–111
*Sound Design: The Expressive Power
    of Music, Voice, and Sound
    Effects in Cinema*, 11, 31
Soundminer, 215
sound pressure levels. *See* SPLs
soundproofing, 104
soundtrack elements, 11–13
Source-Connect software, 151
sources, noise, 48
spaces, simulating, 206
SPAN plug-in, 101
speakers
    calibrating, 101–104
    channels, 24–25
    locations, 99–101
    selecting, 96
    surround-sound issues, 295
special voice effects, 205–207
spectrograms, 192
Spectrum Analysis tool, 186
speech intelligibility, 187–188
Spitfish, 178
splitters, headphones, 78
splitting
    audio, 175
    edits, 165
    recording, 85
    tracks, 74
SPLs (sound pressure levels), 51, 223
SPL Transient Designer, 184, 185
sports-izing, 16
spotting sessions, 30–33
    music, 257–258
*Stand Still*, 272
starting
    mixing, 275–284
    projects, 29–36
    sound, 241
*Star Wars*, 2, 210, 218, 239, 271
*Star Wars: Episode II - Attack of the
    Clones*, 5
Stateman, Wylie, 170
stems, 3
stereo
    backgrounds, 79
    channels, 24
    effects, 109
    in the field, 79–83

recording in, 58, 166
speakers, 99. *See also* speakers
super-sizing backgrounds,
    233–235
surround setups, 100
Stewart, James, 4
stock music, 261–263
storage, microphones, 60–61
storage area networks. *See* SANs
strategies for purchasing equipment,
    121
streamers, 158
stretch, time, 195–196
strips, channels, 131–132
studio floorplans, 106
subfolders, 139. *See also* folders
sub-sonic noise, 186
Suburban Neighborhood sound effect,
    218
subwoofers, surround-sound issues,
    295
super-cardioid microphones, 54
super-sizing stereo backgrounds,
    233–235
supervising sound editors, 28
surround sound, 24
    backgrounds, 235
    issues, mixing, 294–295
sweetening
    fixing and, 11–12
sweet spots, 55
swirly sounds, 172
swishy sounds, 172
synchronization, 11, 35, 239–240
    audio recorders, 91
    double-system recording, 87
    foregrounds, 240–241
    licenses, 259
    phase sync, 90
    slate procedures, 89
    sound, 23


tail slates, 89
talent
    placement of, 153
    voiceovers, 146. *See also*
        voiceovers
talkback systems, 151
*Tangy G*, 272
tape, DV (digital video), 86
Tarquin, Brian, 267
TDM formats, 117
Teague, Addison, 275
technical issues, 36–38
    condenser microphones, 53
    noise, 45–48
    omnidirectional microphones, 54
    production, 39–41
    recorders, 93–94
    signal-to-noise ratios, 59
telephone lines, simulating, 205–206
temp tracks, 260
tension, building, 271
*Terminator 2*, 271
*The Element: How Finding Your
    Passion Changes
    Everything*, 285

themes, 270–271
*They Live,* 266. *See also* John
 Carpenter
thickening sounds, 127
Thom, Randy, 5
Thompson, Kristin, 9
threshold levels, 128, 181
 compression, 199
 expanders, 183
thunder, 127
time
 compression/expansion, 195–196
 crossfades, 168
 FX (audio effects), 126–127
 mixing, 287
 signatures, 269
timecodes, 88
timelines for projects, 37
tinny sounds, 172
tip, ring, and sleeve. *See* TRS
titles, sound effects, 215
*To Kill a Mockingbird,* 271
tonal fixes, 186–187
tone
 FX (audio effects), 125–126
 room, 166, 169. *See also* room tone
tools, 1. *See also* corrections
 audio analysis, 132–134
 burnishing, 78
 Chorus, 193, 194
 DC offset utilities, 177
 Declipper, 191, 192
 FX (audio effects), 125–137
 Hum Removal, 192, 193
 J-cuts/L-cuts, 167
 Little Labs IBP Phase Alignment
  Tool, 173, 235
 Pencil, 179
 Spectrum Analysis, 186
 SPL Transient Designer, 184, 185
 vinyl restoration, 188
*Touch of Evil,* 248
*To Wong Foo, Thanks for
 Everything! Julie Newmar,* 4
tracks, 36
 dialogue, cutting, 169
 layouts, 279
 MIDI, 117
 multitrack recordings, 166
 optimizing, 278–280
 production, 219–220
 recording, 85
 split, 74
 temp, 260
 walla. *See* walla
 wild, 46–47

TRAM lavalieres, 67
Tram TR50, 65
transduction, 22, 51
transitions, sounds, 14–15
*TRON: Legacy,* 275
TRS (tip, ring, and sleeve), 76
tweeters, 99
*Twin Peaks,* 208
*Twin Peaks: Fire Walk with Me,* 5
typanic membranes, 21
types of microphones, 51, 61–62

UAD plug-ins, 131
UltimateSoundBank, 216, 217
unidirectional microphones, 54
Universal Audio, 131
 LA-610, 151
USB (universal serial bus), 107, 108

VASST TrakPaks, 262
Vespa, 220
vibration, 19. *See also* sound
video
 DV (digital video), 22
 monitoring, 95–97
 naming conventions, 88
 slate procedures, 88
vinyl restoration, 188
visuals, editing, 30
Vitaphone process, 23
VO boxes, 92
vocal distortion corrections,
 180–182
Voice123, 145
*Voice Actor's Guide to Recording at
 Home and on the Road,
 The,* 149, 153
voiceovers, 1, 33, 143–153
 casting, 145–146
 optimizing, 146–148
 recording, 147, 148–153
 resources, 153
 scripts, 144–145
voices
 off-camera, 286
 special effects, 205–207
volume, 20, 55
 automation, 172
 corrections, 197–198
 mixing, 287–288
 monitors, 98
Volume Unit. *See* VU
*VO: Tales and Techniques of a
 Voice-over Actor,* 153

VST formats, 117
VU (Volume Unit) meters, 72

wah, 127
walkers, Foley, 226. *See also* Foley
walking, 160
walla, 1, 33, 46
 159
 defining, 159
 optimizing, 160–161
 recording, 159–160
*Wall-E,* 16, 218
Warner Brothers, 218
waveforms, 19
WAV files, 19
websites, sound effects, 221–222
Weir, Peter, 272. *See also* Witness
wild takes, 46–47
 ADR (automatic dialogue
  replacement), 155
Wilhelm scream, 5, 218
Williams, John, 271
wind noise, 47–48
Windows operating systems, 114
*Witness,* 266, 272
woofers, 186
workflow, 3–4, 27–38
 applying corrections, 176–177
 delegation, 28–29
 desk setups, 111
 Foley, 230
 FX (audio effects), 136–137
 managing, 139–140
 picture editorial *versus* sound
  editorial, 27–28
 post-production, 139–142
 starting projects, 29–36
 technical issues, 36–38
worldizing, 247–248
wrist rests, 110

*X-Files, The,* 256
XLR inputs, 76
X-treme FX, 216, 217

Y-adapters, 78

Zaxcom Deva, 91
Zoom
 H2, 79
 H4n, 217, 232

# License Agreement/Notice of Limited Warranty

By opening the sealed disc container in this book, you agree to the following terms and conditions. If, upon reading the following license agreement and notice of limited warranty, you cannot agree to the terms and conditions set forth, return the unused book with unopened disc to the place where you purchased it for a refund.

## License

The enclosed software is copyrighted by the copyright holder(s) indicated on the software disc. You are licensed to copy the software onto a single computer for use by a single user and to a backup disc. You may not reproduce, make copies, or distribute copies or rent or lease the software in whole or in part, except with written permission of the copyright holder(s). You may transfer the enclosed disc only together with this license, and only if you destroy all other copies of the software and the transferee agrees to the terms of the license. You may not decompile, reverse assemble, or reverse engineer the software.

## Notice of Limited Warranty

The enclosed disc is warranted by Course Technology to be free of physical defects in materials and workmanship for a period of sixty (60) days from end user's purchase of the book/disc combination. During the sixty-day term of the limited warranty, Course Technology will provide a replacement disc upon the return of a defective disc.

## Limited Liability

THE SOLE REMEDY FOR BREACH OF THIS LIMITED WARRANTY SHALL CONSIST ENTIRELY OF REPLACEMENT OF THE DEFECTIVE DISC. IN NO EVENT SHALL COURSE TECHNOLOGY OR THE AUTHOR BE LIABLE FOR ANY OTHER DAMAGES, INCLUDING LOSS OR CORRUPTION OF DATA, CHANGES IN THE FUNCTIONAL CHARACTERISTICS OF THE HARDWARE OR OPERATING SYSTEM, DELETERIOUS INTERACTION WITH OTHER SOFTWARE, OR ANY OTHER SPECIAL, INCIDENTAL, OR CONSEQUENTIAL DAMAGES THAT MAY ARISE, EVEN IF COURSE TECHNOLOGY AND/OR THE AUTHOR HAS PREVIOUSLY BEEN NOTIFIED THAT THE POSSIBILITY OF SUCH DAMAGES EXISTS.

## Disclaimer of Warranties

COURSE TECHNOLOGY AND THE AUTHOR SPECIFICALLY DISCLAIM ANY AND ALL OTHER WARRANTIES, EITHER EXPRESS OR IMPLIED, INCLUDING WARRANTIES OF MERCHANTABILITY, SUITABILITY TO A PARTICULAR TASK OR PURPOSE, OR FREEDOM FROM ERRORS. SOME STATES DO NOT ALLOW FOR EXCLUSION OF IMPLIED WARRANTIES OR LIMITATION OF INCIDENTAL OR CONSEQUENTIAL DAMAGES, SO THESE LIMITATIONS MIGHT NOT APPLY TO YOU.

## Other

This Agreement is governed by the laws of the State of Massachusetts without regard to choice of law principles. The United Convention of Contracts for the International Sale of Goods is specifically disclaimed. This Agreement constitutes the entire agreement between you and Course Technology regarding use of the software.

**COURSE TECHNOLOGY**
CENGAGE Learning™
Professional • Technical • Reference

Course Technology PTR
# COURSE CLIPS

*Course Clips* are interactive DVD-ROM training products for those who prefer learning on the computer as opposed to learning through a book. *Course Clips Starters* are for beginners and *Course Clips Masters* are for more advanced users.

**Digital Performer 7
Course Clips Master**
Don Barrett ▪ $49.99

**Pro Tools 9
Course Clips Master**
Steve Wall ▪ $49.99

**Pro Tools 8
Course Clips Starter**
Steve Wall ▪ $29.99

**Ableton Live 8
Course Clips Master**
Brian Jackson ▪ $49.99

# Individual movie clips are available for purchase online at **www.courseclips.com**

# Like the Book?

## Let us know on Facebook or Twitter!

facebook.com/courseptr

twitter.com/courseptr